Soldiers on the Cultural Front

HAWAI'I STUDIES ON KOREA

Soldiers on the Cultural Front

*Developments in the Early History
of North Korean Literature
and Literary Policy*

Tatiana Gabroussenko

University of Hawai'i Press, Honolulu
and
Center for Korean Studies, University of Hawai'i

Library of Congress Cataloging-in-Publication Data

Gabroussenko, Tatiana.
  Soldiers on the cultural front : developments in the early history of North Korean literature and literary policy / Tatiana Gabroussenko.
    p. cm.—(Hawai'i studies on Korea)
    Includes bibliographical references.
    ISBN 978-0-8248-3396-1 (alk. paper)
    1. Literature and state—Korea (North)   2. Socialist realism in literature.
3. Korean literature—Korea (North)—Soviet influences.   4. Politics and literature—Korea (North)   5. Authors, Korean—Korea (North)—Political and social views.   6. Political purges—Korea (North)   7. Communism and intellectuals—Korea (North)   I. Title.   II. Series: Hawai'i studies on Korea.
  PL998.K7G33 2010
  895.7'0995193—dc22

                                 2009039566

 The Center for Korean Studies was established in 1972 to coordinate and develop resources for the study of Korea at the University of Hawai'i. Reflecting the diversity of the academic disciplines represented by affiliated members of the university faculty, the Center seeks especially to promote interdisciplinary and intercultural studies. Hawai'i Studies on Korea, published jointly by the Center and the University of Hawai'i Press, offers a forum for research in the social sciences and humanities pertaining to Korea and its people.

Designed by University of Hawai'i Press production staff
Printed by Edwards Brothers, Inc.

Contents

Introduction

THE AUTHORS of the classic study *Communism in Korea,* by Robert A. Scalapino and Chong-Sik Lee, once claimed that "the cultural life of North Korea (outside the realms of science, technology and purely folk art) is a great desert of unalleviated mediocrity and monotony."[1] This comment may sound extremely dismissive, but as a reader of North Korean fiction with more than twenty years' experience, I am forced to agree that North Korean literature has indeed been a field of exceptional uniformity, unchallenged by any alternatives. Dissenting views might exist, but they have so far remained unheard of. North Korean literary texts will hardly inspire the reader who is searching for beauty of language or complexity of character, an original intellectual concept, or a sparkle of heretical thought. At the same time, a researcher who is interested in the shifts and twists of North Korea's propaganda, hidden modifications of the Party line, North Korea's cultural stereotypes, or the officially endorsed self-portrait of the North Korean people and image of the world around them, will find this literature an invaluable source of information.

When searching for the roots of the exceptional uniformity of North Korea's literature, it makes sense to look back at its formative period of 1945–1960, which coincided with the general formative period of the political and social institutions of the Democratic People's Republic of Korea (DPRK). Beginning as the "Soviet era"—a period of implantation of Soviet institutions into every sphere of North Korean national life—this revolutionary epoch established a long-lasting framework for North Korean literature, with its stocks of notoriously restrictive clichés, politicized images, and rhetoric.[2] It also set up an elaborate system of political control over literary matters and over the people who served in this field. In 1946 the DPRK leader Kim Il Sung first described North Korean writers as "soldiers on the cultural front," thus making quite clear what the nascent Communist regime expected from its intellectuals.

The Soviet era quickly gave way to the Korean version of "national Stalinism," which was even more regimented than its Soviet prototype. Creating proper "soldiers on the cultural front" became one of the first major tasks of North Korean Stalinism. Literature in the DPRK was subjected to harsh political control with a strong patrimonial flavor,[3] and Korea's cultural soil was plowed in quite a revolutionary manner. Many of yesterday's nonentities were elevated to the peak of fame, power, and success (often only to be overthrown within a few years) while many outstanding luminaries of the past were erased from the pages of official publications or even from the face of the earth.

The present work deals with several interwoven processes in this transition: the implantation of the Soviet-originating model of "socialist realism" into the Korean cultural soil, the implementation of the system of political management in literary affairs, and the political campaigns directed against famous North Korean intellectuals. I will examine how these and other developments influenced the lives and activities of three prominent literary personalities: Cho Ki-ch'ŏn, Yi Ki-yŏng, and Yi T'ae-jun. Each of these writers symbolized a typical path in this era, and I have endeavored to consider the various factors that determined their success or failure in the Korean literary scene.

Sources

The research draws on a variety of sources ranging from interviews with Korean and Soviet participants in the events, materials from public and family archives, memoirs of North Korean defectors, items from the contemporary press, original literary and critical texts, and other documents.

The original literary and critical texts are mostly from my personal collection, a large part of which consists of a personal gift from the senior Russian scholar Dr. Leo Kontsevich. I was also fortunate to have the opportunity to use a number of important literary texts that Dr. Brian Myers kindly donated to the Australian National University.

Among the interviews with witnesses to and immediate participants in the events described, some of the most enlightening were those with Chŏng Ryul (Chŏng Sang-jin, Chŏng Yurii Danilovich), who now resides in Kazakhstan. Chŏng's life and career were typically turbulent for a Soviet Korean in the DPRK in the 1950s. Along with other Soviet political commissars, Chŏng Ryul moved to Korea to direct the development of this new Soviet-allied state and quickly reached high official status within the North Korean bureaucracy. From 1952 to 1955 Chŏng occupied the position of deputy minister for culture, guided North Korean literature, and became a close friend of many significant North Korean intellectuals. Chŏng subsequently became the object of a defamation campaign against the Soviet Koreans and barely escaped Kim Il Sung's purges, fleeing the North in 1955. The information that Chǒng Ryul generously shared with me during my visit to Alma-Ata in 2000 has been extremely valuable.[4] Another important informant was Cho Yurii, the only son of the founding father of North Korean socialist realism, the Soviet Korean poet Cho Ki-ch'ǒn.[5] Cho Yurii, who is now living in Moscow, generously shared his family's knowledge of his father and his Korean colleagues and provided me with unique materials from the family archive. Further important information came from a telephone interview with Elena Davydova (Pak Myǒng-sun), then living in Pyongyang, who worked as a translator of Russian literature into Korean in the 1950s and 1960s and knew all the famous intellectuals of the period personally.[6]

The recollections of North Korean intellectuals who defected from the North at different times, and who later published their memoirs in Seoul, make up my third important source.[7] Though in recent South Korean scholarship these memoirs have often been dismissed as biased anti-Communist propaganda,[8] in my opinion these books offer a great deal of useful data about the North Korean intellectual world in its early formative years. In general the information of defectors correlates quite well with the data obtained from other sources.

A Brief Review of Relevant Publications

Against a backdrop of a general scarcity of overseas research on North Korean culture and history, North Korean literature has been studied relatively well. The first foreign studies of North Korean literature began to appear in the Soviet Union in the late 1940s and early 1950s. The primary goal of Soviet academia was to patronize the culture of these "younger brothers in Communism," so this research was subjected to stringent political requirements.[9] However, the Soviet scholars managed to include in their studies valuable analyses and frequently a detectable degree of criticism. V. I. Ivanova, V. N. Li, and others had frequent personal contacts with North Korean writers and had at their disposal a rich lode of otherwise unobtainable information about the contemporary situation in North Korea's literary circles.[10] As a result, the Soviet studies of North Korean literature are not without academic value, even if a reader must ignore the obligatory quotations from Marx and Lenin and the ritualistic praise for the Party's wisdom.

Unfortunately, the dramatic political changes occurring in Russia in the late 1990s and into the new century not only have meant the discarding of the previous Marxian agenda but also have rendered research into North Korean literature highly unpopular. The former Soviet academic tradition of North Korean literary studies has no continuity today.

A different situation obtains in South Korean academic circles. Until the late 1980s, studies of North Korean literature were rare, yet some works of this period are definitely worth attention. Take, for example, Yi Ki-pong's *Puk-ŭi munhak-kwa yesurin* (North Korean Men of Literature and the Arts; 1986).[11] Written by a conservative nonacademic expert on North Korean affairs, this research, despite certain limitations, demonstrates a surprisingly sober and original look at the North Korean literary world.

The change in political atmosphere after the collapse of military rule in 1987 transformed the study of North Korean literature into a popular academic pursuit. Most South Korean publications demonstrate a remarkably thorough acquaintance with North Korean literary texts and offer valuable background information about the historical roots of North Korean literary processes.[12] Many of today's Seoul academics, even those who do not specialize in North Korean literature, incorporate detailed analyses of North Korean works into their studies.[13] However, many of these works are not politically detached. In the light of the leftist nationalist *minjung* discourse that is now dominant in Republic of Korea academia, South Korean scholars today are inclined to treat North Korean literary development as an inseparable part of a conjoined "glorious national tradition" that is to be defended, and they tend, as Myers has noted, to gloss over the deficiencies of this literature and judge it on the basis of the perceived "good intentions" of an author.[14] When accessing North Korean literature, South Korean academics often demonstrate an excessive trust in the thoroughly biased verdicts of North Korean officialdom;[15] many scholars isolate this literature from the political context of the era and overlook the obvious self-serving motives of the activities of North Korean writers.[16]

Western scholarship has not been very prolific in the realm of North Korean literary studies, but the scarcity of such works is compensated for by their quality. The two-volume classic of Scalapino and Lee, *Communism in Korea* (1972), which among numerous aspects also deals with North Korea's literature, must be mentioned. An article by Marshall R. Pihl, "Engineers of the Human Soul: North Korean Literature Today," also considers North Korean literature in the context of its didactic tradition.[17] In 1994, Western scholarship was enriched by Brian Myers' brilliant *Han Sŏr-ya and North Korean Literature: The Failure of Socialist Realism in the DPRK*, which presents an original and coherent picture of North Korean literature in its formative years.

A Word about Socialist Realism

Since this book largely deals with historical, biographical, and political issues, I do not intend to dwell at length on the theoretical problems of literary studies. Before commencing the primary discussion, however, I would like to reflect on a concept that is considered central to North Korean literature: socialist realism.

Socialist realism is a doctrine of Soviet origin that prescribes and describes the artistic form of Communist ideology and politics in literature. Authored by Stalin in 1932, this concept remained obligatory for all Soviet writers until the collapse of the Communist system in the late 1980s.[18] After 1945, in the DPRK as well as in other countries of the Communist bloc, socialist realism was officially pronounced to be "the only method of creative activity in the field of literature and art which is socialist in content and national in form." In charter 1 of the General Federation of Korean Literature and Arts Unions, the fundamental function of the federation was formulated as being "to reward the working masses with Communist ideology and revolutionary tradition through literary and artistic activities under the leadership of the Workers' Party of Korea."[19]

Most overseas scholars agree that the self-professed term "socialist realism" defines quite precisely the real essence of North Korean literature. The sole but important exception to this consensus is Brian Myers, who argues that socialist realism "failed" in the DPRK. According to his view, the exemplary works of North Korean literature are not compatible with the major principles of socialist realism.

To decide whether or not North Korean literature belongs to the realm of socialist realism, it makes sense to answer the question that Soviet dissident critic Abram Terts (Sinyavsky) posed in his classic essay, "What Is Socialist Realism?"[20] The answer is not simple, given the theoretical debates surrounding this issue and that, as George Bisztray once observed, "the classics of Marxism-Leninism hardly established any homogeneous aesthetic tradition."[21]

Stalin, in his meeting with Soviet writers on 19 October 1932, gave the following preliminary interpretation of the future doctrine: "An artist has to depict our life truthfully. And if he depicts it truthfully, he cannot help but reveal the facts that lead our life to socialism. This will be socialist realism."[22] The first official interpretation of socialist realism was given in August 1934 at the First All-Union Congress of Soviet Writers: "Socialist realism is the main method of Soviet literature and [literary] criticism. It demands a truthful, historically concrete depiction of reality in its revolutionary development.

These qualities must be achieved through the ideological reformation of all the working people, nurturing them in the spirit of socialism."[23]

Though this definition has been reiterated in all theoretical works about socialist realism, it obscures more than it explains. Like Stalin's remark cited above, this interpretation stressed that only the description of reality from a particular political (i.e., socialist) angle should be accepted as "truthful." However, socialism itself was hardly more than a working plan of the moment, and the means of producing the art that was supposed to promote this plan were even more unclear. Besides, as Marc Slonim has noted, "the formula . . . confused such different concepts as aesthetic method, artistic intention, and point of view, and also confounded such different elements as the requirements of a literary trend and the practical effects of a finished work on the reader (political education of the masses being the main object of the writer)."[24]

Later official Soviet interpretations also failed to deliver a coherent definition or a precise artistic canon of socialist realism. These definitions, which were prone to infinite variation under the pressure of the changing political and social climate of the USSR, presented quite blurred artistic and ideological criteria, with only some general tendencies traceable. The definitions of Stalin's epoch steered writers in an ascetic, militant direction. Soviet literature was called "the freest literature in the world" and at the same time "the most ideological, the most advanced, the most revolutionary literature"; a writer had to depict life "without embellishment"; a "typical hero" should be endowed with "a sense of socialist duty" and "a selfless readiness to devote one's life to the cause of Communism" and "should not be limited by the confines of personal feelings."[25] During the more liberal "thaw" period of the late 1950s and early 1960s, these rigid phrases were gradually substituted with references to "humanism," "romanticism," and "flights of fancy into the future";[26] and literary works came to include some discussions of personal freedom and of how to approach the "eternal concepts of good and evil, beauty and ugliness," though they still remained spiced with references to "revolution" and "the Party."[27] When in 1965 the distinguished and officially recognized Soviet writer Mikhail Sholokhov defined socialist realism in his Nobel Prize acceptance speech, he mentioned neither "Party spirit" nor "class consciousness." Articulating a new official Soviet vision based on the old doctrine, Sholokhov refrained from any boastful Stalinist catchphrases such as "the most advanced literature in the world" and tried instead to situate socialist realism within a worldwide intellectual tradition.[28]

In the 1970s and 1980s, when the influence of the official ideology was becoming seriously eroded in the USSR, even the stubborn diehards in the

Soviet Writers' Union ceased to raise the issue of Communism anymore. The updated official definitions of socialist realism began to include such hitherto unthinkable notions as "historically open system of artistic form" or "the pathos of the subjective activity of a creator."[29] Even the once heretical idea that the "Party spirit" in a socialist realist work might be "at times controversial, depending on the particular historical situation"[30]—a suggestion that would probably lead an author to the Gulag in Stalin's times—began to surface. When discussing the "aesthetic platform" of socialist realism, the authors of the *Soviet Encyclopedic Dictionary* of 1986 speak not of realism but merely of "realistic origins."[31]

Despite the ambivalence and mutual contradictions of their criteria, all of these different definitions were meant to describe the same cultural phenomenon of socialist realism. In the mainstream opinion of Soviet literary studies, all Soviet literature is perceived as belonging to this realm. Some Western scholars tend to restrict the borders of Soviet socialist realism to the literature of Stalin's era, excluding the period of the Great Patriotic War (1941–1945) when some earlier constraints were lifted or eased.[32] Yet even during this brief period, Western scholars have been unable to discern any definite artistic canon of socialist realism. As Slonim noted, "these Communist writers expressed their faith and support of the regime in different literary forms which did not represent anything new but continued various established literary traditions."[33]

The prominent Western scholar Katerina Clark, in *The Soviet Novel: History as Ritual,* made an original attempt to define the literary conventions of Soviet socialist realism through an analysis of some of what she called its "patristic texts" (works of Mikhail Sholokhov, Aleksandr Fadeev, Dmitrii Furmanov, Nikolai Ostrovskii, and others) and to extrapolate features of these texts to other Soviet works. For all its academic merit, this approach has its limitations. Under the rubric of "patristic texts," Clark includes "a core group of novels that are cited with sufficient regularity to be considered a canon." In Clark's opinion these books represented *obraztsy* (exemplars), which were supposed "to guide the writers in their future works."[34] In fact the novels that she perceives as exemplary were officially recognized as works to be followed and emulated. The problem was, however, that the status of "official classic" did not make those works real exemplars for colleagues in terms of literary conventions, just as the oft-repeated slogan of the Soviet Writers' Union, "Let us learn from the classics of Russian literature," failed to turn the poems of Aleksandr Pushkin into patristic texts of Soviet literature. For all the ritualistic calls to "learn from *Virgin Land,*" it is difficult to identify any attempt to emulate the conventions of Sholokhov's novel, even in the Soviet literature of the 1930s, let alone in the texts of later eras. Although Stalin personally extolled Vladimir Maiakovskii as "the best poet of our epoch," no poet in Stalin's era dared to imitate either the language or the imagery of Maiakovskii's formalistic plays. Nor were the vivid (if over-romantic) images of Maxim Gorky's stories ever reproduced in the writing of his colleagues.

This is no surprise, since, with all their unshakable official standing, patristic texts presented poor material for emulation. Even within the Stalinist period, the exemplary works were not artistically congruent with each other. For example, the "spontaneity-consciousness dialectic" that Katerina Clark sees as a typical feature of the socialist realist "master plot" was traceable in the fiction of Fadeev or Ostrovskii but hardly existed in the novels of the much celebrated Stalinist writer Vera Panova. The exemplary works of Sholokhov—*Quiet Flows the Don* (1928–1940) and *Virgin Land under the Plow* (1931–1960)—were characterized by a degree of sensuality that found no counterpart in other similarly patristic works, such as the classic texts of Furmanov, Fadeev, or Ostrovskii.

Moreover, the patristic texts often violated the very principles that were propagated by the Writers' Union. Fadeev's *Devastation,* with its gloomy ending, did not comply with the idea of revolutionary optimism. The intricate linguistic innovations of Maiakovskii's poems run counter to the principle of popular spirit. Sholokhov's *Virgin Land* could be accused of violating a number of principles, including typicality (the narrator makes it clear that all his positive characters are eccentric *{s chudinkoi}*); revolutionary optimism (the protagonists die in the end); and revolutionary humanism (the Communist hero Nagulnov proclaims his readiness "to kill women, children, or old men for the sake of Revolution").[35] Collectivization is depicted as an extremely painful process, accompanied by the suffering of innocents, and often even the Party spirit is forgotten (Sholokhov's upright Communist protagonists often behave in a less than exemplary Communist manner: they indulge in drinking and womanizing and are rather lazy and unskilled peasants who cannot properly manage their own households).

Thus, with all their artistic variety and contradictions, the patristic texts hardly offered any unified master plot or solid literary convention that would unmistakably define a work of socialist realism.

Perhaps in our search for the real meaning of socialist realism we must look to an article by Lenin entitled "Party Organisation and Party Literature" (Partiinaia organizatsiia i partiinaia literatura), which appeared in 1905, long before the birth of socialist realism, but was later extolled as the theoretical foundation of Communist literary policy and theory. The future leader of Soviet Russia formulated his requirements for literature in an unequivocal manner: "Literature . . . cannot be an individual undertaking. . . . Literature must become part of the common cause of the proletariat, 'a cog and a screw' of one single great Social-Democratic mechanism, set in motion by the entire politically conscious vanguard of the entire working class. Literature must become a component of organised, planned, and integrated Social-Democratic Party work."[36]

As we can see, Lenin boldly defined the primary function of literature as "a cog and a screw"—that is, a useful tool in the Party's work. This idea was repeated in a speech by Andrei Zhdanov at the First All-Union Congress of Soviet Writers in 1934. The prominent Party official candidly claimed that socialist realist literature needed no new specific forms—it could borrow them from previous epochs. The really new thing about this literature, he argued, was that it was to be "consciously tendentious" and was to depict "correct" protagonists.[37] Zhdanov's words were crude but precise. Indeed, Lenin's idea of the transformation of literature into a handmaiden of the Party was fully realized in the first Communist state and became a cornerstone of the theory and practice of socialist realist doctrine elsewhere.

If we look at the history of relations between the authorities and culture in Communist states, we will find that, despite rather inconsistent approaches to artistic form and method, Communist officials always demonstrated a consistent ambition to command literary matters and to make sure that literature served the Party's current and ever-changing political demands. It was these demands, rather than any stable aesthetic principles, that made a literary text truly patristic and socialist realist. As Pihl put it, "The doctrine of socialist realism, a Soviet aesthetic canon, holds that literature may not be a simple 'realistic' or 'naturalistic' reproduction of life but must describe reality as the party defines it."[38] In Terts' opinion, "works of socialist realism differ in form and content" but are unified by their "Purpose with a capital P" or by general faith in the goal of Communism, thus representing a kind of religious and educatory literature.[39] Max Hayward insisted that the purpose was more flexible; in his opinion, the actual "central concept of socialist realism" is "the idea that the Party may use literature *for whatever purpose it may think fit at a given moment*" (my emphasis).[40]

Indeed, in the exemplary works of socialist realism, be it Fadeev's romantic sagas about the Civil War, Sholokhov's sensual depictions of life in a reforming village, or Panova's simple domestic tales, the topics, artistic means, and quantities of sheer ideological messages all differ. Not all the authors strictly follow the fixed literary principles of popular spirit, revolutionary optimism, typicality, and so on. Yet these patristic works all demonstrate the extraordinary ability of their authors to sense the sociopolitical requirements of the time and to present them in the very manner that the Party would approve at that particular historical moment.

It is important to stress that these requirements were not confined by rigid ideological postulates. Even the most ideological literary works of the Stalinist period raised broad social issues to do with the family, love, interpersonal and international relationships, and suchlike, and the way in which these topics were presented was often dictated, not by Party ideological directives, but by public assumptions accepted and supported by the Party. Indeed, the Party strove to patrol the social boundaries within which Soviet writers situated their literary texts and to subordinate these boundaries to ideological dictates. However, too often the concerns and traditions of society proved to be stronger than the Communist postulates, and the Party was forced to compromise the ideological purity of socialist realist writings in order to accommodate these concerns and traditions. This is why, for example, we find in many Soviet patristic texts a patriarchal approach to gender issues, which contradicts the Marxist idea of women's emancipation, or the concept of Great Russian patriotism, which goes against the notion of proletarian internationalism. It seems that the mantra of "socialist in content, national in form" was invented to disguise the Party's inability to make socialist realist culture totally socialist. Thus, in my opinion, the primary "Purpose with capital P" that unites socialist realist literature is to serve, not pure ideology, but the will of the state and society ruled by a Leninist Party.

If we view the literature of the DPRK through this prism, we will find no grounds for excluding North Korean creative writing from the broad literary-cum-political movement of socialist realism. North Korean literature was as politically functional as the literatures of other Communist states. All recognized North Korean writers demonstrated an unquestionable loyalty to the current political climate, a complete readiness to fulfill the tasks defined or approved by the Party, and a total engagement in the political process of the North Korean Communist state.

However, the purposes of the North Korean state and society differed from that of the USSR; indeed the DPRK displayed a considerable degree of deviation from the classical Stalinist model in general. Suffice it to mention the xenophobic idea of "racial purity," which Myers showed to be a significant feature of North Korean propaganda—this idea alone is enough to question the orthodoxy of North Korea's Communism. As Scalapino and Lee put it, "It is extremely doubtful that Karl Marx, were he resurrected, would view the Democratic People's Republic of Korea as a state drawn from his inspiration or as a true socialist society by his definition. Even Lenin would find it difficult to accept as legitimate certain cardinal elements of the prevailing creed and structure of Kim Il Sung's polity."[41]

At the same time, Scalapino and Lee admit that the DPRK shares the essential qualities of a Communist state, such as "single Party structure, state ownership of industrial enterprises, a centrally planned economy, mass participation, [and] elitist control."[42] I would also stress such undeniably Communist features of the DPRK as state control of all economic activities, collectivization of agriculture, and an emphasis on class background. Thus, what we see in North Korea is still a state controlled by Marxism-Leninism, though set in a unique North Korean social context. And the same can be said about North Korean literature.

It is difficult to deny that North Korean socialist realism contains a number of inner inconsistencies and paradoxes. Myers correctly noted that, in terms of artistic method or political theme, North Korean texts often differed remarkably from the model Soviet novels. However, the general paradigm of Pyongyang's literature did not significantly deviate from the Soviet Stalinist originals. As we will see, many social idylls in North Korean literature are strongly reminiscent of those of the Soviet prototype. The adjustments, undertaken by the Pyongyang literary propagandists, seem to be necessary adaptations of the original models to the traditions, tastes, and particular political circumstances of North Korean society.

Structure of the Study

The present work consists of five chapters. The first and second chapters discuss the Soviet intellectual influence in the nascent years of North Korean Communism. I examine the major conventions of Soviet socialist realism that the "soldiers on the cultural front" developed during the Soviet era and trace the development of these conventions in the following decades. The first chapter is devoted to two important channels of Soviet influence: Soviet fiction and *Ssoryŏn kihaenggi*, travelogues written by North Korean intellectuals who visited the Soviet Union in 1946–1955 as members of specially arranged official delegations. The second chapter considers the activity of a "living source"—the Soviet Koreans—and, in particular, the iconic figure of the poet Cho Ki-ch'ŏn (1913–1951), who was considered to be the founding father of North Korean literature.

The third and fourth chapters contain a comparative analysis of the lives and activities of two representative personalities of the early North Korean literary world: Yi Ki-yŏng (1895–1984) and Yi T'ae-jun (1904–?).I investigate the experiences, worldviews, and works of both figures within the political context of the era, scrutinize the reasons for their rise and fall, and examine the legacy their activities represented.

In the fifth chapter, I analyze the phenomenon of North Korean literary criticism in the period 1945–1960 and its role in the formation of North Korean literature. Particular attention is given to the political campaigns and purges of 1947–1960 and to the role of the North Korean critics in these events.

In the conclusion, I summarize the major findings of my study and make a general comparison of the patterns of activity of North Korean and Soviet writers.

1 "Let Us Learn from the Soviets"

THE FIRST STEPS in the development of North Korea's literary policy were marked by a wholesale imitation of the Soviet Stalinist models. It is easy to ascribe this process exclusively to Soviet political domination since, predictably, such a policy was actively promoted by the Soviet administration. However, at the time, the DPRK leader Kim Il Sung had his own reasons for encouraging thorough Sovietization of North Korean culture. Kim, whose aim was to create a Stalinist society in Korea, appeared to understand that the Soviet patterns of socialist realism, being necessarily imbued with Stalinist content, could equip Korean intellectuals with guidelines until such time as some national standard of politically desirable "proper literature" could be worked out. Even if the North Korean leader had any ethnocentric propensities at the time, he swallowed them temporarily.

We should remember, however, that it was neither Kim Il Sung nor the occupation forces that brought Soviet literary patterns to Korean soil. The concept of socialist realism was not alien to indigenous Korean culture, and this was one of the reasons why North Korean intellectuals so readily accepted the necessity of following this concept after Liberation. Let us then briefly consider the roots of Korean socialist realism.

Soviet literature was relatively well known among educated Koreans of the colonial era, as was its predecessor, classic Russian literature, which began to spread into Korea from the 1890s.[1] Many scholars believe that Korean readers differed from the Western public in their perception of Russian literature and were more receptive to the moralizing aspects of Russia's fiction.[2] For instance, the Korean public remained largely indifferent to Tolstoy's internationally acclaimed novels *Anna Karenina* and *War and Peace* but were greatly impressed by his religious and moralistic treatises, which had limited popularity among the Western readership.[3] Influenced by Confucian traditions, Korean intellectuals searched literary texts for useful social recipes; and

Russian fiction, according to its own tradition of preaching at rather than entertaining the reader, satisfied their aspirations.

Soviet literature was also viewed largely through this prism. The writings of Maxim Gorky, a lifelong Communist sympathizer who was recognized as a forerunner of socialist realism in the USSR, gained popularity as didactic material.[4] Gorky was transformed into a kind of guru in Korea in the 1920s and 1930s;[5] he not only contributed to the leftward drift of the Korean intellectual world but also influenced the artistic methods of Korean literature. It is notable that Korean intellectuals appreciated the very traits of Gorky's writing that contemporary Russian critics ridiculed, such as its sentimentality and over-romanticizing. Gorky's influence touched even those unsympathetic to Marxism,[6] and his prestige in Korea remained high in the following decades despite all the changes in the political climate. For example, the bestowal of the supposedly flattering nickname "Korean Gorky" on the "proletarian writer" Ch'ŏe Sŏ-hae for his short story "Diary of Escape" (T'alch'ulgi; 1925) was approvingly referred to in a South Korean book published in 1978, at the height of the anti-Communist hysteria in the Republic of Korea.[7]

According to the *Chronology of the History of Korean Literature (Chosŏn munhaksa nyŏndaep'yo),* Gorky was the only Soviet writer whose short stories had been translated into Korean before Liberation.[8] However, in colonial Korea, contemporary Soviet fiction was also available in Japanese translation, and by the 1930s virtually every educated Korean could read Japanese fluently. V. I. Ivanova, citing a survey undertaken by *Munhak kŏnsŏl (Literary Construction)* magazine in 1932, claims that a number of Soviet writers were known and popular in Korea. These included Aleksandr Serafimovich, Mikhail Sholokhov, Aleksandr Fadeev, Fyodor Gladkov, Sergei Esenin, Demian Bednyi, and Vladimir Maiakovskii, among others.[9]

In pre-Liberation Korean literature, socialist realism was associated with the leftist realm of "new tendency" *(sin kyŏnghyang)* literature and the Korean Proletarian Art Federation "proletarian literature." These movements united writers who not only were well acquainted with Soviet fiction but also tried to implement Communist ideology in their own texts.

The new tendency literature of 1924–1925, which is now widely referred to as the forerunner of proletarian literature, emerged as a response to the challenges of colonial modernity and the impoverishment of the Korean peasantry.[10] While new tendency architect Yim Chŏng-jae presented this literary trend as sympathetic to socialist ideology, the project instead promoted conservative anti-industrialism and anti-urbanism along with "truly Korean" traditional values.[11] In the works of Ch'oe Sŏ-hae (1901–1932), Yi Ik-sang

(1895–1930), the poet Yi Sang-hwa (1901–1943), and others, one can find nostalgic lamentations over "pure village life" having been cruelly spoiled by the foreign economic and cultural invasion. These laments were often accompanied by acts of misguided and substantial violence on the part of the protagonists. The works of Ch'oe Sŏ-hae were especially typical in this regard.[12]

The writings of Gorky strongly affected the new tendency literature, sometimes to the point of plagiarism. For example, Yi Sang-hwa's "Yearning for the Storm" (P'okp'ung-ŭl kidarinŭn maŭm) follows the line of Gorky's "Song of the Stormy Petrel" (Pesnia o burevestnike).[13] The effect of Gorky's images of exoticized paupers rebelling against authority is clearly noticeable in the works of Ch'oe Sŏ-hae.

Yet the rebellious actions of the protagonists in Gorky's works and those of the new tendency novels had different connotations. Gorky, who was openly hostile toward the Russian traditional village culture, never endorsed the myth of the village. He described his characters' outbursts of rage sympathetically, but without illusion.[14] Gorky's rebels have to be tamed and civilized to become socially productive—be it by the positive influence of sympathetic intellectuals ("The Orlov Spouses" [Suprugi Orlovy]) or by the ideological authority of the Party ("Mother" [Mat']). In contrast, the new tendency authors, as Brian Myers puts it, "saw the way to overcome injustice not in tempering the spontaneity of the Korean people—through political organization and the infusion of 'consciousness'—but in unleashing it, in allowing it to erupt with a purging force."[15]

The Korean Proletarian Art Federation (KAPF) was established in 1925 and was meant to be a Korean version of RAPP (Russian Association of Proletarian Writers), the ultraleftist literary group in the early Soviet Union.[16] Up to 1927, the KAPF remained a rather amorphous organization. However, in 1927–1930 it underwent a process of "Bolshevization" under the influence of the young radicals in its Tokyo branch (Yim Hwa, Yi Pung-man, and others), who eventually established control over the federation.[17] The result of their endeavors was a new program for the KAPF, which stated: "In our class struggle, we stand on the side of a Marxist understanding of the historical process. Considering proletarian literature as one of the frontiers of proletarian struggle, we chart our mission as follows: (1) a decisive struggle against feudal-bourgeois ideology; (2) a struggle against barbarian regimes and despotism; (3) a struggle for the creation of conscious class activists."[18] One remarkable aspect of the militants' position was their struggle against the proponents of "nationalist literature," or "the writers who insisted that political appeals should be to Koreans *as Koreans,* not to class differences."[19]

Despite frequent debates within the KAPF, the actual creative output of the federation was modest in terms of both ideology and art—or in terms of implementation of Marxian ideology and artistic quality. For all its Marxian rhetoric, anti-urbanism, traditionalism, and ethnocentrism remained the major features of the rather unrefined KAPF fiction. Only a few authors (Yi Ki-yŏng being one of them) enjoyed a measure of popularity, and this not among the proletariat but within a narrow circle of leftist intellectuals. In fact, the subversive potential of this literature was quite low. However, the loud political declarations of KAPF militants took their toll. In the early 1930s the police started to arrest active members of the federation, and in 1935 the KAPF was dissolved under the pressure of the colonial authorities who lured the writers to join the pro-Japanese Korean Writers Society.[20] Myers remarks that by the late 1930s "all KAPF veterans had renounced the revolutionary cause, either in their literary works or in formal declarations to their probation officers."[21]

With their petty rivalry, overindulgence in theoretical debates rather than practical writing, and ideological inconsistency, the KAPF intellectuals did not leave any stable legacy that could be transformed into a national literary discourse after Liberation. The discourse had to be borrowed anyway, and this was the reason why during the early years of the DPRK the North Korean leader continued to stress the importance of "learning from the Soviets."

Following the Soviet example, in 1946 Kim Il Sung unified the disparate and often quarrelling groups that had mushroomed after Liberation, placing them under the banner of the Pukchosŏn Munhak Yesul Tongmaeng (North Korean Federation of Literature and Art, or NKFLA), overseen by the Party's Department of Agitation and Propaganda (Munhwain Pujang).[22]

At the inaugural meeting of the NKFLA on 25 March 1946, the goals of the new organization and of North Korean literature in general were formulated as follows:

1. The establishment of a national art and culture based on the principles of progressive democracy.
2. The promotion of the national unification of all Korean literary and artistic movements.
3. The extirpation of all antidemocratic and reactionary artistic forces and concepts, be they Japanese imperialist, feudal, treasonous, or fascist.
4. The implementation of a large-scale enlightenment movement for the cultural, creative, and artistic development of the masses.

5. The suitable appraisal and appropriation of the nation's cultural heritage.

6. The exchange of the national culture with international culture.[23]

Unlike the KAPF program with its references to Marxist ideology and the proletarian struggle, the NKFLA's platform employed more nationalist and democratic rhetoric. This was in accordance with the Soviet "theory of the people's democratic revolution," which stated that the nascent Communist regimes in the post–World War II Soviet-controlled societies were to deal first with "general democratic tasks," such as the liquidation of the feudal legacy, and only after that to move toward Communist revolution.[24]

In his 24 May 1946 speech at the "Meeting of Propagandists of the Provincial People's Committees, Political Parties and Social Organizations, Cultural Workers, and Artists in North Korea," the DPRK leader described Korean writers as "soldiers on the cultural front" (a variation on Stalin's reference to Soviet writers as "engineers of the human soul"), exhorted them "to go to the masses," and particularly emphasized the need for the "absorption of Soviet culture."[25] In 1955 Pak Chong-sik cited an even more forthright statement that the Great Leader had made in 1946: "We must keep in mind that *only* through learning the progressive art and literature of the Soviet Union can we construct a glorious North Korean culture" (my emphasis).[26]

For a time, the Soviet influence was successfully maintained through various channels. However, in the mid-1950s the political perspectives of both states visibly diverged. While the Soviet leadership was carefully moving toward de-Stalinization, Kim Il Sung opted for a much more restrictive version of state socialism. The DPRK leader strove to escape from Soviet control, and nationalist rhetoric emerged as a useful tool in this process.

The first signs of these looming changes appeared in Kim Il Sung's speech delivered on 28 December 1955 at a conference of Korean Workers' Party (KWP) agitators and propagandists. The Great Leader criticized Koreans for neglecting their own "glorious traditions" and for fostering a preponderance of all things "foreign," which in the contemporary North Korean context meant things Soviet. The Great Leader pointed out, for instance, that in Korean schools there were portraits of Pushkin and Maiakovskii, but no portrait of a Korean writer. He therefore asked: "How can our children learn about national pride?"[27] This speech announced the end of the Soviet era in North Korean culture.

After 1955–1956 the growing rift with Moscow and the increasingly nationalist bias of North Korea's official ideology meant that the once glorified connections with Moscow and Soviet-derived cultural patterns were to be downplayed or denied. Nonetheless, a large number of stereotypes that had entered Korea in the late 1940s from the USSR survived this de-Russification and have remained an important part of the North Korean literary tradition to this day. Many Soviet conventions were also strengthened and readjusted to suit the new needs of the North Korean Stalinist state.

Soviet Literature in Korea

In the Soviet era, or the late 1940s and early 1950s, the number of Soviet books disseminated in North Korea in Korean translation increased dramatically.[28] The precise number remains unclear, since the DPRK never published a complete national bibliography. However, Pak Chong-sik in 1955 declared that "hundreds of titles" of Soviet books had been published in North Korea.[29] Ivanova mentions that in 1945–1950 "overall seventy titles of Soviet and Russian writers [had] been translated into Korean and distributed in the DPRK" and that these Soviet translations "outnumbered the works created by Korean authors" during this same period.[30] Ivanova also quotes a speech by Yi Ki-yŏng in which he said that in 1945–1954, eight million copies of Soviet books were extant in North Korea.

The North Korean literary authorities fervently supported Kim Il Sung's call for the "absorption of progressive Soviet culture." The leading critic, An Ham-gwang, ecstatically exclaimed: "The Liberation of Korea has at last freed up the path for our assimilation of Soviet literature."[31] In an article titled "On International Cultural Exchange" (Kukche munhwa-ŭi kyoryu-e taehayŏ) in the inaugural issue of *Cultural Front* magazine *(Munhwa chŏnsŏn)*, Han Sŏr-ya, the earliest eulogist of Kim Il Sung, stated that Korean literature lagged behind that of the "great Soviet Union."[32] Han exhorted his colleagues to emulate Soviet patterns in the hope of producing a "Korean Gorky" someday.[33]

Literary magazines of the time widely popularized Soviet models and patterns. The lion's share of the content of the leading literary magazine *Literature and Art (Munhak yesul)* in 1949 consisted of Soviet literary pieces, literary criticism in translation, lectures on the Soviet way of life, and articles on Soviet literature, art, and drama. The titles of the articles speak for themselves: Ko Il-hwan's "The Influence of Soviet Literature and the Successes of Our Literature," Chu Yŏng-bo's "Soviet Films Became the Living Textbooks for Our Film Production Industry," Sin Ko-song's "What Can We Learn from Soviet Drama?"[34]

It seems that North Korean writers saw nothing abnormal in treating Soviet writers as "teachers" and their novels as "textbooks" in this confusing new world.[35] Soviet literature, with its artistic authority and firsthand experience of state socialism, presented North Koreans with a conventional set of themes and images to emulate. Without apparent embarrassment, a prosaic Yi Puk-myŏng in his "Let Us Learn the Creative Methods of the Soviet Writers" (Ssobet'ŭ chakkadŭl-ŭi ch'angjak pangbŏp-esŏ paeuja) described in detail how he had "learned" from a particular novel by the Soviet writer Aleksandr Chakovski and admonished his colleagues to do the same.[36] Analyzing North Korean literature from the period between 1945 and 1955 and, in the first instance, the works of the more established North Korean writers such as Yi Ki-yŏng, Han Sŏr-ya, Hong Sun-ch'ŏl, Min Pyŏng-gyun, Hwang Kŏn, Ch'ŏn Se-bong, and Kim Cho-gyu, the contemporary North Korean critic Pak Chong-sik admitted that "it is practically impossible to separate the achievements of these writers from the profound influence of Soviet literature."[37]

In North Korean and Soviet literary studies of the time, the Soviet influence on North Korean literature became a hot academic issue. Numerous articles and dissertations (by An Ham-gwang, Pak Chong-sik, V. I. Ivanova, E. M. Tsoi, A. N. Taen, V. N. Li, and others) monitored the traces of Soviet "patristic texts" such as the "exemplary works" of Vladimir Maiakovskii, Nikolai Ostrovskii, Aleksandr Fadeev, Mikhail Sholokhov, and others in Korean writings both before and after Liberation.[38] The issue of plagiarism was never raised. Ivanova matter-of-factly remarked that North Korean writers Ch'ŏn Se-bong and Yim Chŏng-suk, in their novels, "chose the same story lines as in the novels of Vanda Vasilevskaya" and that "in terms of artistic manner, Hwang Kŏn's novel *Happiness* [Haengpok] is strongly evocative of Fadeev's *Young Guard* [Molodaia Gvardiia]."[39]

Soviet observers, however, did not fail to notice that for all its similarities to the Soviet prototype, North Korea's literature was confined within much stricter boundaries than was Soviet Stalinist literature. In the late 1940s a visiting group of Soviet writers and artists tried to persuade their North Korean colleagues not to write exclusively about the Party and Kim Il Sung but to extol "eternal subjects" such as love or flowers for a change. Nikolai Gribachev, a poet and a top official in the Soviet Writers' Union who often visited Pyongyang in the late 1940s, lamented the absence of lyrical poetry in contemporary North Korean literature.[40] Attempts to persuade North Korean colleagues to "humanize" their literature became more frequent after the Second Soviet Writers' Congress in 1954, which noted the overt bureaucratization of Soviet literature and called on Soviet writers to express their feelings more freely. In light of the steadily increasing creative freedoms permitted in the USSR, Soviet writer and literary official Aleksei Surkov, on his arrival in Pyongyang in 1955, exhorted his North Korean colleagues to pay more attention to the issue of the individuality of the author.[41]

Soviet scholars of North Korean literature also contributed to this cautious criticism. Amid the obligatory praises of the "new progressive literature of the liberated Korean people," they could claim, for instance, that negative characters in Yi Ki-yŏng's much-praised novel *Land (Ttang),* which, as the author himself freely admitted, was an emulation of Sholokhov's *Virgin Land under the Plow,* were too one-dimensional and plain to move the reader[42] or that *sometimes* (my emphasis) North Korean writers were prone to repeating the clichés of ideal heroes which were "too good to be true" or to using tedious, stereotypical artistic methods. It was also argued that *some* (my emphasis) North Korean writers were too wedded to the theme of industrialization and depictions of technological processes rather than presenting people of flesh and blood.[43]

Initially, these calls for a "humanization" of North Korean literature were heeded, and in 1947–1948 a short "lyrical wave" engulfed the Korean poetic world. This wave was strongly inspired by the visit of Nikolai Gribachev and the spread of translated Soviet romantic verses such as Mikhail Isakovskii's "Katyusha" or Konstantin Simonov's "Wait for Me," which were adapted as the lyrics of North Korean pop-songs. Min Pyŏng-gyun, Kim Cho-gyu, Pak Se-yŏng, and other Korean poets also began to produce lyrical poems, and some of these—such as "The First Snow," by Kim Sang-o, and "Pine Tree," by Kim Sun-sŏk—were popular.[44] Yet this wave was temporary, and Korean poets quickly returned to the initial austere pattern.

What Soviet observers of North Korean culture perceived as a misunderstanding of socialist realism or excessive ideological zeal on the part of their "younger brothers" was in fact an expression of the political course that was leading the DPRK in a direction opposite to Nikita Khrushchev's de-Stalinization. Gradually, Soviet readers began to perceive North Korean literature as an unwitting parody on "normal" socialist realism, with "normalcy" referring to contemporary Soviet literature with its higher level of permissible nonpolitical topics. The critics overlooked that, first, this "normal" literature was not politically free itself, and, second, it was Soviet culture that had initially equipped the literature of the "fraternal Korean people" with the basic Stalinist images and patterns of political servility. As North Korean scholar Pak Chong-sik remarked in the 1950s, "if it were not for Soviet literature with its classic exemplary works, our writers would have had to travel a long, complicated and circuitous route."[45]

Pilgrimages to the "Land of Fulfillment": "We Have Forgotten How to Use Money!"

The first "artistic task" that Kim Il Sung personally gave to North Korean writers in 1946 was the production of accolades to Soviet-Korean friendship and eulogies to the Soviet liberators and the Soviet way of life. North Korean writers quickly responded to this demand by producing pro-Soviet writings in various genres.[46] An important niche in these tributes was occupied by *Ssoryŏn kihaenggi,* travelogues of the carefully stage-managed trips made by North Korean writers to the Soviet Union in 1946–1955.

Before discussing these travelogues, I would like to highlight a few peculiarities of this genre. First, these texts, though ostensibly presented as documentary reports, were not intended to be documentary. Unlike the travelogues written by Western pilgrims to the USSR, which were in most cases expressions of sincere though naive illusions on the part of their authors, *Ssoryŏn kihaenggi* were deliberate fantasies, consciously written for propagandistic purposes and rather standardized in terms of rhetoric and images. These travelogues fitted quite well into the frame of socialist realism and had a significant impact on the development of this doctrine in the DPRK.

Second, *Ssoryŏn kihaenggi* promoted certain artistic models and patterns for North Korean fiction and poetry, thus amplifying the effect of translated Soviet literature. (In fact, the picture of the USSR in these nonfictional texts was an even more embellished one than that found in the Soviet fiction of the era). On the other hand, the writing of these reports was among the first tasks specifically assigned by the Party to DPRK intellectuals—their first exercise in political servility and their first test of loyalty to the new regime. The North Korean writers passed this test with flying colors.

The review that follows is based on the original versions of four works: Yi T'ae-jun's *A Trip to the Soviet Union* (Ssoryŏn kihaeng; 1947); Yi Ki-yŏng's *The USSR Creates a Great Life* (Widaehan saenghwal-ŭl ch'angjohanŭn ssoryŏn; 1952) and *The Sun of Communism Is Shining* (Kongsanjuŭi t'aeyang-ŭn pit'nanda; 1954); and *The Great Friendship* (K'ŭnak'ŭn uŭi; 1954), the latter being a collection of the works of six North Korean writers—Min Pyŏng-gyun, Yi Puk-myŏng, Yun Tu-hŏn, Hong Kŏn, Kang Hyo-sun, and Kim Sun-sŏk—who visited the Soviet Union at different times.[47]

These organized pilgrimages of North Korean intellectuals to the USSR constituted an integral part of the Soviet-sponsored propaganda tours for foreigners, which included visits to exemplary factories and collective farms and meetings with top officials as well as supposedly "ordinary" Soviet people.

These staged trips became especially frequent in the final decade of Stalinism, when the establishment of the "socialist camp" necessitated energetic efforts to convert foreigners to an admiration of the USSR as the new world leader. These sponsored journeys, which required quite sophisticated logistics on the part of the hosts, burdened the straitened budget of the postwar Soviet Union.[48] Yet even foreign observers admitted, "Although the effort to manipulate foreign visitors may be costly in material terms, such costs have . . . been more than offset by [eventual] material and propaganda gains."[49]

North Korean writers were also specifically targeted by this scheme. The treatment they were given in the USSR was lavish and flattering; all the visiting North Korean writers commented on the "politeness and hospitality of the Soviet people" and the "perfectly organized service."[50] Yi T'ae-jun, who visited the USSR in 1946, a year of great food shortages in the postwar USSR, exclaimed: "Everything was free! For the last ten days we have forgotten how to use money!"[51] Yi Puk-myŏng excitedly wrote about the luxurious Hotel National in Moscow, where he resided free of charge.[52] What rendered the Korean guests especially susceptible to this aspect of their Soviet visits was the miserable situation in their own country. Two of Yi Ki-yŏng's visits to the USSR were organized in 1952 and 1953, at the height of and closely following the Korean War. Not surprisingly, the writer appreciated all the luxuries he enjoyed in the USSR, including the entertainment in theaters and the careful choice of the best food, which the Soviet hosts endeavored to make suitable for Yi's chronically sick stomach. When the writer's health problems were exacerbated during his 1953 visit, the Soviet hosts provided him with a comfortable hotel room, separate from the other members of the delegation, with the best-quality medical service and a special diet, and then organized several months of treatment in the best Soviet sanatorium. All this was free of charge.[53]

Such pleasures made it easier for the Korean visitors to fulfill the demands of the Pyongyang authorities and to present the USSR as a "land of fulfillment" or "land of happiness."[54] Without a single exception, the North Korean intellectuals accepted the perspectives offered and wrote what they were supposed to write about their "elder brother and teacher"—often even exceeding their brief and inventing implausible fairy tales about a Soviet land of milk and honey. Many images, ideas, and concepts in these tales soon deeply permeated the North Korean literary discourse and became an inseparable part of the DPRK's self-image.

In the following pages I analyze the major borrowings from the Soviet discourse that *Ssoryŏn kihaenggi,* along with the disseminated Soviet literature, brought to Korea and consider how this was applied to the Korean cultural landscape. A brief look at some recent works of literature confirms that many patterns that were introduced to North Korean literature via the various channels of Soviet influence in the late 1940s and early 1950s outlived the short period of Soviet cultural domination and became an important part of the North Korean imagination. Nevertheless, some borrowed models were also characteristically altered under the influence of later modifications to the Party line.

Major Borrowings from the Soviet Discourse

The Image of the Elder Brother

The positive image of the Soviet Union was the primary intended message of the travelogues, and Korean visitors delivered this without exception. Here are a few typical quotations:

> The sun of Communism is shining above humanity. Who hates the sun? Only hateful insects living in total darkness like mosquitoes, lice, or leeches. Capitalists hate Communism because they are in fact like these bad insects. They want to live in darkness and suck the blood of the working people. . . . There are no peoples who hate Communism! Only capitalists and their acolytes can hate the sun of Communism! (Yi Ki-yŏng, *The Sun of Communism Is Shining*)[55]

> The USSR is a country of wisdom. . . . All the old and ugly human traits have disappeared here. It is a new world with new life, new habits and a new culture of a new people. . . . The Soviet Union is a society with which Korea's present and future are closely connected. (Yi T'ae-jun, *A Trip to the Soviet Union*)[56]

While a positive attitude toward the Soviet Union was not rare among visiting foreign intellectuals,[57] the eulogies of North Korean writers markedly surpassed Western accounts. The Korean visitors often augmented their homage to all things Soviet with characteristic self-humiliation, contrasting the strong and determined Soviet people to the weak and timid Koreans. In Min Pyŏng-gyun's travelogue poem "Yŏngye" (Pride), happy liberated Koreans "hid their faces in the wide chests of their Soviet liberators."[58] Hong Kŏn depicts a Korean student at Moscow State University who "was close to tears when he talked about the help that the Russian students gave to Koreans who were not fluent in Russian."[59] During a meeting with Soviet children, Kang Hyo-sun told them about the Korean War, which was being waged at the time, and the Russian children felt compassion for the poor Koreans. The author appreciatively commented, "Soviet children are so kind—as are all Soviet people who are helping Korea," as if he thought that Koreans did not deserve compassion.[60] Kang also relates his conversation with Samuil Marshak, a prominent Soviet children's poet, in which Kang told Marshak that North Korean children live happily under the loving care of the Party while "South Korean children have a dreary and impoverished life under the pressure of American imperialism." Kang Hyu-sun exclaims: "Listening to our story, Marshak lowered his head. We felt that he genuinely loved the Korean children. Why does he love them so much?"[61] The Korean author failed to ask the other obvious question: why should Marshak not love them?

North Korean poetry of the late 1940s and early 1950s that was devoted to Soviet-Korean relations also assumes the perspective of a powerful and wise Russia versus a weak and helpless Korea. For instance, the protagonist of Pak Sǔng-gǒl's poem from the anthology *Glory to Stalin* (1949) claims that the Soviet liberators "raised the flame of life" in the soul of a Korean who had previously lived "as a submissive animal."[62] Myers observes that the Soviet side was often "embarrassed by these tributes which far exceeded even the Eastern Bloc standards of obsequiousness."[63]

This self-humiliating tendency proved to be short-lived, however. In the mid-1950s, when the DPRK was moving away from Soviet control, the teacher/apprentice pattern in Soviet-Korean relations began to make way for an inverted model. A characteristic example was Han Sǒr-ya's essay —"Fadeev and Me" (P'ajeyebǔ-wa na), which was devoted to the recently deceased Aleksandr Fadeev, chairman of the Soviet Writers' Union.[64] In Han's narrative, Fadeev, a top-ranking Soviet dignitary, appears as a timid and naive creature who readily blushes before Han, habitually seeks Han's company, constantly asks for Han's advice and opinion about his new writings, and is thrilled when he finally receives Han's encouragement. Fadeev impatiently awaits the translation of Han's works into Russian, especially his works "of the anti-Japanese struggle period," because these novels, he hopes, will afford his ignorant self a clear perspective on Korea's heritage. In contrast, Han Sǒr-ya emerges as a self-sufficient and confident personality, slightly condescending to his eager Russian friend. Han kindly grants his company to the timid Russian but also skips meetings if he feels he is too busy.

Certainly, these fantasies reveal much about Han, with all his wishful thinking and hidden inferiority complexes. But more importantly, this picture indicates that the earlier pattern of "a Korean crying on the broad chest of a Soviet liberator" was to be reversed with the growth of Korea's "national Stalinism."

The Notion of the Active Social Position of a Communist Intellectual

Another important message of the travelogues was the endorsement of the Soviet pattern of the proper social place of a Communist writer, which in Soviet official parlance was referred to as the "active social position of a progressive writer." This implied that "progressive literature" should promote only "progressive" ideas, which in reality meant the transformation of the writers into Party propagandists.

Visitors from Pyongyang often met with distinguished Soviet writers, many of whom doubled as high-level literary officials, including Aleksei Surkov, Samuil Marshak, Konstantin Simonov, Leonid Leonov, Boris Polevoi, Nikolai Gribachev, and Sergei Mikhalkov. The North Korean writers visited Soviet literary dignitaries in their offices and homes; they attended official ceremonies and were entertained together at parties. The atmosphere of these meetings was warm and friendly, and the guests, being accustomed to the more hierarchical style of relations common to the Korean bureaucracy, admired the easygoing approach of the Soviet dignitaries.[65] Still, during these contacts the Soviet writers did not forget their role as "teachers of socialist realism" and never ceased to explain how a "progressive writer" was supposed to behave and what he or she should produce.

Yi Puk-myŏng recounts that in his meeting with the North Korean delegation Surkov said: "We have to show you a lot of things here. . . . North Korean writers must learn a lot from the USSR."[66] In the words of Yi T'aejun, the Soviet writers instructed the Koreans in the importance of "learning from real life" and "working in the thick of things" and noted that all the Soviet writers themselves were either "of common origin" or had "lived for a long time immersed in the people."[67] Marshak informed Kang Hyo-sun that "our literature is a Party literature and this principle must be reflected in children's literature as well."[68]

In addition to general guidance, Soviet writers also gave their Korean colleagues concrete instructions. Hong Kŏn's recalled that Aleksandr Shtein, a director of the drama department in the Soviet Writers' Union, indignantly informed the Korean guests about a Western visitor to the USSR who had published his Moscow diary in a foreign newspaper in which he implied that there was no toilet paper in his Moscow hotel. Shtein called this article very "narrow-minded" and stressed that Koreans should write "deeper memoirs" about the Soviet Union. (He did not, however, deny the absence of the toilet paper.)[69]

Soviet officials presented the activity of the Soviet Writers' Union "in a proper light" to their Korean guests. Yi Puk-myŏng relates an interesting episode: When his delegation visited the union's Moscow office in early May, they found no writers there. The Korean guests were told that all Soviet writers had willingly gone to factories and industrial sites to "study real life."[70] Yi admired this enthusiasm of the Soviet writers. As a foreigner he did not suspect that it had not been so much a thirst for real life as a chain of national holidays that had prompted the Soviet writers, like all other Soviet citizens, to empty their Moscow offices in early May. Thus the Soviet guides skillfully turned a potentially embarrassing situation into a morality lesson for their Korean guests.

The Soviet officials demonstrated a similar dexterity when they were forced to reinterpret politically slippery incidents involving Soviet writers. In the final decade of Stalinism, such incidents were not rare: for instance, the campaigns over the literary magazines *Zvezda (Star)* and *Leningrad* (1946), the official criticism of Fadeev's novel *Young Guard* (1947), and the persecution of Jewish writers (1950–1952).[71] Some victims of these campaigns were popular in Korea, and the Korean intellectuals were often perplexed by their sudden downfall.

Yi T'ae-jun was openly frustrated by the 1946 political campaign against Anna Akhmatova, and during his visit to the USSR in 1947 Soviet officials took pains to explain to him personally all the "wrongdoings" committed by his favorite poet—namely, "bourgeois aestheticism," "decadence," and "pessimism."[72] Yi Puk-myŏng broached the topic of Fadeev's *Young Guard*, a work about the young guerrilla resistance against Germany's occupation. Awarded a Stalin Prize in 1945, the novel was later criticized for its "underestimation of the Party's leading role," and the author was forced to rewrite it in 1951.[73] Boris Polevoi explained that the novel was "correct" until the moment the new historical facts about the Party's supervision became known, so Fadeev had supposedly come to an independent decision to rewrite his novel in order to make it more truthful.[74]

It is notable that the Soviet literary dignitaries did not volunteer these issues to their North Korean guests but were forced to address them when asked. The Soviet writers must surely have felt that the message that their North Korean apprentices were to digest was too off-putting. Neither popularity nor the high aesthetic value of one's work (as in the case of Akhmatova) nor "active social position" or high official status (as in the case of Fadeev) could save a writer from public denunciation if that was what the Party wanted at the time. As we shall see in chapter 5, Soviet campaigns inspired a chain of similar purges in the Korean literary world, and the accusations leveled at writers there were often even more nebulous and lacking in logic.

North Korean policy makers not only incorporated the Soviet stereotypes of the "active social position" of an intellectual but also created their own much more regularized system of political involvement for writers. One such specific form was the distribution of obligatory topics to North Korean writers.[75] When this system was first introduced in the late 1940s, many North Korean writers were frustrated by the explicit demand to extol land reform and industrialization.[76] Their voices were ignored, however, and the distribution of obligatory topics in the DPRK continued. It is notable that in the Soviet Writers' Union a similar idea was suggested in the early 1930s by some overzealous members but was discarded as absurd.[77] Stalin often expressed his disappointment over the dearth of novels on contemporary themes in Soviet literature, but even he hesitated to mandate specific topics to writers.[78]

Another specific form of political control over intellectuals in the DPRK was the so-called production plans, which were modeled after those in industry. According to these plans, a writer was required to produce a particular number of novels or poems in a given period of time. Those who failed to fulfill their quota were to be criticized and punished.[79] Chŏng Ryul recalls that the entire production plan system was initiated by Kim Ch'ang-man, the head of the Department of Agitation and Propaganda in the KWP Central Committee.[80]

Chŏng also remembers that Kim Ch'ang-man authorized the system of the obligatory dispatch of North Korean writers to exemplary plants, factories, and farms to extol these "real life" experiences in their works.[81] The roots of this system can be traced to the rhetoric of the Soviet Writers' Union, which, as we have seen, promoted it to their North Korean guests. In practice, however, visits by Soviet writers to plants and factories were encouraged but never deemed compulsory.

The obligatory "real-life experience tours" stimulated the growth of so-called documentary literature *(silhwa munhak)* in the DPRK, with its emphasis on factual rather than artistic aspects of literature. An example of this tendency is Yi Ki-yŏng's novel *The Fate of a Woman (Han nyŏsŏng-ŭi unmyŏng)*, written in the early 1960s and, according to the author, based on real events. Yi readily acknowledged the low artistic quality of his work and its overburdening with factual data, but he justified these deficiencies by the political "usefulness" of his book in terms of the "urgent necessity of class education for young people."[82] "Documentary prose" of this ilk occupies an important place in North Korean literature to this day.[83]

North Korean intellectuals not only subordinated themselves to official demands but often initiated their own forms of control and restriction. The poet Paek In-chun, for instance, advocated the "brigade method," according to which poetry and prose were supposed to be created by collectives ("brigades") of authors in order to avoid individual political mistakes.[84] Though this system was not fully established in the 1940s, it flourished later in the 1960s when many Korean literary works came to be written by anonymous "creative groups."

Soviet Cultural Images and Clichés

A further consequence of the Soviet influence on the DPRK was the absorption of officially endorsed Soviet cultural images and symbols into North Korean discourse. Numerous examples of this tendency can be found—see, for example, the above-cited anthology edited by Han Sŏr-ya, *Glory to Stalin,* which presents Stalin as a national Korean hero.[85]

The visiting North Korean writers strove to keep abreast of this political line. They constantly resorted to Soviet-made images, Soviet figures, and Soviet events, trying to insert them into the North Korean heroic pantheon. In the poem "Two Leaders" (Tu suryŏng), Min Pyŏng-gyun has the Korean narrator weep at the sight of the two deceased Soviet leaders Lenin and Stalin.[86] In another poem, "Mother" (Ŏmŏni), Min depicts the mother of two Soviet Communist martyrs, Zoya and Shura Kosmodemyansky, as a figure meant to touch the hearts of his Korean audience.[87]

Not only Soviet images but also events and personalities of traditional Russian culture were to be injected into Korean discourse. Yi Ki-yŏng reported on a speech that he had delivered in Moscow at a ceremony commemorating the opening of a monument to Nikolai Gogol. Yi declared, "Gogol loved the people of his country and hated its enemies. So, too, must the Korean people, now fighting for their independence against the American invaders, learn from Gogol."[88] Thus Koreans were supposed to draw patriotic inspiration from this foreign figure.

Soviet political symbols were also supposed to inspire Koreans. Writing about "the hero city of Stalingrad," Yi Puk-myŏng, for instance, claimed that Stalingrad was "close to the hearts of all Koreans, who, just like the Soviets before them, are fighting now with the foreign [American] invasion."[89] Moscow, as the Soviet capital, was presumed to occupy a special place in Korean hearts. Yi Ki-yŏng wrote:

> Everybody in Korea has a great desire to visit Moscow at least once. And the reason is not just simple gratitude for the liberation of our country from Japanese colonization. Nor is it simply because of the heartfelt brotherly assistance that the Soviets are providing to Korea nowadays. It is because the Soviet people are in the first ranks of those who are struggling for peace and democratic progress all over the world and they are leading mankind along the road to freedom and happiness.[90]

Soviet images were also often used to reinforce current domestic political trends in Pyongyang. Chapter 19 of Yi Ki-yŏng's travelogue of 1954 ("The Sun of Communism Is Shining"), which is devoted to the "brilliant flourishing" of socialist culture and art, is characteristic in this regard.[91] While depicting the Soviet theaters, museums, music halls, and opera houses that represented "the wealth of great socialist art," Yi stressed that Soviet art did not present any examples of "pure art"—an "anti-people art" that supposedly symbolized "bourgeois interests" and was flourishing in contemporary South Korea, where the enslaved artists had to serve the interests of the American imperialists.[92] Yi extolled "progressive socialist Soviet literature, which was born in the struggle with reactionary tendencies." The implications of these statements were clear: the Soviet authority was being used to rationalize the incipient purges against the "pure artists" of the DPRK.

The travelogues bristle with Soviet political catchphrases and clichés: "Moscow is a harbor of the five seas" and "Moscow is the heart of the whole world" (Yi Ki-yŏng);[93] "the First of May is a festival of hope and peace" and "the Soviet people create a garden out of their land" (Hong Kŏn); "those foreign idiots who trumpet the slogan of Communist danger in fact hate the common workers and peasants who refuse to bow to them" (Hong Kŏn); "the Volga river is the mother of Russia" (Kang Hyo-sun); "people are the main value in the Soviet Union" (Yi Ki-yŏng); and so on. When describing his visit to Lenin's Mausoleum, Yi Ki-yŏng commented that he "deeply empathized with the emotions of the people who gathered before the Mausoleum on this chilly winter's day."[94] This image of devoted people crowding in front of Lenin's Mausoleum despite chilly, snowy weather (normal fare for a Russian winter) was one of the stalest of Soviet clichés.

All these clichés and catchphrases that first appeared in North Korean depictions of Soviet "reality" quickly moved into the political lexicon of the DPRK.

This process was accompanied by the creation of parallel domestic stereotypes that better correlated with the Korean traditional heritage. These newly forged Korean stereotypes of socialist realism tended toward sentimentality, calling to mind the traditions of the Korean "new novels" of the beginning of the twentieth century.[95] For example, North Korean descriptions of Leningrad, which had survived nine hundred days of siege by the Nazi army, differed from those of Soviet discourse. While in Soviet parlance Leningrad was referred to as "a heroic city," "a staunch city," and "a city of indomitable citizens," in North Korean accounts it became "a city of suffering and tears."[96]

The theme of international friendship was also delivered in images that Soviet readers would probably have found too sentimental. Yun Tu-hŏn devoted a whole chapter of his travelogue to a long, syrupy story about his friendship with a little Russian girl with whom he used to speak "through feelings." Before Yun's departure the girl presented him with her favorite toy, a rubber frog, so that he might give it to some Korean child. And now every time he looked at the rubber frog, he "thought about the little Russian girl with her big, kind heart."[97] This narration is inappropriately sweet for the Soviet discourse of the time.

Also characteristic in this regard is Yi Ki-yŏng's account of his visit to the Gorky museum in Gorky City. Speaking about the life of the writer who, in Soviet discourse, was referred to as the Stormy Petrel, Yi concentrated not on struggle and resistance (the standard topic of Soviet authors) but rather on the writer's bitter family background and childhood suffering. Eloquently narrating the story of a "poor talented boy" who could not study because his vicious grandfather refused to support him, Yi tearfully contrasts the grandfather (the embodiment of all evil) with the angelic grandmother.[98] Thus, with a stroke of Yi Ki-yŏng's pen, the indomitable Stormy Petrel is turned into a "poor boy," a pitiful personage somewhat reminiscent of the characters in Yi's own pre-Liberation novels (discussed in chapter 3). Yi's perception of Gorky strongly reflected Korean cultural predispositions; he focused primarily on family and educational issues and was more inclined to lament obstacles than to exalt the fortitude required to overcome them.

In the late 1950s, under the increasing influence of the nationalist rhetoric of the DPRK, images such as Koreans weeping at a mausoleum over a departed Lenin or Stalin, as well as the depiction of Moscow as "the heart of the world," evaporated from North Korean writing. Nevertheless, in today's North Korean press—and in *Nodong Sinmun (Workers' Newspaper)* in particular—one can still find a huge amount of Soviet-derived idioms, and many old Soviet clichés still feature in contemporary North Korean literature.

Curiously enough, even the most militant pieces of DPRK propaganda are tinged with characteristic streaks of sentimentalism. This is especially traceable in North Korean works about the historical past, both distant (such as Yi Ki-yŏng's *The Fate of a Woman,* set in the colonial period) and near (such as the "march of hardships," *konanyu haenggun,* portrayed in Ryu Hŭi-nam's "Story about One Family" [Han kajŏnge iyagi]).[99]

Social Idylls

The travelogues greatly contributed toward the crystallization of the artistic self-image of the DPRK as another socialist Eden. In many respects, the picture of the DPRK that emerged in North Korean fiction mirrored the embellished image of the USSR that appeared in the travelogues rather than in the Soviet patristic texts. Of course, Soviet literature also promoted the idea of the USSR as a socialist paradise. However, the orthodoxy of this literary portrait was often diluted by equivocal subplots. The staged trips represented a much more refined type of propaganda, and the pictures of the socialist paradise that were presented to the foreign tourists surpassed the literary socialist realist depictions in terms of exaltation and gross overstatement. North Korean writers ingested these patterns, not only applying them to their depiction of the Soviet Union but also projecting their basic traits into the propagandistic image of the DPRK. Most of these patterns stood the test of time, and some of them were altered in accordance with changes in North Korean policy. Let us consider the major set of myths as they appeared in Soviet fiction and travelogues and trace their influence on the self-image of the DPRK as it appeared in the North Korean literature of the 1945–1960 era and later.

The "Industrialized Paradise"

The image of the USSR as a developed industrialized country constituted the core of Soviet self-presentation. This picture was based on some real achievements, such as rapid industrialization and successful postwar reconstruction, long holidays, relatively short working hours, free education and medical services, and some legal and social rights for women. At the same time, as in any other type of propaganda, many important issues were misrepresented. Aspects that were falsely advertised with particular regularity were the technical sophistication of Soviet industry (overestimated), the labor conditions and livings standards of the Soviet population (grossly embellished), and the human costs that had been paid for the "Communist miracle" (recognized, but misrepresented as voluntary sacrifices).

Let us begin with the pattern involving the *technical sophistication* of the USSR. Yi Ki-yŏng described a Soviet automated brick factory that he visited during one staged trip as "the most progressive factory in the world" on the grounds that "no manual labor whatsoever was needed." As an example of one entirely unique "miracle machine," Yi mentions a weight-lifting crane (*kijunggi*) that was allegedly invented in the Soviet Union and existed nowhere else in the world.[100] This was not true.

Yi Puk-myŏng in 1954 made the following comment about Soviet aircraft: "The USSR is a country of aircraft. And I mean civil airplanes, which are used for pleasure by everybody. One of my colleagues joked that there are more airplanes in the Soviet Union than chickens in North Korea."[101] Yi was certainly exaggerating the role of aviation in the USSR of 1954, where civil aircraft were by no means a common form of travel for pleasure. Note the self-effacing intonation of the joke, which was, as already noted, typical of the Soviet era.

The exaggeration of Korea's own achievements and material progress soon became a typical hallmark of Pyongyang's propaganda. The image of a heavily industrializing new Korea was actively promoted by the Soviet Korean poet Cho Ki-ch'ŏn (discussed further in chapter 2). In his long epic "The Song of Life" (Saengae-ŭi norae; June 1950), for example, Cho extolled North Korean tractors, airplanes, and the "proud smoke of success" of Korean factories, implying that these features had been brought to Korea by the socialist system.[102] Cho conveniently omitted mentioning that Korea had been heavily industrialized since the colonial era. Other contemporary Korean authors admitted the existence of factories and enterprises in pre-Liberation Korea but stressed that only after Liberation could Koreans work happily and effectively in these factories.[103]

The image of industrialization allegedly brought to North Korea by the socialist system is still popular in Pyongyang's domestic propaganda. Take, for example, the poem "The Words I Would Like to Say More and More" (Hago ttohago sip'ŭn mal), by Chŏn Kŭm-ok. Referring to the achievements of socialist Korea, the author resorts to the stale truism of a country boy who before Liberation "had never heard the sound of a train" but who now enjoyed the opportunity of studying at a university.[104] The early twenty-first-century picture of high-tech North Korean society is still typically delivered in images that have remained unchanged since the 1950s. In a poem titled "Look at the Reality!" (Hyŏnsil-ŭl pora!), Sŏ Chŏng-in, a member of Ch'ongryŏn, protects the reputation of the DPRK from the attacks of unspecified "reactionaries" while simultaneously pointing to what he considers to be the signs of a developed North Korea: young women working on tractors, children sitting in buses, and so on.[105] In the 1990s, Sŏ referred to the same "new tractors" and "merrily laboring factory workers" as were used, for example, in Chŏng Mun-hyang's poem "O My Country, My Endless Joy!" (Chogukiyŏ kkŭt'ŏmnŭn na-ŭi kippŭmiyŏ), which was written in 1956.[106]

Similarly, the real *living and working conditions* of the workers in the post-war USSR were far from comfortable,[107] and this fact was often recognized even by Soviet officialdom. In a Soviet novel or poem of the 1940s–1950s, it is difficult to find a positive protagonist who lives in an individual apartment, eats in a good restaurant, or owns a car. However, the organizers of the staged trips presented the Koreans with a more embellished picture. Yi Puk-myŏng admiringly depicted the "typical" large apartment block of ordinary Soviet workers, with a few supposedly private cars near the entrance and the sound of a piano audible through the window.[108]

North Korean socialist realism also widely promoted myths about the luxurious living conditions of Korean workers and farmers. Yi Ki-yŏng in his 1949 novel, *Land,* constantly used the image of a new house as a symbol of the renewed lives of his heroes.[109] The images of workers' families moving into spacious new houses, a child taking a bath in a big bathtub,[110] and the pretty wife of a worker dressed in new, expensive clothes[111] became extremely popular in North Korean literature, especially after the Korean War, when the real living conditions of the majority of Koreans were destitute. Access to life's essentials was presented as an expression of the Party's benevolence, and new houses (*munhwa chut'aek,* "cultured accommodation") were portrayed as the embodiment of comfort.

Recent Korean writings still widely deploy images of the *munhwa chut'aek* as the symbol of a developed North Korean society. The poet Ch'oe Ch'ang-man, depicting the contented life of North Koreans in 1998, uses the same image of "happy laughter pouring from the open window of the cultured accommodation" as the poet Kim Ch'ŏl had in 1956.[112]

Another common element used to demonstrate the "beautiful life" of Soviet workers was the frequent depiction of the banquets that Korean writers enjoyed in Soviet factories. For example, visiting the GAZ automobile plant in Gorky, Yi Ki-yŏng mentioned a sumptuous dinner he had enjoyed in the factory cafeteria.[113] Yi implied that this feast represented a regular meal for common workers in the plant, which was certainly not the case.

The images of an abundance of food and happy family/neighborhood feasts, which were relatively rare in Soviet texts of the Stalin era, became popular in North Korean literature from the very outset.[114] To demonstrate the socialist achievements of the DPRK barely a year after Liberation, Yi Ki-yŏng included scenes of lavish celebrations, complete with lists of the dishes served, in *Land*.[115]

Such scenes have practically disappeared from the North Korean literature of the 1990s, which have come to reflect the more ascetic approach of contemporary slogans such as *konanyu haenggun* (march of hardships) and *sŏngun chŏngch'i* (military-first policy).[116] Recently published Pyongyang anthologies, along with still-popular eulogies of "the achievements of socialism," also include works that exhort Korean people not to complain about food shortages. Consider, for example, the recommendations of Han Chŏng-gyu in his poem "Words I Often Say to My Children" (Chasikdŭr-ege chaju hanŭn mal):

> *Though today we all keenly sense what rice means to us,*
> *Though we have all suffered*
> *During the brief "march of hardships,"*
> *My family,*
> *Do not say that it is hard!*
> *. . . Do not waste*
> *A stalk of rice in the fields,*
> *A grain of rice in your homes!*
> *Remember what our leader said:*
> *"Rice is socialism!"*
> *The ancients said*
> *That only after the belly is full*
> *And the back is warm*
> *Can people smile and dance.*
> *But is that really so?*
> *Let's smile, and dance, and march ahead.*
> *Today the dead heroes of Paektu Mountain see us*
> *Smiling and dancing in the snow flurries,*
> *With only fresh snowflakes in our bellies.*
> *We should smile and sing songs,*
> *And our Marshal Father*
> *Who leads us forward*
> *Will have more strength.*[117]

When it came to the issue of the *human costs* of the Soviet "economic miracles," the eulogists of socialist construction also tended to hush them up or to reinterpret them as an expression of the willing self-sacrifice of the Soviet people. For instance, Yi Ki-yŏng devoted an entire chapter of *Land* to the glorification of the "heroic construction" of the Volga-Don Canal, which was allegedly undertaken by the willing labor of the masses.[118] The canal was in fact built by Gulag prisoners, whose numbers in January 1952 reached 118,000.[119] Yun Tu-hŏn recounts another characteristic tale. While traveling in Tajikistan, he saw an artificial lake near Dushanbe. The land had been too hard to dig with spades, so young communist workers had supposedly used their bare hands to create the lake.[120]

The idea that sacrifice and suffering are immanent attributes of virtually any achievement in a Communist society was quite popular in Soviet discourse; suffice it to mention the classic *How the Steel Was Tempered*, by Ostrovskii (1932). However, in the North Korean discourse, this martyr syndrome became a special favorite. In *Land*, Yi Ki-yŏng depicts the protagonists as draining marshes and working the fields with their bare hands or with heavy, unwieldy tools, a portrayal presented as an indication of their eager readiness to work.[121] Even the slightest attempt of a North Korean literary hero to consider his or her own personal needs was treated as evidence of reactionary tendencies. In the play *Two Girls* (Tu ch'ŏnyŏ), written by Song Yŏng in 1953, a young female character who is sent to a rural area feels uncomfortable and lonely at first and wants to return home.[122] Then she overcomes her negative feelings and starts to work enthusiastically. Song quickly received a critical reprimand from the critic Kim Myŏng-su, who claimed that the positive heroine should not feel this way or express such "petit bourgeois feelings."[123] In Sŏk In-hae's 1956 short story "The Village Schoolmistress" (Maŭl-ŭi nyŏsŏnsaeng), the protagonist organizes the voluntary work of her colleagues and pupils to construct a new school building.[124] Though the labor is considered to be voluntary, to be done after normal hours, a male colleague who attempts to avoid it for personal reasons is criticized as a "hostile element." When an enthusiastic schoolboy is injured at the construction site and his mother vents her anger on his supervising teacher, this episode is presented as harassment of the progressive teacher.

The motif of enthusiastic workers who must overcome enormous obstacles (and may even die in the process) was widely promoted in North Korean literature. One typical example is a short story by Pyŏn Hŭi-gŭn entitled "Happy People" (Haengbokhan saramdŭl; 1953), in which the female worker T'an-sil, during an American air raid on her factory, receives irreversible facial injuries while saving the factory equipment.[125] Her fiancé, the exemplary fighter Ch'ang-sŏn, enthusiastically asserts that he is "really happy to love such a wonderful girl": "You, comrade, have saved an electric furnace from enemy attack, sacrificing your flowerlike face in the process. This is such a wonderful and proud deed! The scars on your face do not matter. What really matters is how deeply you love the country and what a beautiful and noble heart you have." The young man makes a vow to defeat the wicked enemy and then "to come back to you, comrade, and to the electric furnace that you have saved."[126]

North Korean literature of the late twentieth and early twenty-first centuries still reflects this martyrdom tendency. A minor character in the short story "A Person of the Same Age" (Tonggabi), by Chŏng Ok-sŏn, heroically dies at a construction site.[127] The heroine of Ryu Hŭi-nam's above-mentioned "Story about One Family" exhausts herself to the point of death while caring about the collective herd of goats for her husband's brigade.[128] In a number of stories, well-educated and Pyongyang-born protagonists willingly abandon city comfort to work in shabby remote villages.[129] It seems that North Korean policy makers, like their Soviet predecessors, did not notice the major contradiction between two essential elements of this Communist idyll. On the one hand, the socialist worker supposedly enjoys a wealthy and comfortable lifestyle as a result of the unwavering care of the Party, while on the other the exemplary worker is expected to endure all manner of hardships and often to die heroically, struggling against impossible odds.

The "Agricultural Paradise"

Another range of widely exaggerated tales in the travelogues referred to the well-being of the people in Soviet kolkhozes, or collective farms. Given the particularly miserable reality of Soviet rural areas, this fiction was sadly grotesque.[130] At a time when Soviet collective farmers mockingly sang, "Proletarians of all countries, join us! Treat yourself to one hundred grams of bread a day! Don't hesitate!" Yi Ki-yŏng wrote after visiting a "typical" Ukrainian kolkhoz that a Soviet farmer received a kilo and a half of flour, two kilos of potatoes, and a sum of money for one workday (Rus. *trudoden'*).[131] Hong Kŏn relates the story of some "ordinary farmer" in Abkhazia who supposedly earned fifty thousand rubles in the previous year and then described how he had spent this enormous income: "I bought a new Pobeda [a large car] and constructed a two-story house. The remaining money I just wasted."[132] The poet Kim Sun-sŏk relates a similarly false interview with an "ordinary farmer" from a kolkhoz near Stalingrad who reported, "Last year I spent eight thousand rubles on a car. There are a lot of private cars on our collective farm."[133]

The life of Soviet farmers as presented in the travelogues is not just prosperous but also economically liberated, technologically advanced, and highly cultured.[134] Yi Ki-yŏng claimed that Soviet collective farms sold milk and meat at the local market and distributed the profits among the collective farm members.[135] The writer waxed lyrical about the Soviet miracle machines for potato harvesting and modern tractors that he saw on a Ukrainian collective farm, and he marveled at the TV system in the kolkhoz's school.[136] The poet Kim Sun-sŏk quotes the members of another Soviet collective farm as having said: "Thanks to the care of the Party and the Government, we have all received bright, modern houses. Every evening they show movies in our club. There is a radio, a telephone, and an electrical heating system in every house. There is no difference between the city and rural lifestyles in our country."[137] Likewise Yi Ki-yŏng concludes: "Cities and rural communities in the Soviet Union have the same quality of life. The only distinction between them is the beauty of nature in the countryside that cannot be found in big cities."[138] Yi thus implies that it is only the "beauty of nature" that holds farmers in the countryside.[139]

Some contemporary Soviet literary works, such as *Cavalier of the Gold Star (Kavaler Zolotoi Zvezdy),* by Semyon Babayevsky, and *Happiness (Schastye),* by Pavel Pavlenko, also painted rosy pictures of the affluent life of the Soviet kolkhozes. However, even this Stalinist fiction did not portray Soviet rural areas in such an idealized manner as the Soviet hosts presented to their Korean visitors. Despite their generally triumphant tone, Soviet agricultural novels such as Aleksei Musatov's *Stozhary* (1948), Vera Panova's *Yasnui Bereg* (1949), and Galina Nikolaeva's *Zhatva (Harvesting;* 1950) occasionally referred to material hardships and social discontent in Soviet kolkhozes. The collectivization novels of the 1930s (most prominently, Sholokhov's *Virgin Land under the Plow)* provided anything but a bucolic depiction of happy village life.

In contrast, North Korean writing on rural subjects for decades presented the reality of the newly created "cooperatives" as a paradise for voluntarily united peasants.[140] No social problems were mentioned in the North Korean agrarian novels; all farmers were depicted as simple but honest people, working toward common goals. These tendencies have been noted by Myers in relation to Han Sŏr-ya's writings but are also identifiable in the works of other North Korean writers. The protagonists of Yi Ki-yŏng's *Land* enthusiastically work for the common good and selflessly donate "patriotic rice." The vast majority of the heroes in Ch'ŏn Se-bong's short story "New Spring in Sŏkkaeul" (Sŏkkaeul-ŭi saebom) eagerly work on the collectivized land.

Conflicts, if they appear at all in these chocolate-box environments, are childishly innocuous.[141] Take for instance Pak Hyo-jun's short story "The Ox" (So; 1956).[142] The protagonist, the elderly farmer Un-bo, does not want to pool his precious ox with the cooperative because he is not sure whether the other farmers would take proper care of it. His son, a conscious collectivist, convinces his father that the cooperative needs the ox in order to achieve a good harvest and that the animal would be cared for by everyone in the collective "as if it was their own." The ox finally goes to the collective farm. The cooperative achieves a good harvest, and the old farmer relaxes when he discovers that the ox receives good care from the other members of the cooperative. In the end, Un-bo becomes an enthusiastic supporter of the collective farm. Thus, all the problems of the North Korean postwar village in the story are narrowed to the peculiar stubbornness of an old man that quickly gives way to the norm of collective consciousness.

From the 1990s on, however, the conventions of North Korean agricultural literature have changed slightly. Along with the still-popular images of "fields of gold," "aromatic orchards," "clean houses with snow white walls," and "bathrooms with bathtubs" as sure signs of a prosperous and cultured village life,[143] contemporary North Korean writers often mention the real problems in DPRK rural areas.

This tendency is visible, for instance, in Chŏng Ok-sŏn's short story "A Person of the Same Age."[144] The village-born protagonist, Yŏng-jin, who is studying in Pyongyang, is reluctant to return to his home village after graduation. His female classmate Hye-yŏng, a pretty fashion-lover who is now living in the provincial city with her uncle's family, makes it clear that she would do anything to stay in the city. Yŏng-jin vacillates, but meetings with the mother of his late classmate who died heroically on a construction site, and with a city girl of the same age who has come to their home village to work and "struggle with difficulties," make him understand that "it is time to march in the front ranks of the century" and that he "has no right to be a straggler on the general course of the 'march of hardships,' as proclaimed by our glorious Leader."

Despite the predictable outcome of this soul-searching story, the author mentions certain real problems of the contemporary village and the unwillingness of young people to live there. Thus, the previous stereotype of an agricultural paradise may perhaps be fading away in recent North Korean literature.

An "Educational and Cultural Paradise"

It comes as no surprise that the visitors from Korea, with their deep-rooted Confucian reverence for education, extolled the rich cultural and intellectual life of Soviet citizens and eagerly described Soviet schools, public libraries, theaters, and museums.[145] Nor was their presentation of this aspect of Soviet life completely false; indeed, the Soviet system of free college-level education, a well-developed program of student scholarships, and subsidized theaters, libraries, and museums represented a very real achievement of Soviet socialism. Yet the depictions of these true achievements were often accompanied by gross overstatements. For instance, Hong Kŏn reported that every student at Moscow State University lived in a separate room, each room being eight *p'yŏng,* and that PhD students enjoyed separate, twelve-*p'yŏng* rooms with telephones.[146] Every room also supposedly had a kitchen and a bathroom—and all for a monthly fee of a mere fifteen rubles.[147] According to Yi Ki-yŏng, the student dormitory in Moscow State University looked "like a first-class hotel." The rector of this "palace of science" (the then standard Soviet cliché, which Yi also used) supposedly told him that from now on "all the students of the university will live in separate rooms so as not to disturb each other's studying," since "sharing a room with another student must be a very uncomfortable practice."[148] These supposed pluses of the Soviet educational system in the travelogues were contrasted with the shortcomings in the capitalist world. Yi stressed, for instance, that in capitalist countries like the United States or Great Britain many working people were illiterate, with even primary schools being too costly for ordinary people.[149]

It seems the North Korean visitors expressed a particular admiration for this aspect of Soviet life, yet the motif of the "cultural and educational paradise" appears much less prominently in North Korea's literature than in Soviet creative writings. While Soviet Stalinist novels often depicted the lives of college and university students—for instance, Yurii Trifonov's novel *Students* (*Studenty;* 1951), which won much official acclaim—the protagonist of North Korean poems and novels was rarely a full-time student. This is especially significant if we take into account that students returning from Japan were favorite personages in pre-Liberation Korean novels. The academic activities or studies of the North Korean literary hero, if mentioned at all, always followed long-term engagement in physical labor in either industry or agriculture (see, for example, Cho Ki-ch'ŏn's poem "The Whistle" [Huip'aram])[150] or was considered only to be preparation for such work (Han Sŏr-ya, "The Mining Settlement" [T'an'gaengch'on]).[151]

Not only students but also scientists, engineers, teachers, and university professors were among the favorite characters of the Soviet fiction of the 1940s and 1950s. See, for instance, Konstantin Lokotkov's *Loyalty (Vernost')*, Vadim Ohotnikov's *Roads to the Depths (Dorogi vglub')*, and Frida Vigdorova's *My Class (Moi klass)*.[152] In contrast, North Korean literature of the 1950s seldom dealt with intellectuals. On the rare occasions when the protagonist happened to be an educated person, his or her activity was either overburdened by raw political motive or had little to do with intellectual work at all. In Sŏk In-hae's short story "The Village Schoolmistress," the protagonist, Yŏng-ae, is largely preoccupied with the construction of a new school building, "overcoming difficulties," and repelling "reactionary elements." Only once is Yŏng-ae shown engaged in her professional activity, when she reads with her students a long, propagandistic work about "wicked Americans" and "brave Koreans," lengthy passages of which are given in the text.

This tendency to overlook the intellectual activity of the characters is also visible in North Korean literary works of today. In the short story "Lofty Goal" (Nop'ŭn mokp'yo), by Yang Chae-mo, the characters, who are provincial doctors, are never depicted studying or working. Instead, they indulge in lengthy discussions, one of the main postulates of which is that "real education is to be found not in books but in working among the people." The same tendency to sideline intellectual work is observable in Chŏng Ok-sŏn's "A Person of the Same Age," in which the protagonist, a student, feels deeply inferior before the provincial folk who, unlike him, are "real people" and know how to grow a good persimmon. The protagonist of the science fiction story "Strong Wings" (Ŏksen nalgae; 2004), by Han Sŏng-ho, a talented scientist is able to succeed only after she has listened to the advice of "real people"—construction workers.[153]

Similarly, North Korean fiction rarely depicts its characters visiting a theater or a museum or reading fiction—that is, as being occupied with that very "proper cultural entertainment" that the visiting Korean writers had once admired in Soviet life. The only common sign of a cultural life that I have been able to discover in North Korean literature is "the sound of an accordion" pouring out of the open windows of a new house.[154]

The underrepresentation of intellectuals in North Korean literature is somewhat surprising, given the Confucian background of Korea and its culturally preconditioned respect for intellectuals and contempt for physical labor. It appears likely that this was related to the "deep mistrust of intellectuals" by the North Korean elite, which Myers has mentioned in connection with Kim Il Sung's policies.[155] Unlike the Soviet Stalinist policy makers, many of whom originally came from the intelligentsia and maintained strong connections with this social stratum despite all their "proletarian" rhetoric, the nascent North Korean elite included people of rather low educational levels who distrusted privileged urbanites.

"The Center" and the "Last Hope of the World"

In Stalinist propaganda, the world consisted of two clearly identifiable parts: the progressive camp, which was led, transformed, and inspired by the Soviets, and the reactionary camp, which viciously opposed the "truth of Communism." The Soviet Union was depicted as a protector of the oppressed and a model to be emulated. From the 1920s, special emphasis was placed on the anti-imperialist essence of Soviet policy and the generous aid provided to the "less developed" ethnic groups inside the USSR.[156]

These stereotypes were especially meaningful to the newly decolonized Koreans, and the Soviet propagandists paid particular attention to them. A large number of works by minority writers were translated into Korean in the 1940s, while the propaganda produced an avalanche of Korean-language booklets eulogizing Soviet policy in non-Russian republics. The travelogues followed the same line. Yi T'ae-jun extolled the "wise and noble ethnic policy" of the USSR.[157] Yi Ki-yŏng eulogized the USSR, where "all the ethnic groups live as one big happy family."[158] Min Pyŏng-gyun also repeated the popular Soviet trope: "The USSR is a land of many nations. But you do not feel as if there are too many peoples here. Everybody is happy. Everybody is singing only songs of happiness."[159]

The propagandistic stereotype of the "freedom of minority cultures" in the USSR naturally required the concept of previous shackles, the image of the successfully repelled "other." Yun Tu-hŏn wrote with great regret about pre-Soviet Tajikistan, which had allegedly been "oppressed by Arabs" for centuries. Although the Tajiks had had their own alphabet since the eighth century AD, they were forced to use Arabic letters until liberated from this by the Communist revolution.[160] The author fails to mention, however, which alphabet the Tajiks were actually using at the time of his writing—the Russian Cyrillic alphabet.

Min Pyŏng-gyun wrote about Tajikistan as previously poor and "oppressed by the Muslims" but affluent and exuberant now. The faces of liberated Tajik girls shone with content; they played musical instruments and people gathered around, now free from Muslim tenets, and merrily drank red wine.[161]

References to the non-Communist world in the travelogues have a strong anti-American and anti-Western flavor. Yi Ki-yŏng contrasts the "rich cultural life" of the Soviet collective farms with the situation in capitalist countries, where "even workers in cities live under the strong oppression of illiteracy, not to mention the peasantry."[162] Speaking about the inventions made by the Research Institute for Labor Protection in Leningrad, Yi mentions a machine that had been designed to replace a preexisting American contraption. The American device was too noisy and uncomfortable, because unlike industrial managers in a Soviet state, American capitalists did not care for their workers.[163] Yi comments on the situation: "If Soviet workers live in a living paradise, their Western counterparts work in a real hell." And on the international scene, the United States allegedly behaves like a colonialist power. After visiting Norway, Yi asserted that "Norway is turning into an American colony." As irrefutable proof of his thesis he points out that, unlike in the USSR, "even the soap in Norway's hotels is made in America."[164]

As a rule, Soviet propaganda took pains to distinguish between the "bad" ruling classes of Western countries and the potentially good or at least redeemable "masses," who either supported the Communist cause in the depth of their hearts or would do so if they knew better. As a testimony to the miserable situation of the working class in Norway and Sweden, Yi Ki-yŏng cites the absence of queues in capitalist shops. To his mind, this means that ordinary people in these countries are too poor to buy products, while Moscow's shops with their long queues are overflowing with people who have lots of money to spend.[165]

Still, sometimes in Soviet propaganda the normal ideological line between "good" (exploited) and "bad" (exploiting) Westerners is blurred, offering some concession to the xenophobic generalizations. North Korean travelogues, on the other hand, often resorted to a common cliché of Soviet propaganda according to which "Westerners," independent of their class or nation, were weak, cowardly people who could not conceive of the feats of labor that the tough and energetic Soviet people were able to produce. Yi Puk-myŏng, for instance, retold Soviet stories of "dim-witted foreigners" who refused to believe in the speedy reconstruction of Stalingrad, which had been ruined by war. The Soviet people proved to be much stronger than the "reactionaries" expected.[166]

The place of North Korea in this propagandistic scheme was clear-cut: the nation was supposed to be a recipient of Soviet internationalist benevolence and an object of Soviet protection against the common enemy. Min Pyŏnggyun, eulogizing the "Soviet paradise for the national minorities," made sure that the Korean reader would grasp his message that the Soviet Union was "opening up the same paradise for us Koreans."[167]

From the late 1950s, however, North Korean policy makers started to position the DPRK as a self-sufficient state, equipped with a potentially world-dominating ideology. There emerged an image of North Korea as the sole, independent center of all the truly progressive forces of the globe. This image was strongly reminiscent of the image of the USSR in old Soviet propaganda, with Pyongyang replacing Moscow as the center of the inhabited universe. One of the earliest examples of this emerging trend can be seen in Yi T'ae-jun's short story "Dear People" (Kogwihan saramdŭl; 1951), which dealt with Chinese-Korean friendship.[168] The protagonist, a Chinese volunteer in the Korean War, claims that only his acquaintance with the North Korean Communists and the heroic Korean girl Kim Ok-sil "helped him to understand better his own Chinese People's Liberation Army and the Chinese Communist Party."

However, North Korean writers, being citizens of a monoethnic state and practically devoid of contact with the outside world, could not strictly follow the Soviet model of the "center of the world." While Soviet Stalinist writing readily portrayed Soviet/Russian heroes interacting with people of other specified cultures and demonstrating their cultural and ideological superiority in the process,[169] North Korean fiction seldom depicted its characters dealing directly with foreigners. Though North Korean literature today eagerly uses the image of the DPRK as the main hope of all progressive humankind (or a heroic state that is "saving socialism, which others could not save"),[170] it is reluctant to become more specific when depicting this lucky humankind. The protagonists of Yang Chae-mo's "Lofty Goal," for example, learn unspecified "foreign languages," read "foreign newspapers," sympathize with the people of an unspecified "poor foreign country," and criticize "foreign scientists" from "another country that claims to be developed."[171] It seems that the author of the story has little specific knowledge or experience in the international sphere.

The only discernible "other" in the North Korean creative writings who "has to learn a lot" from North Korea is South Korea. This tendency was already visible in Yi Ki-yŏng's *Land* and Yi T'ae-jun's "Somewhere near the 38th Parallel" (38 sŏn ŏnŭ chigu-esŏ; 1949)[172] and became especially pronounced in the first decade of the twenty-first century, when, with the implementation of the "sunshine policy," North Korean writers were given a chance to see Southerners in person. South Koreans who eagerly look upon the North as their last hope and the center of the universe were popular characters in North Korean fiction in the early 2000s.[173] See, for example, Sŏk Yu-kyun's short stories "Unusual Landscape" (Ryutarŭn p'unggyŏnhwa; 2004) and "Star and Dream: From the Diary of an Ex-Prisoner in a South Korean Jail" (Zvezda I mechta: Is dnevnika byvshego uzdnika yuzhnokoreiskoi tyur'my; 2005).[174]

The role of the negative "other" in North Korean propaganda was bestowed on the "Japs" and the "Yankees." The DPRK world picture did not generally follow the Soviet differentiation between "good" (exploited) and "bad" (exploiting) members of hostile nations. In the DPRK, stereotypes of "bestial Japs" and "weak and vicious Americans with ugly pale faces" versus "strong, vigorous, and generous North Koreans" soon developed to a level of racism that was unimaginable in the multinational USSR. The writings of Han Sŏr-ya, Yi T'ae-jun, and others presented clear examples of out-and-out anti-American bigotry.[175] Yi Ki-yŏng, when writing about the historical past of Korea, eagerly repeated old rumors about the repulsive Japanese who allegedly killed Koreans and used their flesh as bait for fishing.[176]

With the arrival of the *chuch'e* era in the 1960s, anti-Western stereotypes became favorite topics in North Korean propaganda.[177] As a contemporary example of this tendency we need only look to the story "Lofty Goal,"[178] in which the protagonist debunks a "foreign professor" who has stolen an anticancer panacea invented by a rural North Korean doctor. Once again, a very popular topic in Soviet literature of the Stalin era—that of crafty Westerners stealing the discovery of an inventive Russian/Soviet scientist—has been echoed in North Korean literature.[179]

If we look from a historical perspective at the major Soviet-derived patterns that permeated North Korean literature in its early years, we will notice that most of them were successfully embedded into the North Korean discourse. Sometimes they required adaptation to the North Korean environment: some of the more rigid clichés of Soviet propaganda acquired more sentimental forms, the concept of an educational and cultural paradise was less observable, and the pattern of relations between the USSR and the DPRK as that between an elder and a younger brother was eventually obliterated.

The majority of these earlier patterns not only survived the de-Russification of North Korean life in the late 1950s but reemerged in a stronger form. The Soviet notion of the political engagement of the Communist intellectual was transformed into complete servility and reinforced by specific forms of political control over writers. The contrasting of "weak and cowardly Westerners" with "tough and vital Koreans" reached a level of racist rhetoric unseen in the Soviet Union. Many Stalinist propagandistic truisms that had been ridiculed after Stalin's death in the USSR, such as the descriptions of the most mundane chores as struggles (including the proverbial annual "struggle for harvest") or the masochistic images of lakes created by digging with bare hands blossomed in North Korea. And, above all, the basic notion of a social-ist paradise and its accompanying myths still constitute the cornerstones of the national literary ideology of the DPRK. Thus the North Korean appren-tices grasped the torch of Stalinist propaganda at the very moment when their Soviet teachers' own faith in the Communist orthodoxy began to wane.

2   Soviet Koreans in North Korean Literature

The Case of Cho Ki-ch'ŏn

THE SOVIET INFLUENCE upon North Korea's literature, as on other spheres of life in the DPRK, was conducted through a unique and efficient living channel, namely through Russianized or Soviet Koreans.[1] For the Soviet administration, these people, who combined a Soviet upbringing and mentality with a strong sense of belonging to the Korean ethnic community, were invaluable intermediaries in dealing with North Korean society. Among many other political missions in the DPRK, Soviet Koreans were also entrusted with assisting in the transformation of North Korean literature and the arts into crucial propaganda tools of the nascent Communist state.

A majority of the Soviet Koreans who dealt with literature and the arts were employed as political supervisors, officials in the ideological bureaucracy or journalists in the official press. Among these people, one should mention Ki Sŏk-pok, Chŏng Ryul, and Pak Ch'ang-ok in particular. Some of the Soviet Koreans produced works of fiction and poetry themselves, such as Chŏng Ryul, Kang T'ae-su, Chŏng Tong-hyŏk, Yim Ha, and Kim Il-yŏng.[2] All of these figures maintained close connections with the then powerful Soviet faction in the North Korean leadership, and this political alliance greatly contributed to the rise of the Soviet Korean authors to prominence.

The connection with Moscow that made the Soviet Koreans so influential in the late 1940s led to their dramatic downfall in the mid-1950s, when Kim Il Sung began to distance himself from his former sponsors. Most of the Soviet Korean writers either disappeared in purges or fled Korea, and their achievements and contributions to the DPRK were erased from the official history.[3] But there is one Soviet Korean whose significance remains officially recognized in present-day DPRK: Cho Ki-ch'ŏn (1913–1951), a poet and high-ranking official in the early North Korean literary world.[4]

Cho Ki-ch'ŏn's activity in the North did not last long. He arrived in Korea in late August 1945 with the Soviet Army, and in July 1951 he was

killed in his office during an American air raid. During these six years, however, Cho managed to become a leading authority in the Pyongyang literary
world. He achieved a high degree of recognition among young readers and
forged good relations with Kim Il Sung, which allowed him to exercise a profound influence on North Korea's literary politics. An enthusiastic believer in
Communism and a eulogist of the new society, Cho Ki-ch'ŏn received from his
colleagues the symbolic nickname "Korean Maiakovskii," after the founding
father of Soviet poetry.[5] This depiction not only hinted at the special place Cho
occupied in the North Korean literary hierarchy but also indicated such qualities as devotion to Communist ideals, a decisive break with the old literary
style, and impulsive, even eccentric social behavior—all characteristics usually
ascribed to Cho's Soviet archetype.[6] The nickname also implied an emulation
of the well-known images and similes that appeared in Vladimir Maiakovskii's
poems, including the famous remark that a Communist writer's pen equals a
bayonet. Indeed, these features were often displayed in Cho Ki-ch'ŏn's poetry
as well.[7] The epithet "Korean Maiakovskii," which was initially applied to the
poet in his lifetime, was at the time widely used in both a positive and a negative sense.[8] Today Cho Ki-ch'ŏn is still considered to be the pride and glory of
DPRK cultural history and the founding father of North Korean poetry.[9]

A curious testimony to the significance of this figure in North Korean
literary history is the wide range of biographical myths that surround his
name in North Korean, South Korean, and Soviet scholarship. All the mythol-
ogists have their own, mutually contradictory agendas. North Korean academia invented for Cho Ki-ch'ŏn, as it did for Kim Jong Il, a fictional Korean
birthplace and a "purely Korean" biography and strove to downplay his Soviet
connections.[10] South Korean scholars of the anti-Communist era, by contrast,
wanted to portray Cho as an evil outsider, alien to the Korean discourse, and
presented him correspondingly as a wholly foreign figure who could not even
speak proper Korean.[11] Modern South Korean scholarship tends to "domesti-
cate" and "humanize" Cho's legacy, positioning him as a "Korean nationalist,"[12]
even inventing a Korean name for his son, Yurii, or portraying Cho Ki-ch'ŏn
as a secret partisan of pure poetry who felt "animosity toward the Kim Il Sung
dictatorship" and attempted to flee the North.[13] Soviet scholars, along with
North Korean academia, were inclined to spice up this exemplary Communist
figure with a pinch of heroic fantasy, insisting that the poet "died heroically on
the battlefield" or "died saving children from burning houses."[14]

In my article titled "Cho Ki-ch'ŏn: The Person behind the Myths," which
is based on new primary sources, I tease out the figure of the "Korean Maiakovskii" from all these popular political fantasies.[15] In this chapter I consider

Cho Ki-ch'ŏn within the political and literary context of his time and analyze his impact on North Korean literature and literary politics of the late 1940s and early 1950s.

"We Are the Generation of the 1930s"

Cho Ki-chŏn was born in 1913 in a village called Ael'tugeu in the Vladivostok district of the Russian Far East to a family of poor Korean peasants.[16] Though born outside Korea, Cho was raised as a Korean, not a Russian. In the 1920s and 1930s, the Korean community in the Soviet Far East made up about one-third of the total population of the region and possessed a developed system of national education that included not only primary and secondary schools but also junior colleges.[17] Though this educational system was lacking in such aspects as calligraphy, Chinese characters, and Korean history and literature, home education in most Korean families, including Cho's, compensated for these deficiencies. Until the mid-1930s, new publications were imported into Russia from Korea in large numbers, so Soviet Koreans had opportunities to acquaint themselves with both traditional and modern Korean literature.[18]

Cho Ki-chŏn graduated from a Korean school; he spoke Korean at home and often cited modern and classical Korean literature.[19] When Cho was seventeen years old, he published his first poem in the local Korean newspaper *Sŏnbong (Avant-garde).*[20] In the years 1930–1933 he continued to contribute to this newspaper. *Sŏnbong* published his poems under such telling titles as "The Morning of the Construction," "To the Advanced Workers," "The Military Field Study" and "Paris Commune." These unabashedly propagandistic verses were replete with the hyperbolized images that would later become so typical of Cho Pyongyang poetry.[21]

Cho continued his education at the Korean Teachers College in Voroshilov-Ussuriisk (1928–1931). In 1928–1932 he was a member of the Communist Youth League (Komsomol), and in 1946 he became a candidate for membership in the Communist Party (candidate card 8234828). From 1931 to 1933 Cho took courses in Khabarovsk, where young educated Koreans were trained to become editors for the Korean-language press.

The next step in his education was the Faculty of Literature of the Pedagogical University, named after Gorky and located in Omsk, where Cho studied in Russian (1933–1937). Information on this period of Cho's life is well documented in the letters of Liia Yudolevitch (Cho Ki-chŏn's girlfriend and a student in the same faculty) to Cho's only son, Yurii.[22] Yudolevitch first met

Cho in class in 1933 and subsequently became his constant companion in the classroom.

Yudolevitch fondly describes Cho as a "popular student who was loved by his peers," "a marvelous man—very committed, with a steady, uncompromising political worldview," and "our dearest comrade." In her words, Cho was a "gifted student" who read books in Russian very quickly and gave brilliant presentations. With admiration, Yudolevitch reports that Marxist philosophy was one of Cho's favorite subjects and that he was quite adept at polemics, eagerly taking part in the numerous political debates popular at the university. Modest and gentle in everyday life, Cho would become transformed into a fervent, emotional, and often intolerant orator in public meetings and political discussions. The following are some additional quotations from Yudolevitch's letters:

> Cho was a man of principle; he was very honest and direct. He has never made excuses, even for friends. I recollect one incident that shows this clearly. Books and teaching materials in the university library were in short supply, so we used them in turn. One day it so happened that I borrowed a book out of turn. I remember what a dressing-down he gave me! He shamed me for my unfair behavior. His accusation was justified and I was not hurt; I just felt awfully ashamed of myself.

> He was a man with inner pride. When he felt offended, he acted emotionally and he would boil and seethe with indignation.

These characteristics would hardly fit today's expectations of popular behavior. However, they do convey the Soviet atmosphere of the years when young people in love called each other "comrade" and when a "steady, uncompromising political worldview" was considered the ultimate personal trait. As Yudolevitch wrote,

> We are the generation of the 1930s, of those remarkable and wonderful years. My comrades and I have always been proud of our contemporaries as symbolized by Pavel Korchagin. Those years were full of hardships—no paper, no good clothes—but it was a beautiful time. The whole nation lived under the slogans "Let's do it! {Dayosch!}, "Let's do Kuzbass!" "Let's do Magnitka!" . . . It was so exiting![23]

Yudolevitch mentioned that Cho was very concerned about Korea and that he often wrote poems about the people in that "distant country." Yet, in her description, Cho's image of Korea was quite bookish, inspired by the Soviet press and by stories he had heard from other people, not from personal experience:[24]

> He loved Korean people very much, and his later fate is no surprise to me. He told me a lot about the life of Korean farming folk and said that he would go to fight for a better life for the Korean peasantry. . . . He used to write poems in the library after we had finished studying. He would sit nearby and write with great concentration. Sometimes he raised his head and would emotionally start to relate how difficult the life of a Korean peasant was. He insisted that they had to fight against the Japanese yoke. . . . He talked about the industriousness of the Korean people and described poor old Korean men who were exhausted by labor. He depicted the scene *as if he had seen it with his own eyes*. (My emphasis)

As was the case with many other representatives of the "generation of the 1930s," in 1937 Cho Ki-ch'ŏng's Communist belief and loyalty were put to the test. That year, all ethnic Koreans from the Soviet Far East were relocated to Central Asia, and the Korean Pedagogical Institute, where Cho was then teaching world literature, was moved to Kzyl-Orda in Kazakhstan.[25] Russian had become the language of instruction there in 1938. In the words of Chŏng Ryul, who was Cho's disciple and a close friend, Cho expressed resentment at this practice and at the forcible resettlement of Koreans.[26]

The year 1938 was also marked by an even more dramatic episode for Cho Ki-ch'ŏn. During the school vacation that summer, Cho left for Moscow to fulfill his longtime dream—to apply for postgraduate studies at the Moscow Literature University. However, a new law prohibited ethnic Koreans from leaving the officially designated settlements in Central Asia, and as soon as Cho arrived in Moscow and showed his documents at the Literature University, he was detained for violating the registration law.[27] Given the general situation at the time, Cho could have easily been executed on a charge of spying. Fortunately, one of his high-ranking Korean friends, Cho Tong-kyu, who held an influential position in the NKVD (the predecessor of the KGB), intervened on his behalf; he arranged for Cho's release after several months in prison and erased the record of this incident from his files.

After his temporary imprisonment Cho returned to Kzyl-Orda. He kept this episode a secret and told his friends that he had been prohibited from entering Moscow Literature University because of the new legal status of Koreans. Chŏng Ryul reported the bitter words of Cho Ki-ch'ŏn at the time:

"I do not believe in the Leninist national policy anymore. All this 'freedom of all the nations' in the USSR is a fiction. Nobody here needs us Koreans. They do not want our language and schools; they do not want us either."[28]

Cho had to abandon his old dream of studying in Moscow or Leningrad. This was a serious blow, but life continued. From August 1938 to December 1941 he worked as a lecturer in the Pedagogical Institute of Kzyl-Orda. This was essentially the same Korean Pedagogical Institute that had been renamed and transformed into a Russian-language school in 1938. From December 1941 to September 1942 Cho worked as a translator for a local newspaper in Kzyl-Orda and then was drafted into the Soviet Army. According to Cho Yurii, his father was happy to learn that he had been recruited, for it meant that he was trusted, despite his imprisonment and his being of an "unreliable" nationality.[29]

From September 1942 to December 1943 Cho Ki-ch'ŏn served in the Soviet Twenty-fifth Army. He was an instructing writer (*instructor-literator redaktzii*) in the editing office at the army's headquarters, which at the time was located in Voroshilov-Ussuriisk. From November 1943 to July 1945 he served in the Political Department of the Pacific Navy as a writer in the editing office (*literator redaktzii*) in Khabarovsk. From August to October 1945 Cho further served in the Political Department of the Primorskii Military District as a chief of department of local affairs in the editing office (*nachal'nik otdela mestnoi zhizni redaktzii*). From October 1945 he worked as a writer in the editing office (*literator redaktzii*) of the Political Department of the First Far Eastern Front.[30] His main activity was related to psychological operations, such as the writing of propaganda leaflets, an activity run by the network of "seventh departments" within the political departments of the Soviet Army.[31]

In late summer 1945 the thirty-two-year-old Cho Ki-ch'ŏn entered North Korea with the troops of the Soviet Army. This was the first time Cho had left the Soviet Union, the country of his birth and upbringing. The Communist mentality and the Soviet way of life were the only real world in which he had been brought up and had known thoroughly, with all its darkness and light.

"A Visitor from Some Mystical Place"

Cho began his new career in the Red Army's Korean-language newspaper *Chosŏn sinmun (Korean Newspaper)* and happily immersed himself in the new atmosphere. He published a number of poems; translated the Soviet poets Nikolai Gribachev, Dzhambul Dzhambaev, and Vladimir Maiakovskii into

Korean;[32] and gave lectures on Soviet literary theory, politics, and the history of world literature. He also took part in numerous literary conventions and discussions.[33]

According to Chŏng Ryul, Cho enjoyed his new status and responsibility while at the same time appreciating the material stability of his new life. Like other Soviet Koreans, Cho received salaries from both the Soviet Army and the Korean agencies for which he worked. These arrangements rendered the Soviet Koreans affluent by the standards of 1940s Pyongyang.[34]

However, Cho Ki-ch'ŏn's official life was far from trouble-free. The clashes between competing factions that North Korean intellectuals had created in alliance with particular Party leaders and their coteries (or, to be more precise, created as extensions of the Party factions) were rapidly becoming a persistent problem.[35] This problem in the North Korean literary reality was so significant that many defectors to South Korea made factional strife the central topic of their writing. This factional struggle within North Korea's literary world at length in chapter 5, but here let us take a preliminary look at the phenomenon.

From the late 1940s onward, three main groups struggled for domination in the North Korean literary scene. The first included former members of the KAPF (Yi Ki-yŏng, Song Yŏng, Pak Se-yŏng, et al.) and some litterateurs of North Korean origin (Hong Sun-ch'ŏl, Han Hyo, et al.). This group was led by Han Sŏr-ya, who relied on Kim Il Sung and the so-called guerrilla faction for support. Then there was the Soviet Korean faction, which included Soviet Koreans and several native Korean writers such as Yi T'ae-jun. These centered around the Ministry of Propaganda and the Soviet Army newspaper *Chosŏn sinmun,* which was dominated by Soviet Koreans. This group enjoyed the support of highly positioned Soviet Korean officials such as Vice-Premier Ho Ka-i and Pak Ch'ang-ok, chairman of the Central Committee's Propaganda and Agitation Department. The third faction included intellectuals belonging to the South Korean Workers' Party, or Domestic Communists. This group of writers was led by Yim Hwa and was actively supported by Pak Hŏng-yŏng, the leader of the South Korean underground. This Southern faction, being less numerous and influential, tended to ally itself with the Soviet Koreans against the ex-KAPF members, who were the strongest of the three.[36]

Every faction deemed itself the sole legitimate representative of Communist ideology in the Korean literary world. The ex-KAPF members posed as the ultimate heroic bearers of the Korean revolutionary literary tradition, while doing their best to push aside their rivals as "outsiders" (the Soviet Koreans) or "traitors to the revolutionary cause" (the Southerners). They downplayed the fact that Han Sŏr-ya had come to the KAPF much later than the real founding father of the organization, the "Southerner" Yim Hwa. They also failed to mention that in the early 1940s Han Sŏr-ya, Yi Ki-yŏng, and other prominent ex-KAPF writers had also collaborated with the colonial regime.[37]

The Soviet Koreans, meanwhile, emphasized their Soviet origin, implying that their Soviet roots and experiences gave them an advantage over their "indigenous" colleagues. Most of the Soviet Koreans were graduates of Russian universities and enjoyed a higher educational level and broader intellectual horizons than their North Korean counterparts.[38] They strove to position themselves as the only true bearers of the sacred knowledge of "real Communism" and thus the only legitimate arbiters of what was right or wrong in North Korea's arts and literature.[39]

As for the Southerners, their leader Yim Hwa, who enjoyed a standing as a popular Communist poet and critic, endeavored to gather the young intellectuals around himself while also deriding his old enemy Han Sŏr-ya for his lack of artistic achievement.[40] Yim's reputation as a prominent poet and critic was indeed unquestioned—to such an extent that Han Hyo, a critic who belonged to Han Sŏr-ya's faction and was a relative of his, plagiarized Yim's *History of Korean Literature*.[41]

These factions competed for political influence and privilege to such a degree that their long-term mutual animosity and personal rivalries led to ugly sectarian warfare. Ostensible literary discussions became the major weapon in this personal power struggle.

Cho Ki-chŏn naturally belonged to the group of Soviet Koreans, whose political position was strong but was destabilized by several serious impediments. First, the Soviet Koreans were associated with the Soviet troops, whose reputation in Korea was quite low. When entering the Korean peninsula in 1945, the Soviet troops had engaged in large-scale pillage, rape, and plunder, and though swift and stern measures by the Soviet commanders led to a decline in such incidents in 1946,[42] the initial negative impression remained strong. The Nationalist Right, whose leaders enjoyed wide support across the country, also promoted this negative picture, presenting the situation in the North as a simple change of occupying power, with the Russians merely replacing the Japanese. This was the prism through which many locals viewed the Soviet Koreans as well.

Second, the policy of the Soviet authorities that discouraged "excessive" interaction between the Soviet Koreans and locals was also partially responsible for their alienation. The Soviet Koreans were rigorously controlled in their actions, and every contact with native Koreans had to be reported to special agencies of the Soviet embassy. Chŏng Ryul recalls that when celebrating birthdays, he had to give separate parties for Soviet and native Korean guests. Marriages between Soviet Koreans and local Koreans were very rare, and the children of Soviet Koreans in Pyongyang attended Soviet Army schools and, after 1953, "High School Number Six"—both of which were inaccessible to ordinary Koreans.[43] In these schools classes were taught in Russian, and the curricula closely followed the Soviet pattern. This practice vividly reminded Koreans of the special schools for Japanese children in Korean cities during colonial times.[44] Most Soviet Korean children did not communicate with local Korean children and often spoke their erstwhile native language poorly.

The high standards of living of the Soviet Koreans also fed resentment. Like the colonial rulers, many Soviet Korean families, even those with a full-time housewife, employed Korean servants. Their local Korean colleagues could not afford such a luxury and were annoyed by the contradiction between the official image of the Soviets as the repository of the altruistic Communist spirit and the real people who enjoyed a high level of material comfort and isolated themselves from impoverished locals.[45]

The final, but not the least consequential, factor was that, though the Soviet Koreans were physically Koreans, they were perceived culturally and behaviorally as aliens and outsiders even by those locals who supported the Communist government.[46] The enduring Northeastern dialect of the Soviet Koreans was regarded with particular disdain by many Korean intellectuals.[47] (The "outsider" perception played an important role in relationships not only between Soviet and native Koreans but also between Southerners and North Korean native writers.[48])

All these factors alienated the native Koreans from their Soviet Korean colleagues. Cho Ki-chŏn was modest in his daily life and eagerly made friends with local Koreans,[49] but even he was unable to avoid estrangement at times—particularly considering his "Soviet" ways, which Liia Yudolevitch so vividly described in her letters. Cho's emotional fervor and intolerance during political disputes, which in the Soviet Union of the 1930s were considered virtues, often set him against his Pyongyang colleagues. Pak Nam-su also mentions other exotic traits of Cho Ki-chŏn, such as his steady manner of speaking, his unusual "Soviet" manner of declaiming verse with his head tilted backwards, and so on.[50]

In general, however, Cho Ki-chŏn was quite popular among his local Korean colleagues, and this was even admitted by his foes. Though native writers were often shocked by his negative view of Fyodor Dostoevsky, a traditional icon of Korean intellectuals,[51] the high intellectual level of Cho's public speeches and his substantial knowledge of contemporary Soviet and foreign literature could not help but impress them. "Everything he said was so exciting and interesting; he seemed like a visitor from some strange and mystical place," Pak Nam-su observed. "He gave the impression of being a very erudite person."[52]

Cho's career as a writer was steadily ascending. His works soon achieved model status in North Korea. They were published in many editions, used as study materials in universities and literary circles, and awarded the Festival Prize, a Korean analogue of the Soviet Stalin Prize and the nation's highest literary award.[53]

Convinced of the need for the "popular spirit" in socialist literature, Cho used to read his freshly written verses aloud to his friends and ask for their opinion. His first audience was his wife, who, in Chŏng Ryul's opinion, "did not know a thing about poetry." However, Cho used to say, "If she understands, it means that everybody will understand. I must write in the most comprehensible manner possible."[54]

Despite Cho's sincere desire to attract everybody over to his side, his poetic style was very distinctive and thus controversial. His specific style was already apparent in the first verses he wrote in Pyongyang in 1946—namely, "Tumangang"[55] and "Ttang" (Land)[56]—but found its fullest expression in his epic poem *Paektusan (Paektu Mountain)*. At the time, *Paektusan* was regarded as the first masterpiece of Korean Communist literature and brought wide popularity to its author;[57] but it simultaneously gave rise to a significant debate in Pyongyang's literary world.

Paektusan: Nationalist Propaganda or a Pro-Soviet Exercise?

Paektusan, the long epic written in 1947 and published in *Nodong sinmun* (Pyongyang's main daily newspaper) in 1948, was devoted to the theme of the anti-Japanese guerrilla activity of Kim Il Sung (in the poem "Commander Kim") and to the Poch'ŏnbo raid by the Korean guerrillas in 1937. The Korean anti-Japanese guerrilla movement had always fascinated Cho. Chŏng Ryul recollects that the immediate stimulus that prompted Cho to start to write *Paektusan* was his meeting with the former anti-Japanese guerrilla Ch'oe Hyŏn.[58]

In recent North Korean scholarship, *Paektusan* is presented exclusively as a saga about the deeds of the Great Leader.[59] The older generation of South

Korean scholars also holds that the poem, in the first instance, worships Kim Il Sung and that for this reason it represents a typical piece of personality cult literature.[60] The younger generation of Seoul academics argues that the real *Paektusan* hero is not Commander Kim but minor characters in the poem such as the partisans Ch'ŏl-ho, Kkot'-pun, and Sŏk-jun, such that this is not a poem about the Great Leader but one about the Korean people.[61]

Argue as they might, most academics from both North and South Korea on the whole imply that *Paektusan* is a poem about Koreans (be they the people or the Great Leader) who liberated Korea. Arguing for the nationalist essence of *Paektusan,* the authors of *Pukhan 50 nyŏnsa* went so far as to state that "the poem in fact asserts that neither the Soviet Union nor the USA liberated Korea, but rather the heroic anti-Japanese partisans."[62]

In reality, however, *Paektusan* can hardly be fitted into the frame of purely Korean discourse. Written in accordance with Soviet-era practice, the poem, though it deals with the Korean resistance, is saturated with Soviet allusions and parallels.[63] To begin with, the poem was dedicated "to the glorious Soviet Army that liberated Korea." And even in describing the landscape, Cho refers to "the nameless rock on Changbaek Mountain that became a symbol of the victory of the Soviet warriors in this land."[64]

Chŏng Ryul recalls a characteristic debate between himself and Cho. One episode in the poem describes how the partisans, exhausted from four days of hunger in a mountain camp, catch cattle belonging to local farmers. Commander Kim Il Sung, after inspecting the tethers on the cattle, orders that the animals be returned: "Since when did we turn into cattle thieves? Since when do we steal the property of farmers? Look at the tethers! These cattle belong to a Korean farmer or a Chinese farmer!" Nevertheless, a young partisan violates the order and kills one of the animals. Kim Il Sung accuses the boy of collaboration with the "Japanese bastards," because such actions undermine the trust between the local poor and the partisans. The partisan realizes the full depth of his moral degradation and prepares himself for immediate execution, but Commander Kim orders him to find the victim and compensate him for the damage.[65] Chŏng Ryul accused Cho of plagiarism because the same sort of stories about stolen peasant property and righteous commanders always protecting the peasants' interests could be found in a number of Soviet partisan novels, such as Aleksandr Fadeev's *The Last of Udege, Devastation,* and others.[66] Cho assured his friend that he had never come across these particular episodes in Soviet fiction.[67] The episode remained untouched when *Paektusan* first appeared in published form, with the characteristic words of Commander Kim:

"Comrades!
If we want to become a big river, to become a sea,
We should remember that our base is in the people,
Our strength is in the people!
Have we forgotten the Soviet guerrillas
Who became blood brothers with the people?
If we forget this,
How can we become a mass movement?"[68]

The fourth chapter depicts the vigilant Commander Kim at night in the partisans' camp:

Just one person is not sleeping,
He is seated near the fireplace
And reading The History of the Soviet Partisans.
He does not notice how the night is passing.
As the hope of a spring day glimmers in the distance,
And his soul is full of joy,
He reads the book.
As clouds of anxiety cover his soul
And despair enters his mind from some dark recess,
He reads the book,
Acquires new strength, and espies his goal.
When he suffers from hunger
And has to cook leather belts to fill his belly,
He reads the book.
When the childhood memories of his distant home
At the foot of the mountain, covered in pine trees
Comes to mind,
The image of the much-loved house of his birth,
Which was destroyed so long ago,
Or the image of his mother working in the kitchen on a spring day,
The image of a sad, sighing mother appears before his eyes,
He reads the book,
Acquires new strength, and espies his goal.
And this night he also thinks
"The Soviet partisans!
Chapaev, Schors, Lazo . . .[69]
That's how they fought!"[70]

Commander Kim then refers to the USSR as "the country of freedom, the country of justice," and as the hope of all other peoples and the embodiment of progress.[71] Characteristically, Kim Il Sung is portrayed here in accordance with the then obligatory Soviet stereotype of the ever-vigilant and book-loving Stalin. While this officially endorsed image of Stalin had some connections with reality (Stalin, in fact, suffered from insomnia and was an avid reader), the real Kim Il Sung, who was much younger and was never particularly fond of books, had little to do with the Commander Kim of Cho's poem.

After the successful raid, Commander Kim addresses his comrades with a speech in which he reminds them:

> *"Our strength is great.*
> *We are not alone:*
> *There is a savior of all oppressed nations,*
> *The Soviet Union!*
> *It stands in the vanguard of the world*
> *And is led by the genius of Stalin.*
> *The USSR is establishing a new morality in the universe.*
> *With the sword of Justice*
> *The aggressors will be beaten,*
> *Unfairness will be annihilated!"[72]*

In the epilogue, the author asks Paektu Mountain how it happened that "the sun, which had once set, is now rising again over this country"? The mountain answers:

> *"{First came} the liberating Soviet Army,*
> *Which defeated the aggressors in the West and the East*
> *And brought light to the whole world,*
> *Braving gunpowder smoke and the thunder of bullets."*

And only after that,

> *"The person whom the nation longed so much for,*
> *The son of the nation,*
> *My consciousness and will,*
> *My belief and my hope,*
> *My partisan,*
> *Commander Kim."[73]*

Concerning contemporary liberated Korea, the mountain proclaims,

> *"We see Commander Kim leading the nation,*
> *With the big reliable hand of friendship and sincerity,*
> *The hand of the Soviet Union."*[74]

Thus, Cho Ki-ch'ŏn, while indeed worshipping Kim Il Sung as a brave national hero, depicts him not as an independent figure but as a kind of Korean Stalin who is expected to act under the wise protective shadow of the larger Stalin in Moscow.

These examples cast doubt on the idea of *Paektusan* as a piece of nationalist literature. We should also not forget that Cho Ki-ch'ŏn, being a Soviet citizen and a Soviet officer, was tightly controlled in his actions by the Soviet administration and simply could not write the poem from a nationalist Korean point of view. This is well illustrated by one characteristic incident. At the Soviet embassy, where the poem was preliminarily read aloud and immediately translated into Russian,[75] an official noticed that the author refers to Korea as "my native/home land" (Kor. "Kohyang"). The officials reacted immediately: "Comrade Cho was born in the USSR. That is in fact his native land; Korea is not."[76] The objection was accepted without dispute, and in the *Paektusan* edition of 1952, as well as in later editions, Korea is referred to as "the land of the ancestors" *(Chosang-ŭi ttang)*.[77]

Discussions over *Paektusan*

Not only was *Paektusan* filled with Soviet references, but it also was influenced by the aesthetics of Soviet literature, which sometimes significantly diverged from Korean literary traditions. The public reaction to the poem in North Korea was mixed.

While many young people praised the poem as an exciting breakthrough in Korean literary style and a novel exercise in applying Communist culture to domestic material (even Cho Ki-ch'ŏn's detractors mention the public interest in the poem),[78] the very novelty of *Paektusan* annoyed a significant section of the North Korean literary establishment. For example, the literary genre of *Paektusan* was defined as *sŏjŏng sŏsasi* (lyrical epic),[79] and the work appeared strange to some Korean intellectuals who perceived it as an improbable mix of different styles.[80] Pak Nam-su, in particular, insisted that Cho was simply unable to write properly within the established borders of accepted Korean genres and had invented this "eccentric style" in order to justify his own inadequacy.[81]

The language of the poem was another source of public irritation. An Ham-gwang, a member of the rival ex-KAPF faction, criticized the author of *Paektusan* for frequent use of archaic images and outdated expressions. Indeed, the language of the poem differed from the customary form of contemporary Korean poetry. For example, Cho depicts Kim Il Sung in this way:

> *"O Kim, you commander of the Korean partisans!*
> *The Japanese pirates of the Three Provinces tremble when they hear your name!*
> *O ruler of Changpaek!*
> *You hold mountains in your bare hands!*
> *Mysterious rumors spread about your glorious name.*
> *They say you can cross a thousand miles in an instant*
> *Because you know the secret of shrinking the earth to move like lightning!*
> *They say that you, a glorified commander, were born*
> *When Venus had risen in the North,*
> *Above the waves of the Amnokkang, and shone mysteriously over the earth.*
> *O Marshal Kim, sovereign of Paektusan!"*[82]

This depiction of Kim Il Sung owed much to the contemporary Soviet tradition, with its typical portrayal of the Communist leader as a legendary hero of epic proportions, particularly in the poetry of the non-Russian republics. The "ethnic minstrels" of the Stalin cult, such as Dzhambul Dzhambaev of Kazakhstan, Suleiman Stal'sky of Dagestan, and Giorgii Leonidze of Georgia, invented colorful designations like "hero of heroes, son of lightning and thunder," "Stalin, who gives rise to thunderstorms in the sea," and "the hope and light of humanity."[83] Though these epithets mostly referred to Stalin, the same elevated tone can be found in poetic images of Lenin and lesser Communist leaders, such as security police chief Nikolai Ezhov, for instance.[84] This particular influence on Cho Ki-ch'ŏn's literary style may be ascribed to the Kazakh poet Dzhambaev, who used particularly aggrandized hyperbole and intentional archaisms in his servile eulogies to Soviet leaders. Cho Ki-ch'ŏn had lived and worked in Kazakhstan when Dzhambaev was a local celebrity, and he translated Dzhambaev's poetry into Korean.

The question regarding the inappropriateness of the poetic form of *Paektusan* developed into a heated discussion between Cho Ki-ch'ŏn and the critic An Ham-gwang. However, the disagreement over artistic form and the clash of literary tastes were only part of the problem. The confrontation between Cho Ki-ch'ŏn as a Soviet Korean and An Ham-gwang as a member of the rival ex-KAPF faction to a very large extent reflected the ongoing political rivalry between the two groups, and most of their contemporaries appeared to understand this.

According to Chŏng Ryul, the question of the unsuitability of *Paektusan*'s poetic form was first raised in 1948 at a meeting of Korean writers in the office of Kim Ch'ang-man, head of the KWP Central Committee's Department of Propaganda, the body that guided the entire cultural enterprise of the country. The meeting began with a reading of *Paektusan*, followed by a discussion in the course of which An Ham-gwang sharply criticized the poem. He described *Paektusan*'s style as "wooden" and "unnatural" and added that he saw no difference between this so-called poem and ordinary prose.

An Ham-gwang was not the first to compare the poem to prose. Chŏng Ryul cites a characteristically sarcastic remark once made by the prosaic Yu Hang-rim. During a presentation of the poem in 1948 in a restaurant on the banks of the Taedonggang River, Yu Hang-rim proposed a toast to the "good prose of Cho Ki-ch'ŏn," because, Yu explained, being prosaic himself, he preferred the non-verse style and felt happy to meet a prosaic colleague.[85]

Such biting remarks from Yu, a well-known jester in the North Korean literary world, could be safely ignored. But the attack by An Ham-gwang was a different matter. An did not simply ridicule the style of Cho's poem but defined it as "non-Korean" and "nonnational," thus insinuating that his Soviet Korean rival lacked national identity and was a stranger to the authentic Korean culture.[86] An also mentioned that the epic lacked engaging protagonists (with the exception of Kim Il Sung), and he concluded that the net result could be called a fiasco.[87]

Cho Ki-ch'ŏn countered in the following manner:

> You think that the poem is bad, do you? But they read it at the Headquarters of the Soviet Army, in the Council of the People's Commissar of North Korea, in the Workers' Party, and everybody said it was good. How dare you contradict such high opinions? You, comrade, are not right. If you are against the opinion of the Headquarters of the Soviet Army, it means you are anti-Soviet. And if you are against the Council of the People's Commissar of North Korea, you are antigovernment. Moreover, if you are against the opinion of the Workers' Party, you are an anti-Party element.[88]

Cho's argumentative style correlates closely to the traditions of Soviet "literary discussions" in which opponents, instead of discussing literary issues, would appeal to the real or imagined support of political authorities.[89] Yet, no matter how elaborate Cho's polemical skills were, without senior endorsement they would not count for much. At the meeting, Cho received strong support from Kim Ch'ang-man, who upheld *Paektusan* unconditionally as "a new harvest in North Korean literature"[90] and accused An Ham-gwang of acting rudely toward his colleague.[91] Kim understood that it was not yet the right time to alienate the Soviet sponsors and supervisors.[92] Also, Kim was fully aware that Kim Il Sung, who was depicted as the main protagonist in the poem, was quite impressed by *Paektusan,* and neither the exultant style nor the lofty epithets employed in the poem embarrassed the future "Sun of the Nation." After Kim Il Sung read the poem, he made Cho Ki-ch'ŏn one of his personal friends and even began to visit the poet's home.[93] Kim Ch'ang-man rushed to declare that the poem's main protagonist, General Kim, deserved the highest style possible and that Cho Ki-ch'ŏn had established a new tradition to depict the Korean leader and his lofty deeds—a tradition that other Korean writers should follow.

Under these circumstances, An Ham-gwang was doomed. Soon after the discussion, he lost his important official positions, including the post of first secretary of the NKFLA, and only the intervention of Han Sŏr-ya and Yi Ki-yŏng (both fellow ex-KAPF cadres) helped him later to be restored as chairman of the Writers' Union and an editor of *Literature and Art,* the organ of the NKFLA.[94]

After this discussion and the subsequent official endorsement of the poem, the standing of *Paektusan* and its author became unassailable. The poem was hailed as a "new classic," an exemplary work to be studied and emulated. Immediately after its publication the author received the first Festival Prize for it.[95] The poem was later staged at the State Theatre by dramatist Han T'ae-ch'ŏn, and Kim Il Sung personally approved the performance.[96]

Nevertheless, the brief debate over the poem was indicative. It stands as an early example of the ideological campaigns that tore the North Korean literary world apart after 1953. The arguments that opponents used in 1948, while not causing the same devastating effects, were of the same demagogic nature. The participants resorted to political accusation: An Ham-gwang accused his competitor of using non-Korean and nonnational motifs, while Cho Ki-ch'ŏn in turn accused his opponent of harboring anti-Party, antigovernment, and anti-Soviet sentiments. Meanwhile Kim Ch'ang-man hinted that An did not show enough deference to General Kim, and so on.

Paektusan brought new form and new images to the North Korean literary tradition. *Sŏjŏng sŏsasi,* the lyrical epic form, has been widely used in North Korean literature, and the image of Kim Il Sung produced by Cho Ki-ch'ŏn played a meaningful artistic role in inspiring numerous eulogists of the North Korean leader to depict him as an intelligent, persistent, and unbending hero. Nevertheless, this initial approach to the leader was gradually modified by the new image created by Han Sŏr-ya, Hong Sun-ch'ŏl, and other ex-KAPF members. Their portrayal of Kim Il Sung as a naive, impulsive, passive figure, endowed with slightly feminine traits, has been perceptively analyzed by Brian Myers in his book on Han Sŏr-ya.[97] Remarkably, the Soviet Koreans working at the time in Pyongyang were indignant at the newly emerging image of the Korean leader, which appeared almost comical to them.

Cho Ki-ch'ŏn after *Paektusan:* An Exemplary Socialist Realist Poet

Between 1945 and 1950 Cho Ki-ch'ŏn composed a number of poems, including "Tumangang" (1946), about the suffering of the Koreans under Japanese colonial rule; "Our Way" (Uri-ŭi kil; 1949), which glorified the Soviet-Korean friendship; and "Resistance in Yosu" (Hangjaeng-ŭi yŏsu; 1950), about the South Korean communist underground.[98]

All of these works were praised as pioneering and exemplary. So too was the lyrical epic "Land" (Ttang), written in response to the Party's order to extol the recent land reform of 1946. While many North Korean writers felt perplexed by these openly political demands, Cho Ki-ch'ŏn, equipped with his Soviet experience, immediately produced the required product.[99] Fulfilling the Party's order to "immerse [oneself] in the masses," Cho Ki-ch'ŏn traveled around the country, visiting farms and factories, and in the summer of 1949 went to the Hamhŭng plant, where he "participated in the assembly of tools and machines and acquainted himself intimately with work and the everyday life of workers."[100] This was yet another exemplary action, since many of his Korean colleagues "immersed themselves in the masses" rather reluctantly.[101]

As a result of those trips, Cho Ki-ch'ŏn wrote poems glorifying socialist construction and industrialization. The following lines from his long epic "Saengea-ŭi norae" (The Song of Life; June 1950), written after his visit to the Hamhŭng plant, illustrate the style of these writings:[102]

> *Steelworker Kim Yŏng-su is coming to the plant. . . .*
> *Smoke billows in front of him,*
> *The smoke is colored by the morning sunshine.*
> *It is the proud smoke of reconstruction.*
> *A creative energy is blazing there,*

Pounding hearts,
Hot breath,
Developing muscles,
The fire of patriotism is blazing there.
It is the proud smoke of success.[103]

The poem tells of the struggle of progressive workers striving to fill production quotas ahead of schedule. According to the Stalinist literary tradition, they must also overcome sabotage by "class enemies." The backward worker Tŏk-po is manipulated by a vicious former landlord and destroys the electric furnace in order to outstrip the opposing brigade in socialist competition. At the end of the poem Tŏk-po regrets his unforgivable behavior and "unbends his crushed soul."[104] Like *Paektusan,* "The Song of Life" and other poems by Cho were saturated with the same exalted intonation and hyperbolic images that alienated some readers in the earlier poem.

Cho Ki-ch'ŏn's works were permeated by politics and ideology, and lyrical themes were rare. The descriptions of landscapes and romantic relationships in Cho Ki-ch'ŏn's poems always convey some propagandistic message: nature approves or disapproves of the protagonists' political actions, and, depending on the situation, mountains and rivers alternatively cry or laugh. For example, the protagonist of "Sitting on the White Rock" (Hŭin pauie anjaso), written in July 1947 in the Kŭmgansan people's resort, is sitting on a white rock above a fast-flowing spring and "talking with the water."[105] At first glance this is a bucolic picture, quite in tune with the Korean literary tradition. But we come to realize almost immediately that the protagonist is not simply enjoying his leisure; he puts his time to use in honoring his revolutionary spirit, for he is learning to be as swift and tenacious as the flowing water and intends to break his enemies into pieces.

The romantic relationships in "The Song of Life" serve as another example of this tendency. According to the Stalinist tradition, love is supposed to help the heroes fulfill production plans and fight enemies more successfully, and the passion of the two protagonists in Cho's poem, the advanced workers Kŭm-sun and Yŏng-su, is quite in tune with this approach:

It is not just "sweet love,"
Which poets eulogize in their "songs of passion."
It is a relationship where both lovers stand hand in hand
For the construction of democracy,
For the creation of the Motherland.

> *It is an exalted love of the new Korea and one that we must applaud. . . .*
> *Love is not about a supple bosom or starry eyes.*
> *Exalted love is a fight for the spring of a free Korea.*[106]

This is strongly reminiscent of the early Soviet philosophy of love as reflected in the famous poems of Maiakovskii, such as "A Letter to Comrade Kostrov from Paris on the Essence of Love," written in 1929 ("To love does not mean simply to boil with passion. / Love leaps over the mountains of bosoms and jungles of hair. / To love means to rush into the backyard and chop the wood for the fire with the sparkling axe, enjoying your strength") or "A Letter to Tatiana Yakovleva," written the same year ("The red color of my republics / must shine / even in my kissing and hugging / and the trembling of the body that I love").[107]

The other lyrical poems of Cho Ki-ch'ŏn, such as "Willow" (Suyang pŏtŭl), "Swing" (Kŭne), and "Whistle" (Hŭip'aram), were also anything but a concession to "pure art." "Willow" depicts a beautiful spring morning and the rejuvenating mood the youthful protagonist feels on watching the young, growing willow tree under his window. But the author does not fail to notice that the spring mood is fruitful, since it fills the hero with a new invigorating strength that, of course, helps him work productively all day.[108] "Swing" describes the spring folk festival Tano and the traditional entertainment of Korean girls being lifted up on a swing. But even this idyllic picture is saturated with propaganda. One of the girls dreams of a distant Pyongyang, where the national flag is waving in the wind, and of Kim Il Sung University, where her boyfriend, yesterday's farmhand, is now studying.[109] The protagonists of "Whistle" are also not ordinary sweethearts but exemplary workers who outperform labor norms and stay up late every night looking through study materials:[110]

> *Again today you smiled purely,*
> *And said that you have surpassed the production plan threefold,*
> *But I do not envy your achievement,*
> *I can do even better,*
> *But I like your smile.*
> *Why is it so pure?*[111]

These poems are vividly reminiscent of the verses of the Soviet poet Mikhail Isakovskii (1900–1973), who habitually extolled the "useful" relationships of "good," "advanced" boys and girls.[112] Cho Ki-ch'ŏn borrowed not only the simple folkloristic form of Isakovskii's poems but also widely used his imagery and metaphors, and this is one of the possible reasons that nowadays South Korean readers tend to misunderstand the message of Cho's poems. For instance, in recent Seoul newspaper articles, "Whistle" has been described as "a song of unrequited love,"[113] but the truth is precisely the contrary. Both protagonists are in love, and the girl smiles invitingly at the boy, but he is too shy to open his heart. He simply sighs secretly, which to Korean eyes probably represents a picture of unhappy love. The images of the poem were clearly derived from "At Sunset I See a Boy Near My House," a Soviet song popular at the time, with lyrics by Isakovskii ("At sunset I see a boy near my house. / He just sighs and does not say a word. / And I don't know why he sighs").[114] Like Isakovskii, Cho depicts his female protagonist as a resolute and active figure, in contrast to the timid boy. Both characters act in accordance with the Soviet/Russian, not Korean, code of behavior, which might mislead Korean readers.

Cho Ki-ch'ŏn during the Korean War

Soon after the outbreak of the Korean War on 25 June 1950, Cho sent his family to Moscow while remaining in North Korea himself. Contrary to popular myth, Cho was never involved in any military actions during the war. Instead he spent the time continuing his administrative duties in Pyongyang. These included his work at the newspaper *Nodong sinmun* and in the Korean Federation of Literature and Art (KFLA), becoming its vice president in March 1951.[115]

Cho's professional life blossomed. He was producing many new verses, such as "Korea Is Fighting" (Chosŏnŭn ssaunda; February 1951), "Korean Mother" (Chosŏn-ŭi ŏmŏni; September 1950), "On the Burning Street" (Pult'anŭn kŏriesŏ; August 1950), "My Heights" (Na-ŭi koji; June 1951), "We Are Korean Youth" (Urinŭn chosŏn ch'ŏngnyŏnida; April 1951), "Death to the Enemies" (Chugŏmŭn wŏnsu-ege; December 1950), "Greeting the New Dawn" (Ch'ŏtsaebyŏk-ŭl matmyŏnsŏ; New Year's Eve 1950), "Snowy Path" (Nunkil; January 1951), and "Spring Song" (Pomnorae; February 1951), among others.[116] All these poems were essentially wartime propaganda meant to encourage North Korean soldiers; they are permeated with fervent patriotic rhetoric and preach righteous hatred against the enemies. In accordance with the general political line, Cho Ki-ch'ŏn represents the Korean War as a heroic fight by the entire Korean people against the nasty American occupiers—in other words, essentially a "national liberation" struggle. The life of prewar

North Korea is depicted as cloudless bliss. Here is how Cho describes it in "We Are Korean Youth":

> *We did not do a chore without a song.*
> *We did not start a day without a smile.*
> *We remained wide awake on spring nights,*
> *Thinking about newly flourishing flowers,*
> *All inside our beautiful dreams.*[117]

Cho Ki-ch'ŏn contrasted this paradise, full of flowers, love, and cheer, with the wartime tragedy of Pyongyang, contrasting the nightmarish American beasts with virtuous Korean patriots. The enemies in these wartime poems are invariably sadistic "Yankees"; their local South Korean allies do not appear. Like Cho Ki-ch'ŏn's previous verses, his wartime poems are full of hyperbole, exaltation, and images of bloodthirsty enemies who are the embodiment of cruelty and evil.[118]

> *A child who lost his mother,*
> *A child who is crawling along the street in tears,*
> *Both children were pierced*
> *With a hundred bullets*
> *Which were targeted at them*
> *By the blood-loving Yankees! . . .*
> *The animals were laughing madly*
> *While poking people's eyes out and tearing out their nails!*
> *The animals carved {pictures of} atomic bombs*
> *On people's chests with their bayonets!*[119]

In 1950–1951 Cho Ki'ch'ŏn remained prominent in the official circles of the Pyongyang bureaucracy. In a letter to his wife, Cho mentions that he was very busy "checking the innumerable works of other writers."[120] For his "special services to the country" he was decorated in 1951 with the Order of the State Banner in the second degree.[121] In March 1951 he became a vice-chairman of the KFLA, an appointment that made him proud and happy.[122] In a letter to his family in Moscow, Cho wrote:

> Now I am working in the Korean Federation of Literature and Art as a vice-chairman. The KFLA is a very influential organization that determines the artistic life of all Korea. . . . My responsibilities are very complex, but

interesting. This is just the work for me! . . . You love my verses and can imagine what a high position I will gain in the future! . . . Every day when I return home from the KFLA office, they send me a car. This is because I have a lot of work and have made a huge amount of progress.

The poet was killed in the prime of his life and career on 31 July 1951 by a direct hit from a bomb while he was in his office on the banks of the Taedong-gang River.[123]

Cho Ki-ch'ŏn's legacy

When the Soviet authorities sent Cho Ki-chŏn to North Korea in 1945, they expected that he, like his fellow Soviet Koreans, would contribute to the growth of Soviet influence in the country. Time proved that he was an ideal choice for this purpose.

Though Cho had experienced the forcible resettlement of Soviet Koreans as well as ethnic discrimination, he obviously did not hold a long-term grudge against Stalin or the Soviet system in general. Like millions of his Soviet contemporaries who were enthusiastic supporters of Stalin, Cho probably explained away the tragedy of the Soviet Koreans as a mistake or some shortsightedness on the part of certain top officials. Having been brought up inside the Soviet reality, Cho perceived the Soviet way of life as the only correct way to live and was eager to share his knowledge with his Korean colleagues. Cho's aspiration to follow the examples of Maiakovskii, Isakovskii, and other officially acclaimed Soviet authors, as well as the explicit ideological motifs of his works, must be justified by his sincere desire to create a new, supposedly "progressive" Korean literature.

His wartime death prevented Cho from being associated with purged politicians—and indeed probably from being purged himself in the late 1950s. As we will see in chapter 5, during those years not even high status could save a doomed writer who belonged to the wrong faction. In official North Korean history, the poet remained a trusted co-worker of the Great Leader and one of his early eulogizers. Elena Davydova claims, however, that for few years, between the late 1960s and early 1980s, Cho's name was virtually absent from North Korean publications.

This silence was broken in the early 1980s when North Korean television broadcast a documentary about him. From that time onward, his works began to be published again, although in heavily revised *chuch'e* editions. A characteristic example is an updated version of "Whistle" that was published in the April 1990 issue of *Chosŏn munhak*.[124] In this adaptation the original stanza ("Again today you smiled purely, / And said that you have surpassed the production plan threefold. / But I do not envy your achievement, I can do even better, / But I like your smile. / Why is it so pure?") was replaced with a new one: "When today you said that you have surpassed the production plan threefold, / I felt fire in my heart. Why is it so?" / While the original version implies that her lovely smile is what attracted the boy to the girl and that her surpassing of the production quota is good but not relevant, the suggestion of the new version is that it is *because* of her success on the production line that the boy feels fire in his heart. In order to attract the attention of the advanced girl, the boy in the revised version is planning to "whistle, holding a bouquet of flowers that I will receive as an innovator / so Poksuna [the girl] will understand my heart." Again, the implication of the new stanza, absent in the original version, is that the boy's progressive activity as an innovator will attract the girl to him. At the same time, the edited version omits the original stanza in which the boy is absent-mindedly looking through his study materials late at night while thinking of Poksuna. The editors obviously wanted to withdraw the stanza with the politically incorrect inference that a girl may be sometimes more important to a boy than study materials. Thus we can see that in the new edition the protagonists became even more politically correct and conscientious. It is noteworthy that contemporary South Korean researchers of North Korean literature rely not on the original but on the revised versions of Cho Ki-ch'ŏn's poems, and this inevitably influences the results of their research.[125]

In present-day North Korea, Cho Ki-ch'ŏn is one of the most honored literary figures. However, it is clear today that Cho's activities as a translator of the Soviet experience for North Korea had ambivalent consequences. In one sense his Soviet/Russian cultural influence, novel in many ways to the Korean national tradition, enriched the Korean intellectual atmosphere. His *sŏjŏng sŏsasi* poetic style, for example, became common in later North Korean poetry.[126] At the same time, Cho's literary and administrative activities helped subjugate the North Korean arts to the political demands of the day. The poet became one of the earliest creators of the Kim Il Sung cult, and the heavy political rhetoric of his writings also influenced subsequent generations of North Korean authors. Eulogies of the "smoke of construction" and "exemplary workers," as well as the curses of the "wicked Yankees" who "carved pictures of atomic bombs" on their victims' chests, still remain in the inventory of North Korean poetry.

The patterns of Cho's "Swing" and "Whistle" are easily traceable in today's North Korean lyrical poetry. Like Cho's socialist realist characters, the subjects of contemporary North Korean verse, in the words of A. M. Van Der Eng-Liedmeier, "are nearly always shown in relation to their work, to a special task set by society or by the Party."[127] Their romantic expressions are secondary and always carry a political meaning. Take, for example, the poem "A Girl's Heart" (Ch'ŏnyŏŭi maŭm), by Kim Ch'ang-ho, in which the heroine, an "extraordinarily hardworking girl," in her rare moments of rest secretly reads letters from a boyfriend "who is wearing an army uniform."[128] In many respects, however, Cho successors went even further, and even such a politically laden plot is a rarity. In the vast majority of cases, the notions of "love" or "emotion" in today's North Korean literature are invariably related to the figures of Kim Il Sung or Kim Jong Il.

Though Cho Ki-ch'ŏn himself never initiated political campaigns against his competitors, he was one of the first writers to introduce the patterns of Stalinist demagogy and political campaigning into Korean literary circles. This politicization of literary discussions was to have grave consequences in the late 1950s.

3 Yi Ki-yŏng

A Successful Literary Cadre

IN NORTH KOREAN LITERATURE, Yi Ki-yŏng and Yi T'ae-jun occupy special places. These two writers are symbolic figures whose activities both before and after Liberation are perceived as cornerstones in the North Korean literary and historical discourse. They occupy opposite corners of this discourse, however. While Yi Ki-yŏng is extolled as an "unbending hero of proletarian literature," a voice of the revolutionary class struggle, and "the pillar of North Korean socialist realism,"[1] Yi T'ae-jun is portrayed as an antihero, a "pure artist" (and thus a natural opponent of socialist realism) who was swept aside by the victorious march of Communist literature. Both North and South Korean academic circles share this vision of the two Yis, although their respective assessments carry different connotations.

At first glance the vision looks plausible. Yi Ki-yŏng (1895–1984) entered the North Korean literary world in 1945 as a well-known writer in the Korean Proletarian Art Federation and immediately came to be revered as the "founding father of Korean proletarian literature," a standing he retained to the end of his life—a rare occurrence at a time when many other literary figures attained preeminence only to disappear within a few years. Yi's pre-1945 works were continually republished and extolled as the first major oeuvre of Korean socialist realism, and his post-Liberation fiction was also printed in great numbers and met with a eulogizing chorus from the North Korean critics. To the present day, Yi Ki-yŏng's writings remain the core of the North Korean literary canon and are included in textbooks in North Korea.[2] Yi's administrative career was also successful. During his thirty-five years as chairman of the Central Committee of the North Korean–Soviet Friendship Society (Chssoch'insŏn Hyŏphoe Chungang Uiwŏnhoe Uiwŏnjang) and in other important official positions, Yi Ki-yŏng enjoyed a level of public respect and material comfort that corresponded to his high official status.[3]

The fate of Yi T'ae-jun (1904–1969?), however, is completely the opposite. A gifted writer who enjoyed wide popularity before Liberation and positioned himself as a devotee of pure art, Yi T'ae-jun in 1946 willingly went to the North and turned his pen to the service of the nascent Communist regime as another "soldier on the cultural front." However, his North Korean activities ended in crushing failure: his pre- and post-liberation writings were condemned as vicious subversions of the principles of socialist realism, and he himself was purged.

The logical explanation of Yi Ki-yŏng's and Yi T'ae-jun's respective rise and fall might be the compatibility or incompatibility of the writers with the Communist ideology and the dominating principles of socialist realism, or the orthodox or heterodox nature of their literary and social activities. However, a comparative analysis of their pre-Liberation works clearly shows that the actual ideological difference between Yi Ki-yŏng's KAPF works and the allegedly "pure" pre-1945 writings of Yi T'ae-jun was surprisingly small, no matter what each side claimed about themselves. On the one hand, Yi Ki-yŏng, like the other representatives of Korea's proletarian literature, was much less proletarian and Marxist than was claimed and could hardly serve as an example of Communist orthodoxy. On the other hand, a closer investigation of Yi T'ae-jun confirms that the "art for art's sake" that he supposedly represented was not completely divorced from social concerns and political questions. Though Yi T'ae-jun's modernist approach cannot be described as Marxist, his works often came closer to the leftist perspective than the supposedly proletarian writings of Yi Ki-yŏng.

As for the post-Liberation activities of the two, both Yi Ki-yong and Yi T'ae-jun turned into equally exemplary soldiers on the cultural front, and the works of both writers strictly followed Party demands. However, the writers' relationships with the North Korean political bureaucracy were remarkably different, and my research maintains that this was the primary factor that determined the vastly different fates of the two Yis. I first consider Yi Ki-yŏng and discuss Yi T'ae-jun in the next chapter.

The "Minch'on" Experience

Yi Ki-yŏng's literary success appears particularly remarkable if we remember that this best-selling author of *Homeland (Kohyang;* 1933–1934), a novel that had been published and republished five times before Liberation,[4] was a barely educated peasant. Most of his writings are autobiographical, and even his pen name, "Minch'on"—which means "poor village" or "village where no *yangban* (gentry) live permanently,"—was a reference to the village where he spent his childhood. Yi Ki-yŏng was born on May 29, 1895, in Hwaryong village, Paeban township, Asan County, Southern Ch'ungch'ŏng Province, but in 1898 his family moved to Chungŏmri *(minch'on)* village, Pukmyŏn township, Ch'ŏnan County, in the same province, so as to live closer to relatives who were small tenant farmers in the area.[5]

Yi's domestic environment was typical of the Korea of the early twentieth century, when the clash between new realities and long-standing traditions gave rise to countless personal tragedies. One such tradition was *ch'ohon,* or early marriage, whereby a boy in his early teens would be compelled to marry a slightly older girl. After marriage, the boy might be sent to study in Seoul or abroad, where he would acquire new, "liberating" ideas and often refuse to return home. The wife had no choice but to remain with her in-laws and raise the couple's children, frequently without her husband's support.

This had been the case with Yi Ki-yŏng's parents, his mother surnamed Pak, of the Milyang lineage (1869–1905), and his father, Yi Min-ch'ang (1873–1918).[6] Though not officially divorced, they lived separately. At the age of twenty, Yi's father passed the official military examinations, making him eligible for a military commission. He then moved to Seoul in search of a suitable job, while his family remained in the countryside, working the land. The father's attempts to find a decent job were unsuccessful, since he was more interested in politics and socializing than in earning money. Yi Min-ch'ang visited his family once a year and provided them with minimal financial assistance. His wife shouldered all the responsibility for the family.[7]

When Yi Ki-yŏng was eleven years old, the whole family caught typhus, and his mother died. This circumstance forced Yi's father to remain with the family, but even before the mourning period for his deceased wife had ended, he married again.[8] Being a *kaehwa sasangga,* or disciple of enlightenment ideas, Yi Min-ch'ang introduced his son to some popular concepts of the period, including the quest for freedom and education, along with dissent against early marriage.[9] Unfortunately, these "civilizing ideas" contrasted with the life surrounding Yi Ki-yŏng. Captivated by contemporary politics and fashionable ideas, Yi Min-ch'ang would spend all of his money on impractical projects while the family suffered under the weight of mounting debt.[10] Despite his enlightenment rhetoric, the father failed to help Yi Ki-yŏng gain a decent education. The schools the boy attended were inferior and had no modern textbooks; the family could not even afford to buy paper for his school notes, and he had to practice writing on cinnamon leaves.[11]

For financial reasons, Yi Ki-yŏng discontinued his education at the primary school level and joined the family in agricultural work.

Despite Yi Min-ch'ang's frequent harangues against early marriage, he forced his son into such a marriage when the latter was just fourteen years old. This decision was to please the boy's grandmother, who at the time was approaching her sixtieth birthday and was impatient to see her first great-grandson. Yi Ki-yŏng's union with Cho Pyŏng-gi (1891–1957), an uneducated peasant woman, proved to be a disaster.[12] In many of his writings, Yi passionately described the neurotic mixture of physical disgust and guilt that he felt toward his first wife.

Immediately following his marriage, Yi ran away from home to wander across the Korean countryside. This life as a vagabond lasted for five years, and only the sudden death of his father and grandmother in 1918 prompted him to return home and assume the role of breadwinner for the rest of his family.

At this time, while teaching at Yŏnghwa women's school in Ronsan, Yi became temporarily absorbed in Christian ideas, which were strongly associated with the new Western way of life, education, and enlightenment.[13] Under the Christian influence, Yi refused to perform the traditional sacrificial rites, or *chesa,* in honor of his deceased father and grandmother and burned their funeral tablets *(hŭnpaek)*. However, a closer personal acquaintance with Christian missionaries—whom Yi later called "wolves in sheep's clothing"—led to disappointment not only with Christian ideas but religion in general.

After 1918, Yi changed jobs several times. He took part in the activities of the local youth organization and read a lot of books and magazines, which he acquired from Japan.[14] In 1922 he made the decision to continue his education, abandoning his family once again, and traveled to Tokyo, where he studied at the School of English Language and Politics for a year.[15] This was a very active period in his life, full of both hardships and important experiences. Yi took a number of odd jobs in Japan, and in the process he became acquainted with the life of Tokyo's poor and came under the influence of the then popular socialist ideas. In Japan, he read Russian and early Soviet literature for the first time and became close friends with the famous Korean literary personality Cho Myŏng-hŭi.[16] But Yi was again unable to complete his studies. The Tokyo earthquake of 1923 led to a bloody massacre of Koreans resident in Japan, and Yi, like many other Korean students, chose to return home.

Yi had to abandon his long-cherished hope of continuing with his formal education. He also turned his back on the advice of his family to find a proper job.[17] What he now strove for was to express his new thoughts and experiences through literature. Impoverished and undereducated, young and enthusiastic—that was Yi Ki-yŏng when he embarked on his literary journey. So what did he write about?

Agrarian Nationalism

A positive response was to be expected from Soviet and North Korean literary critics, who lauded Yi's "proper Communist worldview," his "progressive characters," and his "truthful representation of the people's spirit."[18] However, Yi's pre-Liberation writings inspired applause in South Korea as well. South Korean scholar Kim Sang-sŏn sentimentally confesses to "warm feelings" that Yi Ki-yŏng's literature triggers in his soul.[19] *Who's Who in Korean Literature,* the contemporary English-language South Korean literary encyclopedia, praises Yi's *Homeland* as "one of the most outstanding achievements in Korean proletarian literature" and "a fine specimen of a proletarian novel."[20] In the introduction to Yi *Collected Works* (*Yi Ki-yŏng sŏnjip;* 1989), it is stated that "the quality and quantity of his writings make Yi Ki-yong the greatest and best writer on the Korean peninsula in the 20th century—and this is not just a rhetorical figure."[21]

For all these tributes, Yi's admirers did not by any means define his works as literary masterpieces. Most admitted that his works lacked originality; the writer widely exploited Japanese, Russian Soviet, and in one case, Spanish literary patterns and often bordered on plagiarism.[22] Even ethnocentric Korean critics admitted that many images in Yi's works, and in *Homeland* in particular, included direct borrowings from Gorky's and Sholokhov's novels[23]—and this occurred before Liberation, when no one was forcing him to follow examples from Korea's future "elder brother." Even the most compassionate critics acknowledged that Yi's artistic arsenal was rather limited; most reviewers noted a monotonous stiffness in his language, stilted images, and a paucity of psychological penetration. While analyzing the formal side of Yi's writings, even the most positive Soviet critics routinely offered such unenthusiastic comments as "oversimplistic story line," "a strong didactic tendency," "a touch of bucolic sentimentalism," "a certain implausibility," "superficiality," "schematization," "excessive use of folk motives," and "excessively detailed."[24] Kim Sang-sŏn admits, "Yi Ki-yŏng's writings may indeed be irritating. They do not touch your heart; they just pass through you. The story does not move smoothly; it is too coarse."[25]

These reservations appear reasonable. Yi's unpolished works can indeed irritate a reader. They are full of clichés and conventional images in which pretty girls are invariably compared to beautiful flowers that "open" when happy and "wither" when sad;[26] a quiet and industrious male character predictably resembles an ox (which in Korean is the nickname for a mute workaholic);[27] the lyrical moods of the protagonists are repeatedly accompanied by a nightingale singing in willow branches on a spring night, an easily recognizable allusion to the classic Korean novel *The Tale of Ch'unghyang (Ch'unhyangjŏn)*;[28] while a frustrated hero struggles with stormy weather.[29] Often even these stereotypes are repeated—for example, the Korean proverbial juxtaposition of white herons and black crows can be found in both "A Story about Mice" (Chwi iyagi) and "Paper Factory Village" (Cheji kongjang ch'on).[30] Yi's approach to his characters is, as a rule, one-dimensional. Instead of presenting a character's actions or thoughts, he tends to describe him or her explicitly as "good" or "bad," or he simply makes his positive protagonists deliver righteous speeches, overburdened with convoluted leftist jargon. These speeches are particularly implausible when they emanate from the lips of his favorite female characters—namely, young, uneducated, and docile peasant women. Most of Yi's writings are clumsily and irregularly composed. Their story lines often lack consistency and are laden with minor characters and irrelevant narratives, and the behavior of the heroes lacks motivation. In short, the aesthetic deficiencies of Yi Ki-yŏng's novels are difficult to ignore.

These shortcomings were never a secret for either the North Korean critics or even for Yi himself. In 1952, North Korean critic Han Hyo, while stressing the laudable ideological content of KAPF writings (which included, first and foremost, Yi Ki-yŏng's works), acknowledged that it was "literature of extremely low artistic quality."[31] Yi himself also candidly confessed that his pre-Liberation novels lacked sophistication, but justified this by the historical circumstances that supposedly made literary quality a less significant consideration. In one of his later theoretical works, "About the Creative Method" (1957), Yi explained his attitude during the KAPF era: "We had no time to decorate the handles of our knives when the enemy was fiercely attacking [us]. Our first task was to sharpen the blade so as to strike the enemy to the very heart."[32]

One might dismiss the conflict between blade and handle or between the content and the form of a literary piece as rather artificial. It may be argued, for example, that the inclusion of a political message in a literary work does not necessarily mean neglecting aesthetics; one need only point to the artistic quality and international success of such unabashedly political writers as Gorky or Orwell. Yet it seems that Yi's readership perceived his writings in much the same manner as he described them, and his pre-Liberation recognition was in fact a public acknowledgment of his specific political agenda and of the topicality of his novels rather than their artistic excellence. This was what his KAPF colleague Kim Nam-ch'ŏn lamented in one of his articles published soon after Liberation.[33]

This, then, raises a vital question: what, precisely, constituted this attractive topicality? While both North and South Korean scholarship define Yi Ki-yŏng as a thoroughly Communist proletarian writer[34] and a representative of socialist values,[35] Communist ideology never ranked first in the real agenda of Yi's writings. It is true that in the 1920s and 1930s Yi undoubtedly sympathized with what may be defined as "popular socialism" in its egalitarian and humanistic manifestations, and that he incorporated some rhetoric of a Marxian bent in his works. However, his writings never presented a proletariat-centered approach to the world and society, ideas of class struggle, or the concept of Communist revolution—all of which were necessary features of Communist orthodoxy. Leftist motifs in Yi's writings appear secondary to other ideas, the most prominent of which being his support for agrarianism, or "agrarian nationalism," which "saw the future of Korea from neither a capitalist nor a communist perspective, but in terms of a self-sufficient communal society with explicit linkages to Korea's agrarian tradition."[36]

The success of the traditional peasant perspective in Korean literature was predictable in the intellectual atmosphere of the colonial period, which was dominated by popular myths of the unspoiled village and strong antiurban, antimodern tendencies among even the most educated.[37] Being removed by an unexpected modernity from their habitual social niches, many disappointed Korean intellectuals were searching for an alternative and hence hailed the voices of peasants, the supposed repository of the national essence. Korea was not unique in this regard; similar trends were prominent among intellectuals in many other societies experiencing colonialism or the early stages of modernization. Samuel L. Popkin, a student of Vietnamese rural society, describes these agrarian illusions:

> The pre-capitalist village is seen as a unique form attributable to special virtues of the race or culture. . . . A way of life that may have existed only for lack of alternatives is extolled as a virtue. Peasants who had little or nothing to eat are assumed to have had a rich spiritual life. Sons who may have stayed with their fathers only in order to survive are credited with filial piety. . . . Somehow what might only have been the necessities or oppressions of one era come to be interpreted as traditional values during the next.[38]

In Korea this tendency was also strengthened by the strong spiritual influence of Russian culture, which itself exhibited a persistent "peasant myth" and was propagated most notably by Tolstoy.[39]

This utopian traditionalist discourse, as Gi-Wook Shin has noted, represented a "sharp contrast to both bourgeois and Marxist discourses."[40] In Yi's case, the contrast is not so sharp, for his agrarian nationalist discourse is diluted with socialist rhetoric. Still, the agrarianism in his writings is too strong to allow us to describe his works as thoroughly revolutionary or Communist.[41]

Yi's writings also presented enlightenment themes that harked back to the slogan *munmyŏng kaehwa* (civilization and enlightenment). This catchcry had been popular in Korea since the 1890s.[42] Topics such as liberal protest against prejudice and superstition, anticlericalism, calls for modern education, and eulogies to personal freedom had been propagated in Korean literature from its *sinsosŏl* (new novel) period of the early 1900s,[43] and in a sense they constituted a base for the worldview of Korean intellectuals at the time. Yi's writings also expressed support for women's liberation and female education, criticism of early marriage, and promotion of the principle of "free love" (which in Korean discourse of the time meant "free choice of marriage partner").

This mix of agrarian nationalism and enlightenment ideas won Yi Ki-yŏng the wide acclaim of his contemporaries. He was welcomed into the Korean intellectual world as a bold peasant who had found a way to express himself and who had done so in a most appealing and ideologically familiar way. Educated readers tended to perceive Yi's works as "truly national" chronicles of the "real life" of the Korean common people and were happy to overlook the artistic imperfections in his writings. (It must be stressed that, for the most part, Yi's works were a success among intellectuals and not farmers or workers, who, as Chung Chin-bae discerningly noted, always favored *The Tale of Ch'unghyang* or *The Tale of Hong Kil-dong* over "class-conscious" KAPF literature.[44])

This same perception can be traced in the works of present-day South Korean intellectuals. For example, the prominent South Korean writer Kim Nam-il admits that, "frankly speaking, Yi Ki-yŏng is one of the most boring writers among his contemporaries, not comparable to Yŏm Sang-sŏp, Chae Man-sik, or the others." Yet Kim extols the Yi's value on the basis that "in the dark days of Japanese colonization Yi Ki-yŏng carefully observed our people's life and engendered a hope for the future," and for this reason alone, Kim asserts, Yi can be "of much help to us."[45]

It is significant that after Liberation the agrarianism and enlightenment motifs, albeit laced with official Pyongyang rhetoric, remained dominant in

Yi's works. Considering that his writings formed the basic canon of North Korean literature, it is important to investigate the ideological core of his works and to question the widespread perception of him as the representative of proletarian-Marxian ideology in Korean literature.

Pre-KAPF Writings

The first works of this future "pillar of socialist realism" dealt with a topic that was quite popular in the Korean literature of the 1920s: the sentimental motif of separated or doomed lovers. Yi Ki-yŏng's first novel, *Darkness* (*Amhŭk;* 1924), which remained unpublished, describes an unhappy love affair between a Japanese girl and a Korean student in Japan. The novel also bore the cumbersome subtitle "White Herons Flying under the Shade of Death" (Chukŭm-ŭi kŭrimjae narŭnŭn paekrotte), in keeping with the recently established tradition of the "new novel." This work, as Yi admitted, was strongly influenced by the Japanese novel *Growing Up in the Red Kaolin* (1921), by Nakanishi Inoshuke, the first Japanese writer to mention the presence of Koreans in Japan in his writings, which made them very popular among Korean youth at the time.[46] In later years, Yi defined his first novel as a failure.[47] In 1957 he joked about his first literary experience: "I was like a toothless baby trying to munch on beans and rice."[48]

Following this initial failure, Yi abandoned novels for a while. His first published work was a short story entitled "Elder Brother's Secret Letter" (Oppa-ŭi pimil p'yŏngji; March 1924), which Yi wrote in a week in order to participate in a literary contest sponsored by *Kaebyŏk* magazine[49] and for which he won third prize in April 1924.[50] The story line of "Secret Letter" is as follows: The protagonist, twenty-year-old Maria, is continually humiliated by her arrogant elder brother. Despite his insolent behavior her brother, being a male, is widely respected, while she is invariably treated as a worthless female. In her heart Maria protests against this injustice and disgrace. "The only weapon my brother uses as an argument with me is: "What on earth can you, a woman, understand?!" she muses. Maria easily sees through her brother's hypocritical religiosity, which other people accept at face value. Thus it comes as no surprise to find that her brother turns out to be a womanizer who betrays many innocent young women in the town, including her close friend Yŏng-sun.[51]

Despite the best attempts of North Korean scholarship to categorize "Secret Letter" as revolutionary (though later ascribing a "class position" to the story's author[52]), the story was in fact written in accordance with the

common liberal conventions of the age.[53] The theme of the inequality of the
sexes in Korean society had been discussed in Korean literature from at least
1906—in the new novels *(sinsosŏl)*—and was particularly prominent in the
works of Yi Kwang-su, a future political opponent of Yi Ki-yŏng's.[54] It is no
accident that Soviet scholarship, while eulogizing Yi Ki-yŏng's "true proletarian" novels of the 1920s and early 1930s, tends to pass over his first published novel or refer to it only briefly.[55]

After the publication of "Secret Letter," Yi broke with his family completely and moved to Seoul to earn a living as a writer. In 1924 he met the
leftist writer Cho Myŏng-hŭi, who had just returned from Tokyo. Both writers began to work as correspondents for the magazine *Chosŏn chigwang (Shining
over Korea),* where Yi also made the acquaintance of Ch'oe Sŏ-hae, Song Yŏng,
Yi Ik-sang, Yi Chŏk-hyo, and other leftist writers. Around this time, he also
remarried. Though his choice, Hong Ŭl-sun (1905–?), was a so-called new
woman *(sin yŏsŏng*—that is, a woman who had received at least some Western education),[56] the extent of her emancipation in the contemporary feminist
sense should not be overestimated. From the recollections of Chŏng Ryul,
Hong was quite a traditional shy Korean housewife who shared all of the
hardships of life with her husband without complaint. Yi Ki-yŏng appeared
to be happy with their relationship.[57]

First KAPF Period (1925–1927)

The period from the publication of "Elder Brother's Secret Letter" to the late
1920s was a remarkable one in Yi Ki-yŏng's literary career. Relatively free of
political responsibilities, Yi was guided largely by his own views and convic-
tions. He joined the Korean Proletarian Art Federation in 1925, but up to
1927 the KAPF was a rather amorphous organization. Japanese censorship
at the time was relatively mild, and Yi had an unparalleled opportunity to
express himself.

Being on friendly terms with the "new tendency" writers and sharing
many of their values, Yi nevertheless appeared less radical than most of his
fellow writers in this group. While the exploitation, social discontent, and
misery he depicted was quite in tune with many of the leftist literary conventions, Yi's early writings were remarkably free of descriptions of spontaneous
rebellion. Nevertheless the critic Yi Sang-gyŏng described Yi Ki-yŏng's most
representative work of this period, the short story "Poor Village" (Minch'on;
November 1925), as mirroring "the class struggle between landlords and
tenants."[58]

Let us look at the plot of the story. All the inhabitants of a poor village live miserable lives, except for the rich *yangban* family, the Paks, whose son indulges himself in buying new concubines. His next target is Chŏm-sun, the young and beautiful daughter of the poor peasant Kim. The girl is in love with an intelligent, well-mannered student who recently returned from Seoul and who is known among the peasants by the respectful nickname "Seoul Taek" ("person from Seoul" or "Seoulite"). While his young peasant friends work, Seoulite preaches ideas of social equality ("there is no actual difference between a small merchant and a nobleman"; "everybody must work"[59]) and entertains the country girls with tales of the "beautiful life that could have been had on this land if the bad guys hadn't grasped power":[60]

> Imagine us living here in these beautiful mountain surroundings, in clean houses. We would live here with no concern for food or clothing. Our parents would work in the fields, and we would go to school to study and have fun. In the evenings, after returning home from school, we would help our parents in the fields or go for walks in the mountains. How beautiful our life would be! If only everyone would work together and we were not all separated into rich and poor! How pleasant it would be to love and respect your neighbors! One day we would gather in your house, the next day you could come to mine. How joyful it would be! The birds would sing about humankind's happiness and the flowers would reflect people's joy. Everything in the world would be for the people's edification. We would be happy even watching the moon!
>
> But look at us. As children we are unable to study. Our aged parents slave away day and night in the fields yet still live in poverty. Women's hands are swollen from grinding grain. Young people, whether boys or girls, cannot love freely of their own choice. We are hungry and poorly dressed; we live in meager huts and suffer fleas and bedbugs. And it is all because bad people have stolen our wealth and forced many who work loyally and tirelessly into the abyss of poverty.[61]

The young women are touched by Seoulite's speeches. "Dreaming about the beautiful life," they cry because Seoulite has "awakened sadness in their hearts that they had never known before."[62]

Meanwhile, *yangban* Pak helps the poor Kim family, lending them two sacks of rice, and suggests that Chŏm-sun should become his concubine. Her father considers the proposal shameful and reacts with fury, "grinding his teeth" and "clenching his fists": "I would rather die of hunger! How dare he!

He is actually suggesting that we should sell our daughter for rice—and give her to him to be his third or fourth concubine!"[63]

After this, Chŏm-sun's father collapses and becomes seriously ill, and to pay for his treatment the family resorts to the very means that led the man to his deathbed—they send Ch'ŏm-sun to Pak's house as a concubine. Ch'ŏm-sun herself initiates the marriage, asking her father's permission, which he grants.

Ch'ŏm-sun's brother delivers a bold speech, affirming that he would rather go to jail than give his sister to Pak and that "to give him a body is worse than death."[64] However, he is as daunted by the obstacles the family faces as are the other family members, who spend the days crying helplessly and lamenting about "how cruel today's world is, where it is impossible to find really noble people" and "today's world, where nobody wants to help each other."[65] Their consternation leads to another collapse, that of the grief-stricken mother.[66]

When Chŏm-sun is about to leave her parents' house to ride in the marriage palanquin, Seoulite approaches her with the following "quiet words": "Chŏm-sun, do not despair! Think over your situation. There must be a way to the new life!"

In the final scene of the story, Chŏm-sun is riding in the marriage palanquin while the last words of Seoulite echo in her ears like a drum, again and again:

> "Chŏm-sun, do not despair! Think over your situation! There must be a way to the new life!" Those words gave her great inspiration. Over and over she pondered: "Well! Whose fault was it that I was sold? Poverty is not a fault. Until this debt is paid, I would rather live like a slave but I will never be a concubine! Never! I would rather die!" Chŏm-sun made a firm resolution. She bit her lips, and her eyes filled with tears.[67]

Certainly, the story fails to glorify struggle of any kind. The writer's endeavors to place expressions of protest into the mouths of the protagonists turn these quite traditional suffering personages, the embodiment of *han* (a mixed feeling of sorrow and regret), into unintentionally comic figures, because their righteous words are in such striking contrast to their actions. The girl's "firm resolution" that she would rather die than be a concubine is made when she is already seated in the palanquin, with an obvious purpose to marry, not to die. Her father's diatribes against Pak and his declaration that he would rather die of hunger than offer his daughter as a concubine is promptly followed by the marriage of Chŏm-sun. Seoulite's sermons about heaven on earth are ardently delivered while his listeners work and he remains idle. His farewell words are awash with empty rhetoric rather than any kind of real help for the girl he supposedly "so innocently loves."

The denunciatory tirades in "Poor Village" do not rise above age-old complaints about the cruelty of "today's world." It is significant that "today's world" is presented as a symbol of all things evil, things that, as the author obviously assumes, did not exist in "yesterday's world," an idealized era of supposed bucolic harmony. In today's world money is "so important," "sly misers have their pride," and "people have no nobility,"[68] while in yesterday's world "the *yangban* could not live if they had money, for they valued their inner pride very highly."[69]

It is therefore difficult to agree with Yi Sang-gyŏng's assertion that "poor peasants in the story, though suffering, are not passive and spiritless."[70] In effect the characters in "Poor Village" are utterly submissive and inert. While the descriptions of the family's emotional outbursts and collapse occupy some six pages of the text,[71] not one character attempts any act of protest, not even in the irrational style of Ch'oe Sŏ-hae's rebelling protagonists. Yi Sang-gyŏng explains this characteristic of "Poor Village," however, in a most complimentary manner: "The story does not finish with an abstract slogan or idealistic act of revenge, like the stories of the fashionable 'new tendency' literature. The reason Yi Ki-yŏng concludes his story with total failure is that he understands the seriousness of social discord much more deeply than the other 'new tendency' writers."[72]

In fact, "Poor Village" does finish with an abstract slogan—namely, Seoulite's "invigorating" farewell. Furthermore, the sole reason that Yi Ki-yŏng puts forward for the contemporary state of social discord is the greed of the "bad guys," an approach that was hardly going to win him the title of insightful social analyst.

Soviet scholars found it difficult to reconcile the submissiveness of the characters in "Poor Village" with the officially sanctioned image of Yi Ki-yŏng as an unbending proletarian writer who supposedly possessed a clear-cut class perspective. In order to rationalize Yi's story, they strove to highlight the discrepancy between the words and deeds of the characters (and in particular between the final fervent words of Seoulite and his actual passivity) as a deliberate ploy of the author to "instill righteous indignation in the reader."[73] However, the author's notion that Seoulite's words gave "great inspiration" to the weeping heroine robs this interpretation of any sense. V. N. Li, true to the trivializing tenor of Soviet Marxist philology, explains the protagonist's behavior in terms of his class position: Seoulite, a "worthless hero," is a "representative of the degenerating gentry."[74] This explanation does not stand up to criticism either, since Yi portrays Seoulite as an unquestionably positive character.

Indeed, to understand this or any other of Yi's works of that period, the scholar has no choice but to reject the conventional view of Yi Ki-yŏng as a revolutionary figure. In fact, nothing in Yi's novels of the period suggests any significant deviation from the values of the social stratum from which he originated—that is, the traditional impoverished peasantry. The implicit values of "Poor Village" are loyalty to one's elders, conservatism, and passive endurance—indeed, the same traditional virtues that were considered positive in classical Korean literature. The utopian ideal, depicted by Seoulite as "the new life," is—like his words of protest—a rather antiquated one. His visions of an ideal society originate from traditional Korean rural community values that include harmonious and moderate manual labor, an education for one's children, and equality and mutual respect among the village community.

The perspectives of Yi Ki-yŏng's other early stories from this period do not differ much from that of "Poor Village." Even the allegory "A Story about Mice" (1925), which in Soviet scholarship was touted as "an appeal for the socialist reconstruction of society,"[75] is no exception in this regard.

The allegory describes a family of mice, surnamed Kwak, that is moving from the house of the poor peasant Sudol to the rich house of the Kim family. The mouse family compares the two ways of life and deduces that the human order of things is unfair because those who work hard cannot live well. Here are some of their observations: "People's money is just like the devil's hat casting a spell on people," "People who steal live well," and "Rich people are as greedy as pigs."[76] The father mouse concludes: "Sudol has the right to demand the return of the land that they took from him. He must stick together with the other peasants because if you submit, things only get worse. . . . To wait for mercy from the rich is just as senseless as to wait for a black crow to turn into a white heron."[77]

As a practical step toward the realization of this social program, the mice decide to seek revenge on the rich family's mean-spirited daughter-in-law, who refused to help a poor neighbor's family by lending them rice. The brave mice urinate on her "ugly face" while she is sleeping. The father mouse then steals a wad of money from the Kim patriarch and carries his loot to the Sudol family's simple hut. The story concludes with a final admonition from the father mouse Kwak: "There are good and evil forces in this world. The good force comes from the unity of people, and the bad one comes from individual violence. Good people must unite their good souls. And we should always use our strength to help the good people."

This was the only story of the period in which Yi suggests any kind of project for social change, yet this work could hardly be interpreted as an "appeal for socialist reconstruction." Instead, "A Story about Mice" evokes the traditional pattern of Hong Gil-dong, a Korean Robin Hood figure who robs the rich to feed the poor, in accordance with a centuries-old pattern of rebel peasant behavior. Rather than change society, peasant riots tend to conserve and stabilize it, "consolidating the traditional political system by purging it" and never challenging "more than the abuses of the traditional regimes."[78] "A Story About Mice" sticks to the egalitarian ethic of the patriarchal Korean peasantry with its condemnation of the more fortunate members who do not help their less fortunate brethren.

These and the other stories by Yi Ki-yŏng from the period, such as "The Peasant Chŏng To-ryŏng" (Nongbu Chŏng To-ryŏng; 1925), "Poor People" (Kananhan saram; 1925), "Father of Five" (Onammae tun abŏji; 1926), and "The Peasant's House" (Nongbu-ŭi chip; 1927), deal mostly with rural life. It is difficult to agree with the assertion of South Korean scholar Kim Chae-yong that Yi, "unlike ordinary peasant writers, observed rural life from the perspective of a worker."[79] Yi's perspectives did not deviate from the discourse of the traditional village community. His "inner character" of the period can be defined as an enlightened peasant who is infuriated by the arrival of capitalist modernity. The only response he can envisage to the harshness of the new life is a return to the imagined social harmony of the past. He is not inclined to protect the traditional ways unconditionally, however. With some basic education he comes to perceive some aspects of traditional rural life as annoying, with the long-established institution of early marriage seen as a major evil.[80]

Second KAPF Period (1927–1934)

The next period of activity in Yi Ki-yŏng's career began to unfold when the KAPF was radicalized. It would appear that Yi accepted the new KAPF policy wholeheartedly. Not only did he profess his support for Bolshevization by publishing a set of articles in *Chosŏn chigwang* magazine,[81] but he also started to fashion his writings according to the new political requirements. Still, these new tendencies failed to offset his old visions.

Let us look at two of his most tendentious short stories of the period, "Wŏn-bo" (1928)[82] and "Paper Factory Village" (1930). The first story,

"Wŏn-bo," describes an accidental meeting between the poor peasant Wŏn-bo and his wife and the worker Sŏk-pong in a Seoul flophouse. Wŏn-bo, an old man whose legs were crippled in an automobile accident, has come to Seoul in a desperate search for medical help, which he fails to receive, because of his lack of money. It is his first visit to a big city, and he observes this new reality through innocent, childlike eyes. Sŏk-pong, the out-of-work miner who is the other guest at the inn, explains to the elderly couple why they, a worker and a peasant who have both worked all their lives, are now completely destitute. "Those who only play and eat stole the wealth of the peasants and the workers," he explains.[83] The only way out, Sŏk-pong insists, is to "struggle against the ruling class." Wŏn-bo is utterly thrilled at Sŏk-pong's words of wisdom. His deathbed desire is to deliver these sage words to his grandson so that he too might come to know the truth about life.

South Korean scholar Kim Sang-sŏn has characterized "Wŏn-bo" as "a story about the unity of the aspirations of workers and peasants,"[84] while North Korean scholar Sin Ku-hyŏn praises it highly as a story about "the awakening of class consciousness" in Wŏn-bo, a peasant with a soul "as pure and clean as a white piece of paper."[85] These were probably the actual intentions of the author. The question is, however, how convincingly Yi Ki-yŏng realized these intentions.

The idea of an instant "awakening of class consciousness" in a peasant character with a mind as clean as "a white piece of paper" might not appear too implausible in itself. However, Wŏn-bo is a totally ignorant man who has spent all his life in a remote rural area; he does not even know what city dwellers do in their everyday life and is surprised when he fails to find his familiar fields and vegetable plots in the city. It is hard to believe that such a childishly innocent soul could grasp in a single day the complicated social theory that is narrated in politicized terms such as "exploitation," "the ruling class," and so on. What is even more incredible is that Wŏn-bo internalizes these new ideas so completely that his lifelong obedience to his superiors is instantly replaced by an eagerness to join the "class struggle." It seems that Yi Ki-yŏng put his favorite peasant hero into an unfamiliar environment that was uncritically borrowed from foreign literary models, Gorky in particular—many scholars have highlighted the common setting of "Wŏn-bo" and Gorky's drama *The Lower Depths*.[86]

Even though the story is steeped in leftist jargon, its Marxian credentials also appear quite doubtful. The main malefactors in Sŏk-pong's social denunciations are not "capitalists" per se but vicious "Seoul folk."

The supposedly Marxist worker Sŏk-pong is infuriated by "city dwell-ers, who took all our possessions and now enjoy life," and by "Seoul resi-dents, who do not work in the fields yet are always well-fed and amused and who do not weave but wear beautiful dresses."[87] Such an antiurban, anti-industrial view can hardly be defined as Marxist or as bespeaking a "clear socialist tendency" in the story.[88] The desired proletarian motifs in "Wŏn-bo" failed to supplant the usual traditionalist perspective of Yi Ki-yŏng's novels.

This same can be said even of Yi's most proletarian story, "Paper Factory Village," which was inspired by another of Gorky's works, *Mother (Mat')*, and describes a workers' strike, a common setting in the literature of social-ist realism. In Yi's story the workers in the paper factory are driven to des-peration by their master's greed and decide to go on strike. The idea comes from an intellectual with the mocking nickname "Saennim" (Know-it-all Smarty-pants, or Egghead) who has come to the factory in order "to be baptized by labor." Initially Saennim's co-workers poke fun at this book-ish creature, but eventually he gains their trust. The strike ends in fail-ure. Saennim, who turns out to be a writer named Hwang-un in disguise, is imprisoned, and petty rivalries tear the workers' ranks apart. However, Hwang-un is happy, for he feels that "the seeds he planted are growing day and night."[89]

Characteristically, in this proletarian story the workers appear not as an active force but rather as a dark mass of wretches who have been crippled by harsh labor. Like Gorky's *Mother*, Yi Ki-yŏng's story starts with a gloomy description of the factory, including the same comparisons of the workers to hellish "machines" or "slaves of machinery," and the factory reality to "a nightmare" where alcohol and prostitutes are the only known forms of relax-ation.[90] However, unlike *Mother* with its lively and distinctive proletarian protagonists, Yi's story includes no vivid personalities among the workmen. The only personal trait of the worker Chang that Yi mentions is that he was "famous for his industriousness." In contrast, the author lavished lengthy pas-sages of description on the main character, who is clearly reminiscent of com-mon intellectual characters in Korean prose at the time, with their immanent weakness and doomed refinement.[91] Yi verbosely describes such things as the love of a factory girl for the main hero or a female servant's appearance,[92] but when conveying Saennim's progressive thoughts and motivations, he turns to a stultified prose that is lifted directly from the Communist propaganda of the era:

Saennim was a person who had abandoned bourgeois prejudices, who stood on the path of the fight for the proletariat. From the beginning he understood the full danger of his fight. But he determined to fight nevertheless, from the moment he entered the factory village. His arrival at the factory was the first step in a new and sincere life. He made the decision in order to thwart his cowardly ego, which was filled with petty bourgeois consciousness. He wanted to become a proletarian, to become a "proper" person. That is why he threw away his writing brush and ink bottle. He wanted to become a worker who constructs life.

Alas for the life he had lived before! He had spent twenty-five years in a feudal patriarchal environment! But he could break out of it, he could enter a new life! It demanded courage; he could not imagine that such a weak person as himself could handle physical labor. But he threw away all his bourgeois superstitions, cowardice, and idleness and stepped onto the bloody path of struggle![93]

This eulogy appears completely unrelated to the other parts of the story. The reader can only guess what prompted the intellectual to abandon his previous life or what exactly he did to impress his simple and initially hostile co-workers.

Though Yi's works from the second KAPF period undeniably contain leftist rhetoric, they are still centered on Yi's favorite personalities: poor young women, wretched elderly peasants, and fragile intellectuals, whom the author describes with far more authenticity and sympathy than the faceless "progressive" workers or revolutionary activists. The obligatory revolutionary conversions of his traditional heroes remain schematic, and their motivations remain largely unexplored.

Homeland (1933–1934)

The inconsistency between Yi Ki-yŏng's essentially traditionalist peasant worldview and his alien, borrowed proletarian motifs appears most clearly in his most popular work, the novel *Homeland* (1933–1934). Critics generally agree that the novel was written under the strong influence of Sholokhov's major agrarian novels *Quiet Flows the Don (Tihii Don)* and *Virgin Land under the Plow (Podniataia tselina)*.[94] North Korean scholar Pak Chong-sik, citing a personal interview with Yi, stated: "The month after his first reading of *Quiet Flows the Don* in Japanese translation, Yi Ki-yŏng started to write *Homeland*. He set the goal of maintaining the same perspective on contemporary Korean village life as Sholokhov did on the rural life of the Don region. This was the reason for the strong similarity between the images in the two novels."[95]

Homeland, like *Quiet Flows the Don,* attempted to construct a broad panorama of Korean village life in the 1920s and 1930s. The main story line of the novel can be summarized as follows: Kim Hŭi-jun, a progressive student, returns from Japan to his native village, which has been rapidly changing under the influence of colonial modernization. He sees that a majority of the honest peasants have been impoverished, while the less scrupulous ones, like the cunning pro-Japanese village administrator An Sŭng-hak, have prospered. Many villagers have lost their land and are forced to slave away in the hellish world of the local textile factory. The mentality of the villagers remains backward. They still follow the old traditions of forced early marriage, polygamy, and worshipping the Confucian norms of total obedience to their parents' will. Traditional religious beliefs of Shamanism, Buddhism, and superstition occupy their minds side by side with the new Christian tenets.

Kim Hŭi-jun feels obliged to improve the life of the people around him. Following his disappointment with Christianity and a local youth organization, he resolves to restore the traditional rural system of *ture* (neighborhood mutual-help groups), which not only help the peasants materially but also unite and enlighten them. Under Kim's leadership, the unified peasants are able to attain a desirable goal—namely, the right of not paying rent after floods destroy their fields.

The social activity of the progressive student is intertwined with a love theme. Kim Hŭi-jun, who had been forced into marriage with an ignorant older woman, falls in love with the young and well-educated Kap-suk (An Yŏng-hŭi), who has forsaken her rich family, changed her name, and become a factory worker. For the sake of loyalty to his wife and in order to "serve society," Kim decides to suppress his feelings and remains Kap-suk's comrade-in-arms. At the end of the novel the protagonists greet the dawning together.

In North Korea, *Homeland* is invariably presented as a profoundly proletarian work, centered on the story of a workers' union.[96] North Korean scholar Sin Ku-hyŏn even claimed that *Homeland* "was written under the direct influence of the anti-Japanese revolutionary struggle of Kim Il Sung."[97] South Korean scholar Na Pyŏng-ch'ŏl insists that *Homeland* is an example of "literature written by a writer with a socialist worldview."[98] V. N. Li maintains that the main hero is a revolutionary and that the novel on the whole is devoted to the theme of the "revolutionary actions of the masses."[99] A. N. Taen has called the main protagonist, Kim Hŭi-jun, "a typical Korean Communist and revolutionary of the preparatory period of the anti-imperialist, antifeudal revolution in Korea."[100] To my understanding, however, all these interpretations overlook the obvious contradiction between the leftist rhetoric that occasionally appears in the novel and the actual traditionalist, antimodernist essence of *Homeland*.

First of all, the idea of a workers' union in the novel is quite vague. A single episode describes a strike at the textile factory, and this strike produces no visible results. The peasants are able to secure the cancelation of their rent payments not through union action but by blackmail. They threaten the village administrator that they will spread rumors about his daughter, and he succumbs to their pressure.

According to the Marxist doctrine of the vanguard role and fighting spirit of the proletariat, the author delivered a number of eulogies to the working masses: "Female workers are marked by a belief in their comrades, enthusiasm, a hatred for injustice, self-confidence, and an independent spirit"; "All we see around us is the result of the labor of the workers and peasants"; and "A worker is the child of a peasant. He is like a newly hatched chicken that looks at the world around him with clear, wide-open eyes. Looking at the workers, peasants understand that the dawn of their life will come someday."[101] But these panegyrics are scarcely connected to the narrative. None of Yi's important characters are workers; at the very best they experience factory life temporarily (as Kap-suk does). The workers in the novel are by no means a vanguard but rather a suffering mass that is to be saved and led by virtuous intellectuals. Modern industry and technology in this supposedly proletarian novel are mostly depicted as evil forces, tearing apart the harmonious world of the traditional village; moreover, Yi's favorite peasant themes constitute the core of the narrative.

The activities of Kim Hŭi-jun—for example, his revival of the traditional peasant *ture* with ritualistic songs and dances can hardly be described as revolutionary either. In fact they constitute a return to the past, which the author once again describes in idyllic terms: "In the olden days our peasants lived another better life, a life full of poetry. . . . Peasants could sit under a tree free from care and drink unrefined rice liquor or play cards. Women would wash in the river, and itinerant conjurers entertained the people."[102] Yi does not connect these good old days with the traditional customs that are particularly appalling to him, such as early and forced marriage, the enslavement of women, and deep-rooted religious superstitions. On the contrary, he somehow associates these evils with the contemporary order of things as if it was capitalism and colonization that brought these problems to a once-virtuous Korea: "Nowadays there is stupidity, greed, and ignorance everywhere."[103]

The return of *ture* in the novel is represented as the return to a lost paradise for the peasants. "The villagers were as happy as if they were attending a feast. . . . The restoration of *ture* unified the peasants. Even the mothers of Paekryong and Soetŭk forgot their old enmity."[104]

The novel's "revolutionary" heroine, Kap-suk, indulges in "progressive" declarations ("First of all we must fight for our common freedom, not for our personal happiness"; "We must fight for freedom and win"; "We should not live for the physical only"; "Happiness is not just the simple enjoyment of your own life. Happiness is offering your life for the sake of others"),[105] but the nature of her actions remains vague. Kap-suk's "revolutionary fight" for the workers' rights at the factory ends in a somewhat predictable manner: her male boss yells at her, and Kap-suk, feeling that she "has no other choice," dutifully returns to her workstation.[106]

Most of *Homeland*'s critics agree on the implausibility of the love theme and of its "progressive" female characters.[107] Certainly Yi failed to show what prompted Kap-suk to attain her high level of political consciousness and to be transformed from the shy heiress of a wealthy family into a determined social activist. The love theme in the novel appears too foreign, bearing an apparent affinity with the early Soviet and Russian liberal literature in which characters were often forced to choose between the personal and the social (for example, Gorky's *Mother,* Turgenev's *On the Eve,* and Chernyshevskii's *What Is To Be Done?*).[108] Yi later admitted that Kap-suk, though conceptually a "correct" character, "contradicts the sense of reality."[109]

The vagueness of the novel's political message left room for vastly different interpretations. Contemporary Korean literary magazines of the "pure art" persuasion, such as *Chosŏn mundan (Korean Literary World)* and *Samch'ŏnri (Three Thousand Li),* greeted *Homeland* as "the pride of modern Korean literature"[110] and stressed such common social themes in the novel as "spring hunger in the village," "peasants' suffering after a flood," "the immoral activity of clergymen," and more.[111] The South Korean *Encyclopedia of Korean Literature* in 1973, published at the height of the anti-Communist hysteria, just after the Yusin coup, describes *Homeland* as "a work with a powerful life force," as a "humanistic" novel whose main topic is a "search for compromise between landlords and tenants and the possibility of finding this through the reasonable consideration of peasants' needs."[112] Interestingly, when Japanese censorship turned especially harsh in 1937, *Homeland* was translated into Japanese and published in the Japanese literary magazine *Bungaku annai (Literary Guide).*[113]

No Hero (1934–1945)

In the early 1930s, the leftist tendencies in Yi Ki-yŏng's writings began to wane. In 1934 the colonial police arrested him along with more than eighty other KAPF members, accused him of subversive activities, and put him in jail for about a year and a half.

According to Soviet and North Korean sources, Yi refused a post in the reactionary Writer's Society, under the pretext of bad health,[114] and also refused to write in Japanese, offering the excuse that he did not know the language well enough. In the few novels that he published at the end of the colonial period, such as *The Lifeline* (*Saengmyŏngsŏn;* 1942), he maintained the same line, depicting progressive intellectuals who could not endure a merciless Seoul full of arrogant Japanese and fled to the countryside.[115] During the campaign in the 1940s to change Korean names to Japanese *(ch'angssi kaemyŏng),* Yi refused to abandon his Korean name. In 1944 he left Seoul for a rural district in Kangwondo Province to support his family by working on the land as a tenant farmer.[116] This picture of Yi's life after 1935 perfectly correlates with the official North Korean image of KAPF members as unbending heroes of proletarian literature.

However, according to other sources, Yi, along with his KAPF colleagues, behaved less bravely. In the words of Brian Myers, he "held the posts of executive secretary of Yi Kwang-su's notorious Writers Society in 1939 and in the equally treasonous Patriotic Society of Korean Writers."[117] Yi also steered a "conversion" course (conversion from his "subversive activity") in the form of so-called industrial novels, which included *The Lifeline, Son of Earth* (*Taeji-ŭi adŭl;* 1939), *Miners' Village* (*Kwangsan-ch'on;* 1943), and *Virgin Land* (*Ch'onyŏji;* 1944). South Korean scholar Yi Sang-gyŏng emphasizes that Yi's pro-Japanese course must be treated "with caution," however, because these novels can equally be seen as signs of the author's "belief in the creativity of the Korean people" or as works that "encouraged the inventiveness of Korean workmen."[118]

Yi was indeed no unbending hero. Like his other literary colleagues, he surrendered under the pressure of the colonial authorities and followed their requests, albeit without enthusiasm. We need to remember this fact, not in order to pass judgment on the writer, but to shatter the myth about the exemplary fortitude of the KAPF writers, which we will encounter later.

After Liberation

Immediately after Liberation, Yi Ki-yŏng entered the North Korean literary and political world. He took part in the organization of the People's

Committee in the town of Naegŭmgang and participated in political rallies. From October 1945, Yi headed the Department of People's Education in Kangwondo Province.[119]

As the most prominent "proletarian" writer, Yi immediately became a member of the North Korean Federation of Literature and Art.. In March 1946 he was granted a personal meeting with Kim Il Sung in Pyongyang, during which the North Korean leader encouraged him to remain in the North and helped him to find accommodation for his family, who at the time still lived in Kangwondo.[120] Soon afterward, Yi became the NKFLA chairman. His chairmanship did not last long, however; in 1948 he was replaced by Han Sŏr-ya, who was widely seen as "the keener political brain."[121] Nonetheless, Yi's lofty position in the North Korean literary and official world had already been secured. After April 1946 Yi was promoted to chairman of the Central Committee of the North Korean–Soviet Friendship Association, a post he retained for the rest of his life. In November 1946 he became a deputy of the People's Assembly and was later made a member of the Provisional People's Committee of North Korea. From August 1948, Yi was a member of the Presidium of the Supreme People's Assembly,[122] and in 1957 he became its vice-chairman.[123]

The NKFLA political program seemed to inspire Yi. Its nationalistic and enlightenment implications resonated quite well with his own pet ideas, and the urge to imitate the "advanced cultures" was also none too foreign to the writer. However, despite his sincere desire to follow the Party's line, the fate of the first big novel Yi wrote in North Korea on a contemporary topic, *Land,* was not trouble-free.

The Troublesome Fate of a Patristic Text

Yi Ki-yŏng wrote *Land* (*Ttang;* 1948–1949) as a direct response to the Party's request that North Korean writers reflect in their work the "tremendous transformation" in the villages in the course of the recent land reform. Yi intended the novel to be a continuation of the themes of *Homeland.*[124] Though *Land* came to be regarded as a classic of North Korean literature, it also became the object of sustained critical attack, which resulted in a radical rewriting of the text.

In the novel, life in the remote village of Pŏlmaŭl, which was full of hardship and suffering under Japanese colonial rule, is transformed into a paradise following Liberation, land reform, and the establishment of the new people's government. The new authorities are represented by the chairman of the town committee, Kang Gyun, a wise and intelligent hero. Kang has come up with the idea of draining the marshes on the outskirts of Pŏlmaŭl and turning the area into rice fields. An overwhelming majority of the village people enthusiastically support the idea, greeting the proposal with shouts of "Long live the Great Leader Kim Il Sung!" The project is gloriously realized.

The main protagonist, Kwak Pa-ui, who was a poor and uneducated tenant in the past and once suffered unjustly in a Japanese jail, is especially zealous. After receiving his share of land, the hardworking and socially active Kwak is transformed into a respectable member of the local community. His personal life also improves. In the past he was betrayed by his wife, who left him for another man while he was in jail. But now Kwak marries the beautiful Chŏn Sun-ŏk, who in the hellish past was sold as a concubine to the rich landowner Yun Sang-yŏl to repay her father's debts. She is now free from her shameful past and becomes an active member of the new society.

The reactionary camp in the village community is represented by a few former landowners who try to sabotage the new development of the village but are easily identified, seized, and sent to prison. Several of their earlier supporters, such as a greedy merchant (referred to as Sun-ŭi's mother), eventually come to recognize their own villainous nature, mend their ways, and join the majority of the villagers.

At the end of the novel, Kwak Pa-ui is chosen to be a member of the People's Assembly and goes to Pyongyang. There he meets Great Leader Kim Il Sung and also listens to the speeches of several deputies who have visited the Soviet Union—the promised land, where "there are no jobless or hungry" and "Man is the most precious thing."[125] The novel concludes with a panegyric to Kim Il Sung and the new people's government, who have brought long-awaited happiness to the Korean land.

Land can certainly be seen as an example of the declared policy of the absorption of the Soviet culture. To begin with, the novel bristles with eulogies to the Soviet Army, Soviet culture, and the Soviet way of life. Most of the information about the latter leans heavily on Yi Ki-yŏng's personal experience, acquired during several guided tours to the USSR in 1946–1947, and for this reason alone it contains a lot of propagandistic falsities (suffice it to mention the notion that in Soviet maternity homes there were personal telephones near each bed).[126]

The absorption of Soviet culture is particularly detectable in the artistic form of the novel. As has been mentioned before, many critics admit the strong influence of Sholokhov's *Virgin Land under the Plow* on Yi Ki-yŏng's work.[127] Both are farming novels that glorify the "new village construction," and many *Virgin Land* characters have their analogues in *Land* (Iakov Lukich and Ko Pyŏng-sang, Varia and Sun-ok, Grandpa Shchukar' and Kang Sa-gwa, to name a few). The similarities between Sholokhov's David Molchun and Yi's protagonist Kwak Pa-ui are especially remarkable. Like Sholokhov, Yi approvingly depicts his hero as a silent, industrious man, undereducated but imbued with an extraordinary will and great physical power. Yi admiringly compares his hero to an ox; indeed his very name Pa-ui means "a rock" in Korean.[128] These traits have positive connotations in Russian culture, but not in Korea, with its Confucian disregard for physical labor and the people engaged in it.

Yet another interesting detail in the depiction of Kwak Pa-ui is that, like Sholokhov's peasant, the Korean hero eats generously and with gusto.[129] Yi portrays this aspect of his character approvingly, which is notable given that the majority of Yi's positive pre-Liberation characters had refined manners.

Between *Land* and *Virgin Land* there are also undeniable affinities in both artistic technique and the authors' approach. Both authors try to enliven the ideologically imposed story lines with comic episodes and with the use of colorful dialect and colloquial expressions. In *Land* Yi uses more than seventy folk songs and legends, often repeating himself (for instance, the popular pattern of the old Korean fairy tale *Ŏndal and the Princess,* a Korean variant of *Beauty and the Beast,* appears in both his pre-Liberation *Homeland* as well as in *Land*). At the same time, there are profound conceptual disparities between Sholokhov's and Yi Ki-yŏng's novels.

First of all, the Soviet and North Korean novels differ in their emphasis on political aspects. As mentioned earlier, in *Virgin Land* the major propagandistic message is blurred by ambiguous subplots. In comparison, Yi's *Land* is an extraordinarily didactic novel, permeated with a stiff dualism of good versus evil. The two contrasting groups of characters in *Land* call to mind an old Korean fairy tale about two brothers, *Hŭngbu and Nolbu (Hŭngbu-wa Nolbu),* and an allusion to this story even appears at one point in the novel.[130] In the fairy tale the angelic Hŭngbu receives rewards from a good spirit, while his devilish brother, Nolbu, is severely punished for his wrongdoings. Like Hŭnbu, the positive protagonists of *Land* are imbued with all the virtues imaginable; they are modest, industrious, socially active and selfless, and beautiful as well. The few negative characters are, like Nolbu, the embodiment of every imaginable evil; they are ugly, lazy, greedy, selfish, lustful, and deceitful.

Such cartoonish villains do not pose a serious threat. Unlike Sholokhov's plausible "enemies," the negative characters in *Land,* in addition to all their other evils, are weak and cowardly. With their laughable greed, comical mutual conflicts, and complete inadequacy, Yi's ex-landowners serve more to enliven the narrative than to create any sense of conflict.

In fact, the conflict between the two camps appears so insignificant that some critics have even failed to take it into account. Analyzing the role of Kwak Pa-ui, North Korean critic Han Hyo pointed out that the character was an example of "the struggle to increase crop output and the struggle for the respect of the new power," but he did not mention any kind of struggle against a real enemy; obviously there was none.[131]

Instead, the conflict between positive and negative unfolds in a safer sphere—in the black-and-white juxtapositions of the hellish colonial past and the joyful Communist present. One typical episode is a celebration in the family of peasant Pak, who has received his parcel in the new regime's redistribution of land.[132] Though no extra rice has yet appeared on the table of the constantly hungry family, all the family members are consumed with exultation. While the old mother cries as she recollects the cheerless past, the youngsters dance and begin to invent a new song about the happy life of the peasants in North Korea.

The scenes of the courtship and marriage of Kwak Pa-ui and Chŏn Sun-ok are delivered in a similar manner.[133] Seeking the girl's hand, Kwak declares to her that the country is now free and land reform has been completed, so now is the time to enjoy their lives. Party secretary Kang Gyun, who acts as a matchmaker to the couple, persuades the girl that under the new social conditions she can finally be happy. She hesitates and cries, recollecting the awful past that has ruined her life, but in the end she succumbs to the persuasion. The village women strongly encourage the couple to marry because "life is so beautiful today that it is precisely the time to have babies." At the wedding party, the guests wish to dance and sing but discover that there are no merry songs about marriage in Korea, since all the marriages in the past were unhappy. They therefore compose a new wedding song. Alone at night, the bride and groom cannot believe their bliss, which, they stress, could happen only in the new Korea. In the morning after their first night, they lie in bed, once again recollecting the horrific colonial past, only to launch into another cycle of praise for their new life ad infinitum. This merry-go-round of bitter recollections about the past and exaltation over the new life, tears and laughter, runs nonstop through the quite lengthy novel.

In addition to the Japanese imperialists of the past, the American imperialists who are occupying South Korea in the present also occasionally perform the role of enemy. The "bad guys" in the novel are invariably distant outsiders, while the life of "authentic" Koreans under Kim Il Sung's rule is associated exclusively with virtue, joy, and happiness. Unlike Sholokhov's *Virgin Land,* in which the reality of the Soviet village in the early 1930s, fifteen years after the October Revolution, is portrayed with ambivalence and antagonisms are not glossed over, in *Land* (as in Han Sŏr-ya's *Growing Village {Charanŭn maŭl},* 1949) the present is depicted as cloudless harmony—even though a mere three years have passed since Liberation.[134] The new regime brings smiles to the faces of everyone and, like Jesus Christ, heals even terminally ill people; after the agrarian reform, the paralyzed Old Ko rises from his deathbed to have a look at the new rice fields and watch a performance staged by the village youth.[135] While *Virgin Land* frequently depicts murder or illness and concludes with the death of the two main Communist protagonists, in *Land* none of the heroes suffer even minor physical discomfort.

In many respects the idealized present in *Land* reiterates the images of a mythologized Korean past, so widely exploited in Yi Ki-yŏng's earlier works.[136] Again, Yi refers to the *ture* leagues as an ideal form of typically Korean mutual help.[137] *Land's* evil characters are depicted as violators of the traditional moral norms of rural community; typical villains in the Confucian mold, they do not help each other and they even cheat their own brothers.[138]

The interaction between the past and the present is especially interesting in the character of Kang Sa-gwa, a positive representative of "the old generation of poor but honest intellectuals."[139] Old Kang resolutely rejects the traditional principles of filial obedience, polygamy, expensive mourning ceremonies, and Confucian scholastics.[140] His speech bristles with anti-Confucian rhetoric: "Chinese characters are useless relics"; "Democracy is the workers' kingdom"; and so forth. These notions of the resolute elder are generally reminiscent of the comic pro-Communist stances of Sholokhov's Grandpa Shchukar, but in Yi's case they are taken seriously and at face value.

Kang's proselytizing negativism toward the Confucian past is not uniform, however. On the one hand, Kang abhors Confucian tradition, and because of this he has long since refused to become a scholar-official.[141] Yet in another scene he refers to this same post of scholar-official as the ultimate prize for a talented youth.[142] Describing Kang's appearance, the author notes with reverence, "The old man was so nobly beautiful that you could take him for an aristocrat"[143]—a notion that would be impossible in Soviet literature, with its "popular spirit."

As regards gender themes, Yi's outrage against Confucian morality was equally inconsistent. He approvingly describes Kang's obedient daughter-in-law, who, "sitting at a distance, listened in reverent silence to the conversation of the elders."[144] The young woman knows her place, and this is very praise-worthy. Through the lips of Kang Sa-gwa, the author expresses his approval of Chŏn Sun-ok's attempt at suicide, which was a traditional means for a Korean woman to protect her dignity. Nevertheless, in general the theme of the progressive Korean woman is probably the most radical in the novel.

The idea of gender equality represented the quintessence of enlightenment for Yi Ki-yŏng, and he apparently tried to portray an advanced image of the new Korean woman. With respect to ideological transformation and adherence to "Communist novelty," the image of Chŏn Sun-ok certainly outshines Sholokhov's realistic images of rural women. In Sholokhov's novel the rural Cossack women are shown as more backward and conservative than the males. They may be independent-spirited and smart, but by no stretch of the imagination are they vanguard revolutionary fighters. Very often it is the women in *Virgin Land* who start to rebel against the new regime and to physically attack the Communists.[145] The main female protagonist of the novel, the sensual beauty Lushka, easily manipulates the Communist males and for a while even manages to lead some of them astray.[146] The most progressive female character, Varia, who is engaged to the Communist protagonist Davudov, decides to study at an agrarian college—not of her own conscious choice but in order to please her fiancé ("I will follow him anywhere"; "I'll do everything he says").[147]

In contrast, *Land*'s positive female protagonists are shown as miraculously transformed into staunch Communist new women under the influence of "the people's rule," within a few short years. The quiet and modest rural Korean woman Chŏn Sun-ok (who once allowed her father to sell her as a concubine and, as a model Confucian heroine, attempted suicide after hearing malicious gossip about herself) becomes in a twinkling the politically active chairwoman of the village Women's Union. She is the first in the village to join the Workers' Party and help mobilize people to accomplish the sowing campaign ahead of schedule and to teach illiterate girls. In the evening she reads newspapers to her illiterate husband, "choosing the most important political news and explaining the Party line to him."[148] At night the newlyweds have long talks about the happiness of the Korean people and the terrible Japanese colonial past (or, for a change, the nightmarish South Korean life under American rule) or they discuss political events. In addition to the "voluntary tax," Sun-ok decides to donate ten extra bags of rice as "patriotic rice" to the new government.[149]

On the rare occasions when this politically conscious heroine happens to occupy herself with ordinary household chores, she feels inappropriately mundane and guilty. For example, one evening after Sun-ok has listened to the politically inspired reasoning of her husband, she feels "deeply ashamed because a philistine love of comfort and decency has become rooted in her soul": "While her husband is so lofty-minded, she thinks too much about hygiene, forces him to wash himself regularly and dress neatly. . . . What petit bourgeois thoughts! Sun-ok falls on her knees and begs her husband's forgiveness for her imperfections."[150]

Nevertheless, Chŏn Sun-ok's image, however stilted and cloyingly "correct," met with a range of critical responses in North Korean literary circles. In the opinion of Pak Chong-sik, the character's life "lacks social activity."[151] Ŏm Ho-sŏk condemns the relationship between Kwak Pa-ui and Chŏn Sun-ok as "too sensual."[152] Considering the total absence of love scenes in the novel, this accusation appears completely unfounded. E. M. Tsoi articulated another improbable claim: "Some critics and readers disapproved of the image of Chŏn Sun-ok. Her flaws appear especially visible in comparison to the irreproachable Kwak Pa-ui. . . . In the past, Sun-ok was a member of a landowning family and lived as a concubine—i.e., not by her own labor."[153] Justifying such accusations, however, Tsoi, attempts to excuse the "sinner": "We must take into account that Yi Ki-yŏng's heroine has only just started to be reclaimed."[154]

The reason for all this unfounded quibbling is simple: the highest arbitrator in North Korea, Kim Il Sung, had already cast his judgment on the "Sun-ok issue." During his meeting with Korean writers, the Great Leader expressed his dissatisfaction at the fact that the companion of the exemplary hero of the novel was a "former mistress": "Everybody needs pure water. I should like to give this tenant farmer, who has slaved and hungered so long in darkness and tyranny, pure water."[155] Myers has wittily pointed out that Kim Il Sung certainly did not believe that "the tenant-hero's own failed marriage should prevent him from marrying another virgin."[156]

The remark from the Great Leader had nothing to do with Chŏn Sun-ok's alleged membership in the class of exploiters or her "social passivity." However, the critics quickly picked up the Great Leader's attitude and busied themselves in finding more and more deficiencies in the character's image. Nobody cared that the patriarchal approach to gender relationships that was articulated by the supreme Pyongyang authority contradicted both the written requirement of the NKFLA "to extirpate feudal concepts" and the usual visions of Soviet literature that North Korean writers were supposed to absorb.[157]

Yi Ki-yŏng himself saw nothing wrong in the status of his heroine as an ex-concubine. First, the institution of concubinage was regarded as a special form of marriage in old Korea, and second, in Chŏn Sun-ok's case this marriage was forced. Yi explained his understanding of the situation through the words of Kang Sa-gwa: "There is nothing wrong with second marriages; the tradition of concubinage is to blame."[158] Yet the writer had to readjust his work according to the demands of the Great Leader and rewrite it several times, with an especially thorough reworking in 1973. In the later version Chŏn Sun-ok has been transformed into a virgin, and Kwak's wife does not betray him but instead dies of hunger. In light of the unofficial demand for ethnocentrism that openly emerged in Kim Il Sung's speech of 28 December 1955 (discussed in chapter 1), Yi's novel was indeed not "correct": a "truly Korean" wife should never be portrayed as a traitor; instead she would rather die as a martyr at the hands of the Japanese. The eulogies to the "Soviet liberators" and the Soviet way of life were also edited out, for any praise for a foreign innovation represented an offense to the "national cultural heritage."

In 1974, in his article "Having Only Loyalty in Mind" (Ojik ch'ungsŏng-ŭi han maŭm-ŭro), Yi humbly admitted his mistake: "How could I marry such a perfect hero to a woman who had been the concubine of a landowner? That was of course a mistake that I committed because I did not understand the new reality of a liberated village. Kwak Pa-ui was a new hero who could marry only a virgin. . . . I am grateful to the Great Leader, who expressly mentioned this fault of mine."[159]

The rewritten *Land* represents a picture that was a far cry not only from Soviet literary patterns but also from the realistic images of Yi Ki-yŏng's earlier writings.[160] *Land* corresponds much more to the conventions of a fairy tale. It presents the reader with mild conflicts that the "good guys" always win, and perfect harmony reigns supreme. A peaceful bunch of positive heroes in the mold of the fabled Hŭngbu are tied to each other by traditional values and playfully subdue a few inept Nolbus. Occasionally some members of the positive group may act out of character, demonstrating, for instance, childish selfishness or stubbornness (as Sun-ŭi's mother does). Yet, under the positive influence of the "truly Korean" community, they are quickly set straight, as badly behaved children would be after being placed in a time-out area. The positive heroes devote their lives to the enthusiastic service of the Communist state, collecting patriotic rice and reading official newspapers. To stress the exemplary niceness of this assemblage, the author from time to time recalls a hellish past under wicked foreign rulers or muses over the other ill-willed foreign power that is allegedly torturing the distant South. All of these are more like fairy-tale monsters than real-life enemies.

This troop of happy and loyal children is wisely ruled by omnipresent and omnipotent father figures. In the first instance this figure is the chairman of the town committee, Kang Gyun, and high above stands the perfect and infallible Great Leader. Taken as a whole, the rewritten *Land* represents the realized ethnocentric peasant paradise that had once been proposed by Seoulite in *Minch'on,* supplemented with some new propagandistic notions.

Land proved to be the only major novel that Yi Ki-yŏng would write on contemporary themes. Soon afterward, he began his lengthy epic *Tumangang,* the first sections of which were published in 1954–1957. This novel was devoted to the past, and the writer could once again safely resort to his familiar realistic images of suppressed women, injustice, and the hard life of the Korean peasantry. In all probability this return to history was Yi's attempt to seek refuge in the past, much as Gorky did in the later years of his life.

Yi's few later works on contemporary themes were short and terse and, in an artistic sense, represented a remarkable decline in quality, as South Korean scholar Yi Sang-gyŏng was quick to point out.[161] If in *Tumangang* Yi still occasionally indulged in rural maxims and folk images, his writings about the present—such as *Red Pocketbook* (*Pulgŭn such'ŏp;* 1961), which describes a group of North Korean youths who initiate the Ch'ŏllima (Flying Horse) movement at a railroad construction[162]—are astonishingly blunt in both imagery and language. Gradually, the plots and characters in Yi's writings were narrowed to complete utilitarianism. For example, his novel *The Fate of a Woman (Han nyŏsŏng-ŭi unmyŏng),* written in the early 1960s, presented a black-and-white didactic contrast between the pre- and post-Liberation lives of the female protagonist P'illye.[163] The writing style of the novel and the language the heroine uses remind one of articles from *Nodong sinmun* rather than a literary piece.

In all probability, these changes were not accidental. After the long process of accommodating *Land* to the ever-changing demands of the new regime, which was insisting on further and further simplification of the novel, Yi may not have found it necessary to use an elaborate artistic technique. Besides, his jealous superior, Han Sŏr-ya, who was unpopular among the public, would not tolerate any competition[164]—and Yi preferred not to irritate him.

Yi Ki-yŏng died at the height of his official recognition and privilege at the age of ninety, on 9 August 1984. As for the actual popularity of his novels among the North Korean reading public, that was a matter of no concern in the DPRK.

"He Never Had Enemies"

Contrary to popular perception, Yi Ki-yŏng demonstrated neither a clear-cut Communist-proletarian worldview nor a particularly brilliant literary talent. The ideology of his pre-Liberation works, often presented as the earliest example of socialist realism in Korean literature, was hardly Marxist. His views could be better described as "peasant utopianism" with strong antimodernist and antiurban tendencies, occasionally spiced with leftist rhetoric.

Still, Yi turned out to be the very figure that the Pyongyang cultural establishment required in the late 1940s. First, his traditional peasant perspectives were quite useful to the Pyongyang literary establishment, whose leaders claimed authentic roots. These perspectives also resonated well with the values of the North Korean regime, which, from the very beginning, placed great emphasis on the promotion of nationalistic ideas. The ordinariness of Yi's literary abilities was of assistance when it came to his participation in propaganda activity—a sphere in which too-distant flights of imagination were not appreciated. His readiness to follow the orders of the regime was also helpful under the circumstances. Thus, Yi Ki-yŏng fitted perfectly into Pyongyang's official design.

Yet anyone familiar with the turbulent situation in North Korean literary circles in the period 1945–1960 might pose this question: if Yi Ki-yŏng made political mistakes serious enough to provoke the displeasure of Kim Il Sung and necessitate the rewriting of some 60 percent of his major novel, how was he able not only to survive but even to prosper within the official bureaucracy? We can only speculate on the reasons and should not rule out luck as one of the possible explanations. However, interviews with people who knew Yi personally have given me reason to conclude that, to a significant degree, Yi's safe North Korean career was made possible because of his ability to maintain good relationships with people in power, his lack of personal ambition, and his remarkable gift for avoiding conflict.

All my informants recall Yi Ki-yŏng with genuine sympathy, as a gentle person who was never spoiled by success or corrupted by power. V. I. Ivanova, who worked with the writer in Pyongyang in 1949 and then met with him several times in Moscow, recalls that Yi was a favorite client of his Russian staff—he was always modest and kind to them—and this presented a great contrast to his arrogant and capricious boss, Han Sŏr-ya, also a frequent visitor to Moscow at the time.[165] Pak Myŏng-sun remembers Yi as a very placid man who always kept away from politics and personal clashes.[166] Yi's KAPF and then North Korean colleague Song Yŏng recalls that Yi's ability to remain silent in the most heated discussions earned him the nickname of "speechless writer" or "silent writer" (*muŏn-ŭi in* or *mal ŏmnŭn chakka*) from his KAPF colleagues.[167] Chŏng Ryul, once a close personal friend of Yi's, reports that Yi "never had enemies"[168] and always avoided criticizing people. When asked about a particular person, Yi would answer unwillingly: "I do not know the man well enough. How can I judge him?" Despite his formal membership of the KAPF faction, Yi managed to maintain good relations with the writers from the other factions as well, even at times of the sharpest sectarian conflict.[169] Characteristically, even political adversaries were remarkably soft on Yi; for example, Pak Nam-su in his negativist memoirs mentions Yi a mere handful of times and in a surprisingly neutral tone.

Yi's relationships with the mighty Han Sŏr-ya, an associate of his from before Liberation and his boss in North Korea after 1945, are noteworthy. Han's major pre-Liberation novel *Dusk* (*Hwanghon;* 1936), highly praised during his golden age (1956–1961) as an "immortal masterpiece of progressive literature," was written under the strong influence of Yi's *Homeland,*[170] yet once Han had established control over the North Korean literary bureaucracy, the official versions of previous events were changed. From the 1950s on, Han was presented as the leader of the entire proletarian literature movement, while Yi Ki-yŏng was relegated to his shadow.

Yi appears not to have been overconcerned about this misrepresentation. He simply accepted the new order of things and began to pay the required tribute to Han's alleged historic significance.[171] Such tactics neutralized Han's ever-jealous attitude to his professionally more prominent colleague. While Han relentlessly destroyed all possible rivals, he let Yi hold the number two position in the literary establishment. In 1958, *Dusk* and *Homeland* were touted as twin pillars of Korean socialist realism.[172]

Most of North Korea's writers regarded Yi as a quiet, courteous old man, slightly eccentric and essentially harmless. Chŏng Ryul recollects a characteristic anecdote about Yi. One day Yi announced his eagerness to enter the Workers' Party. The Party group leader asked the writer about his motives, expecting to hear some lofty phrases, but Yi answered naively: "It is so fashionable now. Everybody is in the Party, and I want to be in it too." The Party officials laughed and said: "No, *harabŏji* [grandfather]. You'd better stay out-of-fashion."[173] It is significant that Yi's political carelessness, which would certainly have entailed serious consequences for anybody else in a Stalinist world, was simply chuckled at. We can therefore surmise that his other political mistakes were probably treated with much the same leniency.

Song Yŏng, however, paraphrasing a Korean proverb, once called Yi a "person of outer tenderness and inner steel."[174] Indeed, along his challenging life journey, Yi, a seemingly feeble and irresolute man, often demonstrated this inner steel. He always refrained from noisy political activism: the obligatory eulogies to the Great Leader in his books and articles did not exceed the level that was commonly required at the time.[175] During the purges of 1953–1956, Yi avoided participating in the slander campaigns against his doomed colleagues under the common excuse of a "sick stomach," a chronic disease that always worsened just at the start of a new defamation campaign. On the rare occasions when Yi was forced to take part in such public events, he remained silent.[176]

Chŏng Ryul recollects with gratitude that at the harshest moments of the witch-hunting campaigns against the Soviet Koreans, Yi was one of the very few Writers' Union members who did not turn his back on his scapegoat colleagues. He continued to meet with the Soviet Koreans and visit them in their homes. This immutable friendliness became a precious moral support to his doomed colleagues, and it was another sure expression not only of Yi Ki-yŏng's outer tenderness but his inner steel as well.

4 Yi T'ae-jun

The Failure of a "Soldier on the Cultural Front"

IF THE POST-LIBERATION LIFE of Yi Ki-yŏng correlated closely with his earlier experiences and views, Yi T'ae-jun's fate left many questions unanswered. How was it that Yi T'ae-jun, a member of the apolitical Nine Members Club and an implacable enemy of the KAPF before Liberation, chose the Communist North? Why did "the most unadulterated *sŏnbi*" (learned gentleman) of Korean literature[1] and "the extoller of pure art"[2] suddenly change direction, becoming a "soldier on the cultural front" and eulogizing bloody scenes of "class struggle" and Communist virtues?

The most popular argument is that Yi T'ae-jun's move to North Korea was, first and foremost, a mistake by this otherworldly intellectual who strove to find an ideal world in the Stalinist DPRK and fell victim to his illusions.[3] The suggested reasons for this mistake vary. Some theorists search for the roots of Yi's ideological shift in his experiences as an orphan and his desire "to reunite himself with his dead father," a leftist sympathizer who had died when the future writer was only five years old.[4] Others stress "the motif of the lost home," which permeated Yi Ki-yŏng's pre-Liberation works and supposedly prompted the writer to seek happiness elsewhere.[5] Sin Hyŏng-gi searches for an answer in the "grammar of Yi T'ae-jun's narrative," since "grammar is an established institution" that "he could not make"; rather, "it makes the writer."[6] Pak Nam-su in his memoirs blames the cunning strategy of the Soviets who lured Yi T'ae-jun to North Korea with special privileges.[7] Kang Hŏn-guk maintains that the forty-year-old writer was driven by "romantic impulse" and "denied reality."[8] In most instances, Yi's choice is presented as unconscious or imposed on him against his will, whether by an unhappy childhood, by the grammar of narrative, or by cunning Soviets.

Like many other personal questions in history, Yi T'ae-jun's unexpected move to the North will never be completely clarified—especially if we remember that he was a quite complicated character and, borrowing Pang Min-ho's expression, an "eclectic personality."[9] All the above-cited speculations may contain a grain of truth, yet to my mind they are all based on an incorrect assumption—that Yi T'ae-jun was truly a "pure artist" whose worldview was inherently incompatible with Communist ideology.[10] This common presumption in fact mirrors the official Pyongyang interpretation of Yi's behavior.[11]

However, a thoughtful investigation into Yi's writings and experiences attests that neither his personality nor his activities were irreconcilably contradictory to Communist ideas per se. His incompatibility with the KAPF and the KAPF-derived North Korean literary bureaucracy is a different story, however. Let us consider three major periods of Yi's professional life: his pre-Liberation experience, his activities in South Korea in 1945–1946, and his activities in North Korea.

The Early Years

Yi T'ae-jun was born in 1904 in the town of Ch'ŏlwŏn in Kangwondo Province. His father, Yi Mun-gyo, a teacher at a local school and a very educated person by the standards of the day, was an active supporter of the Independence Club and other reformist groups.[12] After the failure of their reformist projects, he decided to migrate to Japan with his family. On the way to Vladivostok in August 1909, Yi Mun-gyo suddenly died, and his widow, An Sun-hŭng, returned to Korea, where she tried to support her three children by running a small eatery. She sent Yi T'ae-jun to school, where he was very successful academically.

An Sun-hŭng died in 1912, when Yi T'ae-jun was eight years old.[13] Consequently, Yi and his siblings were forced to rely on the charity of their relatives. The writer later recollected this period as an extremely sad experience. He continued to display great promise at school, but no one was interested in him.[14] In 1918 Yi's uncle pushed the boy to enter an agricultural college, but Yi quit after one month of study and ran away from home, led by the romantic craving "to construct his own world with his own hands."[15]

Wandering around the country, Yi reached Wŏnsan and found a job in a *kaekchuchip,* a kind of merchants' inn that doubled as a moneylender's office. In Wŏnsan he met his maternal grandmother, a small-time shopkeeper, who began to support the boy with great selflessness. With her aid, Yi could spend more time on his education and read many books, including his favorite Tolstoy.[16] Several times Yi made plans to travel to China, but every time he was discouraged by a lack of funds. He finally decided to move to Seoul to study and in 1920 entered Paejae College, but he could not manage to find the money to pay the enrollment fee. Soon he received help again; this time, on a Seoul street, he accidentally ran into an old Wŏnsan acquaintance, a merchant, who gave him a job so he could work in the daytime and study in the evenings at the Youth Center (Ch'ŏngnyŏn Hoegwan).

In 1921 Yi entered Huimun College. Again he had difficulty with the enrollment fee, but his grades were so high that the rector of the college granted him a special favor: an exemption from the fee on the condition that the boy cleaned the rector's office. It was a lucky break, yet Yi T'ae-jun was not able to fully capitalize on the opportunity. In 1924 he took an active part in a student strike, protesting against the oppressiveness and irrationality of the educational process, and was expelled from the college in June 1924 as one of the ringleaders. However, the goodwill of the people around him did not run out. With the financial support of a college friend, Yi traveled to Japan to study. In April 1926 he entered the preparatory Jŏchi University in Tokyo, but again he failed to complete his course. Despite the active support of his American teacher in Tokyo, Yi could not bear the material hardship and loneliness of his life overseas. Once again he quit his studies and returned home in November 1927.

While in Japan, Yi started to write his own prose. His first story, "Omongnyŏ," was written in Tokyo and published in the newspaper *Sidae ilbo (Times Daily Newspaper)* on 13 July 1925. After returning home, he began to work at the Kaebyŏk publishing house and to cooperate with a number of literary magazines.[17]

Yi's literary endeavors proved to be successful from the very beginning, and soon he became one of Korea's most popular writers. His aesthetically appealing prose, written in refined language, full of beautiful scenery and deep psychological portraits, made Yi authoritative enough to be employed in 1932 as a professor of literary composition at Ewha Womans College (Yihwa Yŏjŏn), although the writer had never completed even undergraduate studies.[18]

As we can see, the early lives of Yi T'ae-jun and Yi Ki-yŏng had many similarities. Both writers lost their parents at an early age, experienced poverty (though to different degrees—Yi T'ae-jun was always luckier in finding generous sponsors), and wandered around their country. Both were socially conscious: Yi T'ae-jun, who once participated directly in a student strike and suffered the consequences, had even more experience of political activity. Both loved to read and yearned to receive a modern education but could not achieve their ambitions. So it is perhaps no surprise that the attitudes of both writers had much in common.

Social Concerns in Yi T'ae-jun's Early Writings

Let us take a closer look at Yi T'ae-jun's early writings. The plot of his first work, "Omongnyŏ" (1925), is roughly as follows:[19] Omongnyŏ, a young woman and a licentious and selfish individual, is cheating on her poor and elderly blind husband. She has an affair with the poor young fisherman Kŭm-dol. Her sensuous beauty attracts another man, a policeman called Nam, who kills Omongnyŏ's husband in order to take over his house and take his wife as a concubine. The woman rejects Nam, however, and runs away with her young lover.

Despite the romantic plot, the short story has an important social component that turns "Omongnyŏ" into a sorrowful commentary on the moral degradation of Korea's social order. The author realistically depicts the regular tyranny of police officers who "when drunk beat the poor without exception, curse men who are old enough to be their fathers, and consider the street to be their private property."[20] The young author tries to analyze the actions of his heroes from a social angle and to show how people unwillingly succumb to the pressure of circumstances. The policeman Nam is not vicious by nature. He is actually more tolerant of people than his merciless predecessor Pang-ga, yet when he enters the policing world, where brutality toward the common people is the norm, Nam must play by these rules. The heroine, full of zest for life, had been sold like an animal to a blind old man, so it is no surprise that she rebels against her predicament, striving not just for material well-being but for her human freedom as well (the man of her choice is a poor fisherman, not a rich policeman). The hopelessly impoverished fisherman cannot afford a normal wedding and gives in to the temptation of seducing his neighbor's wife. Thus, if the theme of Yi Ki-yŏng's first story ("Secret Letter") is a politically safe call for women's liberation, the social dimension of "Omongnyŏ" is not only deeper but also politically riskier.

This sharp social criticism is sustained in Yi T'ae-jun's subsequent writings, along with their melancholic mood and sympathy for the underdog. The long-awaited reunion of a poor father and his son is ruined by a sly and vicious policeman in "Happiness" (Haengbok; 1929); a promising student is too weak to liberate his first love, a beautiful girl who has lost both her parents and sees no choice but to sell herself to a brothel in "The Shadow" (Kŭrimja; 1929); an aging *kisaeng* (courtesan) suffers poverty and is despised by the very people who had once exploited her in "The Courtesan Sandŏri" (Kisaeng Sandŏri; 1930), a depiction of the double standards of Korean society; and so on.[21]

Many South Korean scholars have specifically stressed the nationalistic theme in Yi T'ae-jun's early writings.[22] Yet Yi's reflection of this theme is not at all consistent. The motif of national disgrace and the frequent portrayals of victims of colonial modernization are similar to those found in works by Yi Ki-yŏng. An idealization of the good old days can also occasionally be found in Yi T'ae-jun's writings, yet unlike Yi Ki-yŏng with his steady antiurbanism and idealization of preindustrial, precolonial Korea, Yi T'ae-jun did not always equate virtue with the norms (real or imagined) of the traditional rural Korean community.

Take, for example, the short story "The Curse of Marriage" (Kyŏrhon-ŭi anmasŏng; 1931).[23] The heroine, S., an educated heiress from a rich family, is besieged by young men eager to win her hand in marriage, but she sees them only as the scum of a Korean society that is blindly pursuing capitalism: "The offspring of a prime minister! Those Korean ministers who are all covered in feces and whose honor is so dishonorable!"; "Today the Korean people are throwing away their human pride like useless old shoes."[24] Finally the girl meets a poor yet noble man of letters, T., and marries him—only to discover that they need the very money she had earlier cursed as the root of all evil. After several unsuccessful attempts to earn an income through honest labor, T. unwillingly considers an offer of service in some administrative body that, "though not the police, treats the Korean people in a similar manner."[25] The couple understands that this will be a betrayal of their principles, and S. sadly contemplates the situation: why do Korean people always have to choose between poverty and disgrace?

> She compared the lives of Koreans and Westerners. There are no barriers in the Westerners' way. When it is cold, they use steam heaters. When it is hot, they use fans. At night they can enjoy watching the beautiful stars and lying in comfortable beds. In the morning, ham or sausages are waiting for them, prepared for them many miles away in New York or Paris. Wherever they go, there is no place in the world where they face personal or national humiliation. When their children are born, schools and workplaces are ready for them. God did not spread his blessings evenly. What blessings do Korean people have?[26]

Despite her chagrin, the girl decides to overcome "the curse of marriage," fight for an honest family life side by side with her husband, and not fall into the trap of material temptation.

Although "The Curse of Marriage" expresses criticism regarding Korea's loss of national and personal pride under the pressure of an emerging colonial capitalism, the idea of a "blessing" in the story is associated, not with the golden past of Korea, but rather with steam heaters, comfortable beds, and tasty sausages—the products of the very capitalism whose arrival in her country the heroine condemned. It is characteristic, however, that the author (like Yi Ki-yŏng in *Homeland*) obviously saw no connection between the Korean capitalist fortunes made by "bad people" who "are all covered in feces" and the idea of the desirable and much coveted "progress" that allowed Westerners to live in prosperity, enjoying freedom and modern luxuries.

Another of Yi's stories from this era bears a title reminiscent of a work by his contemporary Yi Ki-yŏng—namely, "Homeland" (Kohyang; 1931).[27] In this story, Kim Yun-gŏn is returning home after spending six years studying in Tokyo. All these years, this enthusiastic young man has dreamed of investing his newly acquired knowledge and talent in the development of his native land. Now he feels deeply disappointed in Korea, which had changed beyond all recognition. On the boat, Kim meets former Korean peasants who lost their lands and are now returning home from Japan, where they have been slaving for a pittance—a frightened, pitiful, and helpless crowd of people in "ugly national costumes that did not fit them at all." Observing them, Kim muses, "Is this really the attire of a people with a brilliant national culture and history?"[28] Kim is distressed by the gloomy policemen who are "watching you as if you have done something wrong," the barren Korean hills, deprived of their forests, and the whole "atmosphere of tears and anxiety, which is the atmosphere of the land of Korea."[29] His schoolteacher colleagues are apathetic and unfriendly; one of his schoolmates, a school activist, has been accused of a political crime and is in prison. Distressed by what he sees around him, Kim gets drunk and embarks on a night of wild debauchery—only to end up in a police station.

Unlike Yi Ki-yŏng's *Homeland,* which advocates the restoration of Korea's lost traditional past as a remedy for its social ills, Yi T'ae-jun's short story does not put forward any social recipes. Though the hero is not inspired by the social changes in his country, he does not harbor any illusions about Korea's old culture.

In "Planting Flowers" (Kkoch' namunŭn simŏ nohko; 1933), however, Yi T'ae-jun tends to idealize the past in the manner of Yi Ki-yŏng.[30] Here the peasant Pang family have moved to the city after their land was confiscated by a Japanese company. The Pangs are helpless in their hostile new environment, which is full of insidious and cold people. Pang's wife falls victim to a treacherous pimp, and his sickly little daughter dies in his arms because he has no money to pay for her medical treatment. Pang curses the cruel world and seeks relief in bouts of heavy drinking.

The author recalls the Pangs in the past, in their native village, where the family was confident and skillful, hardworking, and trustworthy. Their former Korean landlord was kind and intelligent, so "the peasants had never felt that the land was not their own." Wandering the city streets in spring, a devastated Pang sees a delicate young Japanese woman admiring a flowering tree, the same kind of tree that he planted in his village before he left it. He feels a deep sadness. He no longer has a right to the beauty of nature—the refined urban Japanese girl now owns it.

This depiction of the rural past is vividly reminiscent of the imagined paradise of Seoulite in Yi Ki-yŏng's "Poor Village." The good-hearted Korean landlord in Yi T'ae-jun's story, like Yi Ki-yŏng's kind and sophisticated *yang-ban* of the olden days, appears as a symbol of an uncorrupted and pure Korean life—an idealized vanishing past that Yi T'ae-jun makes clear has been taken by the Japanese.

In "Country Bumpkin" (Ch'onttŭgi; 1934), another story about a poor peasant in the merciless city, the olden days are less idealized. This protagonist recollects his past life in a small mountain village where, because of a lack of suitable land, people were traditionally forced to rely on odd jobs to feed their families. The protagonist describes this life as "extremely poor," yet he stresses that in the past "nobody in his village died of hunger" and "nobody begged."[31] This judgment at least appears a little more balanced.

As we see, the social analysis of the "national problem" in Yi T'ae-jun's stories is far from consistent. This is not unexpected, taking into account the varied nature of his heroes. A student returned from Japan, a poor peasant and the educated daughter of a rich family all see the social situation from different angles. Yet all of them are concerned about the future of the modernizing Korea, and this may be perceived as the position of the author. The critical social messages of these stories leave no doubt about the deep engagement of Yi T'ae-jun with the social problems of his country.

The Nine Members Club

We may approach the main paradox of Yi T'ae-jun's pre-Liberation life by examining the writer's membership in the so-called Nine Members Club. "Planting Flowers," "Country Bumpkin," and his other socially critical works were written at a time when Yi was involved with the Nine Members Club, a literary group that is invariably presented as the epitome of pure art in Korea. By definition, "pure art" suggests the emancipation of a writer from the social and political issues of the day and an exclusive concentration on the aesthetic aspects of his or her work.[32] How, then, can we reconcile the social criticism of Yi's writings with the demands of pure art?

A widely cited version of events maintains that in August 1933 Yi T'ae-jun, together with Pak T'ae-wŏn, Yi Hyo-sŏk, Yi Sang, and a few other writers, established the Nine Members Club (Kuinhoe) in order to protect the true artistic values of Korean literature from the claims of leftist activists. The KAPF was the club's primary target.[33] However, Cho Yong-man, one of the club's members, claims in his memoirs that the significance of the group and the consistency of its program were grossly exaggerated after Liberation. The Nine Members Club in fact represented a loose group of intellectuals who occasionally spent some time together chatting about literary matters. Yi T'ae-jun, as the most authoritative figure in this circle, used to preside over the gatherings, but the most active member was the poet Yi Sang, who, being unemployed at the time, used the group to promote himself. Cho claims that the group had no fixed program and that its determination "to protect literature from the arrogant political intruders" found expression only in the occasional verbal outbursts of its members against particular members of the KAPF whose political ambitions were not supported by their literary credentials. Like many other contemporary intellectuals, regardless of their political persuasion, the Nine Members despised the KAPF activists—Han Sŏr-ya, in particular—and the feeling was mutual.

It seems that in the confrontation between the KAPF and the Nine Members Club, ideological considerations were less significant than interpersonal relationships. Despite a formal adherence to different political groups, Yi T'ae-jun invariably supported his friend Yim Hwa, the main ideologist of the KAPF. Chŏng Ryul recollects that Yi T'ae-jun sincerely respected Yi Ki-yŏng as a "wise old man" of Korean literature and loved to talk with him about life and the arts.[34] At the same time, Yi T'ae-jun refused to cooperate with Yi Kwang-su and Yŏm Sang-sŏp, writers with similar views on literature and also self-proclaimed proponents of pure art.[35]

In fact, no matter how the writers formulated their artistic credentials, the actual ideological discrepancies between Yi T'ae-jun and the KAPF writers remained minor, as we can see in the example of the KAPF's classic writer Yi Ki-yŏng. Apart from some occasional "progressive" passages that appeared in Yi Ki-yŏng's most militant works, the general content and tone of his supposedly "proletarian" writings did not differ much from those of the "purist" Yi T'ae-jun. Both filled their narratives with similarly wretched characters (fragile intellectuals, miserable old peasants, and poor country girls) who felt uncomfortable in the changing world of a modernizing Korea but failed to find any escape.

Yet even though the existence of any real ideological disparities between Yi T'ae-jun and the KAPF was questionable, the mutual hatred between Yi T'ae-jun and some KAPF members proved to have very real consequences. Unfortunately for Yi, the ambitious KAPF activist Han Sŏr-ya would become the supreme boss of North Korean literature in the early 1950s, and the old animosity would resurface and destroy Yi years later. The weapon in this later personal struggle would be the same old straw man of "pure art," with all its negative connotations of Stalinist discourse, connotations that were not really applicable to Yi. In the opinion of Chŏng Ryul, who would later discuss literature with Yi in North Korea, Yi often did not even understand these connotations. "Pure art" in Yi's interpretation meant not aloofness from society but a high professionalism, the obligation of a writer to do his job well, not distracting himself with any talk of politics.[36]

Failing to Kill Rabbits

As already mentioned, the late 1930s saw the imposition of strict Japanese colonial censorship regulations on Korean literature. Though Yi T'ae-jun did not suffer any personal persecution, he, like the "proletarian writers," had to adjust to the new demands. In the 1930s, the social criticism in Yi's works was visibly and substantially reduced. His writings had a more inward orientation with a strong autobiographical tendency and a gloomy psychological soul-searching.

As an example of this later trend in Yi's works, "Raven" (Kkamakui; 1936) depicts the sad friendship between a desperately poor elderly writer and a terminally ill young woman who is an admirer of his novels.[37] Sensing her approaching death, the girl estranges herself from the living world. She is suffering from a phobia of ravens, the symbols of death, and feels as if their black bodies contain something terrible. The writer decides to kill a raven to prove that there is nothing special inside the ugly bird's black body. But his action is too late; the girl has already died. In another example, "A Story about Rabbits" (T'okki iyagi; 1941), the protagonist is again a poor writer who fails to find a way to improve the lives of his family (his pregnant wife and three children).[38] In order to support the family, the wife raises rabbits, but when the animals are fully grown, a problem emerges: somebody must slaughter them. The writer hates even to think about it, but feels that it is his duty as the man of the family. Still, he procrastinates until his wife, a timid and delicate woman who once studied in a girl's school, loved foreign poems, and dreamed of a beautiful life, does it herself. In the final scene she appears with her trembling hands stained with blood, endeavoring to smile in order to reassure her mortified husband.

The protagonist in each of these artistically very different stories ("Raven" has a strong touch of mysticism, while "A Story about Rabbits" is realistic) is a familiar Yi T'ae-jun character: the helpless intellectual trapped in a ruthless materialistic world. Yet "A Story about Rabbits" reads like a self-accusatory verdict on Yi's favorite nonviolent hero. Eschewing the earthier aspects of life, the gentle idealist does not make them disappear; he simply passes the responsibility for dealing with unsavory reality to his loved ones. The profound passion of this message is particularly impressive if we take into account that the story is autobiographical. In the image of the protagonist's wife, Yi T'ae-jun depicts his wife, Yi Sun-ok, whom he married in 1930 and who became the mother of his five children. Yi always felt gratitude and a sense of guilt for this gentle and well-educated woman, who tolerated his deficiencies and accepted all the various tides of their life without complaint.[39]

"A Story about Rabbits" offers us a clue to the sudden bouts of "revolutionary violence" in Yi's post-Liberation writings. In all probability, Yi had solved the moral dilemma of admitting the necessity for "violence in order to protect virtue" long before publishing his controversial pro-Communist story "The First Fight" (1948), in which totally positive, strong, and energetic protagonists kill in abundance—and their victims are not rabbits.

Like the biographies of the majority of his colleagues of a different political persuasion, Yi T'ae-jun's is tainted by his pro-Japanese activities in the late 1930s to early 1940s. Virtually all Korean writers who were living in the country in the late 1930s and early 1940s, including KAPF members, collaborated with the colonial authorities and published pro-Japanese texts. Still, Yi rarely produced a wholehearted piece of pro-Japanese propaganda in the mold of Yi Kwang-su. Probably the only example in which Yi noticeably backed the colonial regime is his pro-war propagandist article "A Day in the Support Army Training Camp" (Chiwŏnbyŏng hunlyŏnso-ŭi ilil), which was published in the pro-Japanese magazine *Munjang (Composition)* in December 1941.[40] Generally, his apostasy works, as they have been called, bore another kind of pro-Japanese message, which is detectable in *Moonlit Night of Ideas (Sasangŭi worya),* an autobiographical "newspaper," published in *Meil shinbo (Everyday Newspaper)* in 1941. The critic Yang Mun-gyu called the work "a novel of education," or bildungsroman, with clearly didactic functions.[41]

"Moonlit Night of Ideas" narrates the moral searching of young Song Pin (Yi himself was the prototype) who is studying abroad at a Japanese university.[42] After much spiritual turmoil, Song Pin discovers the one true course:

the path of civilization and enlightenment, embodied in the novel by Japan. Korean society and Korean students appear in the background of the novel and are portrayed as ignorant and backward.

Though Yi T'ae-jun's level of apostasy was moderate and found expression first and foremost in a support of the general discourse of enlightenment, modernization and progress in his writings, like the industrial development in Yi Ki-yŏng's "industrial novels," were to be conducted, by definition, under "positive Japanese influence." Being honest, Yi T'ae-jun did not fail to realize this and was deeply ashamed of his occasional support of the colonial regime. He ceased his pro-Japanese literary activities quite early (1939–1941)[43] and in 1943 moved back to his hometown, where he remained until Liberation.[44] It is notable that this unenthusiastic pro-Japanese activity did not bring Yi T'ae-jun, then a famous writer, any material benefit.[45]

In summary, this examination of the initial period of Yi T'ae-jun's literary activities reveals that, despite the self-perception of the writer as a purist and as apolitical, his writings were characterized by strong social concerns and sharp social criticism. A comparison with the writings of Yi Ki-yŏng, a typical representative of the KAPF, shows that the imagery and tone of Yi T'ae-jun's short stories brought them quite close to the actual conventions of what passed for Korean proletarian literature. This similarity remained palpable during the mid- to late 1930s. Nor was there much difference in the social attitudes of Yi T'ae-jun and the KAPF members; all of them were equally involved in pro-Japanese activity.

"Around Liberation" (1945–1946)

The brief period 1945–1946 is of singular importance in the history of Korean literature and thought. It was a period when old colonial restrictions had been removed while a new set of politically motivated restrictions (Stalinist in the North, anti-Communist and Nationalist Right in the South) had not yet been imposed on literature. The political and creative freedom of the period did have limitations, especially in the North, but it was still a unique phenomenon, not to be repeated again until the late 1980s with the political liberalization of South Korea. Yi's writings from this period reveal more about his worldview than do his pre-1945 or post-1946 works. A particularly important work of this period that explains the reasons Yi eventually chose the North over the South is the autobiographical short story "Around Liberation" (Haebang chŏnhu; August 1946).[46]

This story was published first in the South Korean *Munhak (Literature)* monthly, and after Yi moved to North Korea, he immediately received a special literary prize for the text as a socialist realist short story.[47] Some South Korean critics also refer to "Around Liberation" as a proletarian novella and describe its plot as one about "a young man who is desperately looking forward to Liberation" and who, after Liberation, "subscribes to a radical ideology and becomes a leader in the socialist literature movement."[48] In reality, "Around Liberation," one of the most honest texts ever written by Yi T'aejun, has little to do with socialist realism or radical ideology. Instead, this is a confessional story in which Yi admits his pro-Japanese activity and his passivity during the colonial period (notably, none of his ex-KAPF rivals published anything similar) and analyzes the dilemmas Korean intellectuals faced in postcolonial Korea.

In the story, Hyŏn, an artist who has been forced to collaborate with the Japanese, feels unhappy and guilty. Although Korea is now free, he remains frustrated. During conversations with his close friend Kim, an old-fashioned Confucian scholar, Hyŏn says that he wishes his country could choose its own unique path and not have any foreign system imposed on it, but that as long as Korea is poor and backward, it has to follow a particular foreign course. Along with his country, Hyŏn has to make his choice. He chooses the Soviets and joins a pro-Communist literary group, not because he is really "red" but because the Soviets, as the protectors of the poor and oppressed, may be closer to the traditional Korean spirit and thus be of less harm to Korea's independence. In support of his reasoning, Hyŏn quotes Lenin's words about Communist support for all national liberation movements. In comparison, capitalism offers no hope for a better life for ordinary Koreans because the capitalist Americans in Korea behave just as the Japanese had in the past. In the final scene, Hyŏn casts away his doubts and immerses himself in the new activity of the Communist literature union, just as Yi did in real life at the time.

This reasoning on Yi's part is quite sensible and can hardly be dismissed as romantic impulse. The evolution of the fictional Hyŏn mirrors the realities of the writer's own life: Yi too became increasingly involved with Communist front organizations in literature and was known to have played a vital role in the South Korean Communist movement. Scalapino and Lee, in their account of North Korean communism, mention Yi as the head of the cultural Department of the Korean Communist Party immediately after Liberation and later as having served in the temporary Party headquarters under Pak Hŏng-yŏng in Haeju.[49] In late 1946, Yi moved to the Communist North.

A Political Transformation in the North

After moving to the North, Yi T'ae-jun was immediately caught in a whirl-pool of factional struggle and was forced to make another choice. His post-Liberation teamwork with the Southerners (and Pak Hŏn-yŏng in particular) and his long-term animosity toward the KAPF made him a logical recruit for the block of Southerners and Soviet Koreans.

Yi quickly made friends with the Soviet Koreans, who needed his author-ity to win their battle with the ex-KAPF group. The sympathy between Yi and the Soviets was instant, mutual, and quite sincere. Chŏng Ryul remembers Yi T'ae-jun with great admiration, referring to his great literary talent, his elevated intellectual stature and his refined Westernized manners. Yi was also attracted to the exotic Soviets, with their high educational level and diverse life experience, and they pampered his ego in all possible ways. The Soviet Koreans helped Yi with the NKFLA vice-chairmanship in 1948, thus turning him in an instant into a high-ranking writer-bureaucrat.[50] They nicknamed him "Korea's Guy de Maupassant," and this flattering title quickly spread through the North Korean media. Yi's Soviet Korean friends also moved to establish a "society for the study of the works of Yi T'ae-jun."[51] In response, Yi enthusiastically took on the ideas and values of his new friends and admirers.

It is significant that Chŏng Ryul finds nothing peculiar in Yi T'ae-jun's choice of the North in circumstances where the nascent South Korean gov-ernment was so unpopular among the contemporary intellectuals. Chŏng mentions that Yi was greatly influenced by a similar decision of an elderly friend, the famous Korean writer Hong Myŏng-hŭi, and gives an interest-ing account of Yi's attitude toward Communist ideology. In his opinion, Yi was never interested in the political or economic viewpoints of Marx-ism but instead perceived Communism as a desirable moral code. Chŏng remembers that Yi said, "I like Communism. There is nothing wrong in it. People strive to live by strict moral rules and I cannot help but respect this desire."[52] Chŏng also found certain aspects of the Communist program particularly appealing, such as the equality of people and the liberation of oppressed nations. Chŏng recalls having long, theoretical discussions with Yi about pure art during which Chŏng found it necessary to "reeducate" him in a more appropriate Stalinist spirit and to point out to him the long-standing "reactionary" implications of the purist approach to literature. Yet, despite these minor theoretical disparities (which faded quickly as Yi spent more time with his new friends), Chŏng did not find that Yi's writings or behavior contradicted Communism in any way.

The active "reeducation" of Yi T'ae-jun was conducted not only through his personal friendship with the Soviet Koreans but also through his Moscow-sponsored "educational trip" to the Soviet Union in 1946 (mentioned in chapter 1) and his exposure to Soviet literature and arts. In 1946–1947 Yi, always an avid reader, extensively read the socialist realist Soviet literature, which was at the time being translated into Korean in large quantities. The influence of this literature soon became discernible in Yi's writings.

All these factors contributed to the transformation of this socially concerned yet politically unattached Korean intellectual into a staunch soldier on the cultural front who was eager to serve the new regime. The new role brought Yi not only material affluence and recognition but also a sense of purpose and a sturdy system of cohesive spiritual values. To borrow the words of Geoffrey Hosking,

> Acceptance of the doctrine of socialist realism was not only a matter of security and a quiet life. It also offered certain definite, if meretricious, spiritual rewards of its own. The intellectual who had known the intense but isolated and fissiparous life of the 1910–1920s now found himself part of a great national movement, subscribing to a credo accepted at least nominally by the whole reading public, and participating in tasks which were to bring a glorious future to everybody. . . . The writer felt himself again part of the society, a useful person.[53]

Yi T'ae-jun's writings of the period clearly reflected this new worldview, as can be seen in a few significant examples. In "Father's Hempen Clothes" (Abŏji mosi ot; August 1946), a young woman named Ch'ang-ok is living in the newly liberated Seoul with her mother, desperately waiting for the arrival of her father, a Korean patriot who had been forced to live overseas.[54] Instead of returning, however, the father sends a letter in which he informs the family that he will continue his struggle until the country is "truly and completely independent." The letter is an eye-opener to the daughter. Suddenly Ch'ang-ok realizes that Seoul is indeed not truly free; the Americans care more about the well-being of the Japanese than of the Koreans, and Korean patriots are discriminated against while national traitors enjoy social respect. Likewise, the interests of Korea are not taken care of; her own family is impoverished to the extent that her father's best hempen clothes have been taken by a money-lender. The girl feels betrayed, angry, and determined to resist.

This short story was written just a month after Yi moved to the North and probably represents his sincere impression of the situation in the South. The political messages in the story (anti-Americanism, harangues against South Korean policy, and so on) are expressed in relatively moderate terms, and the story preserves the best artistic traits of Yi's previous works—vivid images, detailed depictions of scenery, and a well-developed story line. The characters are portrayed realistically; neither epic heroes nor jet-black villains can yet be found in "Father's Hempen Clothes."

However, his next short story, "The First Fight" (Ch'ŏt ch'ŏnt'u; 1948), displays a dramatic change in Yi T'ae-jun's style and perspective. In this piece, a small Communist guerrilla band is operating somewhere in South Korea, fighting "dirty bastards" who have "sold the country to the Syngman Rhee clique" and the "American bastards." The band is made up of eight guerrillas, led by Kwon P'an-dol, a former railway worker from the Ch'unch'ŏn factory who joined the guerrilla movement after the October Struggle.[55] One particularly zealous fighter, called the Third, is the young brother of Kwon's fallen comrade Kyŏng-su, who was shot while trying to escape from prison. All the fighters are determined to succeed, except for Dr. Yun, the lonely intellectual who at times expresses doubts. Yet even Yun's perplexities fade away when the proletarian commander Kwon reminds him of the exemplary bravery that "Marshal Kim [Il Sung]" demonstrated while fighting the "Japanese bastards." Though the guerrillas are small in number and this is their first fight, they win easily and without losses. Only the Third, young and impatient, is wounded slightly because of his brave but reckless actions. The victorious guerrillas organize a "people's trial" of the "dog-shit bastards." The victims try to appeal to the nationalistic feelings of the guerrillas "as Koreans," but their pleading makes our heroes only laugh because they, like Communists and the exploited, are free from such "reactionary feelings." Revolutionary justice is served, and the guerrillas move on to new battles.[56]

"The First Fight," written under the strong influence of the classical Soviet guerrilla novel *Devastation (Razgrom),* by Aleksandr Fadeev,[57] is shockingly different from anything previously produced by Yi T'ae-jun. The "iron-style" characters, an abundance of expletives that are meant to demonstrate the popular spirit and revolutionary fervor of the heroes, violence depicted with obvious sympathy, wooden "progressive" rhetoric—all these features place an impenetrable barrier between Yi's refined classic works and his first socialist realist endeavor. The only recognizable hero in the story is Dr. Yun, a hesitant intellectual who lacks political awareness. But now he has a mentor, the superior proletarian leader, to correct him—just as in Fadeev's novel, in which the Communist commander Levinson also has to set an uncertain doctor right. The story still bears some familiar features of Yi's writing style, such as vivid depictions of scenery and some psychologically persuasive sketches. Along with the revolutionary justice in the scene of the people's trial, for example, Yi also depicts the temporary bewilderment of the peasants and the tragedy of the family of one of the victims. It must be noted, however, that such ambiguity was normal for exemplary Soviet partisan prose as well.

Yi's reeducation was so radical that it led some researchers to claim that the work had been written "not by the author's choice but under outside pressure."[58] However, this allegation does not appear convincing, because 1948 was a time when a convert to Communism could still change his mind. The abundance of stories Yi wrote at the time confirms that he enthusiastically participated in his reeducation and tried hard to implement the new political requirements in his works. Let us take a look at some of these texts.

"Tiger Grandma" (Horangi halmŏni; 1949) is a short story about the illiteracy eradication movement in a small Korean village.[59] The story's protagonist is an old woman who has been given the nickname "Tiger Grandma" for her tough and outspoken personality. Tiger Grandma is an influential figure among the village women, so her strong opposition to adult education frustrates the young and inexperienced Communist educator Sang-gǔni. Yet the young communist senses that Tiger Grandma is curious about his program but is too proud to reveal her interest. So he has this informal leader head the women's study group and wins her enthusiastic support. The strong-minded woman becomes literate enough to write a letter to her grandson Yŏng-dol, who is serving in the People's Army. She bids him perform his duties diligently and asks him to relay her greetings to Marshal Kim.

The bucolic sweetness of this story, with its uncomplicated peasants and unsophisticated folk humor, which is obviously meant to demonstrate the socialist realist popular spirit, is atypical of the earlier Yi T'ae-jun. Tiger Grandma is strongly reminiscent of the character of Grandpa Shchukar in Sholokhov's *Virgin Land,* who also represents the saccharine image of a comical rural elder who, despite his age, zealously supports the new regime.

In "Somewhere near the 38th Parallel" (38 sŏn ŏnŭ chigu-esŏ; October 1949), the "American bastards" and the "South Korean clique" constantly disturb the happy and peaceful life of North Korea's newly liberated peasants who live near the thirty-eighth parallel.[60] The Communist border guard, comrade Yu Kyŏng-hwan, is wounded in a battle with the "bandits" but does not lose his nerve and manages to cut off the head of one of the "bastards." In the final scenes, the hero slides into unconsciousness as visions of "the faces of his mother, his father, Premier Kim Il Sung's portrait, and the fluttering banners of the Republic" pass through his mind. His last thought is, "Where is my rifle?"[61]

This short story marks the beginning of Yi's purely functional propagandistic writings. Short, terse, and filled with crude expletives addressed to the "enemies" alongside an uncritical adulation of Communist heroes, these black-and-white narratives are completely lacking in the sophistication of Yi's pre-Liberation works.

Other works that followed also demonstrate this tendency. In "The Road to My Homeland" (Kohyang kil; 1950), for example, a guerrilla returning to his native village as an intelligence agent silently witnesses the sufferings of his family at the hands of the "bastards."[62] Because he must accomplish his mission, the agent cannot reveal his identity or do anything for his family. Finally, he turns this tragic personal experience into a positive stimulus for further struggle: "He felt he should be enraged at the larger things, should avenge the more important things."[63] Another story, "For One Hundred Times, One Thousand Times" (Paekpae ch'ŏnbae-ro; April 1951), describes the fight of the heroic North Korean soldiers against the cowardly American and South Korean "bastards."[64] One of the heroes, the young O Ki-ho, dies in battle. When his comrades return to pick up his body, they find him lying among numerous dead Americans, with his hands still grasping his rifle. O's comrades pledge to avenge the hero: "For one hundred times, we'll pay one thousand times."[65] Yet another example is the story "Let's See Who Will Surrender" (Nuga kulbok hanŭnga poja; April 1951), which portrays a young truck driver who has no war experience and is frightened during his first battle.[66] Nevertheless, under the positive influence of his commander, Kim Yŏng-min, an experienced and confident Communist officer, the driver gathers his courage and fulfills his battle task. In the end the officer gives the happy young soldier a hug "as if to an old battle comrade."

Yi's "American Embassy" (Miguk taesagwan; 1951) is a typical example of wartime anti-American propaganda.[67] After an American aircraft is shot down, two American "bastards" appear amid the North Korean positions, carrying a letter with the request that they be given food and delivered to the nearest American embassy. The North Korean soldiers are appalled at the arrogance of the intruders, who expect to receive humane treatment after all the atrocities they have committed on Korean soil. The soldiers have to hold the "bastards" until the servicemen from divisional headquarters pick them up, so they put the Americans in the cell of a former prison where the family members of Korean patriots had been tormented at the hands of the "American and South Korean clique bastards." Finding themselves faced with a room full of dead and mutilated bodies, "the bastards" are scared to death. With trembling lips they ask, "What is this?" to which the ironic answer is,

"This is your bloody American embassy!" The cowardly Americans, certain that they too will be tormented, kneel, whine, and try to bribe the Korean soldiers with wads of dollar bills, only to receive a sturdy rejection: "This is not your bloody America. You can buy your president but not a Korean." The Americans are told that they will not be killed, "because Koreans respect international law," but they are still locked in the cell with the words: "See what you have done, American butchers. Here is your American embassy. A very typical embassy."[68] This story was said to have received the highest of praise from the Great Leader.[69]

Though Yi T'ae-jun's prose was still marked by a higher artistic quality than the writings of his ex-KAPF colleagues, and critics at the time routinely mentioned this strong aspect of Yi's works,[70] his post-1945 stories were grossly inferior to his earlier writings. Like the post-Liberation works of Yi Ki-yŏng, Yi T'ae-jun's texts of this period are greatly simplified in terms of language, composition, and psychological persuasion. This propagandistic functionalism was the very thing that the writer was expected to demonstrate, and even a single attempt to add a personal touch to the obligatory propagandistic utterances was quickly spotted and rebuked by the critics. This occurred when Yi wrote the short story "Dear People" (Kogwihan saramdŭl; 1951), which dealt with the topic of Chinese-Korean friendship, something that was officially encouraged.[71]

In "Dear People" the seriously wounded Chinese volunteer Chin P'yŏng-su is saved by a beautiful Korean nurse named Kim Ok-sil. The young woman gives the soldier her own blood and remains vigilant at his bedside all night, singing Chinese songs. Some romantic feelings begin to develop between them, but the girl dies in a subsequent battle, trying to save another wounded soldier. The Korean commander Pak O-chŏl tells Chin of the heroic life and death of the girl, and Chin confesses that the image of her "helped him to understand his own Chinese Liberation Army and Chinese Communist Party better" and to understand "how nobly a person can live."[72] Chinese and Korean soldiers contemplate together the "noble internationalism" that connects their nations and the future life of their generation, which will certainly be peaceful and happy. During the conversation, the soldiers take inspiration while looking at a wall that boasts the portraits of their "dearest people"—the leaders of China and North Korea, together with Generalissimo Stalin.

While in general this story remains "correct" (it is the supreme Party leaders, not the beautiful girl, who are designated as the "dearest people" in the story), the minor concession to romance did not go unnoticed. The author immediately received a polite reprimand:

The appearance of this story, devoted to the high ideal of Korean-Chinese friendship, is a happy event in our literature. But unfortunately the theme of internationalism was expressed through the romantic relationship of the heroes. Of course there is nothing wrong with love itself. . . . But in this way this urgent political task is turned into a casual melodrama. Despite the perfect artistic quality of this story, we have to stress that romance is not suitable while depicting a lofty political subject.[73]

Yi deftly heeded the message and refrained from allowing himself any such frivolity in his subsequent writings.

In general, in the period between 1946 and 1953, criticism of Yi T'ae-jun was extremely rare. As we have seen, in general the writings of this alleged purist fitted perfectly into the propagandistic discourse of the DPRK, and Yi's prolific endeavors were highly appreciated.[74]

Yi T'ae-jun after 1953: The Purge and Rejection

For all this initial success however, Yi T'ae-jun's fame and prosperity did not last long. After 1953 he found himself subjected to increasingly severe critical campaigns conducted by the very same people who had consistently praised him just a few years earlier. Works that had been fervently eulogized now became objects of harsh criticism. What was the reason behind this abrupt shift in attitude?

According to the official North Korean version, "Yi T'ae-jun conducted subversive activity against 'progressive Communist North Korean literature' and the Great Leader personally, and he was punished for that."[75] The popular South Korean scholarly perception, meanwhile, holds that Yi "could not turn into a full Kim Il Sung–ist and for that reason could not survive in the North."[76] Yet, as we have seen, Yi had been reeducated quite sincerely, and none of his post-Liberation works demonstrated even the slightest trace of dissent or skepticism toward the official values, let alone any tendency toward subversive activity. The actual reason for Yi's purge had nothing to do with ideological incompatibility with—or disloyalty to—the regime.

Like other contemporary North Korean writers whose fortunes were closely connected with particular political factions, Yi T'ae-jun's fall from grace was preordained by the failure of the factions that represented his interests—the South Koreans and the Soviet Koreans. The ascent of the rival KAPF faction after 1953 and the weakening of the positions of his friends made the shift in Yi's fate just a question of time. Unlike the rare cases of some of his more sociable colleagues (such as Yi Ki-yŏng, who seemed to be everyone's friend and no one's enemy, or Min Pyŏng-gyun, who while belonging to the Soviet faction managed to maintain a good relationship with Han Sŏr-ya and enjoyed a stable position in the Pyongyang literary world after the Soviets left Korea),[77] Yi T'ae-jun could not strike a balance between the warring factions in the North Korean literary scene. Yi was known as a reserved person whose circle of friends was quite narrow and who avoided noisy parties and did not drink much. He liked to entertain his close friends, mostly Southerners and Soviet Koreans, in his house, sharing delicious food and pleasant conversation with them, but he did not interact with the wider community.

Yi's lack of political acuity made his defeat even more crushing. Though he was eager to follow the official conventions of North Korean literature, he profoundly misunderstood the unofficial, unspoken rules of the Pyongyang literary world. All informants unanimously remember Yi as a person who was fully focused on his writings, considering them to be of primary importance. At the same time, he ignored and often openly mocked the political games that constituted an essential part of a writer's life in the DPRK of the 1950s.[78]

The Soviet journalist Arkadii Perventsev, who visited Pyongyang in 1950 and met with the members of the newly created NKFLA, reports that Yi complained about the NKFLA's overindulgence in time-consuming political activities that distracted North Korean writers from their professional goals. Yi assumed that "in the Soviet Union the situation must be better in this regard." Predictably, the Soviet journalist rebuffed the Korean writer with bombastic Stalinist clichés to the effect that it was the "honorable duty of every truly progressive writer to be involved in ideological work," and so on.[79] One can only wonder how the forty-six-year-old Yi, who had spent four years in the upper reaches of the Stalinist literary bureaucracy, could be naive enough to share such a heretical view with a visiting journalist.

Yi's daughter recalls another episode that testifies to Yi's lack of political flexibility.[80] While in exile, Yi rejected his family's suggestion that he concoct a novel about the Great Leader on the idealistic pretext that he could not compromise his literary dignity—how could he write a good biographical novel about a person whom he did not know sufficiently well? A proud professional and a bad strategist, Yi T'ae-jun could not mend his ways, even after being purged.

Unlike Yi Ki-yŏng, who skillfully avoided seemingly unavoidable conflicts, Yi T'ae-jun did not care to hide his views about people and ignored the social hierarchy, to his own peril. He continued to ridicule his old foe Han Sŏr-ya for being an incompetent writer, disregarding that the increasing political weight of the artistically mediocre Han made him a very dangerous target.[81]

Yi T'ae-jun's underestimation of the significance of unofficial connections and petty politicking inside the Pyongyang literary world played a further role in his tragic fate. In the next chapter, I discuss the factional struggle in the North Korean literary world in greater detail. For the moment I would like to touch on the particulars of the noisy accusatory campaign against Yi T'ae-jun that began in 1953.

The campaign was conducted by a "wolf pack" of Han Sŏr-ya's close friends and political allies: Ŏm Ho-sŏk, Han Hyo, An Ham-gwang, Hong Sun-ch'ŏl, and other representatives of the ex-KAPF faction. Earlier, these critics had already contemplated attacks on Yi T'ae-jun and his removal from the literary scene,[82] but in each instance the Soviet backers managed to protect him. By 1953 the situation had changed considerably, and the long-term rivals set loose a torrent of defamatory articles against Yi.

To understand the spirit of this campaign, we might look at an article by Yi T'ae-jun's primary "literary executioner," Ŏm Ho-sŏk, entitled "The Reactionary in Yi T'ae-jun's Literature" (Yi T'ae-jun-ŭi munhak-ŭi pandongjŏk ponjil).[83] This work represents a typical example of Stalinist political criticism in its North Korean incarnation—personally abusive, unsubstantiated, illogical, and often plainly hysterical. Here are a few quotations from the work:

> From the very first day when Yi T'ae-jun crawled into North Korea, he never missed a chance to establish himself in the North Korean Federation of Literature and Art, where he began to search for henchmen. He conspired with Pak Ch'ang-ok, Ki Sŏk-pok, Chŏng Tong-hyŏk, and Chŏng Ryul [Southerners and Soviet Koreans who were once prominent in literary politics] and indecently engaged in subversive activity within the NKFLA.

> In the past Yi has written many novels about love—that is, pornographic novels. How could he consider himself to be a "pure artist"?

> Coming to the North, Yi took off the mask of "purity" and took on the mask of realism instead. He camouflaged himself as a progressive writer. But his essence was the same under the masks of both "purity" and realism. His true character is ugly naturalism, and this has never changed. When he wrote wearing the mask of "purity," his literature was naturalistic. And when, after Liberation, he switched to the mask of realism, his ugly face under this new mask was that of a naturalist who continued to frown and grin.[84]

Accusations against Yi covered both his pre- and post-1945 literary activities. Note how Yi's past is presented in articles by Hong Sun-ch'ol and An Ham-gwang:

> All the pre-Liberation activity of Yi T'ae-jun is simply artificial rubbish. . . . Yi T'ae-jun viciously strove to prove that the perfect works of the KAPF writers were worthless. . . . Bourgeois ideology permeated all the works of Yi T'ae-jun before Liberation. They all aimed at one goal—distracting the Korean people from the anti-Japanese struggle. . . . Hysterically striving to repudiate the political and ideological content of art, Yi T'ae-jun countered the KAPF's traditions of true realism, insanely and wildly propagating the ideas of "pure art." The heroes of his literature became bourgeois intellectuals, lechers, dirty *kisaeng,* and other useless people. . . . The heroes of his first story, "Omongnyŏ," are deeply licentious people. Through their images, the author represents the Korean nation as immoral.[85]

> Yi T'ae-jun chose to depict only lowly subjects—depraved people or dreamy youth, driven by desperation. . . . He is certainly nothing but a reactionary bourgeois writer who insisted on the separation of form from content in literature. He organized the reactionary Nine Members Club in order to fight with the KAPF, which produced healthy people's literature, and he tried to destroy the development of such literature. In fact he is a totally ignorant person.[86]

Note how easily the critics resort to personal denunciations such as "totally ignorant person," "wildly propagating," "hysterically striving," and so on, and how they mount accusations without bothering to present any proof. Even more importantly, the critics demonstrated a stunning double standard. While attacking Yi for his collaboration with the Japanese,[87] they omitted acknowledgment of the collaboration of virtually every KAPF writer. Accusing Yi of being passive during the Japanese colonial period, the critics failed to note that helpless images of "dreamy youth, driven by desperation," were an equally common feature of "healthy people's literature"—suffice it to mention Han Sŏr-ya's "Transition Period" (Kwadogi; 1929) or "Pagoda" (T'ap; 1940–1941)[88] and Yi Ki-yŏng's "Poor Village" (Minch'ŏn; 1925).[89]

In addition, note the demagogic nature of the criticism regarding "Omongnyŏ." The licentious behavior of the heroine is presented as no less than national humiliation for all Koreans—even though Yi T'ae-jun unequivocally expressed his disapproval of the heroine. Again, the double standard is evident: Yi Ki-yŏng's first piece of fiction also dealt with a womanizing hero, yet his story has remained a part of the official North Korean literary canon to this day.

The accusations directed against Yi T'ae-jun's post-Liberation works, including "The Road to My Homeland," "The First Fight," and "Tiger Grandma," seem even more absurd. Even if some tendencies or ideas that disagreed with the North Korean state ideology can be found in Yi's pre-Liberation works (and indeed in the KAPF works of the period as well), Yi's post-1945 works perfectly fulfilled their propagandistic mission. Nevertheless, these exemplary socialist realist texts also became the objects of harsh criticism.

A large part of the above-mentioned harangue by Ŏm Ho-sŏk is devoted to condemning Yi's "Tiger Grandma," a story about the reforms in the North Korean countryside during the early years of Communist rule. A comic folkloric character, Tiger Grandma was meant to symbolize the popular support allegedly enjoyed by the new regime. However, Ŏm reinterprets her as a vicious enemy representing "political opposition to the Party,"[90] and he deliberately overlooks that in the final scene this alleged class enemy sends her heartfelt greetings to the Great Leader. The critic claims that Yi was harboring hidden malicious intent by depicting how one person's opposition to the collective could threaten the whole study program. According to his accuser, Yi allegedly wanted to convince readers that "one person is stronger than a collective and hence the Communist party has no influence."[91] Ŏm emphasizes that Tiger Grandma leads the women's group not because of her willingness to study but in order to gain more power. Such an obstinate and uneducated person, he maintains, could not be a leader of the whole village, and he argues that it would also be impossible to find an illiterate person in a North Korean village of twenty families in 1949:

Tiger Grandma is the embodiment of stubbornness. She is an illiterate person, confined to the darkness of superstition. She ensnares the village women with her superstitions, and the author depicts the village women as coming to her on a daily basis to call on her "wisdom." This means that in this village the arbitrator with the wisdom to solve all the difficult problems is Tiger Grandma, the embodiment of superstition and illiteracy. Hence the village women who depend upon this superstition are illiterate and superstitious persons themselves, and the entire twenty-family village is not only a den of unlettered people but also a dark coven of superstition. In 1949, after the great success of the Cultural Revolution and land reform, the spirit of our peasants has risen to a high level. They rely in their daily lives upon solid political rights and cast aside even the faintest shadow of demons with hereditary feudal customs. To depict at this time a whole village still soaked in the dark world of superstition is a fabrication. . . . It is impossible to find such a person in 1949."[92]

"The First Fight" and "The Road to My Homeland," which had also been highly praised at first, were criticized in the early 1950s for alleged "defeatism."[93] With regard to "The First Fight," Ŏm particularly targets the scene of the "people's trial," which was, as we will remember, one of the rare bright spots in the bombastic narrative. The guerrilla leader, acting as an impromptu tribunal chairman, asks the villagers whether the defendant is guilty or not. In response, the mother of the criminal shouts loudly, "He is not guilty!" But hers is a lone voice. All the other villagers at first maintain an awkward silence. They support the accusation and hate the traitor, but feel uneasy at judging their neighbor. Here are Ŏm's comments on the scene: "The villagers don't listen to the guerrilla leader, and by their silence they even support the cries of the reactionary element's mother. . . . In this story Yi showed that the villagers did not support the guerrillas and sympathized with the enemy. The author himself, through the reactionary element's mother's cry of 'Not guilty!' reveals his own position and claims that the enemy is not guilty."[94] Ŏm pretends not to notice that virtually in the next paragraph Yi describes how the public mood quickly changes: people look at the traitor with "eyes flashing with anger," and in response to the guerrilla leader's question as to whether they can forgive the enemy, they shout, "No!" and "He must be killed!"

Criticizing "The Road to My Homeland," Ŏm aims his accusations at the scene in which the guerrilla protagonist witnesses the violence of the US soldiers toward his family, whom he is unable to help. The scene was written with an obvious purpose: to show the enemies as bloodthirsty torturers and to demonstrate the determination of the protagonist to fight the "imperialists." Yet Ŏm again manages to turn the situation upside down, declaring that "Yi T'ae-jun used this scene to suggest to the reader that the family had fallen victim to the guerrillas' fight, so it was better to keep away from the guerrillas."[95]

In another article Ŏm found additional political blunders in this scene from "The Road to My Homeland":

In this story Yi T'ae-jun depicts unrealistic contradictions. . . . The author describes the scene without any emotion—in order to distort the Party's notion of discipline. The Party's discipline comes from a deep love of the native land. But this love cannot contradict love for one's family. Who would sacrifice one's loved ones for the sake of one's native land? In real life the duty of the fighter to protect the country from the American intruders cannot contradict one's love for one's family! . . . The writer's intention was to stress that the discipline of our warriors does not come from high morale but is based on fear and violence.[96]

The demagoguery of these accusations appears especially remarkable if we remember that in 1952 this same Ŏm Ho-sŏk had referred to the pre-Liberation works of Yi T'ae-jun, along with the works of the KAPF writers, as "progressive" and extolled "The First Fight" and "The Road to My Homeland" as "perfect works, created by fervent patriotic feelings."[97] In upholding "The First Fight" as a perfect patriotic story, Ŏm on that occasion extols the scene as portraying "revolutionary justice"—the very scene he would criticize just one year later as "reactionary"—and he lavishes Yi's guerrilla characters with praise: "These heroes know neither romantic feelings nor fear of death. When the enemy removes a comrade from their ranks they do not feel any sentimentalism. Instead these positive heroes fill their hearts with revenge, with a striving for future victory. They step over the cold corpses of their dead comrades and move forward to victory!"[98]

Ŏm Ho-sŏk's allegations constituted only a part of the large-scale campaign that was unfolding against Yi T'ae-jun after the collapse of the South Korean faction in 1952–1953. All of Yi's works that had initially been highly praised became the object of frenzied attacks after 1953. For example, An Ham-gwang comments on "Around Liberation": "The novel definitely promotes anti-Soviet ideas. It is filled with bourgeois nationalism."[99] Regarding "For One Hundred Times, One Thousand Times," An Ham-gwang wrote: "The author looks at the situation from a physiological point of view. The dead bodies of our patriots and the corpses of the American bastards are depicted similarly. . . . Thus Yi T'ae-jun defiles the sacrifice of our soldiers, propagates the idea of the vanity of fighting, of the devotion of their lives."[100]

This same accusation was developed by Hŏ Kyŏng in a more emotional manner:

In the work "For One Hundred Times, One Thousand Times," Yi depicts the dead bodies of the soldiers of our People's Army and the dead bodies of the enemies, the American bastards, in the same manner. He situates these corpses together. If Yi had any feelings for the modern Korean people, he could not observe equally the dead bodies of the soldiers of our People's Army, who were victims in the sacred fight for the freedom and independence of the country, and the disgraceful corpses of the American cannibals, who were hired by the American monopolists to take part in a war to conquer our nation, only to be roundly punished by our people.[101]

Hŏ continues his tirade against Yi:

In "The First Fight," Yi compares the enemy's cannons, which were shooting at our side, with the shining moon. If Yi T'ae-jun felt the same hostility toward the enemy as the Korean nation did, he would never depict the enemy's cannons so beautifully—like the shining moon. . . . All these faults are not accidental. Yi T'ae-jun is stubborn in his bourgeois views. He did not wish to notice the dramatic economic and cultural changes in our country. The reason he turned from the people's side could be explained by the fact that he did not want to acknowledge the great success of our socialist literature and art but instead has been obsessed with rotten West European literature.[102]

For all the absurdity of these accusations, it is significant that the critic attacked the rare vivid image in Yi T'ae-jun's prose as inappropriate.

In yet another example of the criticism of Yi's writing, An Ham-gwang voiced this opinion of "American Embassy": "The author in fact supports the vicious propaganda of our enemies about our army. Our enemies falsely claim that the Korean Army is cruel and that it does not follow international law and the norms of humanity, and Yi T'ae-jun in his story repeats this same lie."[103] This accusation was repeated by Han Sŏr-ya at an "enthusiasts' conference" in Pyongyang in January 1956; he had obviously forgotten the bloody orgies of violence in his own war fiction, such as the novel *History*.[104]

These and other allegations, as parts of a wide political campaign, had nothing to do with literary criticism. The critics simply slung all the mud they could invent at Yi without bothering to substantiate their argument. According to Chŏng Ryul recollection, the all-too-apparent absurdity of these accusations led Yi initially not to take the situation seriously. For quite a long time Yi was sure that the dust would eventually settle and the Party would see who the writer really was. But this was not to happen.

In 1952–1953 all the major leaders of the South Korean faction lost their official positions, and some of them, including the poet Yim Hwa, faced show trials. They were accused of being American spies, saboteurs, and Japanese police informers, then pleaded guilty and were promptly shot or disappeared into the growing ranks of the North Korean prison camps. The Soviet faction was also steadily losing its influence and could not scare off Han and his cronies anymore. The campaign against Yi T'ae-jun reached its climax in January 1956 when a resolution by the Central Committee of the Korean Workers' Party (KWP) castigated Yi as a "reactionary writer" for his long-forgotten participation in the Nine Members Club. Han Sŏr-ya leveled further condemnation at the "Congress of activists of the Pyongyang KWP city committee's literature and art department," after which Yi was purged.[105] Yet for some time Yi remained in Pyongyang—at least until October 1957, the moment when his Soviet friend Chŏng Ryul left North Korea. Chŏng recalls that Yi, who came to say good-bye to him, looked very depressed. Yi repeated: "How lucky you are to have an escape hatch. What am I supposed to do now?" Chŏng tried to encourage his friend but realized that he had nothing to offer.[106]

Information about the subsequent life of Yi T'ae-jun is scarce. According to Min Ch'un-hwan, Yi's exile from Pyongyang occurred later in 1957. After that, Yi worked as an assistant in the *Nodong sinmun* office in remote Hamhŭng, and in 1958 he was working in a concrete block factory in the same city. In 1964 Yi was pardoned, and for a while he worked as a writer attached to the Cultural Department of the KWP Central Committee. He was said to have resided in Kangwondo Province in 1969, in the working compound of the Kangdong mine and living on meager social benefits.[107] Another source, Elena Davydova (Pak Myŏn-sun), maintains that in exile Yi T'ae-jun worked as a ghost writer—that is, he was forced to write novels that were then published in the official press without mentioning his name, largely as part of the so-called creative groups that began to proliferate in the late 1960s.[108]

The recently published diary of Yi T'ae-jun's daughter provides further information. According to this source, Yi was exiled to Haeju in Hwanghae Province, where he worked as a pressman in a factory, and in 1964 he was ordered to write prose, which was then published anonymously. In 1967 he received permission to return to Pyongyang, where he lived happily with his family for a while. In 1974 he was purged again and exiled to Kangwondo Province. Soon after he moved there, his wife died of cerebral thrombosis. The date of Yi T'ae-jun's death is unknown. His purge and exile seriously damaged the personal lives and careers of his five children as well as his own.[109]

Such was the tragic fate of probably the most promising North Korean writer. A recognized literary talent before Liberation, who despite his formal adherence to pure art had always kept a keen eye on social and national issues, Yi T'ae-jun after 1945 became a sincere sympathizer with Communism, which he perceived primarily as a set of lofty moral regulations. The writer consciously chose the DPRK over South Korea and from the outset vigorously immersed himself in Pyongyang's literary activity, eager to serve the new state and new system with his pen. Contrary to the popular perception, Yi T'ae-jun was to be an exemplary Kim Il Sung–ist: all his North Korean writings perfectly fit the North Korean Stalinist discourse, and his bureaucratic endeavors, supported by the once-mighty Soviet Korean faction and the South Korean Communists, were also successful.

Historically speaking, the pattern of an "unadulterated *sŏnbi*" who sincerely and successfully served the Communist dictatorship is much less unusual than it might seem today. One might recall, for example, the lifelong success in Soviet literature of the Russian aristocratic writer Aleksei Tolstoy, who extolled collectivization and the "firm hand" of the Stalinist leadership in his novels, or the high official standing of the *yangban* novelist Hong Myŏng-hŭi in the DPRK literary world. Under different circumstances, Yi T'ae-jun's success in the North could have been lasting. However, the writer was closely tied to his factional protectors and was forced to share their destiny, sinking with the losers. This situation was more or less common in the DPRK literary world at the time, but it was exacerbated even further by Yi's personal lack of political flexibility or wider social contacts.

The figure of the fallen Yi T'ae-jun initially served as a straw man for vicious decadence and naturalism but was eventually erased from the North Korean literary discourse altogether. The *Chronology of the History of Korean Literature (Chosŏn munhaksa nyŏndaep'yo)*, published in Pyongyang in 1957, omits his name even in relation to pre-Liberation literary history. Elena Davydova claims that the average university student in contemporary DPRK has never even heard the name "Yi T'ae-jun."

Although Yi's post-Liberation writings may be of doubtful value, the elimination of his pre-Liberation prose from North Korean libraries and bookshops is certainly a matter for regret. The North Korean readership has been denied access to some of the brightest pieces of Korean creative writing, to works that can be said to represent the quintessence of Korean literature of the 1920s–1940s.

The campaign against Yi T'ae-jun set the real scale of values and priorities for North Korean artists. The fate of this talented and ideologically loyal writer clearly demonstrated to his colleagues that neither professionalism nor eagerness to serve the regime could guarantee success or survival. North Korean writers came to realize that, as Myers has perceptively noted, "their careers would depend less on performance than on access to power."[110]

5 North Korean Critics as Political Executioners

IN 1947–1960 THE NORTH KOREAN intellectual world was beset by recurrent political campaigns and purges whose victims often included famous writers. The campaigns were conducted by the leading North Korean critics, and the victims of these campaigns (of whom Yi T'ae-jun, Yim Hwa, and Kim Nam-ch'ŏn were the most prominent) were formally accused, among other crimes, of deviating from the Party line of socialist realism and of promoting "bourgeois ideology."

It comes as little surprise that official DPRK historians present the events of 1947–1960 as crusades by socialist realist warriors (mostly ex-KAPF writers) who fought for the ideological purity of North Korean literature against vicious reactionaries.[1] The most recent version embellishes this picture with even more fantastic details. It holds, for instance, that the purges of Yi T'ae-jun, Yim Hwa, and Kim Nam-ch'ŏn were a consequence of the exceptional political vigilance of the Beloved Leader, the then nine-year-old Kim Jong Il, who is said to have been the first to spot the reactionary "defeatism" and "pessimism" of Yim Hwa's poem "Where Are You Now?" (Nŏ ŏdie innŭnya?; 1950).[2]

Many of today's South Korean academics also observe the events in the DPRK in 1947–1960 from an angle that differs little from that of North Korea's officials and politically engaged Soviet scholars.[3] The broad scholarly consensus today holds that the ideological and aesthetic purity of socialist realism was the major bone of contention in the battles of 1947–1960. Sin Hyŏn-gi and O Sŏng-ho, addressing the issue of the political campaigns of 1953–1956, recount the North Korean version of events without applying any independent analysis.[4] Sim Wŏn-sŏp has argued that Yim Hwa was purged because of "excessively soft" themes in his poems that contradicted the Party line.[5] Ch'oe Ik-hyŏn represents the campaigns of 1953–1956 as a "struggle of beliefs" between Yim Hwa and Yi T'ae-jun, on the one hand,

and the existing political system on the other.[6] American scholars Robert A. Scalapino and Chong-sik Lee follow a similar line, presenting the dramatic events of 1955 as a struggle between supporters of the "shift from Stalinism" (like Yim Hwa) and Stalinist die-hards.[7]

The majority of South Korea's scholars feel sorry for the victims of the campaigns. Yun Chae-gŭn and Pak Sang-ch'ŏn, for example, who link the purges of Yi T'ae-jun, Yim Hwa, and Kim Nam-ch'ŏn with actual "formalism," "pessimism," and "defeatism" in their writings, express compassion for the doomed victims who lived in a "society where ideology was an absolute and literature was ruled by an absolutely powerful ideology that admitted no free thought."[8]

Not all South Korean academics feel this way, however. Yim Yŏng-t'ae and Ko Yu-han claim that "socialist realism not only played the role of an ideological weapon in realizing the great task of postwar reconstruction but also was used in the struggle against the remnants of reactionary bourgeois ideas and the 'pure art' tendency of the members of the South Korean Workers' Party."[9] Thus Yim and Ko tacitly agree that remnants of bourgeois ideology, as well as "pure art" tendencies, existed in Pyongyang's literary world and constituted real problems that demanded resolute opposition. Kim Sŏng-su supports this view even more ardently.[10] According to him, political campaigns against formalism, revisionism, remnants of bourgeois aesthetics, and other reactionary trends led to a "theoretical deepening" of the theory of socialist realism in North Korea and that this should be appreciated as "the most important success of our literary history of this period."[11] Kim Yun-sik asserts that the conflict between Han Sŏr-ya and Yim Hwa over the latter's anthology *Where Are You Now? (Nŏ ŏdie innŭnya?)* was a result of theoretical disparities between the two and led eventually to North Korean socialist realism's being invested with "revolutionary romanticism."[12]

As we can see, all the above-mentioned accounts imply that there were actual differences between the ideological or aesthetic positions of the purged writers on the one hand and the official Party line on the other and that these differences inspired the political campaigns and purges of intellectuals in North Korea. Only a handful of South Korean scholars disagree with this dominant view. Pak T'ae-sang's approach differs partially, for he connects the purges of 1953–1956 not with supposed deviations from the official line of socialist realism but primarily with the sectarian clashes in the political sphere and the "struggle of inner powers" within Pyongyang's officialdom.[13] However, referring to the later purges that involved An Mak, Sŏ Man-il, and Yun Tu-hŏn, Pak explained them as the ideological incompatibility of these writers with the Ch'ŏllima movement and the political line of Kim Il Sung after 1958.[14] Pak similarly attributes the cases of Pak P'ar-yang and Han Sŏr-ya, who were officially accused in 1963 of revisionism and factionalism,[15] to the "insufficient cooperation" of these authors with the official ideological direction of Kim Il Sung.[16]

Kim Chae-yong also partially disagrees with the leading opinion.[17] On the one hand, Kim, like many of his colleagues, considers the campaigns against Yim Hwa, Yi T'ae-jun, and Kim Nam-ch'ŏn as, first and foremost, a "clash of aesthetic worldviews," and he also claims that the controversy between Ŏm Ho-sŏk and Ki Sŏk-pok in 1952 was an aesthetic dispute over socialist realism and revolutionary romanticism. However, when speaking about the results of this dispute—"the groundless criticism of the writers" on a massive scale, which made North Korean intellectuals "timid and servile"—Kim cannot find any ideological or aesthetic explanation for this; he presumes that these purges might have been of a political rather than a literary nature.[18]

Yi Ki-pong disagrees more radically with the North Korean version.[19] He insists that there were no differences of principle whatsoever between the winners and losers in the political campaigns and argues that the campaigns themselves constituted nothing more than a simple prolongation of clashes between factional interests in the top political hierarchy. In general, Yi Ki-pong's analysis of the purges and political campaigns coincides with the opinion of the defector Yi Chŏl-ju in his book *North Korean Artists.*

In present-day South Korean scholarship, Yi Ki-pong's view is normally discarded as oversimplistic and is overshadowed by fancier concepts, such as the theory of an alleged contradiction between the supposed "Seoulism" and "Pyongyangism" of Yim Hwa's and Han Sŏr-ya's respective literary images and approaches.[20] However, Brian Myers—who, unlike some analysts, read not only the critical articles of the time but the much discussed texts as well[21]—provides convincing arguments in support of Yi Ki-pong's observation. Disagreeing with Scalapino and Lee, Myers argues reasonably that the major victim of the political campaigns, Yim Hwa, was no aesthete but a rather conventional propagandist. Myers also reminds readers of the blatant double standards in the North Korean literary bureaucracy.[22]

My research has brought me to similar conclusions. On the one hand, all the available works of the "reactionary writers" proved to be very similar to the works of "warriors for the purity of socialist realism" in an ideological sense. These writings do not bespeak any "excessively soft" themes, "struggle of beliefs," or "shift from Stalinism." On the other hand, the inconsistency of the principles propagated by North Korea's literary critics, as well as their unashamed duplicity in the application of these principles, forced me to reject the prism of theoretical dicta when analyzing the patterns of North Korean literary critique and to begin looking for nonliterary interests behind the official statements.

Double Standards

Scholars who accept at face value the official statements of the campaigns conducted by the North Korean literary critics will soon find themselves trapped in endless contradictions. Take, for example, the works of Chang Sa-sŏn that deal with the influential critic An Ham-gwang. Analyzing An's post-Liberation activities, Chang cites an "anti-rightist tendency," an "anti-ultraleftist tendency," "absorption of progressive Soviet culture," "Party spirit," and so on. He stresses An's particular interests in the "problem of personality," the "importance of lyricism," and the "beauty of language." Considering all this, Chang concludes that An Ham-gwang "made attempts to look at literature from a rational, objective point of view, taking into account all aspects, such as worldview, imagery, and form."[23]

"Anti-rightist" and "anti-ultraleftist" rhetoric was indeed an important part of An Ham-gwang's vocabulary—at some periods, that is. The problem was, however, that this rhetoric had little to do with the actual essence of the literary policy that An was supposed to be implementing. When writing his criticisms, An tended to forget about the necessity to promote "Party spirit" when he extolled such works as "Brothers and Sisters" (Nammae), written by his boss and sponsor Han Sŏr-ya, in which the characters act in an extraordinarily passive and tearful, blatantly non-Communist manner. At the same time, An rudely lambasted "The Zither" (Kayagŭm), by Kim Sa-ryang, an adherent of the rival Soviet Korean faction, for the same passivity on the part of his protagonist and thus his violation of the ever-present "Party spirit"—although Kim's character actually conducts himself in a more proactive way than Han's "perfect" protagonist.[24] Neither the "lyricism" nor the "beauty of language" that An extolled protected the talented writers Yi T'ae-jun and Yim Hwa from wild attacks during the defamation campaigns of 1953–1956. On the contrary, An later blamed the writers for these very qualities, treating them as reactionary, bourgeois, and naturalist.[25]

Thus the criteria by which An applied such terms as "rightist" and "ultraleftist" to a particular piece of art reflected, primarily, the political fortunes of the authors rather than the literary qualities or ideological messages of their works. A skillful politician, An used the official terminology as a device to achieve particular goals in a political struggle to eliminate his factional enemies and to back up his allies and sponsors.

This pattern was typical of North Korean literary criticism of the time. We have already considered the campaign against Yi T'ae-jun, which demonstrated astonishing bias and subjectivity. Different personalities in the North Korean literary world were judged according to different rules. The official recognition of "serious ideological mistakes" in the first edition of Yi Ki-yŏng's novel *Land* led only to a friendly recommendation to rework and improve the novel, while the identification of at least equivalent political mistakes in Yi T'ae-jun's short story "Tiger Grandma" led to the purge of the writer. The proletarian-born writer Yi Puk-myŏng was a frequent object of criticism for the poor artistic quality and psychological shallowness of his novels, while the equally inferior works of his boss, Han Sŏr-ya, were invariably praised. Still, the criticism of Yi Puk-myŏng's novels for a lack of emotionality did not to lead to any personal complications for the writer,[26] whereas the alleged excessive rationalism in Kim Nam-ch'ŏn's short story "Honey" (Kkul) led to an accusation of the writer's "collaborating with the Japanese and American imperialism,"[27] and he was purged as a result.

The Ruthless Chorus

Most North Korean critics, such as An Ham-gwang, Han Hyo, and Ŏm Ho-sŏk belonged to the ex-KAPF faction. Their pre-1945 activities reflected the general vicissitudes of the KAPF's fate, such as radicalization after 1927 and pro-Japanese apostasy in the late 1930s. However, prior to 1945, each of the critics exhibited his own distinguishing features. An Ham-gwang, though born in a poor peasant family, was respected as an intellectual and known for his moderate ideological position,[28] while Han Hyo's arrogant personality and radical leftist views led to his perception as the antithesis of An.[29] In contrast to An Ham-gwang, Ŏm Ho-sŏk tended to be despised as an ignorant and timid rustic.[30] The pre-Liberation personal relations between these critics were also often difficult.

However, soon after Liberation all these different personalities united into a sturdy coalition. Their attitudes, arguments, and idioms became virtually identical, with no discernible individual features. This is why I have deemed it unnecessary to analyze the North Korean activity of each critic separately. Statements such as "Immediately after the war, Ŏm Ho-sŏk attacked such writers as Yim Hwa, Yi T'ae-jun, and Kim Nam-ch'ŏn," "In the mid-1950s, Ŏm took part in the critique of formalism," or "In the mid-1960s, Ŏm's main interest was the creative problems of the image of the Great Leader in *chuch'e* literature"[31] make little sense, because none of these trends were the expressions of Ŏm's personal interests or initiatives. Rather, his positions and issues, which exactly mirrored those of An Ham-gwang and Han Hyo, were determined exclusively by the changing official line and the outcome of factional conflicts.

The uniformity of the criticism seems startling, even against the backdrop of a highly politicized North Korean literary world. Indeed, despite the political pressure for conformity, there were discernible differences in style and themes between, say, works of Yi Ki-yŏng and those of Han Sŏr-ya, the most prominent North Korean novelists of the period. However, even the most significant North Korean critic had no individual voice; each one was but a part of a chorus.

And a ruthless chorus it was! North Korean writer Yu Hang-rim was not far from the truth when he joked, "An Ham-gwang is eager to crush the heads of his colleagues with a big hammer, just as the ancient Russian warriors crushed their Turkish enemies' heads."[32] Contemporaries report a similar "thirst for blood" in another critic, Han Hyo, from pre-Liberation times.[33] This quality could manifest itself in various ways. Sometimes a critic would not be averse to intercepting the private correspondence of a rival to his mistress and reading it aloud before a gathering of colleagues, presenting the intimate details as a testimony to the moral degradation of the opponent.[34] However, more often this attribute revealed itself in the form of critical articles, as in the following examples:

In this poem the protagonist, an engine driver, misses a mysterious girl who used to linger with him near the well by the railway. Now she has disappeared, and only a broken ladle remains by the well. Though the author implies that the girl has gone to fight on the front, this is just a cunning trick. In fact, he is thinking not about the struggle but about the girl. The meaning of this so-called poem is very clear. This engine driver is definitely a crazed lecher. And the girl is surely a bitch. Who else would think about love at this juncture? He does not even know her name! And why on earth does he mention the broken ladle? It is nonsense. The influence of bourgeois ideology is apparent here.[35]

In this novel the worker protagonist organizes the crash of an enemy locomotive. Yet this episode was included, not for the purpose of demonstrating the bravery of our workers, but to satisfy the author's unhealthy interest in the perverse scene of the crash. We can feel no sympathy for the hero, since the whole episode is depicted with coldly vicious objectivism.[36]

Look how Yim Hwa depicts wartime Pyongyang: "I cannot look on these ruins of the beautiful city / my heart is in pain. . . . Every inch of these streets / is covered with the blood of our brothers." So Yim Hwa sees only ruins. He does not see the heroism and creative labor of our people. And for good reason! Only a nasty naturalist, a pessimist, a reactionary pacifist cannot see this. . . . Or look at his other poem: "I have lost my old mother and sister / I have lost my lover at the hands of the enemy / Now I think only about revenge / I dream of giving my life for my country." Why does he write so much about his personal suffering? Why does he not mention that it was a war of the Korean people against the American imperialists?[37]

The bellicose demagoguery of these articles might appear comical, but it was aimed at striking down their opponents. And they were indeed struck down, often quite literally.

"Looking Upward"

All members of the critical chorus shared one major quality, which Chŏng Ryul colorfully defined as the "hot eagerness to keep looking upward"—in other words, to eagerly follow the slightest nod or wink of the authorities of the moment.

In 1952 Ŏm Ho-sŏk criticized the traditional Korean novel *The Tale of Ch'unghyang (Ch'unghyangjŏn)* for its "excessive eroticism" and "empty love cravings."[38] In 1954, when the nationalistic mood began to grow in Pyongyang, this same Ŏm Ho-sŏk summoned North Korean writers "to learn how to depict people's feelings from our glorious classic *Tale of Ch'unghyang.*"[39] Chŏng Ryul recalls that one day An Ham-gwang advised him in a friendly manner to change his previous positive attitude toward Yi T'ae-jun. Both critics had earlier supported the author, but now, as An just happened to know, the Party line had changed: "We are not allowed to praise him now—didn't you know? You must act carefully!"[40] An himself, indeed, acted very "carefully," showering abusive ideological labels ("nasty spy," "traitor," "empty-headed rustic," and so on) on the writer whom he had lavishly praised just two years earlier.[41]

The reverse shift (from denunciation to praise) was not uncommon either. We might recall that, in 1948, An Ham-gwang attacked Cho Ki-ch'ŏn's poem *Paektu Mountain*—obviously misjudging the political situation at the time. In subsequent years, when Cho's standing became unchallengeable, An Ham-gwang eulogized the same poem as "a great success."[42]

This lack of moral integrity was more than just an individual trait of An Ham-gwang or Ŏm Ho-sŏk. It was a quality that contemporary North Korean literary criticism invited at the time. Let us investigate how this influenced the dramatic events in the North Korean literary world of 1947–1960.

The "Ŭnghyang Incident" (1947)

The first event to demonstrate the political essence of North Korean criticism took place soon after Liberation, in 1947. It is known as the Ŭnghyang incident.[43] On 13–14 August 1946, just before the first anniversary of Liberation, the local chapter of the NKFLA in Wŏnsan published the first North Korean anthology of poems, *Hidden Fragrance (Ŭnghyang),* which included several new works by both distinguished and young poets. Among the contributors were Pak Kyŏng-su, No Ryang-gŭn, Ku Sang, Sŏ Ch'ang-uk, and Chŏng Ryul (the latter was a Red Army officer at the time). Because the anthology was conceived to celebrate the first anniversary of the Liberation of Korea by the Red Army, it contained a number of poems on the topic. The verses written by Chŏng Ryul, for instance, were devoted to the landing of Soviet troops in Korea in August 1945 and described the thrill the author felt when he first stepped onto the land of his ancestors.[44] Yet the anthology also included some lyrical poems by Cho Yŏn-hyŏn and Ku Sang, such as these:

> *Jumping, laughing, and crying, miserable people,*
> *You are like croaking frogs.*
> *This year the leaves that died last year*
> *Will not grow again,*
> *O my friend, my friend!*
> *You used to write me so many letters,*
> *But now you have disappeared somewhere.*
> *The flower wind is blowing.*
> *In the morning you want to die,*
> *In the evening you want to live.*
> *Even one day is hard to survive,*
> *Black thunderclouds are low to the ground.*
> *That genuineness that we have not yet been able to find,*

Where are you?
We will probably find it there,
Behind the next mountain.[45]
　　　—Cho Yŏn-hyŏn

Daybreak
Where the sun is rising,
A crow flies by.
At the point where night and day meet,
In a dark and scary backstreet, as if in a den of debauchery,
Long shadows are wandering about.
In a while
As soon as drumbeats loudly sound,
A castle gate, covered with the moss of resentment,
Breaks.
On the road that is covered with poison, like a snake's spine,
A prophet is carrying a torch,
"Wake up," he cries,
Galloping on a white horse.
The sound of hoofs,
The sound of hoofs.
Swords and spears are clinking,
Wild horror is spreading about;
The loud cries of the people
Sound so gloomy.
Even the bright rising sun
Bleeds red blood from its mouth.
What a beautiful smile of a dying man.[46]
　　　—Ku Sang

The mood of these poems reflected fatalistic and melancholic propensities, quite typical of the colonial-era Korean literary tradition. Ku Sang later admitted that "Daybreak" indeed did not reflect cloudless happiness. Nonetheless, he emphasized, no political dissent was intended.[47] Considering that this confession was published in Seoul in a period of near-hysterical anti-Communism, when it made sense to present oneself as a deliberate enemy of the reds, we have every reason to believe it.

　　Characteristically, the verses alerted neither the editors nor the "politically conscious" Chŏng Ryul. The book was lavishly decorated by the talented artist Yi Chung-sŏp and was a great success among the public. All three thousand copies were sold almost immediately, so Chŏng could not even get a spare copy for himself. All the contributors shared a strong feeling of pride in the anthology.[48]

Yet soon, to borrow Ku Sang's expression, "a lightning bolt descended from Pyongyang." In early January 1947 all the North Korean newspapers published a resolution of the Executive Committee of the North Korean Federation of Literature and Art that prohibited the selling of *Hidden Fragrance.* The resolution accused the anthology of defiance of ideology, skepticism, decadence, escapism, idle fantasy, and other transgressions.[49] Instantly, a group of "investigators," which consisted of distinguished intellectuals such as Song Yŏng, Kim Sa-ryang, Ch'oe Myŏng-ik, and Kim Yi-sŏk, was dispatched to Wŏnsan.[50] At the first meeting with the contributors to the anthology, Song Yŏng launched personally abusive attacks on the writers, forcing them to conduct self-criticism in public.[51] The poet Ku Sang later recalled this moment as extremely shameful: "I will never forget the feeling of frustration and unbearable pain that enveloped me that day when [after the meeting] I strolled aimlessly along the streets of Wŏnsan."[52]

The situation led to a wave of insulting accusations against the participants in "the incident." Han Hyo insisted that the above-cited verse by Cho Yŏn-hyŏn was "slanderous" and "filled with decadent ideas meant to corrupt our people." He argued,

> Today, when all our people are marching in single file in order to create a new life, this silly poet calls them "miserable," stresses that "even one day is hard to survive"—his purpose is definitely to imbue them with his damaging ideas. When he invites readers to find genuineness "behind the next mountain," he is clearly trying to lure them from the new life of North Korea to some different life.[53]

And Pak Chong-sik asserted:

> The authors of the anthology *Hidden Fragrance,* under the influence of the false theory of "art for art's sake," stepped out with brazen propaganda for bourgeois ideas. Their goal was to contaminate the Korean people with the spirit of decadence and bourgeois individualism and to turn the Korean people into the slaves of American imperialism. They tried to slander the democratic system of North Korea. They craved for the reconstruction of the old capitalist society.[54]

Sin Ku-hyŏn continued in the same vein: "The collection of works *Hidden Fragrance,* and the anthology published later in Hamhŭng, adulated vulgar love. The enemies who published these subversive books meant to denigrate and slander the Korean people, who at the moment are entering a new way of life, constructing a new social order."[55]

It was the irrational aggressiveness of the attack that struck Ku Sang most: "It was all so self-important; no one could believe that just a few poems could cause such a fuss."[56] The bullied poet soon afterward left Wŏnsan for South Korea, where he eventually published his memoirs of the event.

This attack may certainly have appeared illogical to the people in North Korea at the time. Unlike Soviet Russia, where the tightening of the ideological noose over literature was slow and appeared as a result of the gradual transformation of Russian Communism,[57] literature in North Korea had, from its first steps, been guided by the extraneous Soviet authority. To a layman, the attack did indeed strike like a lightning bolt. Yet, when considered within the Soviet intellectual tradition, the *Hidden Fragrance* incident was a logical reflection of the Soviet political campaigns that were launched almost simultaneously in the same year (1946) against Mikhail Zoshchenko and Anna Akhmatova.[58] The accusations leveled against North Korean poets—decadence, escapism, and skepticism—were very similar to those put forward against Akhmatova.[59]

Nevertheless, the North Korean criticism demonstrated some traits that distinguished it from its Soviet prototype. One of these was the virtually unanimous conformity of the critics; as Myers notes, "there is no record of anyone voicing even token dissent."[60] Despite the disparities in the previous ideological positions and personal inclinations of the investigators (Song Yŏng, for example, was a fervent proletarian writer, while Ch'oe Myŏng-ik had been known as a mild and politically moderate person),[61] all of them obediently performed the role of ideological prosecutor. In contrast, during the campaign of 1946 in the USSR, which was initiated and guided by Stalin himself, such intellectuals as Nikolai Tikhonov and Sergei Prokofiev made cautious attempts to protect the victims from the supreme wrath.[62]

The Ŭnghyang incident also demonstrated the remarkable harshness of the critics' vocabulary. The rudeness of North Korean literary critics, and of their Chinese counterparts,[63] had its roots in the Soviet critical tradition in which the verbal abuse of an opponent was treated as a positive sign of "proletarian candor." Yet the offensiveness of the North Korean critics, who routinely referred to authors as "silly" or "worthless,"[64] was patently beyond the pale of the Soviet tradition. All the contents of and contributors to the ill-fated anthology were condemned without exception. Another of Ku Sang's verses, "Night" (Pam), an innocuous lyrical depiction of the beauty of night, was denounced along with the politically dubious "Daybreak."[65] Chŏng Ryul's eulogies to the Red Army became a subject for the same political criticism as Cho Yŏn-hyŏn's melancholic poem. Chŏng retells a characteristic passage from a critical article of the day: "Why did Chŏng Ryul, a Soviet officer and a representative of the progressive country, become involved in such a provocative, reactionary anti-Party anthology?" It is obvious that the critic did not even bother to read Cho's poem.

Characteristically, the attackers intimidated their confused victims instead of explaining, let alone discussing, the rules and demands that had been introduced less than a year earlier and still remained unclear. Brian Myers has noted the "ignorance of party cultural policy" of even left-wingers in the North Korean intellectual world at the time.[66] A similar abusive attack was launched soon afterward in an incident with another collection of poetry, *Anthology of Writing (Munjang tokpon).*[67]

The outcomes of both the Soviet 1946 campaign and its Korean analogue turned out to be relatively peaceful: the victims, though humiliated, were not seriously punished. Anna Akhmatova was readmitted to the Soviet Writers' Union after writing two poems in honor of Stalin; and Chŏng Ryul, despite all the political accusations, soon became vice-chairman of the Writers' Union. However, the Ŭnghyang incident established a pattern of Soviet-Stalinist literary "discussion" that was to flourish again a few years later.

In the North Korean political discourse, the *Hidden Fragrance* incident was soon transformed into a myth about an aggressive band of "reactionary poets" who had attempted a malicious encroachment against North Korean Communism and who were stopped only by the valiant effort of "real Party writers."[68]

First Factional Clashes

I have already discussed one of the first conflicts in the North Korean literary world to be motivated by factional interests—namely, the heated argument over the poem *Paektu Mountain (Paektusan)* in 1948. At this time An Ham-gwang, a representative of the ex-KAPF faction, strove to push aside the Soviet Korean poet Cho Ki-chŏn but failed and was pushed back himself. The overall outcome of this discussion turned out to be very mild in comparison with the bloody battles of later eras; the argument was not splashed across the pages of the newspapers, the punishments meted out to the losers were mild, and the relationships of the opponents remained stable and even friendly.[69] Nonetheless, the dispute over *Paektu Mountain* set the pattern for relentless factional confrontations in which not only literary but even ideological issues were practically irrelevant. In the discussion over *Paektu Mountain,* each side was protecting practical benefits and interests. An strove to demonstrate that his rival, being a stranger to Korean culture, could not represent the interests of North Korean literature, whose leadership should consist of the KAPF writers. Cho, in turn, wished to push An aside by stressing his ideological ignorance, while picturing himself and the Soviet Korean faction as the sole legitimate representatives of progressive socialist ideology. Kim Ch'ang-man protected *Paektu Mountain* in order to please his boss, Kim Il Sung, and also to avoid confrontation with the Soviets. The poem itself, meanwhile, was a mere weapon in this struggle of sectarian interests.

Since the winners of these North Korean literary factional battles scarcely evoke much sympathy, scholars have often succumbed to the temptation to present the losers as innocent victims or even heroic dissenters. A typical example is the article by Ch'oe Chae-bong entitled, "An Ham-gwang, a North Korean Critic with a Tragic Fate," which represents An's attack on *Paektu Mountain* as a heroic deed. According to Ch'oe, the critic allegedly stood up against the "exaggeration of the personal role of Kim Il Sung" in the poem and thus acted as a brave fighter against the incipient personality cult.[70]

This claim is not supported by hard evidence, since An proved himself anything but a fighter against dictatorship. Just a few years later, in 1953–1957, the critic actively participated in the defamation campaign against "bourgeois remnants" in North Korean literature—in fact, against the personal opponents of his patron Han Sŏr-ya. Some of the favorite labels An frequently applied to his political enemies (Yi T'ae-jun, Kim Nam-ch'ŏn, Yim Hwa, and others) were those of propagation of the principles of pure art, lack of Party spirit, and, above all, vicious disloyalty to the Great Leader.[71]

The sectarian struggle found another expression a few years later when the Soviet Korean faction moved against a member of Han Sŏr-ya's inner circle, the famous dancer Ch'oe Sŭng-hŭi. Though not belonging to the history of literary criticism in a strict sense, this incident revealed much about the levers that moved the North Korean intellectual world and should therefore be noted here.

After the death of Cho Ki-ch'ŏn in 1951 and the gradual concentration of power in the hands of Kim Il Sung and his guerrilla faction, the position of the Soviet faction in literary affairs was weakened. In order to restore their standing, the Soviet Koreans strove to undermine Han Sŏr-ya's influence wherever possible. In 1951 the object of their intrigue became Ch'oe Sŭng-hŭi—a dancer of international acclaim, a chairwoman of the Dancers' Union, the wife of Han Sŏr-ya's friend An Mak, and a close acquaintance of Kim Il Sung himself. Yi Chŏl-ju describes the situation in his memoirs.[72] In August 1951 Ch'oe's troupe won first prize at the East Berlin Youth Festival, and the forty-year-old actress triumphantly returned home to take part in a grandiose performance in Pyongyang's Underground Theater. However, the Propaganda Ministry was dominated by Soviet Korean officials at the time, and they attempted to cancel the performance. According to Chŏng Ryul, who basically agrees with Yi Chŏl-ju's version of events, the officials claimed that the "level of political content" in the show was not satisfactory.[73]

As Brian Myers has noted, Ch'oe's opponents cited her reputation for sexual promiscuity—they "apparently hoped that she would be too aware of her own vulnerability on this score to stand up to them."[74] Chŏng Ryul, who had himself once enjoyed a romantic relationship with Ch'oe, admits that this flamboyant beauty had indeed frequently violated the accepted moral standards. (In this respect, however, she did not differ much from her male colleagues—practically every prominent writer or literary official in North Korea had a mistress and often several.) However, Chŏng insists that Ch'oe's professional activity and the performance were impeccable in both ideological and artistic senses and definitely did not deserve to be canceled.

Ch'oe's foes had miscalculated. Being a determined or (by Yi Chŏl-ju's definition, brazen) personality, the actress did not hesitate to ask for protection from Kim Il Sung himself. Kim obliged, and the Soviet Koreans were forced to retreat.

As in the episode with *Paektu Mountain,* the attackers, who in this case were Soviet Koreans, did not care about the work they were attacking. They paid scant attention to the state of the North Korean arts, which would have suffered greatly from the removal of Ch'oe, one of a very small number of North Korean artists who enjoyed genuine popularity overseas. Petty political interests and political intrigue clearly dominated the conflict.

Fighting Southerners

The pattern of attack emerged fully fledged in the major campaign by ex-KAPF faction members against Yi T'ae-jun, Kim Nam-ch'ŏn, and Yim Hwa, all three being members of the Domestic faction and, simultaneously, backers of the Soviet Koreans. The intrigue aimed at a dual goal—to rob the Soviet faction of its allies and to weaken the position of the Southerners. The second goal formed a part of Kim Il Sung's grand strategy; though his suspicions of the Domestic faction were mounting, a direct assault on it was impossible until the end of the war, because "the former Southerners had been instrumental in running the South Korean underground network of guerrilla bands and intelligence agents."[75] Thus the initial steps were taken in the relatively peripheral cultural sphere.

In the previous chapter I analyzed the details of the critical accusations against Yi T'ae-jun. Now we shall look at the political campaigns against the other two participants in this incident, Yim Hwa and Kim Nam-ch'ŏn.

Both writers, having once been active members of the KAPF, became prominent officials of the NKFLA after 1945 and enjoyed an unquestioned reputation as Communist activists. The introduction to the Soviet version of an anthology of North Korean poetry in 1950 described Yim Hwa in this way:

> Yim Hwa is a fighting poet who has devoted his whole life to the task of the liberation of the Korean people from feudalism and imperialist aggressors. He is one of the founding fathers of the KAPF. He is currently continuing his struggle on the front line, helping partisans in South Korea with his pen and gun. His poems are full of a belief in the victory of the young fighters for a new life for Korea.[76]

This praise could appear in the Soviet publication only with the endorsement of the NKFLA. Indeed, in 1949, An Ham-gwang in *Munhak yesul* magazine mentioned Yim Hwa and Kim Nam-ch'ŏn as "exemplary proletarian writers."[77] Similar statements were made about Kim Nam-ch'ŏn—for example, in Yi Ki-yŏng's article "On Korean Literature," published in 1949 in the Soviet literary magazine *Zvezda*. Yi Ki-yŏng, a senior official representative of the North Korean literary establishment, introduced Kim Nam-ch'ŏn as "the distinguished proletarian writer" of pre-Liberation days, while he presented Yim Hwa's post-Liberation poems as a "significant new achievement of North Korean literature."[78]

However, the established reputation of the writers counted for little when the positions of their sponsors, the Domestic faction, began to deteriorate. In 1952 both writers were exposed to the opening salvos from Han Sŏr-ya's faction. The pretext for the assault was Kim Nam-ch'ŏn's short story "Honey" (Kkul; 1951) and Yim Hwa's anthology *Where Are You Now?* (*Nŏ ŏdie innŭnya?* 1951). Let us take a brief look at these two works.

The protagonist of "Honey," a heroic border guard, is wounded while on duty.[79] The young soldier persuades his comrade to leave him so they can accomplish the mission, and he prepares to die. He sinks into lyrical thoughts and visions. Yet he does not die. An old peasant woman finds him and nurses him back to health with a simple medicine, honey, and restores his spirits with her care and love. The young soldier is eventually ready to fight again.

This story calls to mind the exemplary Soviet *Novel about a Real Man* (*Povest' o nastoiaschem cheloveke*), by Boris Polevoi, in which a wounded pilot is left to the mercy of the rural people, and an old local woman cures him with another simple medicine, chicken soup. Kim's story is also reminiscent of numerous contemporary North Korean works such as Kim Sa-ryang's "Zither" (Kayagŭm; 1949) and Han Sŏr-ya's "Soldier's Farewell" (Ch'ŏnbuŏl; 1950).[80] The latter work, which also depicts a soldier in a lyrical mood when he is forced to rely on an old woman's care, was frequently praised by Ŏm Ho-sŏk.[81] It is noteworthy that the sentimental passages in "Honey" by no means detract from the general uplifting message of the story: the dying soldier is concerned about the accomplishment of the mission, not about his physical survival;[82] the old peasant woman wholeheartedly supports the People's Army; and the protagonist eagerly returns to the battlefield.

Yim Hwa's anthology *Where Are You Now?*, which included the verses "Where Are You Now?" (December 1950), "Carry, Wind!" (Paramiyŏ chŏnhara; February 1951), and "On My Blood That Colored the White Snow Red" (Hŭnnunŭl pulkke multŭrin na-ŭi p'i uie; March 1951), among others,[83] was also devoted to the theme of war. As Yi Chŏl-ju testified, the anthology "was a real success": "Young writers rushed to emulate Yim Hwa's poetical style. They judged the anthology to be a masterpiece, and there were no young men who did not know Yim Hwa's verses by heart."[84] Yim's work also won high praise from the critics, even those belonging to the KAPF faction.[85]

Soviet influence was also traceable in Yim Hwa's approach to war. Soviet wartime poetry included not only eulogies to heroism but also reference to numerous personal tragedies: separation from loved ones, the suffering and untimely death of young people, and so on. This lyrical side was also present in the verses of many other contemporary Pyongyang writers, such as Kim Cho-gyu, Min Pyŏng-gyun, Yi Chŏng-gu, Yim Chŏng-suk, and Ch'ŏn Se-bong.[86] However, the lyrical mood of Yim's poetry entails no passivity or subordination to the enemy. Witness, for example, the characteristic stanzas of "Carry, Wind!":

> *"Carry, Wind!*
> *Carry our feelings to the people we love,*

To the gray-haired people that we adore! . . .
Carry, Wind!
To our mothers who day and night without sleeping
Long for victory
Even more than for the return of their loving sons,
Carry, Wind!
To our mothers who are loyal daughters of our land,
Who, with a deep desire for revenge,
Fight for the death of our enemies, like soldiers.
Carry them our words.
Tell them to curse, not cry!
Tell them to breathe fire and not to groan!
And a glorious day will come,
The sun will rise above the fields and forests and mountains!
The sun will come to every village, every town!
Your sons and daughters will return to the land
Which they are now missing so much,
They will return—without a doubt.
Carry these words to the mothers,
O wind![87]

Here Yim Hwa expresses even more political consciousness than one would typically find in a wartime-era Soviet poem. It is virtually impossible to find in Soviet literature an image of a mother who longs for victory even more than for the return of her loving sons.[88]

The other poems in Yim Hwa's anthology also combine lyrical moods—such as the sorrow caused by the separation of father and child ("Where Are You Now?"), admiration for the beauty of Korea's nature ("Seoul" [Sŏul; July 1950]), or recollections of a loving family ("The Native Land I Have Never Seen" [Hanbŏndo pon il-i ŏpsnŭn kohyang ttang-e] August 1950])—with clear propagandistic messages of hatred for the enemy or loyalty to Marshal Kim and to the Party. In the poem "Where Are You Now?" the poet expresses his readiness to "obey the order of the Dearest Leader and not to cede to the enemy an inch of Korean land."[89]

Thus, in an ideological sense, the works of Yim Hwa and Kim Nam-ch'ŏn were politically beyond reproach and included no dissent whatsoever. Yet soon these works became the targets of severe attacks. To the best of my knowledge, these attacks were initiated by Ŏm Ho-sŏk in *The Basis of Literature and the Arts (Munye kibon)*, published on 20 January 1952.

Ŏm's text begins with the still-obligatory obeisance to the "great literature of the Soviet Union" and invitations to imitate it. It is also laced with
the customary quotations from Lenin, Gorky, and Stalin and dutifully refers
to the "evil" bourgeois values of the capitalist world—namely, naturalism,
formalism, and art for art's sake—and, once again, harangues the contributors
to the *Ŭnghyang* anthology. Then Ŏm addresses some of his reproof to the
work of contemporary North Korean writers, interspersed with the customary
praise for their endeavors and achievements.

The first, utterly respectful critical remarks refer to writers close to Han
Sŏr-ya's faction. Ŏm criticizes Yi Ki-yŏng's *Land* for the "excessive love relationships of the heroes,"[90] mentions some trivial formal shortcomings in the
works of Hwang Kŏn and Yi Puk-myŏng, and even spots a minor blemish
in a short story "Jackals" (Sŭngnyangi; 1951), written by his mighty boss,
Han Sŏr-ya. Ŏm remarks, "At the end of the story the awakening political
consciousness of the maternal protagonist could be seen as a little exaggerated
and embellished. Yet this is the most splendid story Han has ever written."[91]
Considering that the maternal protagonist does not demonstrate any political consciousness at all except for a lone statement addressed to the American
enemies ("Just you wait and see! Not all Koreans have died"),[92] the critic's
argument sounds more like a compliment than a reprimand.

Kim Nam-ch'ŏn's "Honey," meanwhile, appears to be just one of many
works mentioned in the article for which Ŏm expresses his disapproval: "Unfortunately, this story is not so much the product of a strong love or passion as the
outcome of cold and distant contemplation." What the writer really needs to do
in the future, Ŏm insists, is to invest more emotion in his writings: "Though
we cannot call 'Honey' completely nonrealistic or naturalist, the danger of
objectivism should not be overlooked." Ŏm stresses that "the work would be
excellent had Kim Nam-ch'ŏn been able to develop the private image of the
old peasant woman in the story into something more representative."[93]

Ŏm's remarks on "Honey," unsupported by any examples or quotations,
seem quite random; there is hardly any way to prove whether a text has been
inspired by love or by cold contemplation or whether a given protagonist is
typical or not. However, the application of the strongly negative terms "naturalist" and "objectivism" to Kim Nam-ch'ŏn's writing was a warning sign.
These terms were reflections of the contemporary Soviet critical tendencies,[94]
and North Korean critics had previously used them only in vague admonitions to all writers "to follow the Party line" and not to be carried away by
formalism and naturalism.[95] Ŏm's work was the first to apply these straw
men not to distant "bourgeois writers" of pre-Liberation Korea, capitalist

countries, or even "Seoul puppets" but to a North Korean writer who enjoyed high official standing.

The application was so cautious, however, that the article failed to induce any protest or discussion. The criticism of "Honey" was generously compensated for by friendly advice such as the hint that the work could be wonderful if changes were made, and the praise of Kim Nam-ch'ŏn's previous works such as his major pre-Liberation novel *Big River (Taeha)*.[96]

As positive examples of completely flawless contemporary works, Ŏm cites verses by Cho Ki-ch'ŏn and Yim Hwa ("Pyongyang," "Seoul," "The Native Land I Have Never Seen," "On My Blood That Colored the White Snow Red," "Where Are You Now?"). It is worth remembering that in less than a year Ŏm, along with the other critics of Han's group, would harshly criticize these same poems by Yim Hwa.

As if by a signal, in January 1952 the North Korean literary magazines published articles by KAPF critics, sounding another warning about the danger of formalism and naturalism. Two such examples were An Ham-gwang's "The Successes of Our Literature in 1951 and Its Future Prospects" (1951 nyŏndo munhak ch'angjo-ŭi sŏnggwa-wa cho'nmang) in *Inmin (People)* and Sin Ko-song's "The Fight against the Remnants of Formalism and Naturalism in North Korean Drama" (Yŏnguk-e issŏsŏ hyŏnsikjuŭi mit chayŏnjuŭijŏk chanjae-waŭi t'ujaeng) in *Munhak yesul*.[97] Both works, along with polite and oblique critical remarks, contained the usual acknowledgment of the merits of the Soviet Korean faction and Yim Hwa.

However, Ŏm's next publication, "The Fight against the Remnants of Formalism and Naturalism in Our Literature" (Uri munhak-e issŏsŏ chayŏnjuŭi-wa hyŏngsikjuŭi chanjae-waŭi t'ujaeng), published in *Nodong sinmun* (17 January 1952), revealed an important change in the atmospherics. Its appearance not in a literary magazine but in the leading Party newspaper carried additional significance.

The title of Ŏm's article sounded quite militant—and so was its content. The author claimed that in pre-Liberation Korea the KAPF writers were the only heroes who had sternly opposed the harmful tendencies of formalism and naturalism that had supposedly been promoted by the adherents of pure literature. He quoted "Marshal Kim," who had stated, "Only after we have destroyed naturalism can we achieve real success in our literature of realism." However, Ŏm indignantly claimed, there were some intellectuals who had dared to ignore Kim Il Sung's admonitions. As examples of such "insidious trends" in literature, Ŏm cited the verse "Where Are You Now?" (which, as we have seen, he praised in *Munye kibon*) and the short story "Honey."

Ŏm's charges are of particular interest to this research. In essence, he accused the writers of making their narration too detailed, of caring about psychological depth (naturalism), and of applying excessively elaborate artistic techniques (formalism). Instead of simple short sentences, Ŏm opined, "some writers" use decadently complicated ones. "Many writers and poets," Ŏm noted, "now indulge their own narrow artistic inclinations and methods and overstress insignificant details in the narration. In fact they turn their works into a training ground for their formalistic exercises."

This article too was written in a vague manner, using veiled statements such as this one: "It would be a slight exaggeration to consider that these harmful tendencies have been overcome in our literature. We have ample grounds to claim that they are still present in the short story 'Honey.'" The names of the authors of the texts discussed were not mentioned. Even so, the political message was clear. Ŏm once again stated that the KAPF was the sole representative of "authentic" realism in colonial Korea—and thus the ex-KAPF faction, as its only true heir, was entitled to define the norms in North Korean literature. Second, by quoting Kim Il Sung, Ŏm claimed support from the supreme authority. And third, by presenting the stylistic elaboration of Yim Hwa and Kim Nam-ch'ŏn's texts as villainous formalism and naturalism, Ŏm tried to deprive his victims of their trump card—their widely acknowledged artistic excellence, the quality that made Kim Nam-ch'ŏn and Yim Hwa popular.

The Soviet Korean faction immediately struck back with a sarcastic article by Ki Sŏk-pok, also published in *Nodong sinmun* (28 February and 1 March 1952). The tone of Ki's article was harsh and more personal. The Soviet Korean journalist attacked his rival from the familiar position of bearer of the more authentic Communist knowledge and experience. He accused Ŏm of poor knowledge of the relevant terminology; according to Ki, Ŏm had misunderstood the difference between naturalism and realism. The most important thing in socialist realism, Ki stressed, was the writer's duty to write about concrete reality in real terms. Referring to the episode that Ŏm considered naturalistic in "Honey"—when the dying soldier is left by his comrade and becomes engulfed in his melancholy thoughts—Ki claimed that in reality such episodes were inescapable during wartime.

Like his opponent, Ki Sŏk-pok tried to appeal to the supreme authority, Kim Il Sung. Ki stated that Ŏm had distorted the "true attitude" of Marshal Kim toward literary criticism and disobeyed his instructions. Marshal Kim had said that "criticism must encourage writers and guarantee good-quality literature," not destroy it, but Ŏm was doing just the opposite. Though Ŏm had the official right to look through literary works before they were published and to correct them, he did not do this; instead, he abused talented writers. All of his accusations confirmed that he did not even read the works properly, Ki claimed. Ŏm's intentions were vicious, Ki concluded, since he not only abused the individuals but also tried to weaken Communist literature, which was "bravely struggling with the enemy." Ki supported his invectives with numerous examples of Soviet practice and theory in literary matters.

The logic of Ki Sŏk-pok's commentary differed little from Ŏm Ho-sŏk's reasoning. Both authors were equally eager to resort to political demagoguery in their attempts to settle scores; both appealed to the authorities for support.

This factional clash soon developed into a major discussion, which Yi Chŏl-ju has described in his memoirs. According to his account, most contemporary writers supported Ki Sŏk-pok: "Of course, 'Honey' was not completely flawless. But most writers agreed that it was impossible to write in accordance with Ŏm Ho-sŏk's unreasonable demands. Ŏm insinuated that by depicting the soldier who abandoned his wounded comrade, Kim Nam-ch'ŏn was abusing the lofty feelings of comradeship-in-arms. Of course, Ŏm was just flattering the Party." In response to accusations by Ŏm of "excessively lyrical thoughts" before the soldier's death and "cheap sentimentalism," which, Ŏm claimed, the Communist protagonist should not allow himself, Yi stressed: "It is just normal human psychology. Ki Sŏk-pok was completely correct when he affirmed that such episodes were unavoidable on the battlefield." Yi pinpointed the inner motives of Ŏm's attacks: "What Ŏm wanted to say is that the protagonist on his very deathbed must glorify the Party and Kim Il Sung, not think about himself. . . . In fact this statement is nothing but shameless flattery of the Party."[98] Yi noted that Ŏm's attack had nothing to do with the objective search for truth: "If the wounded soldier had continued to fulfill his duty and died, Ŏm would probably blame Kim Nam-ch'ŏn for that outcome [as well]."[99]

With respect to Yim Hwa's poems, the other object of critical attack, Yi Chŏl-ju admitted that he had read only some parts of the anthology. Yet Yi was convinced that the attack on Yim was unjustified: "Yim Hwa was an executive of the Communist Party and a distinguished writer who upheld the revolutionary tradition. There was no reason for him to write a reactionary poem. . . . Besides, he himself, from time immemorial, was fervently opposed to 'pure lyrical' poetry." Yi also dismissed as absurd Ŏm's claims that Yim Hwa's portrayal of his female protagonist, a mother who worried about her frontline soldier son, was unrealistic or atypical.[100]

Ki Sŏk-pok's prompt response caused Han's faction to back off for a while. According to Yi Chŏl-ju, the writers who had been accused "behaved quite confidently."[101] For about a year the KAPF faction avoided open attacks. Ŏm Ho-sŏk wrote a very positive article, "Our Literature in the Period of the War for the Liberation of the Motherland" (Choguk haebang chŏnjaeng sigi-ŭi uri munhak), in which he again cited Yim Hwa among the "patriotic poets."[102] In response, Ki Sŏk-pok published a short article in the same *Inmin* magazine and with an almost identical title, "War for the Liberation of the Motherland and Our Literature" (Choguk haebang chŏnjaeng-kwa uri munhak). In this article, Ki supported Ŏm's positive evaluation of Yim Hwa and praised a number of writers from the rival KAPF faction, including Yi Puk-myŏng, Yi Ki-yŏng, Hong Sun-ch'ŏl, Song Yŏng, and Han Sŏr-ya. However, the focus of Ki's article was on the recently deceased Soviet Korean poet Cho Ki-ch'ŏn, apparently with the aim of representing him as a founding father of North Korean literature.[103]

The critiques written by the other members of Han Sŏr-ya's circle in late 1952 and early 1953 were similarly serene. In an article published in *Munhak yesul* in June 1952, Han Hyo approvingly mentioned Kim Nam-ch'ŏn and Yim Hwa as the exemplary representatives of progressive KAPF literature.[104] The collection of articles *Literary Theory for Young People* (Ch'ŏngnyŏntŭl wihan munhakron; 1952), which included the works of An Ham-gwang, Ŏm Ho-sŏk, and Han Hyo, contained only a few vague references to "the danger of naturalism";[105] a carefully worded injunction on "the necessity to depict heroes dialectically" and not as isolated heroes, as "our writers sometimes do";[106] and oblique sentiments about "some writers who do not pay enough attention to the connection of the hero with reality."[107]

Interestingly enough, Ŏm Ho-sŏk, in his article in this collection, praised Yim Hwa with particular eloquence. Unlike Han Hyo, who simply mentioned Yim Hwa and Kim Nam-ch'ŏn several times in a positive manner as the founding fathers of the KAPF and "the most talented writers of our day,"[108] Ŏm extravagantly praised the very poet whom he had so recently criticized. Ŏm compared the "beautiful images" of Yim Hwa's verses to those of Shakespeare:

> These perfect verses depict the beautiful experiences of the poet. . . . Despite the hatred a soldier feels toward the enemy, the protagonist is as steady as a rock or as iron and is unable to forget the villagers from his hometown, his mother, and the years of his childhood. The wind inspires his song and his strong feelings. . . . Like Cho Ki-ch'ŏn, Yim Hwa recollects the past. But it is not Korea's past; it is his own past. His lyrical poem depicts the brilliant reality of life.[109]

It is hard to believe that the poem described by Ŏm in such a complimentary way is the same "Carry, Wind!" that he had excoriated only a few months before.

This newfound harmony in the North Korean literary world did not last long, however. Signs of ongoing problems reappeared in Ŏm Ho-Sŏk's November 1952 article, "New Signs of Literary Development" (Munhak paljŏn-ŭi saeroun chingjo), in which, among other oblique remarks, the straw man of formalism emerged again.[110] This time Ŏm included some other writers on his list of formalists (notably, two people close to Han Sŏr-ya—Pak Un-gŏl and Cho Pyŏk-am), but in general his critical statements were relatively polite. The article did not negatively refer to any Soviet Koreans or non-KAPF Southerners negatively. However, the reopening of the discussion was a sign of things to come. Among numerous positive examples, the article surprisingly failed to mention Yim Hwa—an ominous sign after all the compliments Ŏm had lavished on the poet a few months earlier.

The new attack on Yim Hwa was prompted by a dramatic reversal of political fortunes in the upper echelons of the Pyongyang government. By the end of 1952 the major protectors of Yim Hwa, the officials from the Domestic faction, were on the verge of a fall. According to Scalapino and Lee, in autumn 1952 Yim Hwa was the first Southerner to be arrested; the alleged reason for his arrest for "anti-Communist thoughts" was the poem that contained the lines: "Forests were set on fire; houses were burned. If Stalin comes to Korea, there is no house to put him up for the night." Scalapino and Lee also report that Yim's arrest was soon followed by that of his friend Kim Nam-ch'ŏn.[111] However, newly available archive materials contradict some of the details of this version of events. The record of a conversation between the first secretary of the Soviet embassy in Pyongyang (V. A. Vasiukevich) and the secretary of the Central Committee of the KWP (Pak Ch'ang-ok) on 4 April 1953 indirectly demonstrates that the actual arrests of the Southerners did not begin before the late winter or early spring of 1953.[112] This was a time when the Korean War was coming to an end and the importance of the personal contacts between the Domestic faction and the South Korean Communist underground had diminished. Before then, Kim Il Sung still valued those connections and did not arrest or officially accuse Yim Hwa or Kim Nam-ch'ŏn; that was why Ŏm Ho-Sŏk's article of 15 September 1952, published in *Munhak yesul,* was relatively neutral. Also, the accusations that were finally leveled at Yim Hwa during the show trial of the Southerners in August 1953 were much more serious than simply "anti-Communist thoughts"; planning a coup, sabotaging the Communist movement in the South, and cooperating with the Japanese police during the occupation and espionage on behalf of the United States were among the charges.[113]

The Fifth Plenum of the KWP Central Committee on 15 December 1952, at which Kim Il Sung made a speech denouncing anti-Party elements and factionalists, became a signal for the critics to intensify their attacks on the Southerners. Yet Han's people had to be careful not to cross the line, since Kim's harangues, though obviously directed against the Domestic faction, did not mention particular names yet. Brian Myers has stated that until February 1953, when Pak Hŏng-yŏng was arrested, Yim Hwa and Kim Nam-ch'ŏn "were referred to vaguely as 'reactionary elements.'"[114] According to archival materials, however, the timing was slightly different: in April 1953 Pak had been dismissed from his high official positions of minister of foreign affairs and deputy chairman of the Cabinet of Ministers but not yet been arrested.[115]

Han Hyo's "Korean Literature in Struggle with Naturalism" (Chayŏnjuŭi-rŭl pandaehanŭn t'ujaeng-e issŏsŏŭi chosŏn munhak), which was serialized in *Munhak yesul* from January to April 1953, may indirectly indicate that the attack against the Domestic faction began in earnest around March 1953.[116] Han's work, especially when read as one piece, demonstrates a striking lack of consistency; its first and last parts differ markedly in their approach to the same literary figures. In the part published in January 1953 Yim Hwa, along with the "correct" writers, is politely referred to as "Comrade Yim Hwa," even though he is accused of some "theoretical mistakes."[117] The March and April installments of the article, however, were filled with fierce and extremely insulting political accusations against Yim, who was no longer politely referred to as a comrade. The content of these sections also strikingly contradicted the works that Han had written just a year earlier—"Socialist Realism and Korean Literature," "The New Successes of Our Literature," and "The Conditions for the Emergence of Socialist Realism in Korean Literature and the Characteristics of Its Development."[118] In previous works, Han Hyo had extolled Yim Hwa and Kim Nam-ch'ŏn as the founding fathers of the KAPF and the most distinguished contemporary writers in Korea; in 1953 he refers to Yim Hwa as a renegade of the KAPF: "Yim Hwa followed the course of revising socialist realism. This was a deliberate reactionary attempt to halt the progressive ideological course of KAPF literature, which served the needs of proletarian readers. Yim Hwa's term 'social' in the context of literature was in fact a reactionary facade that covered his actual eagerness to disarm us in the face of the enemy. And we will not excuse this."[119]

What Han Hyo in particular was not going to excuse was the dissatisfaction of Yim Hwa with the aesthetic quality of the KAPF writings, which the poet openly expressed in his critical article before Liberation—a sentiment once shared by the majority of KAPF writers, including Han Hyo himself. In his article "Socialist Realism and Korean Literature," published in 1952, Han acknowledges: "Artistically, young KAPF literature was of extremely poor quality. Despite the great creative will of the writers, they failed to find the proper forms and style."[120] Nonetheless, in 1953, less than a year later, Han had to vigorously deny the existence of the problem. Referring to an old work of Yim Hwa's in which the poet summoned his colleagues not to repeat the mistakes of the early Soviet ultraleftist literary organization RAPP and not to indulge in pure ideology, Han exclaims: "It is completely senseless to talk about *any* mistakes of the KAPF and its literature. . . . If, as Yim Hwa claims, the KAPF allegedly made RAPP-like mistakes, how can he explain the undeniable artistic success of KAPF literature?"[121] According to the recollections of Chŏng Ryul, it was at about this time that any parallels between the KAPF and RAPP (which was the KAPF's direct prototype) disappeared from the North Korean political discourse.

Han Hyo also insists that "Kim Nam-ch'ŏn observes our gigantic reality from some aloof position somewhere 'high above' and refuses to enter the world of the deep feelings of our people." Han accuses the writer of taking an "anti-people," reactionary position and of conveying "fear and hatred of reality," which supposedly had its roots in Kim's pre-Liberation activities.[122] Yim Hwa was dangerously wrong, Han Hyo proclaims, when he equated Kim Nam-ch'ŏn's pre-Liberation novel *Big River* with the works of the real KAPF heroes such as Han Sŏr-ya's "Tower" (T'ap) and Yi Ki-yŏng's *Spring (Pom);* characteristically, the critic fails to notice Han Sŏr-ya's loving descriptions of the caring and fearless Japanese soldiers in "Tower."[123] Han Hyo deftly manages to forget that he, along with Ŏm Ho-sŏk, had just one year earlier highly praised Kim Nam-ch'ŏn's work in exactly the same terms as Yim Hwa's.

For the moment the target of the critical attacks was the South Koreans. Obviously, Kim Il Sung felt that the time was not yet ripe for an offensive against the Soviet faction, and the critics behaved accordingly. In an article written in January–April 1953, Han Hyo mentioned Ki Sŏk-pok, a Soviet Korean, as an ally in the righteous fight against the "reactionary writers of South Korea."[124]

After Yim Hwa and Kim Nam-ch'ŏn were prosecuted in August 1953, the critics started the "victory dance" over Yim Hwa and Kim Nam-ch'ŏn's bodies (to borrow Myers' metaphor).[125] Simultaneously, Yi T'ae-jun became the subject of critical attacks, as discussed in chapter 4.

One of the most vigorous victory dancers was Hong Sung-ch'ŏl, Han Sŏr-ya's obedient crony. Known as a Japanophile mining agent before Liberation,[126] Hong is commonly referred to as a person whose extreme vulgarity and immorality set him apart even from the other unscrupulous members of Han's inner circle.[127] The arrest of Kim Nam-ch'ŏn left the position of KFLA secretary vacant, and the intervention of its chairman Han Sŏr-ya granted this post to the highly unpopular Hong.[128] Hong enthusiastically joined the chorus of condemnation with particularly insulting diatribes:

> Soon after Liberation Yim Hwa wrote the article "The Conception of National Literature," in which he stated that "the remnants of feudalism and Japanese militarism" tend to be the most important obstacle facing contemporary Korean literature. . . . What Yim Hwa in fact wants is to destroy the socialist realist literature and to replace it with bourgeois literature. The dirty traitor of the Korean people and the nasty defector from the KAPF, Yim Hwa, understands that he cannot deserve the forgiveness of the Korean people and of the writers of the KAPF. So he just strives to oppose literature that serves the people. . . . He viciously denies the tendency of realism in our literature and zealously works toward the distortion of the principle of socialist realism.[129]

> Casting aside his last remaining human shame, in 1952 Yim Hwa published his false work "Korean Literature," in which he presented himself as the creator of Korean literature. He arrogantly tried to cover his sins of turning the KAPF over to the hands of the Japanese police and to excuse his nasty behavior. He maliciously reckoned the role of the KAPF to be low; he is killing the tradition of socialist realism in Korean literature.[130]

> Kim Nam-ch'ŏn is a spiteful traitor to the KAPF. His pre-Liberation works are all about the lives of drunkards and *kisaeng;* they are all empty and full of moral degradation. His post-Liberation works are very few, but they are also vile because they paralyze the fighting will of the Korean people. . . . In his "Honey," Kim Nam-ch'ŏn merely observes the fight of the Korean people with an air of aloofness, as if it was something distant and irrelevant. This work serves the interests of the American imperialists.[131]

The other critics were not slow to follow Hong Sung-ch'ŏl. Here are a few quotes from Ŏm Ho-sŏk's 1953 article "Problems of the Image of the Working Class and Aesthetics":

Before Liberation, Kim Nam-ch'ŏn, armed with a reactionary ideology, embodied it in some dull, ordinary images, which he tried to insinuate onto the Korean people. Animal instincts, bourgeois decadence, and conscious hatred of the working class and their achievements were typical of his writings. . . . Yim Hwa wrote reactionary works that depicted the fight of the Korean working class as pointless. . . . It is not accidental that there is pessimism in the demeanor of Kim Nam-ch'ŏn and Yim Hwa. They just do not see the reason for optimism. Everyone knows that pessimism permeates all the writings of Yim Hwa, an American spy. It is not even necessary to explain this. But the worst thing is that the pessimism of this insignificant malcontent does not come from his nature. It is not the result of a melancholic mind or a part of his literary style. It is a part of his reactionary bourgeois ideas.[132]

These statements are remarkable for their demagoguery. The terms "pessimism" and "decadence" were applicable to nearly all pre-Liberation Korean novelists, including the much praised proletarian writers Yi Ki-yŏng and Han Sŏr-ya. The allegedly "dull" pre-Liberation writings of Yim Hwa and Kim Nam-ch'ŏng had enjoyed a degree of popularity that proved to be inaccessible to Han Sŏr-ya. Hysterical, abusive expressions like "insignificant malcontent," "American spy," "spiteful traitor," "bourgeois decadence," and "animal instincts" surely indicated that North Korean literary criticism had totally split from the realm of culture and turned into an instrument of the witch hunt.

At the same time, the critics continued their search for more and more fantastic similes with which to glorify the KAPF. From 1953 the KAPF faction members began to be promoted by any and every means, including the most blatant falsifications.[133] For example, one passage in Ŏm Ho-sŏk's "Problems of the Image of the Working Class and Aesthetics" contains at least three distortions: "All the heroes of the KAPF writers are progressive workers" (there were practically no proletarian heroes in the works of the KAPF writers; most protagonists were petty intellectuals); "distinguished proletarian works such as Yi Ki-yŏng's 'Paper Factory Village' and Han Sŏr-ya's 'Prime of Youth'" (in 1937 Han had apologized to his readers for the "emptiness" of "Prime of Youth," a harmless love story written during his apostasy period);[134] "the KAPF writers did not succumb under the pressure of the Japanese"[135] (all KAPF writers collaborated with the colonial authorities).[136]

Soviet Koreans under Fire

Though in 1953 Yim Hwa and Kim Nam-ch'ŏn were purged and disappeared from the cultural scene, the story did not end there. In 1955 the campaign against disgraced writers took another form.[137] Now Kim Il Sung launched an open attack against the Soviet Koreans.

Although Andrei Lankov has argued that early signs of the impending attack on the Soviet Koreans can be traced to as early as 1954,[138] Chŏng Ryul insists that the first assault on the Soviet Koreans in late 1955 came as a complete surprise. In the summer of 1955, just before the purges began, Chŏng, then one of the most prominent Soviet Korean literary officials, was sufficiently relaxed to undertake an entertaining trip to the USSR with a group of Korean artists in order to participate in the celebration of the tenth anniversary of the Liberation of Korea. During the Korean group's performances he met with his Soviet friends, including Anna Akhmatova and Aleksandr Gitovich, who at the time were both actively engaged in translating Korean poetry. Yet, as soon as he returned to Pyongyang, his boss, Hŏ Chŏng-suk, the minister for culture and propaganda, warned him that "the Soviet Koreans have gotten into real trouble." The troubles had indeed begun. Lankov reports that, "as early as August, Kim Il Sung ordered the collection of information critical of the Soviet Korean unofficial leader, Pak Ch'ang-ok, the chairman of the State Planning Committee."[139] In late October 1955, Chŏng Ryul and a few other high-ranking Soviet Korean officials (Pak Ch'ang-ok, Chŏng Tong-hyŏk, and Pak Yŏng-bin among them) were summoned to the personal office of Kim Il Sung, no less, where all the members of the Politburo were gathered. They were accused of "the ill-intentioned propagation of South Korean literature and art, the vicious implantation of foreign artistic standards, and agitation for the reactionary writers of the past."[140] In Chŏng Ryul's words, "propagation" simply meant translation of Soviet literature into Korean—an activity in which Soviet Koreans were indeed active, along with the advocacy of pre-1945 Korean literature, such as Kim So-wŏl's poetry.

Han Sŏr-ya became one of the most zealous prosecutors in the case. He accused the Soviet Koreans of being "too friendly with Yim Hwa, Yi T'ae-jun, and Kim Nam-ch'ŏn" while "despising real proletarian writers." Han publicly recalled an episode when Chŏng Ryul refused to translate one of Han's novels into Russian. Han ascribed Chŏng's reluctance to his loathing of the "truly revolutionary" literature of the KAPF. Chŏng's explanation—that being a native speaker of Korean, not Russian, he had never undertaken literary translation from his native language into Russian and that he only translated in the opposite direction—was in vain. Han, who knew no foreign languages, never forgave Chŏng for this. The story was repeated a few months later when Song Chin-p'a—the chief editor of *New Korea* magazine (an overseas North Korean foreign-language propaganda monthly)—was accused of "being hostile toward Han Sŏr-ya" because Song was allegedly reluctant to publish Han's novel *Taedonggang*.[141]

None of those involved in either episode dared to question the quality of Han Sŏr-ya's works or of the eligibility of Han's texts to represent North Korean literature overseas. Nobody asked why Russian translators of Han's stories, being the most detached in this respect, found it necessary to "adapt" (actually, rewrite) Han Sŏr-ya's works before presenting them to the Soviet readership.[142] Han was never modest enough to ask these questions of himself, and the Great Leader did not care about these issues at all.

During the meeting in October 1955, Kim Il Sung openly supported Han's claims to supreme control over literary matters. He accused the Soviet Koreans of constantly interacting with Yim Hwa, Yi T'ae-jun, and Kim Nam-ch'ŏn to the detriment of contacts with the members of Han's group. Chŏng Ryul admitted to his friendship with the ill-fated writers, saying that they had indeed often met and talked about literature and the arts. At this juncture Kim Il Sung interrupted indignantly: "I ordered Pak Ch'ang-ok to support the KAPF writers, the real proletarians in our literature. Did he inform you about this Party decision?" Chŏng responded that he had heard of this idea but had never perceived it as an order. According to Chŏng, the final document drafted at the meeting stated that "the Soviet Koreans, guided by personal antipathy, viciously ignored the order of Kim Il Sung."[143]

This meeting finally lifted the remaining restrictions that had limited Han Sŏr-ya's domination over North Korean literature. In Chŏng Ryul's view, "it was the point after which the most shameless public promotion of the KAPF was launched."[144] The era of KAPF domination began in 1956 and lasted for the following seven to eight years—until the purge of Han Sŏr-ya led to a new rewriting of Korean literary history. Though the official campaign against the Soviet Korean officials was launched later, in December 1955,[145] in the estimation of Chŏng Ryul, late October 1955 was the moment when Han finally managed to annihilate all his rivals and achieve unchallenged domination of North Korean literary politics.

From then on, the Soviet Koreans were subjected to increasingly humiliating public criticism. A representative example of this situation was the famous speech that Kim Il Sung delivered on 28 December 1955 at a conference of KWP agitators and propagandists. In this speech the Great Leader berated the Soviet Koreans for their numerous "political mistakes" and in particular for the negligence they allegedly demonstrated toward "Korea's truly proletarian writers": "When I asked Pak Ch'ang-ok and his adherents why they stood against the KAPF, they answered that there had been traitors in the KAPF's ranks. Does this mean that the KAPF, whose core constituted such brilliant writers as Han Sŏr-ya and Yi Ki-yŏng, was a senseless organization? We must highly value these people's accomplishments in struggle; we must allow them to play a major role in our literature."[146]

Unlike Yi Ki-yŏng, who, despite being frequently eulogized as a classic KAPF member, kept a low profile during this campaign,[147] Han Sŏr-ya enthusiastically initiated attacks against his now-doomed rivals. He incorporated the names of Yim Hwa and Kim Nam-ch'ŏn into a new picture of treason and subversion, which now came to include the Soviet Koreans as well. Han Sŏr-ya described the situation in a speech that was published in *Chosŏn munhak* in February 1956:

> The purge of the treasonous clique does not put an end to our ideological struggle. The problem is that there are people who have conspired with the reactionary bourgeois ideas of the accomplices of the clique of Pak Hŏng-yŏng and Yi Sŭng-yŏp, Yim Hwa, Kim Nam-ch'ŏn, and Yi T'ae-jun. In the spheres of literature and art, these people stood against the correct policy of our Party and were largely responsible for the situation whereby the venom of incorrect ideology, which was seeded by the clique of Yim Hwa and Yi T'ae-jun, was not eradicated completely.
>
> The first example was Ho Ka-i [a top Party bureaucrat and leader of the Soviet Koreans until 1953], who promoted sectarian anti-Party activity and supported the clique of Yim Hwa in order to satisfy his craving for power and expand his influence on the ideological frontiers of literature and art. Then, after the death of Ho ka-i, it was comrades Pak Ch'ang-ok and Pak Yŏng-bin who did not enforce the essential Party line on the eradication of the evil influence of Ho Ka-i and the clique of Pak Hŏng-yŏng and Yi Sŭng-yŏp, but instead continued Ho Ka-i's strategy of sectarian bureaucratism. The others were comrades Ki Sŏk-pok, Chŏng Tong-hyŏk, and Chŏng Ryul, who caused enormous damage to the Party when instead of encouraging the Party's policy in literature and the arts and on the propaganda front, they supported bourgeois reactionary ideas. Those comrades conspired ideologically with Yim Hwa, Yi T'ae-jun, and Kim Nam-ch'ŏ, and undertook anti-Party actions, attacking writers who were truly loyal to the Party while encouraging Yim Hwa, Yi T'ae-jun, and Kim Nam-ch'ŏn.[148]

In the same speech, Han Sŏr-ya lavished praise upon the KAPF.

For several months afterward, the image of a dangerous bunch of treasonous outsiders striving to destroy "truly progressive" literature was constantly invoked in the leading literary magazine *Chosŏn munhak.* The March 1956 issue contained an article titled "The Reactionary Essence of Yi T'ae-jun's Literature," in which Ŏm Ho-sŏk represented the purged Soviet Koreans as the depraved supporters of the "reactionary writer."[149] By way of contrast, in the same issue the magazine published an article that extolled Han Sŏr-ya's new novel, *Taedonggang.*[150] In April 1956, *Chosŏn munhak* published an article by Han Sŏr-ya under the title "Our Literature and Arts, Which Are Developing According to the Cultural Policy of Our Party," in which Han repeated the accusations he had made against the Soviet Koreans in the *Chosŏn munhak* piece the previous month.[151] In the May 1956 issue of *Chosŏn munhak* an article by Yun Si-ch'ŏl, titled "The Poison of Reactionary Literature That Slandered the Korean People (Based on the Post-Liberation Works of Kim Nam-ch'ŏn)," was full of extremely harsh abuse of Kim Nam-ch'ŏn as well as his alleged "accomplices," the Soviet Koreans.[152]

Beginning with the June 1956 issue of *Chosŏn munhak,* all accusations of the Soviet Koreans in connection with the out-of-favor writers suddenly ceased. Though the victory dance over the demise of Yim Hwa, Kim Nam-ch'ŏn, and Yi T'ae-jun continued, the Soviet Koreans were temporarily excluded from the scene. Around March 1956, for some political reason, the ongoing anti–Soviet Korean campaign had cooled, and the February issues of *Nodong Sinmun* in 1956 reflected this trend quite quickly.[153] The literary magazine *Choson munhak* responded a little more slowly, presumably because it took more time to transform an accepted manuscript into printed text. The reprieve was short-lived, however. The unsuccessful coup attempt launched by the Soviet and Yan'an factions in August 1956 sparked a revival of the briefly abandoned campaign about treacherous activity instigated by outsiders against the "truly proletarian literature."[154]

Waning of Political Campaigns

In 1957 the list of unmasked villains was supplemented by another member, Hong Sun-ch'ŏl. Hong's behavior and abuse of power in his influential secretarial post in the Writers' Union gave cause for his demotion and expulsion from the union in 1957.[155] Officially, his case was tied to the condemned trio (Yim-Kim-Yi) and the Soviet Koreans. Han Sŏr-ya, striving to distance himself from his now-compromising connection with his supporter, announced in one of his speeches that Hong had only pretended to be a KAPF collaborator; in fact, he had "prospered" under Soviet Korean patronage as a "typical reactionary, anti-Party element" who in cooperation with Yim Hwa, Yi T'ae-jun, and Kim Nam-ch'ŏn had propagated pernicious bourgeois ideas.[156]

The major events in the early history of North Korean literary criticism were reflected later in some peripheral episodes, such as the critical attacks against Ch'oe Myŏng-ik that occurred around the same time.[157] The demagogic logic of the offensives against this respected writer differed little from the cases described above, which suggests that Ch'oe's only fault was his close friendship with Yi T'ae-jun.[158] In any case, Ch'oe was relatively lucky. To my knowledge he was not purged in the 1950s, although he disappeared from the literary scene in the 1960s.

In an ironic twist, Han Sŏr-ya, the initiator of many purges, whose top position at first seemed unshakable, eventually fell victim to a similar campaign. In 1962 it was his turn to be accused of traditionalism and liberalism and subsequently purged. Though Han's demotion was probably welcomed by many of his colleagues, this purge, like the earlier campaign against Hong Sun-ch'ŏl, was anything but a triumph of justice. As with the cases of Yim Hwa and Kim Nam-ch'ŏn, the campaign against Han Sŏr-ya in 1962 was the outcome of successful manipulation arranged by Han's longtime rival Kim Ch'ang-man (who in turn was also purged in the mid-1960s). It was conducted in much the same vein as the campaigns Han himself had waged against his enemies: with outbursts of insulting rhetoric and the extensive use of pseudopolitical labels. Once again it was not literature that was at stake but a lucrative place in the official bureaucracy.

In the 1960s the noisy political campaigns in the North Korean literary world began to wane. This change was a reflection of the general political situation in the country, which became quite stable after Kim Il Sung had destroyed his rivals one by one and established absolute supremacy in North Korean politics. As a logical result of the end of the faction-based system in politics, the factions in the literary world disappeared as well. To make the North Korean literary world even more evenhanded, in the 1960s top DPRK politicians strongly encouraged "collective authorship," a system according to which literary writings were claimed to be products of unnamed "creative collectives" with no names of individual writers attached to a work. The new situation presupposed neither personal fame nor a public fall from grace for a particular author. All the conflicts in the North Korean literary world, if there were any, were henceforth to be hidden from public view. Under these circumstances, North Korean critics, as attested watchdogs of factional interests and public executioners of political rivals, also lost their significance.

Literary Criticism (1947–1960): The Historical Results

The nascent years of North Korean literary history vividly demonstrated that the real role of North Korean critics was not to assess literary texts, nor even to provide ideological guidance to literature, but to announce the position of officialdom with regard to a particular writer. Literary texts were mere tools in the political games of the time. Quite often the same critic would produce diametrically opposing evaluations of the same work within the space of a few months. A novel lauded one day could be subjected to the most humiliating criticism a year later if the political fortunes of its author began to fade. In most cases these political fortunes were determined by factional clashes within the North Korean power structure. Hence the purge of the South Korean (Domestic) faction in 1952–1954 resulted in the downfall of writers associated with it; the fall of the Soviet Korean bureaucrats after 1956 led to the expulsion of the Soviet Korean writers. Sometimes, as in the cases of Hong Sun-ch'ŏl and Han Sŏr-ya, it was personal conflicts within the literary bureaucracy itself that determined the fate of a writer and his or her works. In all these cases, the critics acted not as judges of literature but as executioners who carried out predetermined sentences against particular individuals. My investigation of almost the complete run of the leading North Korean literary journal, *Chosŏn munhak,* over this period attests that journal was the only existing form of literary criticism at the time. The rigidly controlled North Korean society knew no alternative discourse. How then did a form of criticism that was centered not on literature but on personal and factional gain exert such influence on the North Korean cultural landscape? As would be expected, the constant intimidation did not help North Korean writers in their creative activity. In order to survive, the writers had no choice but to turn their full attention to political games, not to their professional duties. The logical consequence of this state of affairs was the gradual decline in artistic quality of North Korean literature and its transformation into the "great desert of unalleviated mediocrity" (as Scalapino and Lee put it) that we see today.

Conclusion

Soldiers on the Cultural Front versus
Engineers of the Human Soul

FROM ITS INCEPTION, North Korean literature demonstrated not only obvious similarities with its acknowledged Soviet prototype but also a number of particular traits that set it apart from the practice and traditions accepted in the Soviet Union. Let us reconsider these commonalties and specifics of North Korea's literature in comparison with the Soviet model.

When the Communist regime was inaugurated in North Korea, Korea had no established Communist intellectual tradition. Though the colonial period was marked by the emergence of leftist rhetoric in Korean literature and the arts, leftist Korean intellectuals could hardly be defined as orthodox Communist. Rather, the writings of "proletarian" Korean writers reflected the general social concerns of contemporary Korean literature. Their texts included antimodernist lamentations over the "lost paradise" of the traditional way of life, embarrassment over the backwardness of their native land, disappointment about the supposed moral degradation of Korean society, grief about the powerlessness of Korean intellectuals, and the like. As we have seen from the examples of Yi Ki-yŏng and Yi T'ae-jun—who are usually perceived as typical representatives of opposing camps in the North Korean intellectual world, a "proletarian writer" and a "purist," respectively—the commonalities in their pre-Liberation writings were more obvious than their differences. It is worth noting that formal adherence to the radical program of the KAPF barely changed the values of Yi Ki-yŏng, who, despite his self-description as a proletarian writer, largely remained a "peasant writer," predisposed to traditionalist sentiment and a gross idealization of premodern rural life. One important factor was that in the late 1930s and early 1940s practically every Korean writer of significance was somehow involved in collaboration with the colonial authorities, and the self-proclaimed proletarian writers of the KAPF were no exception.

Thus the pre-Liberation Korean literary world had neither a comprehensive tradition of creative activity driven by leftist beliefs nor the experience of acting in accordance with the steady program of an influential political organization. Under these circumstances it was only logical that the newly born

North Korean Communist regime decided to "learn from the Soviets" and adopted the theory and practice of Soviet "socialist realism" as a political and artistic strategy. The Soviets, pursuing their own political objectives, eagerly provided support and practical guidance to their "younger brothers in socialism." Through various channels of influence—such as orchestrated excursions to the USSR, large-scale translations of Soviet literature, and the activity of Soviet Koreans as living carriers of Soviet values—the Stalinist principles of managing culture and intellectuals permeated the North Korean literary and political world. The Soviet Stalinist model promoted specific artistic images and sets of social idylls that corresponded with the general propagandistic idea of a "socialist paradise." The Soviet experience also demonstrated forms of official control over intellectuals and prescribed the particular mode of behavior of an officially recognized writer.

The Soviet-modeled socialist realist scheme was successfully introduced into the DPRK in 1945–1950. Soviet clichés, artistic images, and "socialist paradise" idylls were quickly absorbed into the North Korean discourse and, with some important alterations, adjusted to the cultural traditions and perspectives of North Korea. This impact proved to be a lasting one. Even the deterioration of Pyongyang's relations with Moscow from the late 1950s onward failed to eradicate these visions from North Korean culture. In fact, the imagery and vocabulary first borrowed in the 1940s still largely define North Korean culture today. Only one pattern totally failed to stand the test of time, that of the teacher/apprentice model of relations between Moscow and Pyongyang and the ritualistic presentation of the Soviet Union as a leader of the Communist world. After the early 1960s this initial approach was replaced by an ethnocentric picture in which North Korea appeared as the sole exemplar to be emulated by an admiring world.

The North Korean literary world readily incorporated Soviet methods of control over intellectuals and evolved its own techniques, such as the distribution of obligatory topics, the implementation of production plans, mandatory tours by the writers to industrial sites, and "brigade methods" in creative writing. With the help of these methods, the North Korean literary cadre was successfully transformed into yet another example of "engineers of the human soul" or, for that matter, "soldiers on the cultural front," with all the usual ramifications of this phenomenon.

The degree of ideological dissent in the activity of the North Korean literary "soldiers" was virtually zero. Close investigation of supposedly heretical texts whose authors were purged for alleged ideological transgressions provides no proof of any ideological defiance. North Korean literature appeared to be remarkably homogeneous in terms of ideological and Party loyalties, and all writers, including the victims of the political campaigns of the 1950s, eagerly responded to Party demands. Both Yi Ki-yŏng and Yi T'ae-jun took pride in their supposed role of educating the people in the Party spirit and enjoyed a material affluence that corresponded to their newly acquired social status.

Thus, for all practical purposes, we may say that the basic social function of the newly born North Korean literature did not differ much from its prototype, the Soviet literature of Stalin's socialist realism era. Yet the literary politics of the DPRK and the USSR revealed some profound disparities that were rooted in the different political conditions and traditions in each country.

Considering the specifics of the North Korean literary world, one must agree with Brian Myers, who has referred to a "patrimonial functioning of cultural apparatus" in the DPRK as a part of the general bureaucratic tradition in which "the first loyalty is to the boss, not to official ideology."[1] This dynamic often interfered with the ideological consistency of North Korean literature, as in the case of Yi Ki-yŏng. Yi tried to present gender issues in *Land* according to the official demand "to extirpate the feudal concept" but was eventually forced to accommodate his vision to the more traditional, patriarchal, and ethnocentric values of the Great Leader.

The patrimonial approach to cultural politics in the DPRK was complicated by factionalism. This meant that an intellectual not only had to follow the orders of his or her superior but also had to choose such a person carefully, taking into account the existence of a number of rival factions. Very often the orders and approaches advocated by various persons in authority contradicted each other, and these contradictions were dictated not by diverging personal visions but by factional considerations or personal rivalry. What on the surface looked like literary discussions in fact reflected the ongoing factional rivalry and power struggle. In the uneasy situation of the late 1940s and early 1950s, even the shrewdest officials occasionally miscalculated. Thus the critic An Ham-gwang in 1948 found himself in a dangerous situation when he followed the orders of his ex-KAPF faction superior and tried to undermine the standing of the Soviet Korean Cho Ki-ch'ŏn by criticizing his poem *Paektu Mountain.* This action clashed with the interests of Kim Il Sung, who was charmed by *Paektu Mountain*'s personal eulogies to himself and did not want to jeopardize the still-vital relations with his Soviet patrons.

The third peculiarity was the special role of literary critics in the DPRK. North Korean literary criticism began under the strong influence of the Soviet political campaigns of the last decade of Stalinism, and it employed similar labels and idioms. However, the campaigns in the DPRK had little to do with literature. The primary concern of North Korean critics was neither the ideological appropriateness nor the artistic quality of a literary work, but the political standing of its author or his or her closeness to the "correct" group or person in authority.

Arbitrariness and double standards deeply permeated the practice of North Korean literary criticism. Totally orthodox writing by Yim Hwa, Yi T'ae-jun, and Kim Nam-ch'ŏn was condemned as reactionary only because the writers were associated with the losing side of the conflict between the Domestic and KAPF factions. The pre-Liberation works of the unlucky trio were constantly criticized for passivity and a melancholic mood, presented as signs of their immanent "bourgeois" inclinations. At the same time, similar expressions of passivity and melancholy in the pre-1945 writings of Han Sŏr-ya and Yi Ki-yŏng, the leaders of the winning KAPF faction, were either ignored or praised as signs of their alleged anti-Japanese disposition. The artistic credentials of Yim Hwa and Yi T'ae-jun were evidenced by the genuine popularity of their work both among the reading public and in literary circles. Yet these achievements were either ignored, brazenly denied, or even criticized as signs of vicious "formalism." At the same time, quite primitive works by KAPF writers, which enjoyed no popularity whatsoever, were extolled as literary masterpieces.

The North Korean critics, most of whom belonged to the KAPF faction, acted as a well-synchronized chorus, eulogizing or vilifying literary works according to changes in the political fortunes of an author. The appearance of one criticized work was the unmistakable harbinger of a coming defamation campaign against a particular writer. During such a campaign, all his or her writings, including those that may have been officially praised only a few months earlier by the same critics, would be condemned. Thus, rather than conducting literary analysis and providing authors with particular aesthetic or ideological guidance, North Korea's critics played the role of political executioners.

If we compare the North Korean peculiarities with the state of affairs in Stalin's USSR, we will notice that the atmosphere in Soviet literature, while also being far from relaxed, was nonetheless ruled by more predictable dicta. This was a reflection of the different political situation in the USSR and, paradoxically, of the more active involvement of the Soviet dictator in artistic matters.

In Stalin's USSR, literature was under the personal control and patronage of the Soviet "Great Leader." Stalin was inspired by the model of tsarist

Russia, and in literary matters he often followed the old pattern of the tsar who acted as the supreme censor—to the extent that he, like the Russian tsar Nicholas I, often took pains to analyze some literary works personally and offered technical advice to the authors.[2] In addition to political considerations, there may have been personal reasons for this involvement: Stalin, a promising poet in his youth, enjoyed high-quality literature and art. Kim Il Sung, in contrast, showed no personal interest in literature and was never known as an avid reader.

Stalin's guidance in literary matters could hardly be defined as patrimonial. The Soviet "father of socialist realism" established a set of taboos and norms for Soviet authors. The norms could change according to the political situation,[3] but in general these prescriptions were commonly known and understood. Violators would be immediately spotted, punished, and/or forced to correct their "mistakes," no matter what position they held in the official hierarchy at the time. Even the most established Soviet writers such as Ehrenburg, Fadeev, or Sholokhov were at various times forced to "improve" their works that had been deemed as deviating from the established set of requirements. Neither personal considerations nor other secondary preferences played a major role in the evaluation of a particular author. Campaigns against intellectuals in Stalinist USSR were aimed mainly at unorthodox literary writings whose authors somehow dissented from the common ideological norms or prescriptions, the critical campaign against Zoshchenko and Akhmatova in 1946 being quite typical in this regard.

Stalin often demonstrated exemplary objectivity while judging writers; his personal sympathies and antipathies were hardly relevant when it came to his assessment of literature. No matter how much the Soviet dictator personally disliked Demian Bednyi, he still supported the poet as "necessary"— that is, until the moment Bednyi's works came to contradict the resurrected "Russian idea" of Stalinist literature and the arts.[4] On the other hand, Stalin could sympathize with Mikhail Bulgakov and even personally intervened to provide the blatantly non-Communist author with some income, but this did not facilitate the publication of the works of this writer whose activity was too obviously incongruent with the ideological and political norms of the regime. Unlike the DPRK literary world, where the officially propagated principles faded before the caprice of a superior, the Soviet cultural environment had rules, both spoken and unspoken, that were meant to be mandatory for everybody. As far as we can judge, the situation in China was similar to the Soviet one—D. E. Pollard, for instance, has identified a set of particular common taboos in Chinese literature of the Cultural Revolution period.[5] At the same time, it is hard to imagine in the Soviet literary world a situation like the "Ŭnghyang incident," in which the rain of critical wrath poured down on both the just and the unjust and all the writings in this ill-fated anthology were equally condemned, despite the obvious differences in their ideological messages and artistic imagery.

Unlike in the DPRK, attacks on politically deviant intellectuals in the USSR were rarely driven by factional considerations. Factionalism in literary affairs barely existed in the USSR after the mid-1930s, and all attempts to create coalitions inside the Soviet Writers' Union were spotted and promptly suppressed by Stalin or his trusted lieutenants.[6]

Literary critics in the USSR were less prominent, and their activities were mainly confined to their professional function as literary analysts. Soviet literary critics maintained a low profile in purely political matters—indeed, too low in some estimations.[7] Stalin, who maintained vigilant personal control over literary matters in the Soviet Union, did not trust intellectuals enough to let them interfere in the substantial matter of ideological control.[8] The purges and defamation campaigns against dissenting artists in Soviet Russia were initiated exclusively by Party leaders and conducted by representatives of the Party's Central Committee, such as Zhdanov, or through anonymous editorials in the Party organ *Pravda* and public speeches by Party officials. Literary critics played no greater part in the campaign than that of "representatives of the indignant masses"—workers, peasants, or intellectuals who signed "letters of protest" written by Party committees or delivered speeches at prearranged political meetings.[9] Critics in the USSR merely supported the accusations that were initially leveled at writers by members of the Party bureaucracy, whereas published critiques in North Korea usually signaled the beginning of purges.

In fact, on the rare occasions when Soviet literary critics tried to assume more influence over literary politics, they were promptly stopped. The fates of two notorious literary organizations, Proletkult (Proletarian Culture) and RAPP (Russian Association of Proletarian Writers), were characteristic in this regard. The leaders of these organizations, which launched a number of witch hunts in the 1920s, often tried to present themselves as full representatives of the Party and emphasized their closeness to the Soviet nomenclature. However, they were never officially recognized in that capacity. The attempts of these radical groups to usurp power in the literary world proved to be short-lived. Both organizations were disbanded by the authorities (Proletkult in the mid-1920s and RAPP in 1932), after which the Party bureaucracy established its supreme control over literary matters in Russia.[10]

Thus, there were significant differences in the way the Soviet engineers of the human soul and the North Korean soldiers on the cultural front conducted their activities. Certainly the creative activity of the "engineers" was seriously restricted by the ideological and social regulations and aesthetic taboos of Soviet socialist realism, yet these regulations were mostly predictable and some free space remained for a writer to express himself or herself. In comparison, the activity of the "soldiers" was subjected primarily not to common restrictions but to the chaotic whims of the political climate that could in an instant alter the status of a particular work or the fate of a writer.

An unfortunate consequence of this political situation in North Korea was the steep decline in the quality of its literature, since North Korean writers had to concentrate more on factional relationships and jockeying for official positions than on their professional performance. At least some writers, if not many, may also have become reluctant to sharpen their literary abilities or demonstrate any special talents for fear of rising above the mediocre, in particular rising above the level of Han Sŏr-ya, whose position as a living classic and omnipotent literary boss had been cemented by the campaigns of 1953–1956.

North Korean writers may even have found artistic refinements to be somehow incompatible with the necessity to propagate the constricted Party line. Indeed, any excessive "decorating of the knife's handle" could turn into a dangerous pastime when a writer became involved in propagandistic activities in a Stalinist society. As the American scholar of Chinese literature T. A. Hsia pointed out, even if a writer remains a sincere devotee of the Communist ideology, his dedication to art inevitably leads him to stray from the strict ideological instructions. Hsia made the following perceptive remark after analyzing the cases of Chinese Communist novelists Zhou Libo, Wu Qiang, Yang Mo, and others whose works (much like Sholokhov's) were intended to be propagandistic but also had many other, sometimes anti-Communist layers:

> When a writer persists in reducing his personal study of life to words, he is deviating from ideology. . . . His narration which, by the force of political reality, has to satisfy the demands of ideology, but which, owing to his own ambition, has now also to satisfy the demands of art, will eventually burst out of the bounds of the formula within which he would otherwise live happily. He has swallowed a monster, which is art. His book will be kicking with the life beyond the control of ideology.[11]

Established North Korean writers might instinctively have felt this danger, and the unique political environment in their literary arena strongly discouraged them from swallowing the monster that is art. So they produced writings of dull images, stereotyped story lines, and lifeless language, in order to live happily ever after. The near-complete absence of readership attention to these writings in South Korea, despite the leftist sympathies of many South Korean intellectuals, may serve as a proof of this literature's artistic deficiencies.

An important caveat is necessary here, however. I would like to stress that all of the above is applicable only to the published North Korean texts. We have no information about underground literature, which possibly exists in some form in North Korea despite the rigid control. As for the fate of North Korean culture as a whole, it should be noted that the remarkable decline in the quality of officially recognized writing did not irreversibly desolate the North Korean cultural soil. Among other invigorating cultural sources that may be mentioned are the translated works of Russian, Soviet, Western, and Chinese literature, which were prohibited in the mid-1960s but have, since the early 1980s, begun to reappear in DPRK bookshops. Meanwhile, premodern Korean literature, which has remained at least partially available throughout DPRK history, has also been a great source of education, entertainment, and hope to the long-suffering North Korean reader.

Notes

Introduction

1. Robert A. Scalapino and Chong-sik Lee, *Communism in Korea* (Berkeley and Los Angeles: University of California Press, 1972), 890.

2. Describing the late 1940s–early 1950s, Scalapino and Lee noted that "in cultural as well as in political terms, this was the Soviet era, with Russian literature, Russian movies, and the Russian language featured everywhere." Ibid., 375.

3. Regarding the "patrimonial functioning" of Korea's cultural administration, see Brian Myers, *Han Sŏr-ya and North Korean Literature: The Failure of Socialist Realism in the DPRK* (Ithaca, NY: East Asia Program, Cornell University, 1994), 1–2. Myers uses the term "patrimonialism" in accordance with the model presented by sociologist Norman Jacobs in *The Korean Road to Modernization and Development* (Urbana and Chicago: University of Illinois Press, 1985). Describing Korean society as "patrimonial," Jacobs explains that in Korea "the right to authority is determined primarily by moral-intellectual considerations, monopolized by a self-asserted elite and validated by the dissemination of moral service (termed prebends) in the society through political means by that elite" (Jacobs, *Korean Road*, 1–2). Jacobs explains that, in Korea's patrimonial bureaucracy, devotion to ideology has rarely been able to overcome parochial loyalties, and Korean patrimonial allegiance is to superiors, not to an organization or a task. Jacobs, *Korean Road*, 18–19, cited in Myers, *Han Sŏr-ya*, 2.

4. Chŏng Ryul, interviews, Alma-Ata (Kazakhstan), 9–13 December 2001.

5. Cho Yurii, interviews, Moscow (Russia), October–November 2001.

6. Elena Davydova (Pak Myŏng-sun), telephone interview, Yanji (China), 6 July 2000.

7. Pak Nam-su, *Chŏkch'i 6 nyŏn-ŭi pukhan mundan* (Seoul: Pogosa, 1999); Yi Chŏl-ju, *Puk-ŭi yesurin* (Seoul: Kyemongsa, 1966).

8. See, for instance, Kim Chae-yong, "Pukhan-ŭi namnodanggye chakka sukch'ŏng," *Yŏksa pip'yŏng* 27 (Winter 1994): 328–364.

9. Soviet scholar V. I. Ivanova claimed that political censorship in academic studies on North Korean literature appeared excessive even by the notorious standards of the USSR in the late 1950s. Referring to her research on Korean literature in the early 1950s, she said: "It was a nightmare. We had to rewrite and rewrite endlessly in order to pander to all the necessary political emphases of the moment" (V. I. Ivanova, telephone interview, Moscow, 3 February 2002). According to senior Soviet scholar

Leo R. Kontsevich, there always existed a palpable disagreement between most Soviet Koreanists and the DPRK political line, and some managed to express it through indirect, Aesopian language (Leo R. Kontsevich, telephone interview, Moscow, 10 October 2003).

10. V. I. Ivanova, *Li Gien: Zhizn' i tvorchestvo* (Moscow: Vostochnaia literatura, 1962); V. I. Ivanova, "Sovetskaia literatura v Koree," in *Problemy Dalnego Vostoka,* 1974, no. 3:187–193; V. I. Ivanova, "Sovetskaia voenno-patrioticheskaia literatura v Koree," in *Literatura stran zarubezhnogo vostoka i sovetskaia literatura* (Moscow: Nauka, 1977), 124–138; V. N. Li, "Koreiskaia literatura pervyh let posle osvobozhdeniia (1945–1950)," in *Hudozhestvennyi opyt literatur sotsialisticheskih stran* (Moscow: Nauka, 1967), 339–354; V. N. Li, *Sotsialisticheskii realizm v koreaiskoi literature* (Tashkent: Fan, 1971).

11. Yi Ki-pong, *Puk-ŭi munhak-kwa yesurin* (Seoul: Sasayŏn, 1986).

12. A few examples of the scholarship that particularly impressed me in this regard: Kim Yun-sik, *Yim Hwa yŏngu* (Seoul: Munhwa sasangsa, 1989); Kang Yŏng-ju, *Pyŏkch'o Hong Myŏng-hŭi yŏngu* (Seoul: Ch'angjak-kwa pip'yŏngsa, 1999); Yi Sang-gyŏng, *Yi Ki-yŏng sidae-wa munhak* (Seoul: P'ulpit', 1994).

13. See, for instance, the works of South Korean scholar Na Pyŏng-ch'ŏl, who in his literary studies often resorts to North Korean literary patterns. Na Pyŏng-ch'ŏl, *Sosŏl-ŭi ihae* (Seoul: Munye ch'ulp'ansa, 1998); Na Pyŏng-ch'ŏl, *Munhak-ŭi ihae* (Seoul: Munye ch'ulp'ansa, 1995).

14. Myers, *Han Sŏr-ya,* 9. *Minjung* is a combination of the two Chinese characters *min* (people) and *jung* (the mass). *Minjung* literally means "the mass of the people," or simply "the people." Regarding *minjung,* or "progressive" ideology, see Hahm Chaibong, "The Two South Koreas: A House Divided," *Washington Quarterly* 28, no. 3 (Summer 2005): 57–72.

15. See, for example, Yim Yŏng-t'ae and Ko Yu-han, *Pukhan 50 nyŏnsa* (Seoul: Tŭlnyŏk', 1999), vol. 1; and Sin Hyŏng-gi and O Sŏng-ho, *Pukhan munhaksa* (Seoul: P'yŏngminsa, 2000).

16. This tendency clearly emerged in Kim Yun-sik's *Yim Hwa yŏngu,* which tends to ignore the political constituent in Yim Hwa's activity and presents him exclusively as a highly motivated idealistic poet. See also Kim Chae-yong, *Pukhan munhak-ŭi yŏksajŏk ihae* (Seoul: Munhak-kwa chisŏngsa, 1994); and Ch'oe Ik-hyŏn, "1956 nyŏn 8 wŏl chongp'a sakŏn chŏnhuŭi pukhan munhak chilsŏ," in Yi Myŏng-jae, ed., *Pukhan munhak-ŭi inyŏm-kwa silch'e* (Seoul: Kukhak charyowŏn, 1998), 59–91.

17. Marshall R. Pihl, "Engineers of the Human Soul: North Korean Literature Today," *Korean Studies* 1 (1977): 63–110.

18. Evgenii Gromov, *Stalin: Vlast' i iskusstvo* (Moscow: Pespublika, 1998), 157.

19. Ryu Hun, *Study of North Korea* (Seoul: Research Institute of International and External Affairs, 1966), 287.

20. Abram Terts, "Chto takoe sotsialisticheskii realizm?" in *Fantasticheskii mir Abrama Tartsa* (New York: Inter-Language Literary Associates, 1967), 399–446.

21. George Bisztray, *Marxist Models of Literary Realism* (New York: Columbia University Press, 1978), 48.

22. Gromov, *Stalin,* 155.

23. *Pervyi Vsesoiuznyi s'ezd sovetskih pisatelei, 1934: Stenograficheskii otchet; Prilozheniia* (Moscow: Sovetskii pisatel', 1990), 24.

24. Marc Slonim, *Soviet Russian Literature: Writers and Problems, 1917–1977* (New York: Oxford University Press, 1977), 165.

25. *Bolshaia sovetskaia entsiklopediia,* vol. *Sovetskii Soyuz* (Moscow: Sovetskaia entsiklopediia, 1948), 1472–1475.

26. Ibid., vol. 40 (1957), 181.

27. *Malaia sovetskaia entsiklopediia* (Moscow: Sovetskaia entsiklopediia, 1960), 8:800–801.

28. Mikhail Sholokhov, "Rech' na vruchenii Nobelevskoi premii," *Literaturnaia gazeta,* 14 December 1965, 1.

29. *Sovetskii entsiklopedicheskii slovar',* 4th ed. (Moscow: Sovetskaia entsiklopediia, 1986), 1251.

30. *Kratkaia literaturnaia entsiklopediia* (Moscow: Sovetskaia entsiklopediia, 1972), 97.

31. *Sovetskii entsiklopedicheskii slovar',* 1251.

32. For examples of this perception, see Max Hayward, introduction to Max Hayward and Leopold Labedz, eds., *Literature and Revolution in Soviet Russia, 1917–1962* (London: Oxford University Press, 1963); Geoffrey Hosking, *Beyond Socialist Realism: Soviet Fiction since Ivan Denisovich* (New York: Holmes and Meier, 1980); and Katerina Clark, *The Soviet Novel: History as Ritual* (Chicago: University of Chicago Press, 1981).

33. Slonim, *Soviet Russian Literature,* 168.

34. Clark, *Soviet Novel,* 4, 261–263.

35. Ibid., 60.

36. V. I. Lenin, "Party Organisation and Party Literature," in *Collected Works* (Moscow: Foreign Languages Publishing House, 1962), 10:45.

37. Cited in Bisztray, *Marxist Models of Literary Realism,* 43–45.

38. Pihl, "Engineers of the Human Soul," 77.

39. Terts, "Chto takoe sotsialisticheskii realism?" 399–446.

40. Hayward, introduction, xv.

41. Scalapino and Lee, *Communism in Korea,* 1296.

42. Ibid., 1297.

Chapter 1: "Let Us Learn from the Soviets"

1. Mun Sŏk-u, "Rŏsia sasiljuŭi munhak-ŭi suyong-kwa kŭ hakmunjŏk pyŏnyong, torŭsŭtoi chungsim-ŭro," in Yi Poyŏng et al., eds., *Hangukmunhak sokŭi segye munhak* (Seoul: Kyujanggak, 1998), 214.

2. See Brian Myers, *Han Sŏr-ya and North Korean Literature: The Failure of Socialist*

Realism in the DPRK (Ithaca, NY: East Asia Program, Cornell University, 1994), 16; V. I. Ivanova, *Novaia proza Korei* (Moscow: Nauka, 1987), 133–152; Mun Sŏk-u, "Rŏsia sasiljuǔi munhak-ǔi suyong-kwa kǔ hakmunjŏk pyŏnyong, torǔsŭtoi chungsim-ǔro," in Yi Poyŏng et al., *Hangukmunhak sokǔi segye munhak,* 214.

    3. Ivanova, *Novaia prosa Korei,* 133–152.

    4. V. I. Ivanova, "Sovetskaia literatura v Koree," *Problemy Dalnego Vostoka,* 1974, no. 3:187.

    5. Regarding the particular influence of Gorky on Korean literature, see Mun Sŏk-u, "Tturǔgenep'ǔ-wa Korikki Munhak-ǔi kyŏngu," in Yi Poyŏng et al., *Hangukmunhak sokǔi segye munhak*, 293–335.

    6. Myers, *Han Sŏr-ya,* 16.

    7. Ch'u C'hŏn and Ku An-hwan, *Hanguk myŏgjak tanp'yŏn sosŏl* (Seoul: Chiphyŏnjŏn, 1978), 1:240.

    8. *Chosŏn munhaksa nyŏndaep'yo* (Pyongyang: Kyoyuk tosŏ ch'ulp'ansa, 1957), 82, 84.

    9. Ivanova, "Sovetskaia literatura v Koree," 187.

    10. The term "new tendency" was first used by Yim Chŏng-jae in an article titled "Munsa chegune yohanun ilmun" [One Sentence to Men of Intelligence], published in *Kaebyŏk* 7 (1923), cited in Mun, "Tturǔgenep'ǔ-wa Korikki Munhak-ǔi kyŏngu," 297. For South Korean scholarship's view of the new tendency, see Yun Pyŏng-no, *Hanguk-ǔi hyŏndae chakka chakp'umron* (Seoul: Sŏnggyunkwan taehakkyo ch'ulp'anbu, 1993), 17–18. The North Korean view is represented by Han Hyo, "Chayŏnjuǔi-rǔl pandaehanǔn t'ujaeng-e issŏsŏǔi chosŏn munhak," in Yi Sŏn-yŏng et al., eds., *Hyŏndae munhak pip'yŏng charyo chip 2 (Ibukp'yŏn)* (Seoul: T'aehaksa, 1993), 391–522.

    11. Myers, *Han Sŏr-ya,* 18.

    12. Ch'u and Ku, *Hanguk myŏgjak tanp'yŏn sosŏl,* 1:228–244; *Who's Who in Korean Literature,* published by Korean Culture and Arts Foundation (Seoul: Hollym, 1998), 47–48.

    13. Yi Sang-hwa, "P'okp'ung-ǔl kidarinǔn maǔm," http://www2.knu.ac.kr/~psy/kyngsim/space/exhibit/lee_sw/lsw_frm.htm; Maxim Gorky, "Pesnia o burevestnike," in *Izbrannye proizvedeniia v treh tomah* (Moscow: Gosudarstvennoe izdatel'stvo hudozhestvennoi literatury, 1951), 1:408–409.

    14. Maxim Gorky, "Konovalov," "Foma Gordeev," and "Na dne," in *Izbrannye proizvedeniia v treh tomah,* 2:81–130, 2:144–408, 2:524–591.

    15. Myers, *Han Sŏr-ya,* 19.

    16. Chŏng Ryul, interviews, Alma-ata (Kazakhstan), 9–13 December 2001. Regarding KAPF literature, see Yi Hun, "1930 nyŏndae Yim Hwaǔi munhakron kǔndaesŏng," in *Minjŏk munhak-kwa kǔndaesŏng* (Seoul: Munhak-kwa chisŏngsa, 1995), 407–427.

    17. Myers, *Han Sŏr-ya,* 26.

    18. "Koreiskaia literatura," in *Literaturnaia entsiklopediia* (Moscow: Akademiia nauk, 1931), 5:460–470.

19. Robert A. Scalapino and Chong-sik Lee, *Communism in Korea* (Berkeley and Los Angeles: University of California Press, 1972), 121. Emphasis in original.

20. V. I. Ivanova, *Li Gien: Zhizn' i tvorchestvo* (Moscow: Vostochnaia literatura, 1962), 47.

21. Myers, *Han Sŏr-ya*, 29.

22. As an example of such quarreling groups, many scholars believe that the Chosŏn P'ŭrolletaria Yesul Tongmaeng (Korean Proletarian Art Federation), founded on 17 September 1945 by Han Sŏr-ya and Yi Ki-yŏng, was deliberately set up as a counter to the Chosŏn Munhak Kŏnsŏl Ponbu (Center for the Construction of Korean Literature), which had been established earlier in August by Han's long-term enemies Yim Hwa and Kim Nam-ch'ŏn. Notably, the ideological platforms of both groups did not significantly differ (U Tae-sik, "Haebang hu pukhan mundan-e koch'al," introduction to Pak Nam-su, *Ch'ŏkch'i 6 nyŏn-ŭi pukhan mundan* [Seoul: Pogosa, 1999], 9–14). In March 1951 after the official announcement of the unification of the South Korean Writers organization and the NKFLA, the NKFLA was renamed Chosŏn Munhak Yesul Ch'ong Tongmaeng, or Korean Federation of Literature and Art (KFLA). After the First Congress of Writers and Artists in 1953, the KFLA was dissolved; each of its units became a separate entity. KFLA leadership was transferred to the Writers' Union (WU), whose chairman at the time was Han Sŏr-ya.

23. Cited in Myers, *Han Sŏr-ya*, 42.

24. Andrei Lankov, *From Stalin to Kim Il Sung: The Formation of North Korea, 1945–1960* (New Brunswick, NJ: Rutgers University Press, 2002), 8–9.

25. Kim Il Sung, "Munhwawa yesulŭn Inmin-ŭl wihan kŏsuro toeŏya handa" [Literature and the Arts Must Serve People], in *Kim Il-sung sŏnjip* [Kim Il Sung's Selected Works] (Pyongyang, 1955), 1:96–104, as quoted in Myers, *Han Sŏr-ya*, 43.

26. Pak Chong-sik, "Chosŏn munhak-e issŏsŏŭi ssobet'ŭ munhak-ŭi yŏnghyang," in *Haebang hu 10 nyŏngan-ŭi chosŏn munhak* (Pyongyang: Chosŏn chakka tongmaeng ch'ulp'ansa, 1955), 417. No such statement can be found in the available publications of Kim Il Sung's works. The remarks were most probably deleted from later editions after relations with the USSR soured in the late 1950s.

27. Kim Il Sung, *Sasang saŏp-esŏ kyojojuŭiwa hyŏngsikjuŭi-rŭl t'oejihago chuch'e-rŭl hwangnip hal te taehayŏ* (Pyongyang: Chosŏn nodongdang ch'ulp'ansa, 1960), 6.

28. As the main channels for spreading Soviet cultural influence, Charles Armstrong names the Soviet Information Bureau, the international book agency Mezhdunarodnaia kniga (which distributed Soviet books and journals in Korean translation), the Soviet news agency TASS, and Sovexportfilm, a branch of the Cinema Ministry. See Charles K. Armstrong, *The North Korean Revolution, 1945–1950* (Ithaca, NY, and London: Cornell University Press, 2003), 171. However, there is reason to believe that Mezhdunarodnaia kniga was not the only channel for the distribution of Soviet literature in Pyongyang and that the North Korean state had its own channels. If we consider the numerous Korean translations of Soviet texts that are now kept in the collection of the Russian State Library, it is easy to see that the majority of these

books were translated and published by Korean publishing houses such as Pyongyang kungnip ch'ulp'ansa, Kungnip tosŏ ch'ulp'ansa, Minju ch'ŏngnyŏnsa, Chosso ch'ulp'ansa (Pyongyang), Kyoyuksŏng p'yŏnch'an kwanliguk, Nodongsinmunsa, Chosŏn chakka tongmaeng ch'ulp'ansa, and others.

29. Pak Chong-sik, "Chosŏn munhak-e issŏsŏŭi ssobet'ŭ munhak-ŭi yŏnghyang," 435.

30. Ivanova, "Sovetskaia literatura v Koree," 189; V. I. Ivanova, "Sovetskaia voenno-patrioticheskaia literatura v Koree 40–50 godov," in *Literatura stran zarubezhnogo vostoka i sovetskaia literatura* (Moscow: Nauka, 1977), 129.

31. An Ham-gwang, *Chosŏn munhaksa* (Pyongyang: Kyoyuk tosŏ ch'ulp'ansa, 1956), 346.

32. The publication of this article is specifically mentioned in *Chosŏn munhaksa nyŏndaep'yo*, 105. The name of the magazine, *Cultural Front*, was probably an allusion to Kim Il Sung's above-mentioned speech about "soldiers on the cultural front" in May 1946.

33. Myers, *Han Sŏr-ya*, 45.

34. Ko Il-hwan, "Sobet'ŭ munhak chakp'umesŏ padŭn yŏnghyang-kwa uri munhak-ŭi sŏnggwa," *Munhak yesul*, 1949, no. 10:52–55; Chu Yŏng-bo, "Ssoryŏn yŏnghwanŭn uri yŏnghwachak-ŭi san kyojae-ga toenda," *Munhak yesul* 1949, no. 10:55–59; Sin Ko-song, "Ssobet'ŭ yŏngŭk-esŏ uri-nŭn muŏs-ŭl paeunŭnga?" *Munhak yesul* 1949, no. 10:64–69.

35. An, *Chosŏn munhaksa*, 346.

36. Quoted in Pak Chong-sik, "Chosŏn munhak-e issŏsŏŭi ssobet'ŭ munhak-ŭi yŏnghyang," 438.

37. Pak Chong-sik, "Chosŏn munhak-e issŏsŏŭi ssobet'ŭ munhak-ŭi yŏnghyang," 418.

38. An, *Chosŏn munhaksa*, 346–349; Pak Chong-sik, "Sovremennaia koreiskaia literatura posle osvobozhdenia: Formirovanie i stanovlenie sotsrealisma v koreiskoi literature po tvorchestvu Li Giena" (doctoral thesis, Moscow State University, 1953); Ivanova, "Sovetskaia literatura v Koree"; E. M. Tsoi, "Otrazhenie velikih peremen v koreiskoi derevne v romanah Li Giena" (PhD thesis, Moscow State University, 1955); A. N. Taen, "Ocherki sovremennoi koreiskoi literatury (demokraticheskie natsional'nye tendentsii i sotsialisticheskii realizm v koreiskoi literature)" (PhD thesis, Herzen Pedagogical Institute, Leningrad, 1954); V. N. Li, "Koreiskaia literatura pervyh let posle osvobozhdeniia (1945–1950)," in *Hudozhestvennyi opyt literatur sotsialisticheskih stran* (Moscow: Nauka, 1967). A long list of important "exemplary" Soviet works is given in Pak Chong-sik, "Chosŏn munhak-e issŏsŏŭi ssobet'ŭ munhak-ŭi yŏnghyang," 437–438.

39. Ivanova, "Sovetskaia literatura v Koree," 190.

40. Pak Nam-su, *Chŏkch'i 6 nyŏn pukhan mundan* (Seoul: Pogosa, 1999), 126–136; Chŏng Ryul interviews.

41. Myers, *Han Sŏr-ya*, 89.

42. V. I. Ivanova, "Li Gien i ego roman 'Zemlia,'" in *Kratkie soobscheniia instituta vostokovedeniia*, no. 18 (Moscow: Izdatel'stvo AN SSSR, 1955), 38.

43. V. N. Li, "Koreiskaia literatura pervyh let posle osvobozhdeniia," 345–346.

44. Chŏng Ryul interviews; Pak Nam-su, *Chŏkch'i 6 nyŏn pukhan mundan,* 129–130.

45. Pak Chong-sik, "Chosŏn munhak-e issŏsŏŭi ssobet'ŭ munhak-ŭi yŏnghyang," 436.

46. For an original analysis of North Korean fiction on the theme of Soviet-Korean friendship, see Brian Myers, "Mother Russia: Soviet Characters in North Korean Fiction," *Korean Studies* 16 (1992): 82–93; and Myers, *Han Sŏr-ya,* 67.

47. Yi T'ae-jun, *Ssoryŏn kihaeng* (Pyongyang: Pukchosŏn ch'ulp'ansa, 1947); Yi Ki-yŏng, *Widaehan saenghwal-ŭl ch'angjohanŭn ssoryŏn* (Pyongyang: Chosso munhwahyŏphoe, 1952); Yi Ki-yŏng, *Kongsanjuŭi t'aeyang-ŭn pit'nanda* (Pyongyang: Chosso ch'ulp'ansa, 1954); *K'ŭnak'ŭn uŭi (Ssoryŏn kihaengjip)* (Pyongyang: Chosŏn chakka tongmaeng ch'ulp'ansa, 1954).

48. For an insider's account of the staged Soviet trips in the 1930s, see the memoirs of the established Soviet interpreter Valentin Berezhkov: *Kak ia stal' perevodchikom Stalina* (Moscow: Daem, 1993), 170–185, 235.

49. Sylvia Margulies, *The Pilgrimage to Russia: The Soviet Union and Treatment of Foreigners, 1924–1937* (Madison, Milwaukee, and London: University of Wisconsin Press, 1968), 211.

50. *K'ŭnak'ŭn uŭi,* 143–149.

51. Yi T'ae-jun, *Ssoryŏn kihaeng,* 67.

52. *K'ŭnak'ŭn uŭi,* 44–54.

53. Yi Ki-yŏng, *Kongsanjuŭi t'aeyang-ŭn pit'nanda,* 170–188.

54. Yi Ki-yŏng persistently stressed that "dear Marshal Kim Il Sung" was the very first person who had inspired Koreans "to learn from the USSR." Ibid., 88.

55. Ibid., 210–212. Being the chairman of the Soviet-Korean friendship society and having particularly good relations with his Soviet colleagues, Yi Ki-yŏng enjoyed Soviet hospitality more frequently than other DPRK writers. It cannot be said for sure how often Yi Ki-yŏng visited the USSR during his lifetime, but his collection of Soviet travelogues published in 1960 in Pyongyang refers to four such trips. The first took place in 1946, when Yi headed a delegation of North Korean writers to the USSR. Yi T'ae-jun was a member of this delegation. The second occurred in 1949, when Yi Ki-yŏng received a personal invitation to visit the USSR to take part in the celebration of the 150th anniversary of the birth of Russian classic poet Aleksandr Pushkin. The third time was in 1952, when Yi Ki-yŏng visited the USSR as a representative of North Korean litterateurs to attend the celebration of the 100th anniversary of another classic Russian writer, Nikolai Gogol. On the fourth occasion, Yi Ki-yŏng visited the USSR in 1953–1954 to participate in the celebration of the 36th anniversary of the October Revolution. This trip was the longest, since at this time Yi stayed in a Soviet sanatorium. Yi Ki-yŏng, *Kihaeng munjip* (Pyongyang: Chosŏn chakka tongmaeng ch'ulp'ansa, 1960).

56. Yi T'ae-jun, *Ssoryŏn kihaeng,* 5, 92–93, 122.

57. See Paul Hollander, *Political Pilgrims: Travels of Western Intellectuals to the Soviet Union, China and Cuba, 1928–1978* (New York and Oxford: Oxford University Press, 1981).

58. *K'ŭnak'ŭn uŭi,* 6–8.

59. Ibid., 136–137.

60. Ibid., 170–173.

61. Ibid., 198.

62. Han Sŏr-ya, ed., *Yŏnggwang-ŭi Ssŭttalinege: Ssŭttalin t'ansaeng 70-chunyŏn kinyŏm ch'ulp'ansa* (Pyongyang: Pukchosŏn munhakyesul ch'ongtongmaeng, 1949), 86.

63. Myers, *Han Sŏr-ya,* 70.

64. Han Sŏr-ya, "P'ajeyebŭ-wa na," *Chosŏn munhak,* 1956, no. 8:97–106.

65. *K'ŭnak'ŭn uŭi,* 56, 160, 196–220.

66. Ibid., 55–59.

67. Yi T'ae-jun, *Ssoryŏn kihaeng,* 195–198.

68. *K'ŭnak'ŭn uŭi,* 200.

69. Ibid., 161–162.

70. Ibid., 55–59.

71. For more information about these political campaigns, see Evgenii Gromov, *Stalin: Vlast' i iskusstvo* (Moscow: Pespublika, 1998), 452.

72. Chŏng Ryul, interviews; Yi T'ae-jun, *Ssoryŏn kihaeng,* 123–125. The resolution of the Central Committee of the Soviet Communist Party on 14 August 1946 stated that Akhmatova's verses were "typical representatives of apolitical poetry": "Her verses are soaked with the spirit of pessimism and decadence, frozen in the shape of bourgeois aestheticism and 'art for art's sake' ideologies that are harmful to the education of our youth and cannot be tolerated in our literature." Regarding Akhmatova, see Edward J. Brown, *Russian Literature since the Revolution* (Cambridge, MA, and London: Harvard University Press, 1982), 180–181. Also see *O partiinoi i sovetskoi pechati* (Moscow: Pravda, 1954), 346, quoted in Gromov, *Stalin,* 391.

73. See Aleksandr Nemzer, "Razgromlennyi generalnyi," http://www.ruthenia .ru/nemzer/FAD.html.

74. *K'ŭnak'ŭn uŭi,* 80–86.

75. Chŏng Ryul interviews. Chŏng Ryul recollects that the Soviet Koreans viewed this system somewhat ironically. Cho Ki-ch'ŏn, a Soviet Korean poet, was more positive toward the system, however. For more information concerning Cho Ki-ch'ŏn, see chapter 2.

76. Pak Nam-su, *Chŏk-ch'i 6 nyŏn-ŭi pukhan mundan,* 59.

77. One of the most fervent critics of the "obligatory themes" was the prominent Soviet writer Yurii Olesha. See George Bisztray, *Marxist Models of Literary Realism* (New York: Columbia University Press), 42–43.

78. Konstantin Simonov, *Glazami cheloveka moego pokoleniya: Razmyshleniia o I. V. Staline* (Moscow: Respublika, 1989), 183.

79. Pak Nam-su, *Chŏkch'i 6 nyŏn pukhan mundan,* 126–136.

80. Chŏng Ryul interviews.

81. Ibid.

82. Li Gien (Yi Ki-yŏng), *Sud'ba odnoi zhenshchiny* (Pyongyang: Izdatel'stvo literatury na inostrannyh iazykah, 1964), 8.

83. See these collections of contemporary North Korean literary writings: *Pit'nanŭn rojŏng* (Pyongyang: Munhakyesul chonghap ch'ulp'ansa, 1998); *Yŏngyŏnhan noŭl* (Pyongyang: Munhakyesul chonghap ch'ulp'ansa, 1998); *Pokpadŭn kangsan* (Pyongyang: Kŭmsŏngch'ŏngnyŏn ch'ulp'ansa, 1998).

84. Chŏng Ryul interviews.

85. Han Sŏr-ya, *Yŏnggwang-ŭi Ssŭttalinege.*

86. Min Pyŏng-gyun, "Tu suryŏng," in *K'ŭnak'ŭn uŭi,* 12–14.

87. Min Pyŏng-gyun, "Ŏmŏni," in *K'ŭnak'ŭn uŭi,* 15–18.

88. Yi Ki-yŏng, *Widaehan saenghwal-ŭl ch'angjohanŭn ssoryŏn,* 11–20.

89. *K'ŭnak'ŭn uŭi,* 59–67.

90. Yi Ki-yŏng, *Kongsanjuŭi t'aeyang-ŭn pit'nanda,* 13.

91. Ibid., 158–163.

92. Ibid., 160.

93. The latter cliché was particularly popular in Soviet discourse. See, for example, the contemporary collection of poems by Aleksei Surkov, *Serdtse mira: Stihi o Moskve* (Moscow: Moskovskii rabochii, 1946).

94. Ibid., 8–9.

95. For a discussion of these "new novels," see Ivanova, *Novaia proza Korei;* and Yun Pyŏng-no, *Hanguk-ŭn hyŏndae chakka chakp'umron,* 10–13.

96. Min Pyŏng-gyun, "Leningradesŏ," in *K'ŭnak'ŭn uŭi,* 19–22.

97. Ibid., 97–106.

98. Yi Ki-yŏng, *Kongsanjuŭi t'aeyang-ŭn pit'nanda,* 55–60.

99. Ryu Hŭi-nam, "Han kajŏnge iyagi," *Chosŏn munhak,* 2004, no. 5:26–40. The motto "march of hardships" was created in 1996 in response to the DPRK's dire economic hardships. The Party used the slogan to define the current era of DPRK history, which had begun a few years earlier, thus drawing a parallel with the march of the anti-Japanese guerrilla troops led by Kim Il Sung in 1938–1939 in Manchuria.

100. Ibid., 25.

101. *K'ŭnak'ŭn uŭi,* 69.

102. Cho Ki-ch'ŏn, "Saengae-ŭi Norae," in *Cho Ki-ch'ŏn sŏnjip* (Pyongyang: Munhwa chŏnsŏnsa, 1952), 1:153–360.

103. See Yi Sang-hyŏn's novel *Namyŏnbaek-esŏ on p'yŏnji,* in *Chosŏn munhak,* 1956, no. 4:22–35; and Han Myŏng-ch'ŏn's poem "Pot'ong nodongil," in *Chosŏn munhak,* 1956, no. 2:76–79.

104. Chŏn Kŭm-ok, "Hago ttohago sip'ŭn mal" in *Pit'nanŭn rojŏng,* 169–172. The remark about the sound of a train is especially curious since the North Korean railway network has remained unchanged since the colonial era. Most of the existing

lines were built by the Japanese, and the railway technology has not changed much. See Ch'oe Hyŏn-su, "Pukhan-ŭi ch'ŏldo hyŏnhwang," *Kukmin ilbo,* 19 September 2000, 5.

105. Sŏ Chŏng-in, "Hyŏnsil-ŭl pora!" in *Pit'nanŭn rojŏng,* 100–102. Ch'ongryŏn was a pro–North Korean organization in Japan. For a discussion of its activities, see Sonia Ryang, *North Koreans in Japan: Language, Ideology, and Identity* (Boulder, CO: Westview, 1997).

106. Chŏng Mun-hyang, "Chogukiyŏ kkŭt'ŏmnŭn na-ŭi kippŭmiyŏ," *Chosŏn munhak,* 1956, no. 1:13–15.

107. See Elena Zubkova, *Poslevoennoe sovetskoe obshchestvo: Politika i povsednevnost' 1945–1953* (Moscow: Rosspen, 2000).

108. *K'ŭnak'ŭn uŭi,* 66. In reality, most of the Soviet workers at the time lived in dugouts, barracks, or communal flats with kitchens and toilets shared by a dozen or so families. See Zubkova, *Poslevoennoe sovetskoe obshchestvo,* 55–56; and Bryon MacWilliams, "Communism at Uncomfortably Close Quarters," *Chronicles of Higher Education,* 26 April 2002, A56. Private cars were relatively rare even in the USSR of the late 1980s.

109. Yi Ki-yŏng, *Ttang* (Pyongyang: Chosŏn chakka tongmaeng ch'ulp'ansa, 1955), 343.

110. Kim Ch'ŏl, "Irhagi do chok'ho salgi do chot'ha!" *Chosŏn munhak,* 1956, no. 5:96–99.

111. Ch'ŏn Se-bong, "Sŏkkaeul-ŭi saebom," *Chosŏn munhak,* 1956, no. 6:21–64; Kim Kwang-sŏp, "Pidan," *Chosŏn munhak,* 1956, no. 6:65–67.

112. Ch'oe Ch'ang-man, "Onŭldo ch'ŏngsanbŏl-e kyesine uri suryŏngnim," in *Pit'nanŭn rojŏng,* 107; Kim Ch'ŏl, "Irhagi do chok'ho salgi do chot'ha!" 96–99.

113. Yi Ki-yŏng, *Kongsanjuŭi t'aeyang-ŭn pit'nanda,* 72.

114. Soviet authors, by contrast, tended to stress the simplicity of the food that their heroes enjoyed. See, for instance, Yurii Trifonov, *Studenty,* in *Sobranie sochinenii* (Moscow: Hudozhestvennaia literatura, 1985), 1:68–70, 158, 200.

115. Yi Ki-yŏng, *Ttang* (1955), 100, 200–211, 377–384.

116. See Kim Kap-sik, "1990 nyŏntae 'konanŭi haenggun' kwa 'sŏngunchŏngch'I': Pukhanŭi insikkwa taeŭn," in *Hyŏndaepukhan yŏngu* (2005), 1:9–38; Pang Chŏng-pae, "Pukhan 'sŏngun chŏngch'I' ŭi chŏngch'ichŏk hamŭi," *T'ongil munje yŏng* 25–26 (2003–2004): 143–162.

117. Han Chŏng-gyu, "Chasikdŭr-ege chaju hanŭn mal," in *Pit'nanŭn rojŏng,* 130–132.

118. Yi Ki-yŏng, *Kongsanjuŭi t'aeyang-ŭn pit'nanda,* 23–30.

119. M. B. Smirnov, ed., *Sistema ispravitelno-trudovyh lagerei v SSSR* (Moscow: Zvenia, 1998), 128–130.

120. *K'ŭnak'ŭn uŭi,* 122.

121. Yi Ki-yŏng, *Ttang* (1955), 156–161.

122. Song Yŏng, "Tu ch'ŏnyŏ," *Munhak yesul,* 1953, no. 9:65–79.

123. Kim Myŏng-su, "Uri munhak-e issŏsŏŭi chŏnhyŏng-kwa kaldŭn munje," *Chosŏn munhak,* 1953, no. 11:135–137.

124. Sŏk In-hae, "Maŭl-ŭi nyŏsŏnsaeng," in *Chosŏn munhak,* 1956 no. 8:80–112.

125. Pyŏn Hŭi-gŭn, "Haengbokhan saramdŭl," *Munhak yesul,* 1953, no. 6:75–85.

126. Ibid., 85.

127. Chŏng Ok-sŏn, "Tonggabi," in *Pit'nanŭn rojŏng,* 260.

128. Ryu Hŭi-nam, "Han kajŏnge iyagi."

129. For examples of this tendency, see Yang Chae-mo, "Nop'ŭn mokp'yo," in *Pit'nanŭn rojŏng,* 304–323; Kim Ch'ang-su, "Nae kohyang-ŭi tŭl changmi," *Chosŏn munhak,* 2004, no. 10:44–55; and Kim Kyo-sŏp, "Pot'ong saramtŭr-ŭi iyagi," *Chosŏn munhak,* 2005, no. 34:61–68.

130. The period of 1946–1947 was a time of acute food shortages in the Soviet Union, often described as famine by modern historians of the USSR. See V. F. Zima, *Golod v SSSR 1946–1947 godov: Proishozhdenie i posledstviia* (Moscow: IRI, 1996).

131. Yi Ki-yŏng, *Kongsanjuŭi t'aeyang-ŭn pit'nanda,* 98. Even according to official statistics, 75.8 percent of the Soviet kolkhozes in 1946 provided their members with less than 1 kg of grain per workday and 7.7 percent of kolkhozes paid nothing, leaving their members entirely to their own devices. See Zubkova, *Poslevoennoe sovetskoe obshchestvo,* 61–62. As for the potatoes and other vegetables, in most cases the farmers were supposed to grow these themselves in their tiny backyard patches after a full day's work on the kolkhoz.

132. *K'ŭnak'ŭn uŭi,* 151–152.

133. Ibid., 215.

134. In this regard too, the reality of the Soviet village was very different. In 1949 Olga Berggolts, a Soviet poet who was famous at the time, spent a few weeks in a village located between Moscow and Leningrad (a relatively prosperous part of the country) and wrote in her diary: "The sowing has been transformed into the hardest, almost penal, corvée: the authorities exert great pressure in regard to the time and area [to be sown] while there is nothing to use for plowing—few horses (14 horses for 240 households) and only two tractors. The women used hoes to prepare the fields for wheat. . . . Yesterday I saw women dragging a plow themselves" (cited in Zubkova, *Poslevoennoe sovetskoe obshchestvo,* 69.

135. By spreading this falsehood, Soviet propagandists intended to make parallels between kolkhozes and farmers' cooperatives in capitalist countries—a leitmotif that is also prominent in Sholokhov's *Virgin Land under the Plow* (1932), a Soviet saga of agricultural reform. See Mikhail Sholokhov, *Podniataia tselina* (Moscow: Prosveshchenie, 1973), 123, 221.

136. Yi Ki-yŏng, *Kongsanjuŭi t'aeyang-ŭn pit'nanda,* 101–103.

137. *K'ŭnak'ŭn uŭi,* 215.

138. Yi Ki-yŏng, *Kongsanjuŭi t'aeyang-ŭn pit'nanda,* 104.

139. In reality, it was not the beauty of nature that tied Soviet collective farmers to the rural areas but a strictly enforced system of administrative controls. In Stalin's

time Soviet collective farmers did not have their own ID documents and thus were not able to move freely around the country or get regular employment outside their native village. For more information on the control of population movement in the USSR, see "70-letie sovetskogo pasporta," *Demoscope Weekly*, 2002, no. 93, http://www.demoscope.ru/weekly/2002/093/arxiv01.php.

140. In fact, the reality of the North Korean village in the 1950s was even harsher than that of its Soviet counterpart. In 1956 Yi P'il-gyu, then a prominent North Korean statesman, relates how he described the situation in contemporary villages during a meeting with a senior Soviet diplomat: "Farmers comprise 80 percent of the population of [North] Korea. After Liberation they were offered an excellent opportunity for a better life; however, they remain very poor. The government has been following an incorrect taxation policy. During the past ten years, instead of 23–27 percent tax, they have been taking more than 50 percent from the farmers. Such a policy continues to this day. It is not necessary to recount the methods employed in 1954–1955 to gather taxes. Tax collecting was accompanied by beatings, murders, and arrests. The Party's activities are based on violence, not persuasion. The cooperative movement is based on violence. The workers live poorly; [they] do not have enough grain or soybeans. Intellectuals and students live in difficult conditions." Document kindly provided by Andrei Lankov and quoted at greater length in his *Crisis in North Korea: The Failure of De-Stalinization, 1956* (Honolulu: University of Hawai'i Press, 2004).

141. Ch'ŏn Se-bong, "Sŏkkaeul-ŭi saebom," *Chosŏn munhak,* 1956, no. 6:21–64.

142. Pak Hyo-jun, "So," *Chosŏn munhak,* 1956, no. 3:16–44.

143. Pak Chŏng-ae, "Nae kohyang-ŭi irŭm," in *Yŏngwŏnhan noŭl* (Pyongyang: Munhak yesul chonghap ch'ulp'ansa, 1998), 101–103; Ch'oe Ch'ang-man, "Onŭldo ch'ŏngsanbŏl-e kyesine uri suryŏngnim," in *Pit'nanŭn rojŏng,* 107–109.

144. Chŏng Ok-sŏn, "Tonggabi."

145. Yi Ki-yŏng, *Kongsanjuŭi t'aeyang-ŭn pit'nanda,* 158–163.

146. A *p'yŏng* equals 3.954 square yards.

147. *K'ŭnak'ŭn uŭi,* 133–137.

148. Yi Ki-yŏng, *Kongsanjuŭi t'aeyang-ŭn pit'nanda,* 42. The reality of Soviet student dormitories in the 1940s and 1950s was very different from Yi's description. Separate rooms were a luxury for the majority of the Soviet people, and separate bathrooms and kitchens were an unbelievable extravagance for most Soviet families. Ten to twenty students living in the same room was the norm in most university dormitories at the time. At the highly privileged Moscow State University, the number of students sharing the same room might be smaller. But providing every student with a separate room would have been beyond the means of even the most prestigious Soviet universities of the day. Only foreign students could sometimes enjoy this luxury. Telephone interviews with Valentina Lankova (Moscow, 22 October 2002), Leo R. Kontsevich (Moscow, 3 September 2002), and Valeri and Irina Gabroussenko (Novosibirsk, 5 November 2003), all of whom were students of major Soviet colleges and universities from the late 1940s through the late 1950s.

149. Yi Ki-yŏng, *Kongsanjuŭi t'aeyang-ŭn pit'nanda,* 160.

150. *Cho Ki-ch'ŏn sŏnjip,* 2:69.

151. Concerning this short story, see Myers, *Han Sŏr-ya,* 54–60.

152. K. Lokotkov, *Vernost'* (Novosibirsk: Novosibirskoe knizhnoe izdatel'stvo, 1951); Vadim Ohotnikov, *Dorogi vglub'* (Moscow: Molodaia gvardiia, 1950); Frida Vigdorova, *Moi klass* (Novosibirsk: Novosibirskoe knizhnoe izdatel'stvo, 1951).

153. Han Sŏng-ho, "Ŏksen nalgae," *Chosŏn munhak,* 2005, no. 3:59–72.

154. See, for example, Pyŏn Hŭi-gŭn, "Haengbokhan saramdŭl," 75.

155. Myers, *Han Sŏr-ya,* 38.

156. For a profound study of the early Soviet ethnic minority policy, see Terry Martin, *The Affirmative Action Empire: Nations and Nationalism in the Soviet Union, 1923–1939* (Ithaca, NY: Cornell University Press, 2001).

157. Yi T'ae-jun, *Ssoryŏn kihaeng,* 102, 104, 113–116, 133–136, 191.

158. Yi Ki-yŏng, *Kongsanjuŭi t'aeyang-ŭn pit'nanda,* 12.

159. Min Pyŏng-gyun, "Myŏngnanhan saram," in *K'ŭnak'ŭn uŭi,* 32–35.

160. *K'ŭnak'ŭn uŭi,* 107–124.

161. Ibid., 32–35, 36–39. In reality, red wine is quite rare in this area, where strong distilled liquors have always been much more popular.

162. Yi Ki-yŏng, *Kongsanjuŭi t'aeyang-ŭn pit'nanda,* 103.

163. Ibid., 123.

164. Yi Ki-yŏng, *Widaehan saenghwal-ŭl ch'angjohanŭn ssoryŏn,* 53–63.

165. Ibid., 100–105.

166. *K'ŭnak'ŭn uŭi,* 64.

167. Ibid., 32–35, 36–39.

168. Yi T'ae-jun, "Kogwihan saramdŭl," in *Yi T'ae-jun munhak sŏnjip* (Seoul: Kip'ŭn saem, 1995), 3:147–159.

169. See, for instance, Trifonov, *Studenty,* 40.

170. Han Chŏng-gyu, "Chasikdŭr-ege chaju hanŭn mal," 130–132.

171. Yang Chae-mo, "Nop'ŭn mokp'yo."

172. Yi T'ae-jun, "38 sŏn ŏnŭ chigu-esŏ," in *Yi T'ae-jun munhak sŏnjip,* vol. 3 (1995), 121–129. This work and Yi Ki-yŏng's *Land* are discussed further in the chapters to come.

173. See Brian Myers, "Kim Jong Il Mania: The Depiction of South Korea in Contemporary North Korean Propaganda," in Proceedings of the 2006 international conference "North Korean Strategy and Propaganda," Seoul, 19 May 2006.

174. Sŏk Yu-kyun, "Ryutarŭn p'unggyŏnhwa," *Chosŏn munhak,* 2005, no. 5:44–52; Sŏk Yu-kyun, "Zvezda I mechta: Is dnevnika byvshego uznika yuzhnokoreiskoi tyur'my," *Korea segodnya* (in Russian), 2004, no. 8:37–38; no. 9:36–37; no. 10:42–43.

175. For a discussion of the racist implications of wartime North Korean literature, see the insightful and well-researched account in Myers, *Han Sŏr-ya,* 94–109. Anti-American racism in Yi T'ae-jun's writings is discussed in chapter 4 of this book.

176. Yi Ki-yŏng, *Han nyŏsŏng-ŭi unmyŏng* (Pyongyang: Chosŏn sahoejuŭi nodong ch'ŏngnyŏn ch'ulp'ansa, 1965).

177. Brian Myers even suggests that the anti-Western tendencies in subsequent North Korean literature might be part of Han Sŏr-ya's legacy. See Myers, *Han Sŏr-ya*, 153. *Chuch'e/juche* is an official ideology of the DPRK. The main propagated principle of *chuch'e* is self-reliance. According to Myers, "the word *juche* came into use well before 1945 as the Korean translation of the term 'subject'—as in 'acting force'—that is common in Western philosophical and especially Marxist contexts, e.g. 'The masses are the subject/*juche* of history.' The word derives from the same ideograms (主體) with which 'subject' has always been written in Chinese and Japanese translations of Marxist texts." See Myers, "Ideology as Smokescreen: North Korea's Juche Thought," *Acta Koreana* 11, no. 3 (December 2008): 161–182.

178. Yang Chae-mo, "Nop'ŭn mokp'yo."

179. In 1949, *Sud chesti* (Tribunal of Honor), a film directed by Abram Room that dealt with this theme, was awarded the Stalin prize.

Chapter 2: Soviet Koreans in North Korean Literature

This chapter is based on my 2005 article in *Korean Studies*. See Tatiana Gabroussenko, "Cho Ki-ch'ŏn: The Person behind the Myths," *Korean Studies*, 2005, no. 29:55–95.

1. Soviet Koreans, most of whom were trusted Soviet Party members, often with a good education and useful experiences, arrived in North Korea soon after Liberation and in 1945–1951 "occupied as many as two hundred key posts." See Robert A. Scalapino and Chong-sil Lee, *Communism in Korea* (Berkeley and Los Angeles: University of California Press, 1972), 383. Regarding Soviet Koreans in the initial period of the DPRK, see Andrei Lankov, *From Stalin to Kim Il Sung: The Formation of North Korea, 1945–1960* (New Brunswick, NJ: Rutgers University Press, 2002), 110–135.

2. Chŏng Ryul, interviews, Alma-Ata (Kazakhstan), 9–13 December 2001.

3. Andrei Lankov, "Kim Il Sung's Campaign against the Soviet Faction in Late 1955 and the Birth of *Chuch'e*," *Korean Studies* 23 (1999): 43–67.

4. Sin Hyŏng-gi and O Sŏng-ho, *Pukhan munhaksa* (Seoul: P'yŏngminsa, 2000), 29.

5. Vladimir Maiakovskii (1893–1930) was a popular and talented Soviet poet.

6. The Soviet journalist N. Hohlov describes Cho Ki-ch'ŏn in this way: "In Korea they call Cho Ki-ch'ŏn a 'Korean Maiakovskii.' This is a very precise definition! Both poets were so close spiritually. The grand revolutionary scale of Cho's poetry, its grandiose topics, the specific meter and rhythmic system of his poetry—all these he inherited from Maiakovskii." The Soviet journalist depicts Cho as a "strongly passionate," emotional person, a "revolutionary in Korean poetry," who, like Maiakovskii, preferred new aesthetic forms and "burning political topics of the day" to eternal themes. See N. Hohlov, *Koreia nashih dnei* (Moscow: Molodaia gvardiia, 1956), 153–156. All these depictions are very close to the way Maiakovskii's

Soviet contemporaries perceived him. See V. O. Perzhov and I. M. Serebrianskii, eds., *Maiakovskii: Materialy i issliedovaniia* (Moscow: Gosudarstvennoe izdatel'stvo "Hudozhestvennaia literatura," 1940); and Elena Usievich, *Vladimir Maiakovskii* (Moscow: Sovetskii pisatel', 1950), 32.

7. V. N. Li, "Koreiskaia literatura pervyh let posle osvobozhdeniia (1945–1950)," in *Hudozhestvennyi opyt literatur sotsialisticheskih stran* (Moscow: Nauka, 1967), 341.

8. For the positive sense, see, for instance, Yi Ch'ŏng-gu's detailed North Korean biography of Cho Ki-ch'ŏn, by entitled *Siin Cho Ki-ch'ŏn ron* (Pyongyang: Munye ch'ong ch'ulp'ansa, 1953), or L. K. Kim's Soviet article titled "Poeziia Cho Kich'ona," in *Koreiskaia literatura* (Moscow: Izdatel'stvo vostochnoi literatury, 1959), 150–179. For the negative sense, see, for instance, an anti-Communist work by the South Korean scholar Yi Ki-pong written when the cold war between Seoul and Pyongyang was at its height. This book represents Cho Ki-ch'ŏn as an arrogant intruder into Korean literature, but still employs the same epithet. See Yi Ki-pong, *Puk-ŭi munhak-kwa yesurin* (Seoul: Sasayŏn, 1986), 219–224.

9. Elena Davydova (Pak Myŏng-sun), telephone interview, Yanji (China), 6 July 2000; "Famous Korean Poet," an article distributed by the Korean Central News Agency, 5 July 2001.

10. See, for example, *Chosŏn munhaksa,* vol. 10, *Haebang hu p'yŏn* (Pyongyang: Sahoe kwahak ch'ulp'ansa, 1994), 60–79.

11. Yi Ki-pong, *Puk-ŭi munhak-kwa yesurin.*

12. Yim Yŏng-t'ae and Ko Yu-han, *Pukhan 50 nyŏnsa* (Seoul: Tŭlnyŏk', 1999), 1:144.

13. See, for example, Hong Chŏng-sŏn et al., "Cho Ki-ch'ŏn chaejomyŏng: 'Na' poda 'uri' kangyohan sunsujuŭija," *Hanguk ilbo,* 8 August 1992, 4; and Yi Ch'ang-ju, "Puk-ŭi huip'aram siin Cho Ki-ch'ŏn," *Koryo Times: Weekly Magazine for the Foreign Korean Community,* 10 August 1992, 21.

14. See, for example, Hohlov, *Koreia nashih dnei,* 156; L. K. Kim, "Poeziia Cho Kich'ona," 147; "Famous Korean Poet"; and "Aeguk siin ko Cho Ki-ch'ŏn-ŭl ch'umohayŏ yugo 'pihaenggi sanyangkkun-ŭl' naemyŏnsŏ," *Munhak yesul,* 1953, no. 7:78.

15. Tatiana Gabroussenko, "Cho Ki-ch'ŏn: The Person behind the Myths," *Korean Studies,* 2005, no. 29:55–95. The new primary sources include Cho's personal dossier, letters, and private papers and my interviews with his friends and relatives, along with analysis of the original versions of his works.

16. Cho Ki-ch'ŏn, "Lichnyi listok po uchetu kadrov," official questionnaire completed by Cho, 18 June 1946. A copy is now kept in the author's archive. Such personal files were compiled in the former USSR every time a person took a new job. The file forms were filled out by the employee and then checked by the employer. Often people were given an extra form or two, to better prepare a draft. One such draft was kept by Cho's family.

17. See Kim German and Sim Yŏng-sop, *Istoriia prosveshcheniia koreitsev Rossii i Kazahstana* (Alma-Ata: Kazak universiteti, 2000), 93–96, 113.

18. Chŏng Ryul, interviews.

19. Ibid.; Cho Yurii, interviews, Moscow, October–November 2001.

20. Yi Myŏng-jae, *Pukhan munhak sajŏn* (Seoul: Kukhak charyowŏn, 1995), 942.

21. L. K. Kim, "Poeziia Cho Kich'ona," 150–151. Kim gives the Korean titles of Cho's poems in Russian translation.

22. Liia Grigorievna Yudolevitch, undated letters written to the poet's son, Cho Yurii, in 1976–1977, originals in the author's archive.

23. Pavel Korchagin was a protagonist of the popular novel by Nikolai Ostrovskii, *How the Steel Was Tempered*, written in 1932. See Ostrovskii, *Kak zakalyalas' stal'* (1932; reprint, Moscow: Gosudarstvennoe izdatel'stvo detskoi literatury Ministerstva prosveshcheniia, 1948). Kuzbass and Magnitka were major Soviet industrial projects of the early 1930s.

24. Stories about anti-Japanese guerrillas, which were sometimes embellished, filtered across the Soviet-Korean border, and some exploits of the resistance fighters were described by the Soviet press. One of the people who particularly inspired Cho Ki-ch'ŏn in this regard was the famous Cho Myŏng-hŭi, a Korean nationalist writer who had arrived in the Soviet Far East in 1928. Chŏng Ryul interviews.

25. Cho Ki-ch'ŏn, "Lichnyi listok po uchetu kadrov."

26. Chŏng Ryul interviews.

27. Cho Yurii interviews.

28. Chŏng Ryul interviews.

29. Cho Yurii interviews.

30. Cho Ki-ch'ŏn, "Lichnyi listok po uchetu kadrov."

31. Chŏng Ryul, interviews.

32. Yi Myŏng-jae, *Pukhan munhak sajŏn*, 943; Chŏng Ryul interviews.

33. Yi Myŏng-jae, *Pukhan munhak sajŏn*, 81–83.

34. Chŏng Ryul interviews.

35. Concerning factional struggle in the DPRK, see Lankov, *From Stalin to Kim Il Sung*, 77–154.

36. Pak Nam-su, *Chŏkch'i 6 nyŏn-ŭi pukhan mundan* (Seoul: Pogosa, 1999), 104–107. For some reason the Chinese Communist faction, which was quite powerful in Pyongyang politics and included a number of renowned intellectuals (like Kim Tu-bong, the titular head of state in the DPRK), was not represented in the literary sphere.

37. Brian Myers, *Han Sŏr-ya and North Korean Literature: The Failure of Socialist Realism in the DPRK* (Ithaca, NY: East Asia Program, Cornell University, 1994), 29.

38. While the general educational level of Korean leftist writers was above that of the average Korean, it was still quite low. In contrast to the early Russian Bolsheviks and their supporters, who were often graduates of the best universities, most Korean leftist writers attended Japanese universities only briefly and left them

in the first or second year without completing their courses. Their education at the tertiary level thus tended to be rather superficial and fragmentary. Myers, *Han Sŏr-ya*, 20; Chŏng Ryul interviews.

39. Chŏng Ryul interviews.

40. Yi Chŏl-ju, *Puk-ŭi yesurin* (Seoul: Kyemongsa, 1966), 22–24.

41. Pak Nam-su, *Chŏkch'i 6 nyŏn-ŭi pukhan mundan,* 114.

42. Chŏng Ryul interviews.

43. Andrei Lankov, *Severnaia Koreia: Vchera i Segodnia* (Moscow: Vostochnaia literatura, 1995), 174–175.

44. Chŏng Ryul interviews.

45. Ibid.

46. Sŏng Hye-rang, *Tŭngnamu chip* (Seoul: Chisik nara, 2000), 56.

47. A refugee, Yi Chŏl-ju, referring to the Soviet Koreans and to Ki Sŏk-pok in particular, scorns the latter's "clumsy Hamgyŏng dialect" in his memoirs (Yi Chŏl-ju, *Puk-ŭi yesurin* [Seoul: Kyemongsa, 1966], 199, quoted in Myers, *Han Sŏr-ya,* 88). Sŏng Hye-rang, writing quite recently, also refers to the same accent as a telltale mark of Ki Sŏk-pok and other Soviet Koreans (Sŏng Hye-rang, *Tŭngnamu chip,* 170–171). Pak Nam-su, another defector, describes Hamgyŏng-do natives ironically as primitive and uneducated rustics (Pak Nam-su, *Chŏkch'i 6 nyŏn-ŭi pukhan mundan,* 209).

48. Elena Davydova interview.

49. Ibid.

50. Pak Nam-su, *Chŏkch'i 6 nyŏn-ŭi pukhan mundan,* 78.

51. As Pak Nam-su reports, Cho Ki-ch'ŏn, in answer to a question by a member of the public at a meeting with Korean writers, described the famous Russian novelist as a reactionary, which bewildered the writers (ibid., 81). Cho's response reflected the official Soviet view on Dostoevsky at the time. See, for example, an article by D. Zaslavskii, "Protiv idealizatsii reaktsionnyh vzglyadov Dostoevskogo," *Kultura I zhizn',* 20 December 1947, 3–4.

52. Pak Nam-su, *Chŏkch'i 6 nyŏn-ŭi pukhan mundan,* 83.

53. Ibid., 88, 94.

54. Interviews with Chŏng Ryul and Cho Yurii.

55. Pak Nam-su, *Chŏkch'i 6 nyŏn-ŭi pukhan mundan,* 79.

56. L. K. Kim, "Poeziia Cho Kich'ona," 153.

57. Yi Myŏng-jae, *Pukhan munhak sajŏn,* 503–508.

58. Chŏng Ryul interviews.

59. *Chosŏn munhaksa,* 10:70.

60. Kwŏn Yŏng-min, *Hanguk hyŏndae munhaksa* (Seoul: Midŭmsa, 1993), 358–359; Yi Ki-pong, *Puk-ŭi munhak-kwa yesurin,* 221.

61. Sin Tong-ho, "Hanguksiesŏ nat'anan paektusan sangjing yŏngu" (MA thesis, Chungang University, Chungang taehakkyo yesul taehakwŏn, 1999), 54.

62. Yim Yŏng-t'ae and Ko Yu-han, *Pukhan 50 nyŏnsa,* 1:144.

63. Of course I am speaking here only about the original version of the poem, not its heavily revised *chuch'e* editions, which were published well after the author's death.

64. Cho Ki-ch'ŏn, *Paektusan,* in *Cho Ki-ch'ŏn sŏnjip* (Pyongyang: Munhwa chŏnsŏnsa, 1952), 1:6, 13.

65. Ibid., 73–84.

66. In Aleksandr Fadeev, *Sobranie sochinenii* (Moscow: Pravda, 1987), vols. 1 and 2. Take, for instance, the episode when a peasant's melons are stolen by the careless young partisan Morozko in Fadeev's *Razgrom* (Devastation; 1927). The righteous Commander Levinson uses the same tactic as Commander Kim. First, Levinson raises the anger of the guerrilla collective toward the wrongdoer. The comrades berate the offender and threaten him with exile or worse, causing Morozko to feel deeply ashamed of himself. Then the commander and comrades show mercy and decide to help the peasants, and the victim of the robbery in particular, by working together with them in the fields. See Aleksandr Fadeev, *Razgrom* (Moscow: Hudozhestvennaia literatura, 1972), 44–53.

67. Chŏng Ryul interviews.

68. Cho Ki-ch'ŏn, *Paektusan,* 1:82.

69. These are the names of popular Soviet partisan leaders from the Civil War period (1917–1922).

70. Cho Ki-ch'ŏn, *Paektusan,* 1:69–71.

71. Ibid., 71–73.

72. Ibid., 140.

73. Ibid., 145–146.

74. Ibid., 148–149.

75. At that time, North Korean literary officials did not dare publish this poem without the Soviet embassy's approval. Chŏng Ryul interviews.

76. Ibid.

77. Cho Ki-ch'ŏn, *Paektusan,* 1:10, 29.

78. Pak Nam-su, *Chŏkch'i 6 nyŏn-ŭi pukhan mundan,* 91.

79. Soviet and North Korean scholars maintain that Cho Ki-ch'ŏn borrowed this form from Maiakovskii (L. K. Kim, "Poeziia Cho Kich'ona," 167; Pak Chong-sik, "Sovremennaia koreiskaia literatura posle osvobozhdenia: Formirovanie i stanovlenie sotsrealisma v koreiskoi literature po tvorchestvu Li Giena" [doctoral thesis, Moscow State University, 1953]). One may question this assumption, given that the lyrical epic genre was popular in Russian and Soviet poetry apart from Maiakovskii. In any case, the Korean contemporaries had little doubt about the foreign roots of the literary form of *Paektusan.*

80. Pak Nam-su, *Chŏkch'i 6 nyŏn-ŭi pukhan mundan,* 91.

81. Ibid., 96.

82. Cho Ki-ch'ŏn, *Paektusan,* 1:23–24.

83. G. S. Cheremnin, *Obraz Stalina v sovetskoi hudozhestvennoi literature* (Moscow: Pravda, 1950).

84. In a characteristic poem by Dzhambul Dzhambaev entitled "Narkom Ezhov" (People's Commissar Ezhov; 1937, http://cray.onego.ru/~solvio/gostinaya/albom/literatura/ezhov.html), Ezhov, the chief of the NKVD secret police during the Great Purge of 1937–1938, is referred to as "a stern sword," the "eye of the country, which is clearer than a diamond," and the like.

85. Chŏng Ryul interviews.

86. Ibid.

87. Pak Nam-su, *Chŏkch'i 6 nyŏn-ŭi pukhan mundan,* 86.

88. Ibid., 87.

89. For more information about "literary discussions" in the USSR in Stalin's era, see Evgenii Gromov, *Stalin: Vlast' i iskusstvo* (Moscow: Pespublika, 1998), 130–142. This same trend is observable in North Korea—for example, during the discussion over Yi T'ae-jun's short story "The First Fight" (Ch'ŏt chŏnt'u). Protecting the novel from the attacks of Han Hyo, another critic of the ex-KAPF faction, "a certain writer" cites the following words of Han Hyo: "Had I worked in the department of publishing affairs, this novel would never have been allowed to pass." The critic then proceeds to give a political interpretation of these words: "Does this mean that comrade Han Hyo is not satisfied with the management of the department? It sounds as if he opposes the Party's opinion." Pak Nam-su, *Chŏkch'i 6 nyŏn-ŭi pukhan mundan,* 117.

90. Sin Hyŏng-gi and O Sŏng-ho, *Pukhan munhaksa,* 29.

91. Pak Nam-su, *Chŏkch'i 6 nyŏn-ŭi pukhan mundan,* 87.

92. Kim Ch'ang-man himself was by no means pro-Soviet. In the late 1950s he would play a major role in the campaign against Soviet influence. For more details of his participation in this campaign, see chapter 5 of this study and also Andrei Lankov, *Crisis in North Korea: The Failure of De-Stalinization, 1956* (Honolulu: University of Hawai`i Press, 2005), 149, 161.

93. Cho Yurii interviews.

94. Yi Myŏng-jae, *Pukhan munhak sajŏn,* 762.

95. Brian Myers suggests that the prize was received in 1947 (Myers, *Han Sŏr-ya,* 51), but the Soviet sources maintain that it was bestowed in 1948 (L. K. Kim, "Poeziia Cho Kich'ona," 147). The latter date seems more convincing, since the first publication of *Paektusan* in *Nodong sinmun* was in 1948.

96. Chŏng Ryul interviews.

97. Myers, *Han Sŏr-ya,* 135–142.

98. Yi Myŏng-jae, *Pukhan munhak sajŏn,* 942–943.

99. Pak Nam-su, *Chŏkch'i 6 nyŏn-ŭi pukhan mundan,* 59–60.

100. L. K. Kim, "Poeziia Cho Kich'ona," 147.

101. Han Sŏr-ya, for instance, spent "just one day in the industrial zone of Sadong" and "did not seek contact with the workers, choosing instead to join the students of the local engineering school on a class excursion to an adjacent mine." Myers, *Han Sŏr-ya,* 44, 54.

102. *Cho Ki-ch'ŏn sŏnjip,* 1:153–360.

103. Ibid., 161–163.

104. Ibid., 235.

105. Ibid., 2:52–54.

106. Ibid., 1:308–309.

107. Vladimir Maiakovskii, "Pis'mo tovarishchu Kostrovu o sushchnosti liubvi" and "Pis'mo Tatianie Iakovlevoi," both in *Sobranie sochinenii* (Moscow: Pravda, 1973), 6:150–157.

108. *Cho Ki-ch'ŏn sŏnjip,* 2:47.

109. Ibid., 49; L. K. Kim, "Poeziia Cho Kich'ona," 154.

110. *Cho Ki-ch'ŏn sŏnjip,* 2:69.

111. Ibid., 70.

112. See, for instance, Isakovskii's "Ya ne klala v pechku drov" (I Did Not Put Wood in the Stove; 1927). The poem is about a girl's separation from her boyfriend. The girl, who initiated the breakup, explains that "it is more fun to love a teacher" than to waste time "lazily singing songs." Isakovskii, *Stihi, poemy i pesni* (Moscow: Gosudarstvennoe izdatel'stvo hudozhestvennoi literatury, 1951), 1:74–75. The protagonist of the famous song "Katyusha," a young woman, is waiting for her boyfriend while he is serving in the army "far away." Not surprisingly, the boy is not a simple country lad but an advanced frontier guard who is protecting the great Soviet motherland while Katyusha is "guarding their love" (ibid., 217).

113. See, for instance, Kim Chin-guk, "Chchaksarang naeyong-ŭi ch'oedae hit'ŭ kok Hŭi p'aram," *Chungang ilbo,* 15 January 1995, 17.

114. Mikhail Isakovskii, "Na zakate hodit paren,'" in *Stihi, poemy i pesni,* 1:215–216.

115. L. K. Kim, "Poeziia Cho Kich'ona," 147.

116. *Cho Ki-ch'ŏn sŏnjip*, vol. 2.

117. Ibid., 137.

118. L. K. Kim, "Poeziia Cho Kich'ona," 162.

119. *Cho Ki-ch'ŏn sŏnjip,* 2:132–133.

120. Cho Ki-ch'ŏn, last letter (undated) to his wife, in the family archive.

121. L. K. Kim, "Poeziia Cho Kich'ona," 147.

122. Ibid.

123. Chŏng Ryul interviews; Yi Myŏng-jae, *Pukhan munhak sajŏn,* 943.

124. Cho Ki-ch'ŏn, "Huip'aram," *Chosŏn munhak,* 1990, no. 4:81.

125. See, for example, Chŏn Yŏng-sŏn, "Pukhanŭi yŏnguŏnhan siin Cho Ki-ch'ŏn," *Pukhan,* 2000, no. 3:194–203. When discussing "Whistle," this article quotes the revised version that was published in *Chosŏn munhak* in 1990.

126. See, for instance, the anthology *Yŏngyŏnhan noŭl* (Pyongyang: Munhakyesul chonghap ch'ulp'ansa, 1998).

127. A. M. Van Der Eng-Liedmeier, *Soviet Literary Characters: An Investigation into the Portrayal of Soviet Men in Russian Prose, 1917–1953* (The Hague: Mouton and Co., 1959).

128. Kim Ch'ang-ho, "Ch'ŏnyŏŭi maŭm," *Chosŏn munhak,* 2007, no. 10:67.

Chapter 3: Yi Ki-yŏng

1. See An Ham-gwang, *Chosŏn munhaksa* (Pyongyang: Kyoyuk tosŏ ch'ulp'ansa, 1956), 602–634; and *Chosŏn munhaksa (1926–1945)* (Pyongyang: Kwahak, paekkwa sajŏn ch'ulp'ansa, 1981), 378–379, 435–448.

2. See, for example, *Chosŏn munhaksa,* vol. 10, *Haebang hu p'yŏn* (Pyongyang: Sahoe kwahak ch'ulp'ansa, 1994), 139–158.

3. According to Sŏng Hye-rang, a sister of Yi Ki-yŏng's daughter-in-law, in the 1950s Yi Ki-yŏng's house was "the richest in Pyongyang." The author explains this by the privileged position Yi Ki-yŏng enjoyed as the most prominent writer of the DPRK, his chairmanship of the North Korean–Soviet Friendship Society, and his frequent visits to the Soviet Union, which gave him access to much-coveted foreign luxury items. Sŏng Hye-rang, *Tŭngnamu chip* (Seoul: Chisik nara, 2000), 362.

4. V. I. Ivanova, *Li Gien: Zhizn' i tvorchestvo* (Moscow: Vostochnaia literatura, 1962), 44.

5. Ibid., 5; Yi Ki-yŏng and Han Sŏr-ya, *Yisang-kwa noryŏk* (Pyongyang: Minch'ŏng ch'ulp'ansa, 1958), 6–7; Sin Ku-hyŏn, "Minch'ŏn Yi Ki-yŏng," in *Hyŏndae chakka ron* (Pyongyang: Chosŏn chakka tongmaeng ch'ulp'ansa, 1960), 2:91.

6. Yi Sang-gyŏng, *Yi Ki-yŏng sidae-wa munhak* (Seoul: P'ulpit', 1994), 44.

7. Sin Ku-hyŏn, "Minch'ŏn Yi Ki-yŏng," 91.

8. Yi Sang-gyŏng, *Yi Ki-yŏng sidae-wa munhak,* 50.

9. Yi Myŏng-jae, *Pukhan munhak sajŏn* (Seoul: Kukhak charyowŏn, 1995), 367.

10. Sin Ku-hyŏn, "Minch'ŏn Yi Ki-yŏng," 93.

11. Yi Sang-gyŏng, *Yi Ki-yŏng sidae-wa munhak,* 45.

12. Ibid., 50.

13. Yi Ki-yŏng and Han Sŏr-ya, *Yisang-kwa noryŏk,* 19. For an analysis of the social functions of Christianity in Korea, see Kenneth Wells, *New God, New Nation: Protestants and Self-Reconstruction Nationalism in Korea, 1896–1937* (Sydney: Allen and Unwin, 1990).

14. Yi Ki-yŏng and Han Sŏr-ya, *Yisang-kwa noryŏk,* 25.

15. Yi Myŏng-jae, *Pukhan munhak sajŏn,* 367.

16. V. I. Ivanova, "Li Gien i ego roman 'Zemlia,'" in *Kratkie soobscheniia instituta vostokovedeniia,* no. 18 (Moscow: Izdatel'stvo AN SSSR, 1955), 29.

17. Yi Sang-gyŏng, *Yi Ki-yŏng sidae-wa munhak,* 78.

18. See, for example, Ivanova, *Li Gien,* 22, 31, 71, 80; V. N. Li, *Sotsialisticheskii realizm v koreaiskoi literature* (Tashkent: Fan, 1971), 73; Li Gien, *Zemlia* (Moscow: Izdatel'stvo inostrannoi literatury, 1953), introduction, 10.

19. Kim Sang-sŏn, *Minch'ŏn Yi Ki-yŏng munhak yŏngu* (Seoul: Kukhak charyowŏn, 1999), 4.

20. *Who's Who in Korean Literature,* published by the Korean Culture and Arts Foundation (Seoul: Hollym, 1998), 500–501.

21. *Yi Ki-yŏng sŏnjip* (Seoul: P'ulpit', 1989), 1:7.

22. Yi Ki-yŏng himself admitted that *Ingan Suŏp* (Human Lesson; 1936) was written under the strong influence of Cervantes' *Don Quixote.* See Ivanova, *Li Gien,* 50.

23. As an example of the North Korean critical approach, see Pak Chong-sik, "Chosŏn munhak-e issŏsŏŭi ssobet'ŭ munhak-ŭi yŏnghyang," in *Haebang hu 10 nyŏngan-ŭi chosŏn munhak* (Pyongyang: Chosŏn chakka tongmaeng ch'ulp'ansa, 1955), 424–425. The South Korean case can be represented by the work of Mun Sŏk-u, "Tturŭgenep'ŭ-wa Korikki Munhak-ŭi kyŏngu," in Yi Poyŏng et al., eds., *Hangukmunhak sokŭi segye munhak* (Seoul: Kyujanggak, 1998), 312–316.

24. Ivanova, *Li Gien,* 22, 31, 71, 80 (first five quotations); V. N. Li, *Sotsialisticheskii realizm v koreaiskoi literature,* 73, 79 (sixth and seventh quotations); Li Gien, *Zemlya,* introduction, 10 (last quotation).

25. Kim Sang-sŏn, *Minch'ŏn Yi Ki-yŏng munhak yŏngu* (Seoul: Kukhak charyowŏn, 1999), 4.

26. Yi Ki-yŏng, *Kohyang* (Pyongyang: Chosŏn chakka tongmaeng ch'ulp'ansa, 1955), 77.

27. Yi Ki-yŏng, *Ttang* (Pyongyang: Chosŏn chakka tongmaeng ch'ulp'ansa, 1955), 4.

28. Yi Ki-yŏng, *Kohyang,* 80.

29. Yi Ki-yŏng, "Kananhan saram," in *Hyŏndae chosŏn munhak sŏnjip* (Pyongyang: Chosŏn chakka tongmaeng ch'ulp'ansa, 1958), 3:56–58.

30. Yi Ki-yŏng, "Chwi iyagi," in *Hyŏndae chosŏn munhak sŏnjip,* 3:63; Yi Ki-yŏng, "Cheji kongjang ch'on," in *Hyŏndae chosŏn munhak sŏnjip,* 3:199.

31. Han Hyo, "Sahoejuŭi reallijŭm-kwa chosŏn munhak," in *Ch'ŏngnyŏntŭl wihan munhakron* (Pyongyang: Minju ch'ŏngnyŏnsa, 1952), 170. However, after 1953, when Yi Ki-yŏng became a part of the North Korean ideological canon, the criticism of the artistic quality of his writings disappeared from the pages of North Korean literary journals.

32. Quoted in V. N. Li, *Koreiskaia proletarskaia literatura: Proza 20–30-h godov* (Moscow: Akademiia nauk SSSR, 1967), 11.

33. Kim Yun-sik, *Haebang konggan-ŭi munhak saron* (Seoul: Taehakkyo ch'ulp'anbu, 1989), 177.

34. An Ham-gwang, *Chosŏn munhaksa* (Pyongyang: Kyoyuk tosŏ ch'ulp'ansa, 1956), 602–634; *Chosŏn munhaksa (1926–1945)* (Pyongyang: Kwahak, paekkwa sajŏn ch'ulp'ansa, 1981), 378–379, 435–448.

35. Na Pyŏng-ch'ŏl, *Munhak-ŭi ihae* (Seoul: Munye ch'ulp'ansa, 1995), 307–311.

36. Gi-Wook Shin, "Agrarianism: A Critique of Colonial Modernity in Korea," *Comparative Studies in Society and History* 41, no. 4 (October 1999): 785.

37. For a good account of the antiurban feelings expressed by Korean intellectuals, see Im Hŏn-yŏng, "The Meaning of the City in Korean Literature," *Korea Journal* 27 (May 1987): 24–25.

38. Samuel L. Popkin, *The Rational Peasant: The Political Economy of Rural Society in Vietnam* (London: University of California Press, 1979), 3.

39. Mun Sŏk-u, "Rŏsia sasiljuŭi munhak-ŭi suyong-kwa kŭ hakmunjŏk

pyŏnyong, torŭsŭtoi chungsim-ŭro," in Yi Poyŏng et al., eds., *Hangukmunhak sokŭi segye munhak* (Seoul: Kyujanggak, 1998), 207–255.

40. Shin, "Agrarianism," 788.

41. Notably, in prerevolutionary Russia a similar agrarianist perspective (that of the so-called Narodniks) was harshly criticized by Russian Marxists and primarily by Lenin, who derided the Narodniks' standpoint as "economic romanticism."

42. Regarding *munmyŏng kaehwa,* see Andre Schmid, *Korea between Empires, 1895–1919* (New York: Columbia University Press, 2002), 32–38.

43. Yun Pyŏng-no, *Hanguk-ŭi hyŏndae chakka chakp'umron* (Seoul: Sŏnggyunkwan taehakkyo ch'ulp'anbu, 1993), 13.

44. Chung Jin-bae, "Korean and Chinese Experience of Marxism: Hermeneutic Problems and Cultural Transformation," in *Korean Journal* 35, no. 2 (Summer 1995): 55.

45. Kim Nam-il, "Ije nuga Yi Ki-yŏngŭl ilgŭl gosinga?" *Silch'ŏn munhak,* Autumn 1999, 79–85.

46. Yi Ki-yŏng, "Silp'aehan ch'ŏnyŏ changp'yŏng," *Chogwang,* 1939, no. 12:35.

47. Yi Ki-yŏng and Han Sŏr-ya, *Yisang-kwa noryŏk,* 42.

48. Yi Ki-yŏng, "KAPF sidae-ŭi hoesanggi," *Chosŏn munhak,* 1957, no. 8:85.

49. Yi Sang-gyŏng, *Yi Ki-yŏng sidae-wa munhak,* 81.

50. Ivanova, *Li Gien,* 15; Yi Myŏng-jae, *Pukhan munhak sajŏn,* 367.

51. Yi Ki-yŏng, "Oppa-ŭi pimil p'yŏnji," in *Hyŏndae chosŏn munhak sŏnjip,* vol. 3.

52. Sin Ku-hyŏn, "Minch'ŏn Yi Ki-yŏng," 99.

53. Concerning liberal conventions, see Yun Pyŏng-no, *Hanguk-ŭi hyŏndae chakka chakp'umron,* 13–15.

54. See, for instance, Yi Kwang-su's famous novel *Heartlessness,* first published in 1917. Yi Kwang-su, *Mujŏng* (Seoul: Sŏ mundang, 1997).

55. V. N. Li, "Koreiskaia assotsiatsija proletarskih pisatelei i proza 20–30 godov," in *Natsional'nye traditsii i genesis sotsialisticheskogo realizma* (Moscow: Vostochnaja literatura, 1965), 589; V. I. Ivanova, "Poiski polozhitel'nogo geroia v rannem tvorchestve Li Giena," in *Koreiskaia literatura* (Moscow: Izdatel'stvo vostochnoi literatury, 1959), 95; Ivanova, *Li Gien,* 15.

56. Yi Sang-gyŏng, *Yi Ki-yŏng sidae-wa munhak,* 130.

57. Yi Ki-yŏng's views on gender issues were quite inconsistent. Sŏng Hye-rang recollects that "the feminist" Yi was an extremely conservative father-in-law who treated his female family members in a very traditional Confucian way. Sŏng Hye-rang, *Tŭngnamu chip,* 366–367.

58. Yi Sang-gyŏng, *Yi Ki-yŏng sidae-wa munhak,* 105.

59. Yi Ki-yŏng, "Minch'on," in *Hyŏndae chosŏn munhak sŏnjip,* 3:76, 83.

60. Ibid., 3:76, 84.

61. Ibid., 87.

62. Ibid., 88.

63. Ibid., 90.

64. Ibid., 92.

65. Ibid., 93.

66. Ibid., 93–99.

67. Ibid., 100.

68. Ibid., 70, 89.

69. Ibid., 71.

70. Yi Sang-gyŏng, *Yi Ki-yŏng sidae-wa munhak,* 106.

71. Yi Ki-yŏng, "Minch'on," 3:93–99.

72. Yi Sang-gyŏng, *Yi Ki-yŏng sidae-wa munhak,* 108.

73. Ivanova, *Li Gien,* 21; V. N. Li, "Koreiskaia assotsiatsija proletarskih pisatelei i prosa 20–30-h godov," 590.

74. V. N. Li, "Koreiskaia assotsiatsija proletarskih pisatelei i prosa 20–30-h godov," 590.

75. Ivanova, *Li Gien,* 21.

76. Yi Ki-yŏng, "Chwi iyagi," 62, 63.

77. Ibid., 63.

78. Jean Chesneaux, *Peasant Revolts in China, 1840–1949,* translated by C.A. Curwen (London: Thames and Hudson, 1973), 21.

79. Kim Chae-yong, "Iljeha nonch'on-ŭi hwangp'yehwa-wa nongmin-ŭi chuch'ejŏk kaksŏng," in *Yi Ki-yŏng sŏnjip,* 1:568.

80. One should not, however, overestimate the degree of Yi Ki-yŏng's devotion to the theme of women's liberation in general. Kenneth Wells has convincingly argued that Yi in fact dismissed a feminist position in his articles. See Kenneth Wells, "The Price of Legitimacy: Women and the Kŭnuhoe Movement, 1927–1931," in Gi-Wook Shin and Michael Robinson, eds., *Colonial Modernity in Korea* (Cambridge, MA, and London: Harvard University Press, 1999), 191–221.

81. Yi Sang-gyŏng, *Yi Ki-yŏng sidae-wa munhak,* 450.

82. Yi Ki-yŏng, "Wŏn-bo," in *Hyŏndae chosŏn munhak sŏnjip,* 3:182–194.

83. Ibid., 189.

84. Kim Sang-sŏn, *Minch'on Yi Ki-yŏng munhak yŏngu,* 508.

85. Sin Ku-hyŏn, "Minch'on Yi Ki-yŏng," 115–116.

86. See, for instance, Mun Sŏk-u, "Tturŭgenep'ŭ-wa Korikki Munhak-ŭi kyŏngu," 312–316; and V. I. Ivanova, "Sovetskaia voenno-patrioticheskaia literatura v Koree," in *Literatura stran zarubezhnogo vostoka i Sovetskaia literaturae* (Moscow: Nauka, 1977), 124–138.

87. Yi Ki-yŏng, "Wŏn-bo," 189, 190.

88. Mun Sŏk-u, "Tturŭgenep'ŭ-wa Korikki Munhak-ŭi kyŏngu," 314.

89. Yi Ki-yŏng, "Cheji kongjang ch'on," 213.

90. Maxim Gorky, *Mat',* in *Izbrannye proizvedeniia v treh tomah* (Moscow: Gosudarstvennoe izdatel'stvo hudozhestvennoi literatury, 1951), 2:410–413; Yi Ki-yŏng, "Cheji kongjang ch'on," 195–196.

91. Yi Ki-yŏng, "Cheji kongjang ch'on," 196.

92. Ibid., 198, 210.

93. Ibid., 210.

94. See *Samch'ŏlli,* 1936, no. 4:319, quoted in Ivanova, *Li Gien,* 21; Pak Chong-sik, "Chosŏn munhak-e issŏsŏŭi ssobet'ŭ munhak-ŭi yŏnghyang," 432.

95. Pak Chong-sik, "Sovremennaia koreiskaia literatura posle osvobozhdenia: Formirovanie i stanovlenie sotsrealisma v koreiskoi literature po tvorchestvu Li Giena (doctoral thesis, Moscow State University, 1953), 141.

96. Sin Ku-hyŏn, "Minch'on Yi Ki-yŏng," 130.

97. Ibid., 127.

98. Na Pyŏng-ch'ŏl, *Munhak-ŭi ihae,* 301. For Na's definition of socialist realism, see ibid., 268; and Na Pyŏng-ch'ŏl, *Sosŏl-ŭi ihae* (Seoul: Munye ch'ulp'ansa, 1998), 271.

99. V. N. Li, *Sotsialisticheskii realizm v koreaiskoi literature,* 46, 47.

100. A. N. Taen, "Ocherki sovremennoi koreiskoi literatury (demokraticheskie natsional'nye tendentsii i sotsialisticheskii realizm v koreiskoi literature)" (PhD thesis, Herzen Pedagogical Institute, Leningrad, 1954), 322.

101. Yi Ki-yŏng, *Kohyang,* 320–321, 268, 223.

102. Ibid., 114–117.

103. Ibid., 110–113.

104. Ibid., 193. The mothers of Paekryong and Soetŭk are two secondary characters, village women who used to fight a lot with each other about trivial matters.

105. Ibid., 228, 407.

106. Ibid., 403.

107. For an example of South Korean scholarship on the novel, see Kim Chae-yong, "Iljeha nonch'on-ŭi hwangp'yehwa-wa nongmin-ŭi chuch'ejŏk kaksŏng," in *Yi Ki-yŏng sŏnjip,* 580. For an example of Soviet scholarship, see Ivanova, *Li Gien,* 43. For an example of North Korean scholarship (published in Russian), see Pak Chong-sik, "Sovremennaia koreiskaia literatura posle osvobozhdenia," 184.

108. Tsoi, "Otrazhenie velikih peremen v koreiskoi derevne v romanah Li Giena" (PhD thesis, Moscow State University, 1955), 73.

109. Yi Ki-yŏng's article on the topic, titled "Ideal Heroine," was published in *Chonggwang* 1939, no. 4:152. Quoted in Ivanova, *Li Gien,* 43.

110. *Samch'ŏnri,* 1936, no. 4:319, quoted in Ivanova, *Li Gien,* 43.

111. *Chosŏn mundan,* 1935, no. 3:124, quoted in *Hanguk munhak taesajŏn* (Seoul: Munwŏngak, 1973), 452.

112. *Hanguk munhak taesajŏn,* 452.

113. Yi Sang-gyŏng, *Yi Ki-yŏng sidae-wa munhak,* 452.

114. Aleksandr Gitovich and Boris Bursov, *My videli Koreiu* (Leningrad: Lenizdat, 1948), 86, 48.

115. Ivanova, *Li Gien,* 66.

116. Yi Ki-yŏng and Han Sŏr-ya, *Yisang-kwa noryŏk,* 38; Yi Sang-gyŏng, *Yi Ki-yŏng sidae-wa munhak,* 453; Gitovich and Bursov, *Mu videli Koreiu,* 86; Taen, "Ocherki sovremennoi koreiskoi literatury," 259.

117. Brian Myers, *Han Sŏr-ya and North Korean Literature: The Failure of Socialist Realism in the DPRK* (Ithaca, NY: Cornell University, 1994), 38.

118. Yi Sang-gyŏng, *Yi Ki-yŏng sidae-wa munhak*, 296.

119. Ivanova, *Li Gien*, 68.

120. Yi Sang-gyŏng, *Yi Ki-yŏng sidae-wa munhak*, 454.

121. Pak Nam-su, *Chŏk-ch'i 6 nyŏn-ŭi pukhan mundan*, 54.

122. Ivanova, *Li Gien*, 68.

123. Robert A. Scalapino and Chong-sik Lee, *Communism in Korea* (Berkeley and Los Angeles: University of California Press, 1972), 797–799.

124. Sin Ku-hyŏn, *Koreiskaia literatura posle osvobozhdeniia* (Pyongyang: Izdatel'stvo literatury na inoistrannyh iazykah, 1957), 12.

125. Yi Ki-yŏng, *Ttang* (Pyongyang: Chosŏn chakka tongmaeng ch'ulp'ansa, 1955), 423–427.

126. Ibid.

127. Mikhail Sholokhov, *Podniataia tselina* (Moscow: Prosveshchenie, 1973).

128. Ibid., 52; Yi Ki-yŏng, *Ttang* (1955), 4.

129. Yi Ki-yŏng, *Ttang* (1955), 96–100.

130. Ibid., 46–61.

131. Han Hyo, "Chosŏn munhak-e issŏsŏ sahoejuŭi reallijŭm-ŭi palsaeng chokŏn-kwa kŭ paljŏn-e issŏsŏŭi che t'ŭkching," *Munhak yesul*, 1952, no. 6:92.

132. Yi Ki-yŏng, *Ttang* (1955), 46–52.

133. Ibid., 231–243.

134. Ibid., 60–67. See the analysis of Han's story in Myers, *Han Sŏr-ya and North Korean literature*, 60–67.

135. Ibid., 384–389.

136. Myers spotted the same trait in Han Sŏr-ya's work *Growing Village (Charanŭn maŭl)*. See Myers, *Han Sŏr-ya*, 60–67.

137. Yi Ki-yŏng, *Ttang* (1955), 298–320.

138. Ibid., 132–142.

139. Ibid., 121–124.

140. Ibid., 124–125.

141. Ibid., 124.

142. Ibid., 130–132.

143. Ibid., 124.

144. Yi Ki-yŏng, *Ttang* (1955), 122.

145. Sholokhov, *Podniataia tselina*, 261–268.

146. Ibid., 442–444, 453.

147. Ibid., 567.

148. Yi Ki-yŏng, *Ttang* (1955), 264.

149. Ibid., 405–410.

150. Ibid., 348.

151. Pak Chong-sik, *Sovremennaia koreiskaia literatura posle osvobozhdenia*, 220.

152. Ŏm Ho-sŏk, *Munye kibon* (Pyongyang: Kunnip ch'ulp'ansa, 1952), 64.

153. Tsoi, "Otrazhenie velikih peremen v koreiskoi derevne v romanah Li Giena," 143.

154. Ibid., 146.

155. Cited in Myers, *Han Sŏr-ya,* 84.

156. Ibid.

157. In the canons of Soviet literature, the loss of a heroine's virginity because of a previous marriage or rape has never been regarded as an indelible stain on her reputation. See, for example, an episode in an exemplary work of socialist realism, Ostrovskii's *How the Steel Was Tempered* (1932–1934). When a male protagonist in the novel expresses his discontent with a "female comrade" who has supposedly lost her virginity during a rape, he is immediately chastised by his other comrades as a backward, possessive, even reactionary person. Nikolai Ostrovskii, *Kak zakalyalas' stal'* (1932; reprint, Moscow: Gosudarstvennoe izdatel'stvo detskoi literatury Ministerstva prosveshcheniia, 1948), 140.

158. Yi Ki-yŏng, *Ttang* (1955), 122–124.

159. Quoted in Yi Sang-gyŏng, *Yi Ki-yŏng sidae-wa munhak,* 352.

160. Yi Ki-yŏng, *Ttang* (Pyongyang: Minch'ŏng ch'ulp'ansa, 1973).

161. Yi Sang-gyŏng, *Yi Ki-yŏng sidae-wa munhak,* 42.

162. Yi Ki-yŏng, *Pulgŭn such'ŏp* (Pyongyang: Minch'ŏng ch'ulp'ansa, 1961).

163. Yi Ki-yŏng, *Han nyŏsŏng-ŭi unmyŏng* (Pyongyang: Chosŏn sahoejuŭi nodong ch'ŏngnyŏn ch'ulp'ansa, 1965).

164. The conflict between Han Sŏr-ya and Yim Hwa, who was a much more popular literary figure than Han, led to the disappearance of Yim from the literary scene. This episode, as well as the role of Han Sŏr-ya in the North Korean literary world, is discussed in chapter 5 of this study.

165. V. I. Ivanova, telephone interview, Moscow, 3 February 2002.

166. Elena Davydova (Pak Myŏng-sun), telephone interview, Yanji (China), 6 July 2000.

167. Song Yŏng, "Chakka minch'ŏn," *Munhak sinmun,* 1960, no. 5:27.

168. Chŏng Ryul, interviews, Alma-Ata (Kazakhstan), 9–13 December 2001.

169. Ibid.

170. Yi Myŏng-jae, *Pukhan munhak sajŏn,* 368.

171. See, for instance, Yi Ki-yŏng, "KAPF sidae-ŭi hoesanggi," 81–86.

172. Myers, *Han Sŏr-ya,* 119.

173. Chŏng Ryul interviews.

174. Song Yŏng, "Chakka minch'ŏn," 27.

175. Details of an interview with Pak Sang-ho, Leningrad, November 1989, have been kindly provided by Andrei Lankov.

176. Chŏng Ryul interviews.

Chapter 4: Yi T'ae-jun

1. Yi Ki-pong, *Puk-ŭi munhak-kwa yesurin* (Seoul: Sasayŏn, 1986), 203.

2. Yi Pyŏng-ryŏl, "Ch'ŏtchŏnt'u-wa kohyang kilŭi ŭimi," in *Yi T'ae-jun munhak chŏnjip* (Seoul: Kip'ŭnsaem, 2000), 3:377.

3. See, for instance, Chŏng Hyŏn-gi, *Yi T'ae-jun, chŏngch'i-ro chukki, chakka-ro sŏgi* (Seoul: Kŏnmin taehakkyo ch'ulp'anbu, 1994); Min Ch'un-hwan, "Yi T'ae-jun-ŭi chŏngijŏk koch'al," in *Yi T'ae-jun munhak yŏngu* (Seoul: Kip'ŭnsaem, 1993), 33–54; Yi Ki-pong, *Puk-ŭi munhak-kwa yesurin*, 198–207; *Who's Who in Korean Literature*, published by Korean Culture and Arts Foundation (Seoul: Hollym, 1998), 522.

4. Tomomi Wada, "Aeguk munhak-ŭrosŏŭi Yi T'ae-jun munhak," in *Kŭndae munhak-kwa Yi T'ae-jun* (Seoul: Kip'ŭnsaem, 2000), 83–119; Pak Hŏn-ho, *Yi T'ae-jun-kwa hanguk kŭndae sosŏl-ŭi sŏnggyŏk* (Seoul: Somyŏng ch'ulp'an, 1999), 34–39.

5. Min Ch'un-hwan, "Yi T'ae-jun-ŭi chŏngijŏk koch'al," 46–47; Chŏng Hyŏn-gi, *Yi T'ae-jun, chŏngch'i-ro chukki, chakka-ro sŏgi*, 96–97.

6. Sin Hyŏng-gi, "Haebang ihu-ŭi Yi T'ae-jun," in *Kŭndae munhak-kwa Yi T'ae-jun* (Seoul: Kip'ŭnsaem, 2000), 63–83.

7. Pak Nam-su, *Chŏkch'i 6 nyŏn-ŭi pukhan mundan*(Seoul: Pogosa, 1999), 122–123.

8. Kang Hŏn-guk, "Wolbukŭi ŭimi," *Yi T'ae-junŭi kyŏngu pip'yŏng munhak* 18, no. 66 (2004): 29–30.

9. Pang Min-ho, "Ilche malgi Yi T'ae-jun tanp'yŏng sosŏlŭi sasosŏl yangsang," in *Sanghŏ hakpo* 14, no. 2 (2005): 260.

10. Chang Yŏng-u, *Yi T'ae-jun sosŏl yŏngu* (Seoul: T'aehaksa, 1996), 260.

11. Elena Davydova (Pak Myŏng-sun), telephone interview, Yanji (China), 6 July 2000.

12. The Independence Club was a group of scholar-officials who urged reform and modernization from 1870 onward. See Keith Pratt and Richard Rutt, with additional material by James Hoare, *Korea: A Historical and Cultural Dictionary* (Richmond, Surrey, UK: University of Durham, Curzon, 1999), 187.

13. Chŏng Hyŏng-gi, *Yi T'ae-jun, chŏngch'i-ro chukki, chakka-ro sŏgi*, 16.

14. The writer recalls especially how in 1918 he graduated brilliantly from the Pongmyŏng school and received, as the best student, various awards—but no relative came to congratulate him. Returning home, the boy threw himself on the ground and started to cry: "Why do I not have a mother!" Ibid., 17.

15. *Hanguk myŏngjak tanp'yŏn sosŏl* (Seoul: Chiphyŏnchŏn, 1992), 1:262.

16. Chŏng Hyŏng-gi, *Yi T'ae-jun, chŏngch'i-ro chukki chakka-ro sŏgi*, 17.

17. Ibid., 18–20.

18. Ibid., 107.

19. Yi T'ae-jun, "Omongnyŏ," in *Wŏlbuk chakka-ŭi taep'yo munhak sŏnjip*, 388–402.

20. Ibid., 394.

21. Yi T'ae-jun, "Haengbok," in *Puk-ŭro kan chakka sŏnjip* (Seoul: Ŭryu munhwa sa, 1988), 4:5–15; Yi T'ae-jun, "Kŭrimja," in *Puk-ŭro kan chakka sŏnjip*, 4:15–35; Yi T'ae-jun, "Kisaeng Sandori," in *Puk-ŭro kan chakka sŏnjip*, 4:35–44. On traditional Korean courtesans, see Pratt and Rutt, *Korea*, 223.

22. For example, Chang Yŏng-u, *Yi T'ae-jun sosŏl yŏngu*, 260.

23. Yi T'ae-jun, "Kyŏrhon-ŭi anmasŏng," in *Puk-ŭro kan chakka sŏnjip*, 4:44–61.

24. Ibid., 47, 54.

25. Ibid., 58.

26. Ibid, 59.

27. Yi T'ae-jun, "Kohyang," in *Puk-ŭro kan chakka sŏnjip*, 4:61–83.

28. Ibid., 68.

29. Ibid., 69–71.

30. Yi T'ae-jun, "Kkoch' namunŭn simŏ nohko," in *Yi T'ae-jun munhak sŏnjip*, (Seoul: Kuiinsa, 1988), 76–87.

31. Yi T'ae-jun, "Ch'onttŭgi," in *Wŏlbuk chakka-ŭi taep'yo munhak sŏnjip*, 436.

32. For information on Korea's pure art movement, see Yun Pyŏng-no, *Hanguk-ŭi hyŏndae chakka chakp'umron*, 18–20.

33. Min Ch'un-hwan, "Yi T'ae-jun-ŭi chŏngijŏk koch'al," 45; Chŏng Hyŏn-gi, *Yi T'ae-jun, chŏngch'i-ro chukki, chakka-ro sŏgi*, 19.

34. Chŏng Ryul, interviews, Alma-Ata (Kazakhstan), 9–13 December 2001.

35. Cho Yong-man, "Ch'ago chajonsim kanghan sosŏlga," in *Yi T'ae-jun munhak yŏngu*, 409–415.

36. Chŏng Ryul interviews.

37. Yi T'ae-jun, "Kkamakui," in *Hanguk myŏngjak tanp'yŏn sosŏl*, 1:247–261.

38. Yi T'ae-jun, "T'okki iyagi," in *Yi T'ae-jun munhak sŏnjip*, 225–237.

39. See Chŏng Hyŏn-gi, *Yi T'ae-jun, chŏngch'i-ro chukki chakka-ro sŏgi*, 107; Chŏng Ryul interviews; Kim Hong-gyun, "Wŏlbuk chakka Yi T'ae-jun-ŭi t'onggok-ŭi kajŏksa," *Wolgan Chungang*, no. 300 (November 2000), http://www.kinds.or.kr.

40. Yi Myŏng-hŭi, *Sanghŏ Yi T'ae-jun munhak segye* (Seoul: Kukhak ch'aryowŏn, 1994), 35.

41. Yi T'ae-jun, *Yi T'ae-jun munhak chŏnjip* (Seoul: Kip'ŭn saem, 1988), 7:281.

42. Yi T'ae-jun, *Sasangŭi worya*, in *Yi T'ae-jun munhak chŏnjip*, vol. 7.

43. Yi Myŏng-hŭi, *Sanghŏ Yi T'ae-jun munhak segye*, 37; *Hanguk myŏngjak tanp'yŏn sosŏl*, 1:263.

44. Yi Myŏng-hŭi, *Sanghŏ Yi T'ae-jun munhak segye*, 37.

45. Chŏng Ryul interviews; *Hanguk myŏngjak tanp'yŏn sosŏl*, 1:264.

46. Yi T'ae-jun, "Haebang chŏnhu," in *Yi T'ae-jun munhak chŏnjip*, vol. 3 (1995), 13–52.

47. *Yi T'ae-jun munhak yŏngu*, 421.

48. *Who's Who in Korean Literature*, 522.

49. Robert A. Scalapino and Chong-sik Lee, *Communism in Korea* (Berkeley and Los Angeles: University of California Press, 1972), 282, 295.

50. Brian Myers, *Han Sŏr-ya and North Korean Literature: The Failure of Socialist Realism in the DPRK* (Ithaca, NY: East Asia Program, Cornell University, 1994), 50.

51. Chŏng Ryul interviews.

52. Ibid.

53. Geoffrey Hosking, *Beyond Socialist Realism: Soviet Fiction since Ivan Denisovich* (New York: Holmes and Meier, 1980), 8.

54. Yi T'ae-jun, "Abŏji mosi ot," in *Yi T'ae-jun munhak chŏnjip,* 3:53–57.

55. The October Struggle was a wave of Communist-inspired strikes and riots in 1946.

56. Yi T'ae-jun, "Ch'ŏt chŏnt'u," in *Yi T'ae-jun munhak sŏnjip,* 3:59–103.

57. Aleksandr Fadeev, *Razgrom* (Moscow: Hudozhestvennaia literatura, 1972).

58. Chang Yŏng-u, *Yi T'ae-jun's sosŏl yŏngu,* 307.

59. Yi T'ae-jun, "Horangi halmŏni," in *Yi T'ae-jun munhak chŏnjip,* vol. 3 (2000), 105–120.

60. Yi T'ae-jun, "38 sŏn ŏnŭ chigu-esŏ," in *Yi T'ae-jun munhak chŏnjip,* vol. 3 (2000), 121–129.

61. Ibid., 129.

62. Yi T'ae-jun, "Kohyang kil," in *Yi T'ae-jun munhak chŏnjip,* vol. 3 (1995), 197–198.

63. Ibid., 165–202, 197–198.

64. Yi T'ae-jun, "Paekpae ch'ŏnbae-ro," in *Yi T'ae-jun munhak chŏnjip,* vol. 3 (1995), 131–134.

65. Ibid., 134.

66. Yi T'ae-jun, "Nuga kulbok hanŭnga poja," in *Yi T'ae-jun munhak chŏnjip,* vol. 3 (1995), 35–140.

67. Yi T'ae-jun, "Miguk taesagwan," in *Yi T'ae-jun munhak sŏnjip,* vol. 3 (1995), 141–146.

68. Ibid., 144, 145, 146.

69. Yi Chŏl-ju, *Puk-ŭi yesurin* (Seoul: Kyemongsa, 1966), 235.

70. Chŏng Ryul interviews; Om Ho-sŏk, *Munye kibon* (Pyongyang: Kukrip ch'ulp'ansa, 1952), 190, 195.

71. Yi T'ae-jun, "Kogwihan saramdŭl," in *Yi T'ae-jun munhak chŏnjip,* vol. 3 (1995), 147–159.

72. Ibid., 157.

73. Om Ho-sŏk, *Munye kibon,* 193–195.

74. For positive critical accounts of Yi T'ae-jun, see An Ham-gwang, "Munhak-ŭi kinŭng-kwa ponjil," in *Ch'ŏngnyŏntŭl wihan munhakron* (Pyongyang: Minju ch'ŏngnyŏnsa, 1952), 36–38; and Han Hyo, "Sahoejuŭi reallijŭm-kwa chosŏn munhak," in *Ch'ŏngnyŏntŭl wihan munhakron* (Pyongyang: Minju ch'ŏngnyŏnsa, 1952), 189. In a 1949 article Yi Ki-yŏng mentions Yi T'ae-jun's prose among the "progressive" works created by writers of "new Korea." Li Gien (Yi Ki-yŏng), "O koreiskoi literature," *Zvezda,* 1949, no. 12:147–148.

75. Elena Davydova interview.

76. Yi Pyŏng-ryŏl, "Ch'ŏtchŏnt'u-wa kohyang kilŭi ŭimi," 390.

77. Chŏng Ryul interviews.

78. Elena Davydova interview; Chŏng Ryul interviews; Pak Nam-su, *Chŏkch'i 6 nyŏn pukhan mundan,* 122–123; Yi Chŏl-ju, *Pukhan yesurin,* 190–191.

79. Arkadii Perventsev, *V Koree* (Moscow: Sovetskii pisatel', 1950), 23.

80. Kim Hong-gyun, "Wŏlbuk chakka Yi T'ae-jun-ŭi t'onggok-ŭi kajŏksa," 12.

81. Chŏng Ryul interviews.

82. Pak Nam-su, *Chŏkch'i 6 nyŏn-ŭi pukhan mundan,* 117.

83. The article was first published in 1956 and then reprinted in 1961 in a collection of articles. Ŏm Ho-sŏk, "Yi T'ae-jun-ŭi munhak-ŭi pandongjŏk ponjil," in *Munhak-kwa hyŏndae chŏngsin* (Pyongyang: Chosŏn chakka tongmaeng ch'ulp'ansa, 1961), 436–477.

84. Ibid., 443, 444, 453.

85. Hong Sun-ch'ŏl, "Munhak-e issŏsŏ tangsŏng-kwa kyegŭpsŏng," *Chosŏn munhak,* 1953, no. 12:76–94.

86. An Ham-gwang, "Munhak-ŭi kyegŭpsŏng," in *Munhak-ŭi chihyang* (Pyongyang: Chosŏn chakka tongmaeng ch'ulp'ansa, 1954), 3–41.

87. The accusations presented here were typical. See Yi Sŏn-yŏng et al., eds., *Hyŏndae munhak pip'yŏng charyŏ chip 3: Pukhan p'yŏn* (Seoul: T'aehaksa, 1995), 24, 63.

88. See the analysis of these Han works in Myers, *Han Sŏr-ya,* 25–26 ("Transition Period") and 29–30 ("Pagoda").

89. The pre-Liberation works of Han Sŏr-ya are filled with the same apolitical pastoralism, melancholic lamentations about the good old days, and a dislike of modernity and urban life. See Myers, *Han Sŏr-ya,* 25–26. Yi Ki-yŏng's "Poor Village" is discussed in chapter 3 of this book.

90. Ŏm Ho-sŏk, "Yi T'ae-jun-ŭi munhak-ŭi pandongjŏk ponjil," 459, 467–470.

91. Ibid., 460–461.

92. Ibid.

93. Ibid., 467.

94. Ibid., 468.

95. Ibid., 469.

96. Ŏm Ho-sŏk, "Munhak ch'angjak-e issŏsŏŭi chŏnhyangsŏngŭi munje," in *Munhak-ŭi chihyang,* 152–153.

97. Om Ho-sŏk, *Munye kibon,* 178, 210, 214–215.

98. Ibid., 255–256.

99. An Ham-gwang, "Munhak-ŭi kyegŭpsŏng," 29. In the late 1950s, however, An would play an active part in the struggle against Soviet influence.

100. Ibid.

101. Hŏ Kyŏng, *Munhak yesul punya-esŏŭi kyegŭp t'ujaeng* (Pyongyang: Munhaksŏnjŏnsŏng, 1953), 35.

102. Ibid.

103. An Ham-gwang, "Munhak-ŭi kyegŭpsŏng," 29.

104. Myers, *Han Sŏr-ya,* 109. The full title of the conference is "A Conference of Enthusiasts of Publication Section of Literature, Arts, and Propaganda under the

Jurisdiction of Pyongyang Party Organization." The text of Han's speech can be found in "Pyongyangsi tang kwanha munhak yesul sŏnjŏn ch'ulp'an pumun yŏlsŏngja hoeŭi-esŏ Han Sŏr-ya tongji-ŭi pogo," *Chosŏn munhak*, 1956, no. 2:187–218.

105. *Yi T'ae-jun munhak yŏngu,* 422.
106. Chŏng Ryul interviews.
107. *Yi T'ae-jun munhak yŏngu,* 420–422.
108. Elena Davydova interview.
109. Kim Hong-gyun, "Wŏlbuk chakka Yi T'ae-jun-ŭi t'onggok-ŭi kajŏksa."
110. Myers, *Han Sŏr-ya,* 152.

Chapter 5: North Korean Critics as Political Executioners

1. See, for example, Hŏ Kyŏng, *Munhak yesul punya-esŏŭi kyegŭp t'ujaeng* (Pyongyang: Munhaksŏnjŏnsŏng, 1953); *Munye chŏnsŏne issŏsŏŭi pandongjŏk purŭjyoa sasangŭl pandaehayŏ* (Pyongyang: Chosŏn chakka tongmaeng ch'ulp'ansa, 1956); Ch'oe T'ak-ho, "Uri Munhak-ŭi sasangjŏk sungyŏlsŏng-ŭl wihan tang-ŭi t'ujaeng," in *Kongsangjuŭi kyoyang-kwa uri munhak* (Pyongyang: Kwahakwŏn ch'ulp'ansa, 1959), 24–76; and Ŏm Ho-sŏk, "Yi T'ae-jun-ŭi munhak-ŭi pandongjŏk ponjil," in *Munhak-kwa hyŏndae chŏngsin* (Pyongyang: Chosŏn chakka tongmaeng ch'ulp'ansa, 1961), 436–476.

2. Chang Hyŏng-jun, *Widaehan suryŏng Kim Il Sung tongji munhak puŏngdosa* (Pyongyang: Munye ch'ulp'ansa, 1993), 2:428–435, quoted in Pak T'ae-sang, *Pukhan munhak-ŭi hyŏnsang* (Seoul: Kip'ŭnsaem, 1999), 178–179.

3. Pyongyang used to promulgate its official view on literature in the USSR through a multitude of propagandistic booklets, such as *Pastsvet i razvitie koreiskoi kul'tury* (Pyongyang: Izdatel'stvo literatury na inostrannyh iazykah, 1959); and Sin Ku-hyŏn, *Koreiskaia literatura posle osvobozhdeniia* (Pyongyang: Izdatel'stvo literatury na inostrannyh iazykah, 1957. Soviet scholars were often reluctant to reflect this view in their works and, being unable to avoid the topic of purges, tended to mention it only vaguely, without naming any "bourgeois reactionary writers," some of whom they knew personally. See, for example, V. I. Ivanova, "Sovetskaia literatura v Koree," *Problemy Dalnego Vostoka,* 1974, no. 3:190; V. I. Ivanova, "Sovetskaia voenno-patrioticheskaia literatura v Koree," in *Literatura stran zarubezhnogo vostoka i sovetskaia literatura* (Moscow: Nauka, 1977), 131; and S. G. Nam, *Formirovanie narodnoi intelligentsii v KNDR* (Moscow: Nauka, 1970), 50–51. However, some early Soviet researchers sided completely with the official North Korean line. See, for instance, A. N. Taen, "Ocherki sovremennoi koreiskoi literatury (demokraticheskie natsional'nye tendentsii i sotsialisticheskii realizm v koreiskoi literature)" (PhD thesis, Herzen Pedagogical Institute, Leningrad, 1954).

4. Sin Hyŏng-gi and O Sŏng-ho, *Pukhan munhaksa* (Seoul: P'yŏngminsa, 2000).

5. Sim Wŏn-sŏp, "1950 nyŏndae pukhan si kaegwan," in *1950 nyŏndae nampukhan munhak* (Seoul: P'yŏngminsa, 1991), 107.

6. Ch'oe Ik-hyŏn, "1956 nyŏn 8 wŏl chongp'a sakŏn chŏnhuŭi pukhan munhak chilsŏ," in Yi Myŏng-jae, ed., *Pukhan munhak-ŭi inyŏm-kwa silch'e* (Seoul: Kukhak charyowŏn, 1998), 72.

7. Robert A. Scalapino and Chong-sik Lee, *Communism in Korea* (Berkeley and Los Angeles: University of California Press, 1972), 493–494.

8. Yun Chae-gŭn and Pak Sang-ch'ŏn, *Pukhan-ŭi hyŏndae munhak* (Seoul: Koryŏwŏn, 1990), 2:199–203.

9. Yim Yŏng-t'ae and Ko Yu-han, *Pukhan 50 nyŏnsa* (Seoul: Tŭlnyŏk', 1999), 1:333.

10. Kim Sŏng-su, *T'ongilŭi munhak pip'yŏng nonli* (Seoul: Ch'aek sesang, 2001), 153–186.

11. Ibid.

12. Kim Yun-sik, *Pukhan munhaksaron* (Seoul: Saemi, 1995), 52–58.

13. Pak T'ae-sang, *Pukhan munhak-ŭi hyŏnsang:* Pak T'ae-sang, *Pukhan munhak-ŭi tonghyang* (Seoul: Kip'ŭnsaem, 2002).

14. Pak T'ae-sang, *Pukhan munhak-ŭi hyŏnsang,* 209. Ch'ŏllima was a major mass mobilization campaign launched in 1957. Workers were encouraged to work hard and do their utmost to achieve unrealistically high production targets.

15. Kim Yun-sik, *Pukhan munhaksaron,* 100.

16. Pak T'ae-sang, *Pukhan munhak-ŭi tonghyang,* 163.

17. Kim Chae-yong, *Pukhan munhak-ŭi yŏksajŏk ihae* (Seoul: Munhak-kwa chisŏngsa, 1994).

18. Kim Chae-yong, "Pukhan-ŭi namnodanggye chakka sukch'ŏng," *Yŏksa pip'yŏng* 27 (Winter 1994): 328–364.

19. Yi Ki-pong, *Puk-ŭi munhak-kwa yesurin* (Seoul: Sasayŏn, 1986).

20. Kim Sŭng-hwan, "Haebang Kongganŭi pukhan munhak: Munhwajŏk minju kiji kŏnsŏl ronŭl chungsim-ŭro," *Hanguk hakpo* no. 63 (Summer 1991): 201–224.

21. Kim Chae-yong has candidly admitted that his assessment could hardly be deemed objective, since he had read a lot of North Korean critical articles on the subject but none of the disputed works. Kim Chae-yong, *Pukhan munhak-ŭi yŏksajŏk ihae,* 134–135.

22. Brian Myers, *Han Sŏr-ya and North Korean Literature: The Failure of Socialist Realism in the DPRK* (Ithaca, NY: East Asia Program, Cornell University, 1994), 82.

23. Chang Sa-sŏn, "An Ham-gwang haebang ihu hwaldong yŏngu," *Kukŏkuk munhak,* no. 126 (May 2000): 355–374.

24. Myers, *Han Sŏr-ya,* 49.

25. An Ham-gwang, "Munhak-ŭi kyegŭpsŏng," in *Munhak-ŭi chihyang* (Pyongyang: Chosŏn chakka tongmaeng ch'ulp'ansa, 1954), 3–41. Take, for instance, the following statement from this work: "The characteristic trait of the reactionary worldview of Yim Hwa is his inclination toward the wide use of concrete details in his poetical descriptions. The abundance of images like 'deep dark night,' 'the cold of night that penetrates the body to the very bones,' 'his head is white because of endless

suffering,' et cetera, beckons the reader to enter a world of sadness and distracts him from the struggle." Ibid., 30.

26. Ŏm Ho-sŏk, "Saenghwal-ŭi chinsil-kwa sasiljuŭi-rŭl wihayŏ," in *Sae hyŏnsil kwa munhak* (Pyongyang: Chosŏn chakka tongmaeng ch'ulp'ansa, 1954), 13–19.

27. Hong Sun-ch'ŏl, "Munhak-e issŏsŏ tangsŏng-kwa kyegŭpsŏng," *Chosŏn munhak,* 1953, no. 12:93.

28. See Yi Myŏng-jae, *Pukhan munhak sajŏn* (Seoul: Kukhak charyowŏn, 1995), 762–765; and Chang Sa-sŏn, "An Ham-gwang haebang ihu hwaldong yŏngu."

29. Chang Sa-sŏn, "Han Hyo-ŭi haebang ijŏn-e pip'yŏng hwaldong yŏngu," *Kukŏkuk munhak,* no. 117 (November 1996): 303–325.

30. Chŏng Ryul, interviews, Alma-Ata (Kazakhstan), 9–13 December 2001; Elena Davydova (Pak Myŏng-sun), telephone interview, Yanji (China), 6 July 2000.

31. Yi Myŏng-jae, *Pukhan munhak sajŏn,* 782.

32. Pak Nam-su, *Chŏk-ch'i 6 nyŏn-ŭi pukhan mundan* (Seoul: Pogosa, 1999), 109.

33. Chang Sa-sŏn, "Han Hyo-ŭi haebang ijŏn-e pip'yŏng hwaldong yŏngu."

34. Chŏng Ryul recollects that one day Hong Sun-ch'ŏl, widely known as a lecher himself, read aloud a love letter from Yi T'ae-jun to his mistress at a Party meeting. Chŏng Ryul interviews.

35. Kim Myŏng-su, "Purŭjoa ideorrogijŏk chanjae-waŭi t'ujaeng-ŭl wihayŏ," in *Munhak-ŭi chihyang,* 80–81.

36. Ŏm Ho-sŏk, "Nodong kyegŭp-ŭi hyŏngsang-kwa mihaksang-ŭi myŏtkaji munje," *Chosŏn munhak,* 1953, no. 11:124.

37. An Ham-gwang, "Munhak-ŭi kyegŭpsŏng," 32–35.

38. See Ŏm Ho-sŏk, "Munhak chakp'um-ŭi hyŏngsanghwa-e taehayŏ," in *Ch'ŏngnyŏntul wihan munhakron* (Pyongyang: Minju ch'ŏngnyŏnsa, 1952), 74; Ŏm Ho-sŏk, *Munye kibon* (Pyongyang: Kukrip ch'ulp'ansa, 1952), 64.

39. Ŏm Ho-sŏk, "Munhak ch'angjak-e issŏsŏŭi chŏnhyangsŏngŭi munje," in *Munhak-ŭi chihyang,* 159.

40. Chŏng Ryul, interviews.

41. It is interesting to compare the attitudes expressed several works by An Ham-gwang. In the article "8.15 haebang ihu sosŏl munhak-ŭi paljŏn kwajŏng," written in July 1950, he expressed total reverence for Yi T'ae-jun as "our talented novelist." See An Ham-gwang, "8.15 haebang ihu sosŏl munhak-ŭi paljŏn kwajŏng," in Yi Sŏn-yŏng et al., eds., *Hyŏndae munhak pip'yŏng charyo chip 2 (Ibukp'yŏn)* (Seoul: T'aehaksa, 1993), 25, 43. An expressed this same attitude toward Yi T'ae-jun in 1952. See An Ham-gwang, "Munhak-ŭi kinŭng-kwa ponjil," in *Ch'ŏngnyŏntŭl wihan munhakron* (Pyongyang: Minju ch'ŏngnyŏnsa, 1952), 36. In an article written in August 1951 An called Yim Hwa one of the most distinguished poets of Korea. See An Ham-gwang, "Ssaunŭn Chosŏn-ŭi simunhak-i chegihanŭn chungyohan myŏtkkaji t'ŭkching," in Yi Sŏn-yŏng et al., *Hyŏndae munhak pip'yŏng charyo chip 2 (Ibukp'yŏn),* 121, 123, 137, 138. Yet in an article written in 1954 An refers to the very same—but now doomed—Yim Hwa and Yi T'ae-jun with such rudeness that it leads us to doubt

the pre-Liberation reputation of An Ham-gwang as a "well-educated person." See An Ham-gwang, "Munhak-ŭi kyegŭpsŏng."

42. For instance, An's article "Ssaunŭn Chosŏn-ŭi simunhak-i chegihanŭn chungyohan myŏtkkaji t'ŭkching," written in August 1951, is steeped in expressions of servility to Cho Ki-ch'ŏn.

43. Concerning this incident, see Ku Sang, *Siwa salmŭi not'ŭ* (Seoul: Chayu munhaksa, 1988), 145–146; Yi Ki-pong, *Puk-ŭi munhak-kwa yesurin,* 186–198; and Yi Myŏng-jae, *Pukhan munhak sajŏn,* 876–878.

44. Chŏng Ryul interviews.

45. Quoted in Han Hyo, "Saeroun simunhak-ŭi paljŏn," in Yi Sŏn-yŏng et al., *Hyŏndae munhak pip'yŏng charyo chip 2 (Ibukp'yŏn),* 78–79.

46. Quoted in Ku Sang, *Siwa salmŭi not'ŭ,* 146–147.

47. Ku Sang, *Siwa salmŭi not'ŭ,* 145–155.

48. Ibid., 145–146; Chŏng Ryul interviews.

49. Ku Sang, *Siwa salmŭi not'ŭ,* 154.

50. Yi Myŏng-jae, *Pukhan munhak sajŏn,* 876–878.

51. Yi Ki-pong, *Puk-ŭi munhak-kwa yesurin,* 194.

52. Ku Sang, *Siwa salmŭi not'ŭ,* quoted in ibid.

53. Han Hyo, "Saeroun simunhak-ŭi paljŏn," 79.

54. Pak Chong-sik, "Sovremennaia koreiskaia literatura posle osvobozhdenia: Formirovanie i stanovlenie sotsrealisma v koreiskoi literature po tvorchestvu Li Giena," 13.

55. Sin Ku-hyŏn, *Koreiskaia literatura posle osvobozhdeniia* (doctoral thesis, Moscow State University, 1953), 6.

56. "Sijip Ŭnghyang p'irhwa sakkŏn chŏnmalgi" [The Details of the Ŭnghyang Incident], in *Ku Sang munhak sŏnjip* [Collected Works of Ku Sang] (Seoul, 1975), 404, quoted in Myers, *Han Sŏr-ya,* 47.

57. Between 1918 and 1932 there was an atmosphere of relatively free discussion in Soviet literature. Even works with explicit anti-Communist content could occasionally be published and discussed in the Soviet mass media. For instance, V. V. Veresaiev's novel *Deadlock (V tupike),* which criticized the state security police, Cheka, was published in 1923 and became the topic of widespread discussion. Evgenii Gromov, *Stalin: Vlast' i iskusstvo* (Moscow: Pespublika, 1998), 48–209.

58. Pak Chong-sik, "Sovremennaia koreiskaia literatura posle osvobozhdenia," 13.

59. *O partiinoi i sovetskoi pechati* (Moscow: Pravda, 1954), 346, quoted in Gromov, *Stalin,* 391.

60. Myers, *Han Sŏr-ya,* 47.

61. Chŏng Ryul interviews.

62. Gromov, *Stalin,* 388, 390.

63. Li Hsiao-t'i, "Making a Name and a Culture for the Masses in Modern China," *East Asia Cultures Critique* 9, no. 1 (2001): 55.

64. Han Hyo, "Saeroun simunhak- ŭi paljŏn," 79.

65. Ibid., 79–80.

66. Myers, *Han Sŏr-ya,* 39.

67. Han Hyo, "Uri munhak-ŭi 10 nyŏn," *Chosŏn munhak,* 1955, no. 6:142–143.

68. Take, for example, the characteristic speech by Han Sŏr-ya, first published in *Chosŏn munhak* in October 1953. See Han Sŏr-ya, "Chŏnguk chakka yesulga taehoeesŏ chinsulhan Han Sŏr-ya uiuŏnjangŭi pogo," in Yi Sŏn-yŏng et al., *Hyŏndae munhak pip'yŏng charyo chip* 3 *(Ibukp'yŏn),* 23.

69. According to Chŏng Ryul's account, An and Cho continued to work together as colleagues; the whole episode was presented as a "mistake by comrade An." Chŏng Ryul interviews.

70. Ch'oe Chae-bong, "Pundan sidae piun-ŭi p'yŏngnongga An Ham-gwang," *Hankyŏrye,* 16 June 1998, 12.

71. See, for instance, An Ham-gwang, "Munhak-ŭi kyegŭpsŏng," 3–41.

72. Yi Ch'ŏl-ju, *Puk-ŭi yesurin* (Seoul: Kyemongsa, 1966), 34–38.

73. Chŏng Ryul interviews.

74. Myers, *Han Sŏr-ya,* 80.

75. Andrei Lankov, *From Stalin to Kim Il Sung: The Formation of North Korea, 1945–1960* (New Brunswick, NJ: Rutgers University Press, 2002), 92.

76. *Sovremennaia koreiskaia poeziia* (Moscow: Izdatel'stvo inostrannoi literatury, 1950), 10.

77. An Ham-gwang, "Kosanghan realizŭmŭi nonŭi-wa ch'angchak paljŏn tosang-ŭi munje," *Munhak yesul,* 1949, no. 10:13.

78. Li Gien, "O koreiskoi literature" (in Russian translation), *Zvezda,* 1949, no. 12:147–148.

79. Kim Nam-ch'ŏn, "Kkul," *Chosŏn munhak,* 1951, no. 4:36–45.

80. Myers, *Han Sŏr-ya,* 81.

81. As an example of this kind of critical tendency, see Ŏm Ho-sŏk, "Munhak paljŏn-ŭi saeroun chingjo," *Munhak yesul,* 1952, no. 11:95.

82. This motif was especially popular in the Soviet tradition of war literature. For example, the theme of a terminally wounded soldier who holds back the whole guerrilla troop's movement appears in Fadeev's *Devastation,* which is considered to be an exemplary work of the 'glorious Soviet literature.' The positive protagonist of the novel orders the doctor to poison Frolov in order to free the others. This work was officially prescribed for emulation in North Korea. See Ivanova, "Sovetskaia literatura v Koree," 187.

83. *Yim Hwa chŏnjip* (Seoul: Pakijŏng, 2000) 1:317–323, 332–336, 337–342.

84. Yi Ch'ŏl-ju, *Puk-ŭi yesurin,* 93.

85. An Ham-gwang, "Ssaunŭn Chosŏn-ŭi simunhak-i chegihanŭn chungyohan myŏtkkaji t'ŭkching," 121, 123.

86. Taen, "Ocherki sovremennoi koreiskoi literatury," 190–199; Ivanova, "Sovetskaia voenno-patrioticheskaia literatura v Koree," in *Literatura stran zarubezhnogo vostoka i sovetskaia literatura* (Moscow: Nauka, 1977), 131, 133.

87. *Yim Hwa chŏnjip,* 333, 336.

88. In the tradition of Soviet poetry on war, the relationship of mother and child is usually presented as a contradiction between the mother as a troubled apolitical caregiver and the son (or daughter) as a bold fearless fighter, a hero in the making. Take, for instance, "The First Letter to Kama" (Pervoe pis'mo na Kamu), a popular wartime poem by Olga Berggolts. In the poem, the maternal protagonist thinks exclusively about the health of her daughter who is in Leningrad under siege, while the daughter is protecting the city and pays no attention to herself. See Olga Berggolts, *Stihi* (Moscow: Gosliizdat, 1962), 224.

89. *Yim Hwa chŏnjip,* 321.

90. Ibid., 64.

91. Ibid., 178.

92. See the translation of this story by Han Sŏr-ya in Myers, *Han Sŏr-ya,* 157–187.

93. Ŏm Ho-Sŏk, *Munye kibon,* 151, 154.

94. In the USSR the harangues against "formalism" and "bourgeois tendencies" increased just prior to Stalin's death.

95. See, for instance, An Ham-gwang, "Kosanghan realizŭmŭi nonŭi-wa ch'angchak paljŏn tosang-ŭi munje," 11–12.

96. Ibid., 210.

97. An Ham-gwang, "1951 nyŏndo munhak ch'angjo-ŭi sŏnggwa-wa cho'nmang," in Yi Sŏn-yŏng et al., *Hyŏndae munhak pip'yŏng charyo chip 2 (Ibukp'yŏn),* 143–163, first published in *Inmin,* 1952, no. 1; Sin Ko-song, "Yŏnguk-e issŏsŏ hyŏngsikjuŭi mit chayŏnjuŭijŏk chanjae-waŭi t'ujaeng," in Yi Sŏn-yŏng et al., *Hyŏndae munhak pip'yŏng charyo chip 2 (Ibukp'yŏn),*164–173, first published in *Munhak yesul,* 1952, no. 1. According to Chŏng Ryul, Sin Ko-song was the director of one of Pyongyang's theaters, as well as a playwright and critic who was popular among the actors and his acquaintances. Sin was never active in the political campaigns and strove to avoid confrontation. Yet, belonging to the KAPF faction and being a writer with a high profile, Sin sometimes could not avoid participation in the sectarian struggles. This is one example of such participation. Chŏng Ryul interviews.

98. Yi Chŏl-ju, *Puk-ŭi yesurin,* 92, 93.

99. Ibid., 92.

100. Ibid., 94.

101. Ibid., 95.

102. Ŏm Ho-sŏk, "Choguk haebang chŏnjaeng sigi-ŭi uri munhak," in Yi Sŏn-yŏng et al. *Hyŏndae munhak pip'yŏng charyo chip 2 (Ibukp'yŏn),* 185–208.

103. Ki Sŏk-pok, "Choguk haebang chŏnjaeng-kwa uri munhak," in Yi Sŏn-yŏng et al. *Hyŏndae munhak pip'yŏng charyo chip 2 (Ibukp'yŏn),* 223–240.

104. Han Hyo, "Chosŏn munhwa-e issŏsŏ sahoejuŭi reallijŭm-ŭi palsaeng chokŏn-kwa kŭ paljŏn-e issŏsŏŭi chet'ŭkching," *Munhak yesul,* 1952, no. 6:89.

105. An Ham-gwang, "Munhak-ŭi kinŭng-kwa ponjil," 48–54.

106. Ŏm Ho-sŏk, "Munhak chakp'um-ŭi hyŏngsanghwa-e taehayŏ," 86, 90.

107. Han Hyo, "Sahoejuŭi reallijŭm-kwa chosŏn munhak," in *Ch'ŏngnyŏntŭl wihan munhakron* (Pyongyang: Minju ch'ŏngnyŏnsa, 1952), 200.

108. Ibid., 170, 185, 197.

109. Ŏm Ho-sŏk, "Munhak chakp'um-ŭi hyŏngsanghwa-e taehayŏ," 108, 110.

110. Ŏm, "Munhak paljŏn-ŭi saeroun chingjo."

111. Scalapino and Lee, *Communism in Korea*, 438.

112. Beseda pervogo secretarja posol'stva SSSR v KNDR Vasiukevicha V. A. s sekretarem TsK TPK Pak Changokom, in the personal archive of Dr. Andrei Lankov. I thank Andrei Lankov for generously granting me access to this document in his personal archive.

113. Lankov, *From Stalin to Kim Il Sung*, 95.

114. Myers, *Han Sŏr-ya*, 85.

115. Beseda pervogo secretarja posol'stva SSSR v KNDR Vasiukevicha V. A. s sekretarem TsK TPK Pak Changokom.

116. Han Hyo, "Chayŏnjuŭi-rŭl pandaehanŭn t'ujaeng-e issŏsŏŭi chosŏn munhak," in Yi Sŏn-yŏng et al., *Hyŏndae munhak pip'yŏng charyo chip 2 (Ibukp'uŏn)*, 391–522.

117. Ibid., 419–420.

118. Han Hyo, "Sahoejuŭi reallijŭm-kwa chosŏn munhak"; Han Hyo, "Uri munhak-ŭi saeroun songgwa," *Munhak yesul*, 1952, no. 8:34–56; Han Hyo, "Chosŏn munhak-e issŏsŏ sahoejuŭi reallijŭm-ŭi palsaeng chokŏn-kwa kŭ paljŏn-e issŏsŏŭi che t'ŭkching," *Munhak yesul*, 1952, no. 6:89.

119. Han Hyo, "Chayŏnjuŭi-rŭl pandaehanŭn t'ujaeng-e issŏsŏŭi chosŏn munhak," 438.

120. Han Hyo, "Sahoejuŭi reallijŭm-kwa chosŏn munhak," 170.

121. Han Hyo, "Chayŏnjuŭi-rŭl pandaehanŭn t'ujaeng-e issŏsŏŭi chosŏn munhak," 442. The RAPP was disbanded by Stalin in 1932.

122. Ibid., 497–498.

123. Ibid., 467.

124. Ibid., 504.

125. Ibid., 109.

126. Myers, *Han Sŏr-ya*, 86.

127. Chŏng-Ryul interviews; Yi Ch'ŏl-ju, *Puk-ŭi yesurin*, 184; Pak Nam-su, *Chŏk-ch'i 6 nyŏn-ŭi pukhan mundan*, 118–119.

128. Myers, *Han Sŏr-ya*, 86.

129. Hong Sun-ch'ŏl, "Munhak-e issŏsŏ tangsŏng-kwa kyegŭpsŏng," 86.

130. Ibid., 88.

131. Ibid., 92–93.

132. Ŏm Ho-sŏk, "Nodong kyegŭp-ŭi hyŏngsang-kwa mihaksang-ŭi myŏtkaji munje," 122, 124.

133. Chŏng Ryul interviews.

134. Myers, *Han Sŏr-ya*, 32.

135. Ŏm Ho-sŏk, "Nodong kyegŭp-ŭi hyŏngsang-kwa mihaksang-ŭi myŏtkaji munje," 120.

136. Myers, *Han Sŏr-ya,* 20–25, 29.

137. Andrei Lankov, "Kim Il Sung's Campaign against the Soviet Faction in Late 1955 and the Birth of *Chuch'e,*" *Korean Studies* 23 (1999): 43–67.

138. Ibid., 47.

139. Ibid., 49.

140. Chŏng Ryul interviews.

141. Andrei Lankov, "Kim Il Sung's Campaign," 48. The transcription of Song Chin-p'a's name has been given in accordance with an oral communication from Andrei Lankov.

142. Myers, *Han Sŏr-ya,* 70, 100.

143. Chŏng Ryul interviews.

144. Ibid.

145. Lankov, "Kim Il Sung's Campaign," 49.

146. Kim Il Sung, *Sasang saŏp-esŏ kyojojuŭiwa hyŏngsikjuŭi-rŭl t'oejihago chuch'e-rŭl hwangnip hal te taehayŏ* (Pyongyang: Chosŏn nodongdang ch'ulp'ansa, 1960), 4–5.

147. Chŏng Ryul interviews.

148. Han Sŏr-ya, "Pyongyangsi tang kwanha munhak yesul sŏnjŏn ch'ulp'an pumun yŏlsŏngja hoeŭi-esŏ Han Sŏr-ya tongji-ŭi pogo," *Chosŏn munhak,* 1956, no. 2:201.

149. Ŏm Ho-sŏk, "Yi T'ae-jun-ŭi munhak-ŭi pandongjŏk chŏngch'e," *Chosŏn munhak,* 1956, no. 3:160–161.

150. An Ham-gwang, "Chosŏn-ŭi hyŏnsil-kwa p'yŏnghwa-ŭi yŏkryang," *Chosŏn munhak,* 1956, no. 3:119–139.

151. Han Sŏr-ya, "Tang-ŭi munye chŏngch'aek-kwa hamkke paljŏnhanŭn uri munhak yesul," *Chosŏn munhak,* 1956, no. 4:119.

152. Yun Si-ch'ŏl, "Inmin-ŭl pibanghan pandong munhak-ŭi tokso (Kim Nam-ch'ŏn 8.15 haebang hu chakp'um-ŭl chungsim-ŭro)," *Chosŏn munhak,* 1956, no. 5:142, 146.

153. Lankov, "Kim Il Sung's Campaign," 56.

154. Lankov, *From Stalin to Kim Il Sung,* 154–193.

155. Myers, *Han Sŏr-ya,* 110–111.

156. Han Sŏr-ya, "Uri munhak-ŭi saeroun ch'angjakchŏk angyang-ŭl wihayŏ," *Chosŏn munhak,* 1957, no. 12:17–19.

157. See, for instance, Kim Myŏng-su, "Purŭjoa ideorrogijŏk chanjae-waŭi t'ujaeng-ŭl wihayŏ," 45–55.

158. Chŏng Ryul interviews.

Conclusion

1. Brian Myers, *Han Sŏr-ya and North Korean Literature: The Failure of Socialist Realism in the DPRK* (Ithaca, NY: East Asia Program, Cornell University, 1994), 151–152.

2. For accounts of Stalin's involvement in literary matters, see the memoirs of Denis Babichenko, *Pisateli i tsenzory: Sovetskaia literatura 1940 godov pod politicheskim kontrolem TsK* (Moscow: Rossia molodaya, 1994); Ilia Erenburg, *Liudi, gody, zhizn* (Moscow: Sovetskii pisatel', 1961); Konstantin Simonov, *Glazami cheloveka moego pokoleniya: Razmyshleniia o I. V. Staline* (Moscow: Respublika, 1989); and Elena Bulgakova, *Dnevnik Eleny Bulgakovoi* (Moscow: Knizhnaja palata, 1990).

3. Take, for example, the following typical comment by Stalin regarding two poems by Aleksandr Bezymensky: "There is nothing petit-bourgeois or anti-Party in these poems. Both poems may be viewed as exemplary pieces of proletarian art *for the present moment*" (my emphasis). Quoted in Evgenii Gromov, *Stalin: Vlast' i iskusstvo* (Moscow: Pespublika, 1998), 78.

4. Roi Medvedev, *O Staline i stalinisme* (Moscow: Progress, 1990), 364–365.

5. D. E. Pollard, "The Short Story in the Cultural Revolution," *China Quarterly*, no. 73 (March 1978): 99–121.

6. Gromov, *Stalin*, 104, 146–159.

7. See the resolution of the Central Committee of the All-Soviet Communist Party of Bolsheviks (VKPb) of 1940, "On Literary Critique and Bibliography," which states that "nowadays literary criticism does not influence the development of Soviet literature enough." *O partiinoi i sovetskoi pechati* (Moscow: Pravda, 1954), 488.

8. Gromov, *Stalin*, 308.

9. Ibid., 146, 308, 313.

10. "Rezolutziya TsK VKP (b) 'O perestroike literaturno hudozhestvennyh organizatzii'" [Resolution of the Central Committee of the All-Russian Communist Party of Bolsheviks "On the Reconstruction of Literary and Artistic Organizations"], *Pravda*, 24 April 1932, 1.

11. T. A. Hsia, "Heroes and Hero-Worship in Chinese Communist Fiction," *China Quarterly*, no. 13 (January–March 1963): 115.

Bibliography

Interviews and Unpublished Documents

Beseda pervogo sekretarja posol'stva SSSR v KNDR Vasiukevicha V. A. s sekretarem TsK TPK Pak Changokom [Record of a talk by the first secretary of the embassy of the USSR in the DPRK V. A. Vasiukevich with the secretary of the Central Committee of the Korean Workers' Party Pak Ch'ang-ok]. In the personal archive of Dr. Andrei Lankov.

Cho Ki-ch'ŏn. "Lichnyi listok po uchetu kadrov" [Personal record of an employee]. Official questionnaire completed by Cho, 18 June 1946. Photocopy in the author's archive.

Cho Ki-ch'ŏn. Undated letter to his wife. In the family archive; photocopy in the author's archive.

Cho Yurii. Interviews, Moscow, October–November 2001.

Chŏng Ryul. Interviews, Alma-Ata (Kazakhstan), 9–13 December 2001.

Davydova, Elena (Pak Myŏng-sun). Telephone interview, Yanji (China), 6 July 2000.

Gabroussenko, Valeri V., and Irina P. Gabroussenko. Telephone interview, Novosibirsk (Russia), 5 November 2003.

Ivanova, V. I. Telephone interview, Moscow, 3 February 2002.

Kontsevich, Leo R. Interviews, Moscow, 3 September 2002 and 10 October 2003.

Lankova, Valentina. Telephone interview, Moscow, 22 October 2002.

Pak Sang-ho. Interview, Leningrad, November 1989. Transcript kindly provided by Andrei Lankov.

Yudolevitch, Liia Grigorievna. Undated letters written to the poet's son, Cho Yurii, in 1976–1977. Originals in the author's archive.

Published Materials

"70-letie sovetskogo pasporta" [The 70th Anniversary of the Soviet Passport]. *Demoscope Weekly,* no. 93, 2002. http://www.demoscope.ru/weekly/2002/093/arxiv01.php.

"Aeguk siin ko Cho Ki-ch'ŏn-ŭl ch'umohayŏ yugo 'pihaenggi sanyangkkun-ŭl' naemyŏnsŏ" [In Memory of the Late Cho Ki-ch'ŏn, the Patriotic Poet: His Unpublished Poem "Enemy Plane Hunters"]. *Munhak yesul,* 1953, no. 7:78–82.

An Ham-gwang. "1951 nyŏndo munhak ch'angjo-ŭi sŏnggwa-wa cho'nmang" [The

Successes and Prospects of Our Literature in 1951]. In Yi Sŏn-yŏng et al., *Hyŏndae munhak pip'yŏng charyo chip 2 (Ibukp'yŏn)*, 143–163.

———."8.15 haebang ihu sosŏl munhak-ŭi paljŏn kwajŏng" [The Process of the Development of Fiction after 15 August 1945]. In Yi Sŏn-yŏng et al., *Hyŏndae munhak pip'yŏng charyo chip 2 (Ibukp'yŏn)*, 7–48.

———. *Chosŏn munhaksa* [History of Korean Literature]. Pyongyang: Kyoyuk tosŏ ch'ulp'ansa, 1956.

———. "Chosŏn-ŭi hyŏnsil-kwa p'yŏnghwa-ŭi yŏkryang" [Korean Reality and Potentials for Peace]. *Chosŏn munhak*, 1956, no. 3:119–139.

———. "Kosanghan realizŭmŭi nonŭi-wa ch'angchak paljŏn tosang-ŭi munje" [Discussions about "High Realism" and Questions of the Development of Creative Writing]. *Munhak yesul*, 1949, no. 10:4–36.

———. "Munhak-ŭi kinŭng-kwa ponjil" [The Capacity and Meaning of Literature]. In *Ch'ŏngnyŏntŭl wihan munhakron* [Literary Theory for the Youth], 2–70. Pyongyang: Minju ch'ŏngnyŏnsa, 1952.

———. "Munhak-ŭi kyegŭpsŏng" [Class Consciousness in Literature]. In *Munhak-ŭi chihyang* [Literary Tendencies], 3–41. Pyongyang: Chosŏn chakka tongmaeng ch'ulp'ansa, 1954.

———. "Ssaunŭn Chosŏn-ŭi simunhak-i chegihanŭn chungyohan myŏtkkaji t'ŭkching" [A Few Important Characteristics of the Poetry of the Fighting Korea]. In Yi Sŏn-yŏng et al., *Hyŏndae munhak pip'yŏng charyo chip 2 (Ipukp'yŏn)*, 116–142.

Armstrong, Charles. *The North Korean Revolution, 1945–1950*. Ithaca, NY, and London: Cornell University Press, 2003.

Babichenko, Denis. *Pisateli i tsenzory: Sovetskaia literatura 1940 godov pod politicheskim kontrolem TsK* [Writers and Censors: Soviet Literature of the 1940s under the Political Control of the Central Committee]. Moscow: Rossia molodaya, 1994.

Berezhkov, Valentin. *Kak ia stal' perevodchikom Stalina* [How I Became Stalin's Interpreter]. Moscow: Daem, 1993.

Berggolts, Olga. *Stihi* [Poems]. Moscow: Gosliizdat, 1962.

Bisztray, George. *Marxist Models of Literary Realism*. New York: Columbia University Press, 1978.

Bolshaia sovetskaia entsiklopediia [Great Soviet Encyclopedia]. Vol. 40. Moscow: Bolshaia sovetskaia entsiklopediia, 1957.

———. Vol. *Sovetskii Soyuz* [Soviet Union]. Moscow: Sovetskaia entsiklopediia, 1948.

Brown, Edward J. *Russian Literature since the Revolution*. Cambridge, MA, and London: Harvard University Press, 1982.

Bulgakova, Elena. *Dnevnik Eleny Bulgakovoi* [Diary of Elena Bulgakova]. Moscow: Knizhnaja palata, 1990.

Chaibong, Hahm. "The Two South Koreas: A House Divided." *Washington Quarterly* 28, no. 3 (Summer 2005): 57–72.

Chang Hyŏng-jun. *Widaehan suryŏng Kim Il Sung tongji munhak puŏngdosa* [The Directions of the Great Leader Kim Il Sung in Regards to Literary Criticism], 2:428–435.Pyongyang: Munye ch'ulp'ansa, 1993.

Chang Sa-sŏn. "An Ham-gwang haebang ihu hwaldong yŏngu" [A Study of An Hamgwang's Activity after Liberation]. *Kukŏkuk munhak,* no. 126 (May 2000): 355–374.

———. "Han Hyo-ŭi haebang ijŏn-e pip'yŏng hwaldong yŏngu" [A Study of the Critical Activity of Han Hyo before Liberation]. *Kukŏkuk munhak,* no. 117 (November 1996): 303–325.

Chang Yŏng-u. *Yi T'ae-jun sosŏl yŏngu* [A Study of Yi T'ae-jun's Literature]. Seoul: T'aehaksa, 1996.

Cheremnin, G. S. *Obraz Stalina v sovetskoi hudozhestvennoi literature* [The Image of Stalin in Soviet Fiction]. Moscow: Pravda, 1950.

Chesneaux, Jean. *Peasant Revolts in China, 1840–1949.* Translated by C. A. Curwen, London: Thames and Hudson, 1973.

Cho Ki-ch'ŏn. "Huip'aram" [Whistle]. *Chosŏn munhak,* 1990, no. 4:81.

———. *Paektusan* [Paektu Mountain]. In *Cho Ki-ch'ŏn sŏnjip* [Collection of Cho Ki-ch'ŏn's Works], 1:5–152. Pyongyang: Munhwa chŏnsŏnsa, 1952.

———. "Saengae-ŭi norae" [The Song of Life]. In *Cho Ki-ch'ŏn sŏnjip* [Collection of Cho Ki-ch'ŏn's Works], 1:153–360. Pyongyang: Munhwa chŏnsŏnsa, 1952.

Cho Yong-man. "Ch'ago chajonsim kanghan sosŏlga" [Cold and Dignified Literary Man]. In *Yi T'ae-jun munhak yŏngu* [A Study of Yi T'ae-jun's Literature], 409–415. Seoul: Kip'ŭnsaem, 1993.

Ch'oe Chae-bong. "Pundan sidae piun-ŭi p'yŏngnongga An Ham-kwan" [An Hamgwang, a North Korean Critic with a Tragic Fate]. *Hankyŏrye,* 16 June 1998, 12.

Ch'oe Ch'ang-man. "Onŭldo ch'ŏngsanbŏl-e kyesine uri suryŏngnim" [Even Today Our Leader Is in Ch'ŏngsanbŏl]. In *Pit'nanŭn rojŏng,* 107.

Ch'oe Hyŏn-su. "Pukhan-ŭi ch'ŏldo hyŏnhwang" [The Contemporary State of Railways in North Korea]. *Kukmin ilbo,* 19 September 2000, 5.

Ch'oe Ik-hyŏn. "1956 nyŏn 8 wŏl chongp'a sakŏn chŏnhuŭi pukhan munhak chilsŏ" [The Situation in North Korean Literature around the Event of August 1956]. In Yi Myŏng-jae, ed., *Pukhan munhak-ŭi inyŏm-kwa silch'e* [The Ideas and the Reality of North Korean Literature], 59–91. Seoul: Kukhak charyowŏn, 1998.

Ch'oe T'ak-ho. "Uri Munhak-ŭi sasangjŏk sungyŏlsŏng-ŭl wihan tang-ŭi t'ujaeng" [The Struggle of Our Party for the Ideological Purity of Our Literature]. In *Kongsangjuŭi kyoyang-kwa uri munhak* [Communist Education and Our Literature], 24–76. Pyongyang: Kwahakwŏn ch'ulp'ansa, 1959.

Chŏn Kŭm-ok. "Hago ttohago sip'ŭn mal" [The Words I Would Like to Say More and More]. In *Pit'nanŭn rojŏng,* 169–172.

Ch'ŏn Se-bong. "Sŏkkaeul-ŭi saebom" [New Spring in Sŏkkaeul]. *Chosŏn munhak,* 1956, no. 6:21–64.

Chŏn Yŏng-sŏn. "Pukhanŭi yŏnguŏnhan siin Cho Ki-ch'ŏn" [The Eternal Revolutionary Poet Cho Ki-ch'ŏn]. *Pukhan,* 2000, no. 3:194–203.

Chŏng Hye-gyŏng. "Inmin-ŭi sahoejuui chŏngch'esŏng kŏnsŏl-kwa 'kosanghan' riŏllijŭm" [Construction of People's Socialism and High Realism]. In Choe Tong-ho, ed., *Nambukhan hyŏndae munhaksa* [History of Contemporary North and South Korean Literature], 183–201. Seoul: Nanam ch'ulp'ansa, 1995.

Chŏng Hyŏn-gi. *Yi T'ae-jun, chŏngch'i-ro chukki, chakka-ro sŏgi* [Yi T'ae-jun: Killed by Politics but Survived as a Writer]. Seoul: Kŏnmin taehakkyo ch'ulp'anbu, 1994.

Chŏng Mun-hyang. "Chogukiyŏ kkŭt'ŏmnŭn na-ŭi kippŭmiyŏ" [O My Country, My Endless Joy!]. *Chosŏn munhak,* 1956, no. 1:13–15.

Chŏng Ok-sŏn. "Tonggabi" [A Person of the Same Age]. In *Pit'nanŭn rojŏng,* 255–276.

Chosŏn munhaksa [History of North Korean Literature]. Vol. 10, *Haebang hu p'yŏn* [After Liberation]. Pyongyang: Sahoe kwahak ch'ulp'ansa, 1994.

Chosŏn munhaksa (1926–1945) [History of Korean Literature (1926–1945)]. Pyongyang: Kwahak, paekkwa sajŏn ch'ulp'ansa, 1981.

Chosŏn munhaksa nyŏndaep'yo [Chronology of the History of Korean Literature]. Pyongyang: Kyoyuk tosŏ ch'ulp'ansa, 1957.

Ch'u C'hŏn and Ku An-hwan, eds. *Hanguk myŏgjak tanp'yŏn sosŏl* [Famous Korean Short Stories]. Seoul: Chiphyŏnjŏn, 1978.

Chu Yŏng-bo. "Ssoryŏn yŏnghwanŭn uri yŏnghwachak-ŭi san kyojae-ga toenda" [Soviet Films Became the Living Textbooks for Our Film Production Industry]. *Munhak yesul,* 1949, no. 10:55–59.

Chung Jin-bae. "Korean and Chinese Experience of Marxism: Hermeneutic Problems and Cultural Transformation." *Korean Journal* 35, no. 2 (Summer 1995): 54–73.

Clark, Katerina. *The Soviet Novel: History as Ritual.* Chicago: University of Chicago Press, 1981.

Durdin, A. A. *Etiudy o Mihaile Sholokhove: Tvorchestvo pisatelja klassika v duhovnoi kulture Rossii* [Essays about Mikhail Sholokhov: His Activity in Russian Spiritual Culture]. Ulyanovsk, Russia: UI GTU, 1999.

Dzhambaev, Dzhambul. "Narkom Ezhov" [People's Commissar Ezhov]. 1937. http://cray.onego.ru/~solvio/gostinaya/albom/literatura/ezhov.html.

Erenburg, Ilia. *Liudi, gody, zhizn* [People, Years, Life]. Moscow: Sovetskii pisatel', 1961.

Fadeev, Aleksandr. *Razgrom* [Devastation]. Moscow: Hudozhestvennaia literatura, 1972.

———. *Sobranie sochinenii* [Collected Works]. Vols. 1 and 2. Moscow: Pravda, 1987.

"Famous Korean Poet." Article distributed by the Korean Central News Agency, 5 July 2001.

Gabroussenko, Tatiana. "Cho Ki-ch'ŏn: The Person behind the Myths." *Korean Studies,* 2005, no. 29:55–95.

Gitovich, Aleksandr, and Boris Bursov. *My videli Koreiu* [We Have Seen Korea]. Leningrad: Lenizdat, 1948.

Gorky, Maxim. "Foma Gordeev." In Gorky, *Izbrannye proizvedeniia v treh tomah,* 2:144–408.

———. *Izbrannye proizvedeniia v treh tomah* [Collected Works in Three Volumes]. Moscow: Gosudarstvennoe izdatel'stvo hudozhestvennoi literatury, 1951.

———. "Konovalov." In Gorky, *Izbrannye proizvedeniia v treh tomah,* 2:81–130.

———. *Mat'* [Mother]. In Gorky, *Izbrannye proizvedeniia v treh tomah,* 2:410–729.

———. "Na dne" [The Low Depths]. In Gorky, *Izbrannye proizvedeniia v treh tomah,* 2:524–591.

Gromov, Evgenii. *Stalin: Vlast' i iskusstvo* [Stalin: Power and the Arts]. Moscow: Pespublika, 1998.

Han Chŏng-gyu. "Chasikdŭr-ege chaju hanŭn mal" [Words I Often Say to My Children]. In *Pit'nanŭn rojŏng,* 130–132.

Han Hyo. "Chayŏnjuŭi-rŭl pandaehanŭn t'ujaeng-e issŏsŏŭi chosŏn munhak" [Korean Literature in Struggle with Naturalism] (1953). In Yi Sŏn-yŏng et al., *Hyŏndae munhak pip'yŏng charyo chip 2 (Ibukp'yŏn),* 391–522.

———. "Chosŏn munhak-e issŏsŏ sahoejuŭi reallijŭm-ŭi palsaeng chokŏn-kwa kŭ paljŏn-e issŏsŏŭi che t'ŭkching" [The Conditions for the Emergence of Socialist Realism in Korean Literature and the Characteristics of Its Development]. *Munhak yesul,* 1952, no. 6:83–100.

———. "Saeroun simunhak-ŭi paljŏn" [The Development of New Poetry]. In Yi Sŏn-yŏng et al., *Hyŏndae munhak pip'yŏng charyo chip 2 (Ibukp'yŏn),* 49–82.

———. "Sahoejuŭi reallijŭm-kwa chosŏn munhak" [Socialist Realism and Korean Literature]. In *Ch'ŏngnyŏntŭl wihan munhakron* [Literary Theory for the Youth], 138–204. Pyongyang: Minju ch'ŏngnyŏnsa, 1952.

———. "Uri munhak-ŭi 10 nyŏn" [Ten Years of Our Literature]. *Chosŏn munhak,* 1955, no. 6:138–172.

———. "Uri munhak-ŭi saeroun songgwa" [The New Successes of Our Literature]. *Munhak yesul,* 1952, no. 8:34–56.

Han Myŏng-ch'ŏn. "Pot'ong nodongil" [The Ordinary Course of Labor]. *Chosŏn munhak,* 1956, no. 2:76–79.

Han Sŏng-ho. "Ŏksen nalgae" [Strong Wings]. *Chosŏn munhak,* 2005, no. 3:59–72.

Han Sŏr-ya. "Chŏnguk chakka yesulga taehoeesŏ chinsulhan Han Sŏr-ya uiuŏnjangŭi pogo" [Report by Chairman Han Sŏr-ya Presented at the All-Writers' Congress]. In Yi Sŏn-yŏng et al., *Hyŏndae munhak pip'yŏng charyo chip 2 (Ibukp'yŏn),* 7–46.

———. "P'ajeyebŭ-wa na" [Fadeev and I]. *Chosŏn munhak,* 1956, no. 8:97–106.

———. "Pyongyangsi tang kwanha munhak yesul sŏnjŏn ch'ulp'an pumun yŏlsŏngja hoeŭi-esŏ Han Sŏr-ya tongji-ŭi pogo" [The Speech of Comrade Han Sŏr-ya Given at a Meeting of Activists in the Spheres of Literature, the Arts, Propaganda, and Publishing under the Leadership of the Pyongyang Party Committee]. *Chosŏn munhak,* 1956, no. 2:187–213.

———. "Tang-ŭi munye chŏngch'aek-kwa hamkke paljŏnhanŭn uri munhak yesul"

[Our Literature and Arts That Are Developing According to the Cultural Policy of Our Party]. *Chosŏn munhak*, 1956, no. 4:107–123.

———. "Uri munhak-ŭi saeroun ch'angjakchŏk angyang-ŭl wihayŏ" [For a New Rise in Creativity of Our Literature]. *Chosŏn munhak*, 1957, no. 12:17–19.

———, ed. *Yŏnggwang-ŭi Ssŭttalinege: Ssŭttalin t'ansaeng 70-chunyŏn kinyŏm ch'ulp'ansa* [Glory to Stalin: An Anthology of Works Dedicated to the 70th Birthday of Stalin]. Pyongyang: Pukchosŏn munhakyesul ch'ongtongmaeng, 1949.

Han Sŭng-ok. *Yi Kwang-su: Pigŭkjŏk segye insik-kwa ch'owŏr ŭji* [Yi Kwang-su: A Tragic Perception of the World and an Extraordinary Will]. Seoul: Kŏnguk taehakkyo ch'ulp'anbu, 1995.

Hanguk munhak taesajŏn [Encyclopedia of Korean Literature]. Seoul: Munwŏngak, 1973.

Hanguk myŏngjak tanp'yŏn sosŏl [Famous Korean Short Stories]. Seoul: Chiphyŏnchŏn, 1992.

Hayward, Max. Introduction to Max Hayward and Leopold Labedz, eds., *Literature and Revolution in Soviet Russia, 1917–1962*, xv. Edited by Max Hayward and Leopold Labedz. London: Oxford University Press, 1963.

Hŏ Kyŏng. *Munhak yesul punya-esŏŭi kyegŭp t'ujaeng* [Class Struggle in Literature and the Arts]. Pyongyang: Munhaksŏnjŏnsŏng, 1953.

Hohlov, N. *Koreia nashih dnei* [The Korea of Our Times]. Moscow: Molodaia gvardiia, 1956.

Hollander, Paul. *Political Pilgrims: Travels of Western Intellectuals to the Soviet Union, China and Cuba, 1928–1978*. New York and Oxford: Oxford University Press, 1981.

Hong Chŏng-sŏn et al. "Cho Ki-ch'ŏn chaejomyŏng: 'Na' poda 'uri' kangyohan sunsujuŭija" [Re-illumination of Cho Ki-ch'ŏn: The Purist Who Worshiped "Us" More Than "I"]. *Hanguk ilbo*, 8 August 1992, 4.

———. "Cho Ki-ch'ŏn chaejomyŏng: Ŭnp'ye, waegok . . . Kim Il Sung's ch'eje 'hŭisaengyang'" [Re-illumination of Cho Ki-ch'ŏn: Silenced and Distorted . . . Scapegoated by Kim Il Sung's "System"]. *Hanguk ilbo*, 5 August 1992, 4.

Hong Sun-ch'ŏl. "Munhak-e issŏsŏ tangsŏng-kwa kyegŭpsŏng" [Party Spirit and Class Consciousness in Literature]. *Chosŏn munhak*, 1953, no. 12:76–94.

Hosking, Geoffrey. *Beyond Socialist Realism: Soviet Fiction since Ivan Denisovich*. New York: Holmes and Meier, 1980.

Hsia, T. A. "Heroes and Hero-Worship in Chinese Communist Fiction." *China Quarterly*, no. 13 (January–March 1963): 113–138.

Hyŏndae chosŏn munhak sŏnjip [Anthology of Contemporary Korean Literature]. Vol 3. Pyongyang: Chosŏn chakka tongmaeng ch'ulp'ansa, 1958.

Im Hŏn-yŏng. "The Meaning of the City in Korean Literature." *Korea Journal* 27 (May 1987): 24–36.

Isakovskii, Mikhail. *Stihi, poemy i pesni* [Verses, Poems and Songs]. Moscow: Gosudarstvennoe izdatel'stvo hudozhestvennoi literatury, 1951.

Ivanova, V. I. "Li Gien i ego roman 'Zemlia'" [Yi Ki-yŏng and His Novel "Land"]. In *Kratkie soobscheniia instituta vostokovedeniia* [Short Reports of the Oriental Studies Institute], no. 18, 28–40. Moscow: Izdatel'stvo AN SSSR, 1955.

————. *Li Gien: Zhizn i tvorchestvo* [Yi Ki-yŏng: His Life and Works]. Moscow: Vostochnaia literatura, 1962.

————. *Novaia proza Korei* [The New Prose of Korea]. Moscow: Nauka, 1987.

————. "Poiski polozhitel'nogo geroia v rannem tvorchestve Li Giena" [Searching for the Positive Hero in the Early Works of Yi Ki-yŏng]. In *Koreiskaia literatura* [Korean Literature], 89–116. Moscow: Akademiia nauk SSSR, Izdatel'stvo vostochnoi literatury, 1959.

————. "Sovetskaia literatura v Koree" [Soviet Literature in Korea]. *Problemy Dalnego Vostoka*, 1974, no. 3:187–193.

————. "Sovetskaia voenno-patrioticheskaia literatura v Koree" [Soviet Patriotic War Literature in Korea]. In *Literatura stran zarubezhnogo vostoka i sovetskaia literatura* [Literature of the Overseas Oriental Countries and Soviet Literature], 124–138. Moscow: Nauka, 1977.

Kang Hŏn-guk. "Wolbukŭi ŭimi" [The Meaning of Going to the North]. *Yi T'aejunŭi kyŏngu pip'yŏng munhak* 18, no. 66 (2004): 7–27.

Kang Yŏng-ju. *Pyŏkch'o Hong Myŏng-hŭi yŏngu* [A Study of Pyŏkch'o Hong Myŏng-hŭi]. Seoul: Ch'angjak-kwa pip'yŏngsa, 1999.

Ki Sŏk-pok. "Choguk haebang chŏnjaeng-kwa uri munhak" [War for the Liberation of the Motherland and Our Literature]. In Yi Sŏn-yŏng et al., *Hyŏndae munhak pip'yŏng charyo chip 2 (Ibukp'yŏn)*, 223–240.

Kim Chae-yong. "Iljeha nonch'on-ŭi hwangp'yehwa-wa nongmin-ŭi chuch'ejŏk kaksŏng" [The Devastation of the Peasants under Japanese Colonial Rule and Awakening of Their National Consciousness]. In *Yi Ki-yŏng sŏnjip,*1:567–581.

————. *Pukhan munhak-ŭi yŏksajŏk ihae* [A Historical Understanding of North Korean Literature]. Seoul: Munhak-kwa chisŏngsa, 1994.

————. "Pukhan-ŭi namnodanggye chakka sukch'ŏng" [Purges of the North Korean Writers from the "Southern Party"]. *Yŏksa pip'yŏng* 27 (Winter 1994): 328–364.

Kim Ch'ang-ho. "Ch'ŏnyŏŭi maŭm" [A Girl's Heart]. *Chosŏn munhak,* 2007, no. 10:67.

Kim Ch'ang-su. "Nae kohyang-ŭi tŭl changmi" [Wild Rose of My Hometown]. *Chosŏn munhak,* 2004, no. 10:44–55.

Kim Chin-guk. "Chchaksarang naeyong-ŭi ch'oedae hit'ŭ kok Hŭi p'aram" [The Great Hit "Whistle," a Song of Unrequited Love]. *Chungang ilbo,* 15 January 1995, 17.

Kim Ch'ŏl. "Irhagi do chok'ho salgi do chot'ha!" [It Is Good to Work, It Is Good to Live!]. *Chosŏn munhak,* 1956, no. 5:96–99.

Kim, German, and Sim Yŏng-sop. *Istoriia prosveshcheniia koreitsev Rossii i Kazahstana* [History of the Education of Koreans of Russia and Kazahstan]. Alma-Ata: Kazak universiteti, 2000.

Kim Hong-gyun. "Wŏlbuk chakka Yi T'ae-jun-ŭi t'onggok-ŭi kajŏksa" [The Tragic Family History of Yi T'ae-jun, a Writer Who Went to the North]. *Wŏlgan Chungang,* no. 300 (November 2000). http://www.kinds.or.kr.

Kim Il Sung. "Munhwaintŭlŭn munhwachŏnsŏnŭi t'usaro toeyŏya handa" [Intellectuals Must Become Soldiers on the Cultural Front]. In *Kim Il-sung chŏnjip* [Complete Collection of Kim Il Sung's Works], vol. 3 (January–June 1946): 424–428. Pyongyang: Chosŏn rodongtang ch'ulp'ansa, 1992.

———. *Sasang saŏp-esŏ kyojojuŭiwa hyŏngsikjuŭi-rŭl t'oejihago chuch'e-rŭl hwangnip hal te taehayŏ* [About the Eradication of Doctrinism and Formalism and the Establishment of Chuch'e]. Pyongyang: Chosŏn nodongdang ch'ulp'ansa, 1960.

Kim Kap-sik. "1990 nyŏntae 'konanŭi haenggun' kwa 'sŏngunchŏngch'I': Pukhanŭi insikkwa taeŭn" [March of Hardships and Military First Policy: North Korean Attitude and Responses]. *Hyŏndaepukhan yŏngu* (2005): 1:9–38.

Kim Kwang-sŏp. "Pidan" [Silk]. *Chosŏn munhak,* 1956, no. 6:65–67.

Kim Kyo-sŏp. "Pot'ong saramtŭr-ŭi iyagi" [A Story of Ordinary People]. *Chosŏn munhak,* 2005, no. 34:61–68.

Kim, L. K. "Poeziia Cho Kich'ona" [The Poetry of Cho Ki-ch'ŏn]. In *Koreiskaia literatura* [Korean Literature], 150–179. Moscow: Academiia nauk SSSR, Izdatel'stvo vostochnoi literatury, 1959.

Kim Myŏng-su. "Purŭjoa ideorrogijŏk chanjae-waŭi t'ujaeng-ŭl wihayŏ" [For the Fight with the Remnants of Bourgeois Ideology]. In *Munhak-ŭi chihyang* [Literary Tendencies], 41–97. Pyongyang: Chosŏn chakka tongmaeng ch'ulp'ansa, 1954.

———. "Uri munhak-e issŏsŏŭi chŏnhyŏng-kwa kaldŭn munje" [The Problems of Typicality and Conflict in Our Literature]. *Chosŏn munhak,* 1953, no. 11:135–137.

Kim Nam-ch'ŏn. "Kkul" [Honey]. *Chosŏn munhak,* 1951, no. 4:36–45.

Kim Nam-il. "Ije nuga Yi Ki-yŏngŭl ilgŭl gosinga?" [Who Will Read Yi Ki-yŏng Today?]. *Silch'ŏn munhak,* Autumn 1999, 79–85.

Kim Pŏm-su. "Koŭnŭi si" [The Poems of Ko Ŭn]. *Hankuk ilbo,* 24 August 1999, 33.

Kim Sang-sŏn. *Minch'ŏn Yi Ki-yong munhak yŏngu* [A Study of Minch'ŏn Yi Ki-yŏng's Literature]. Seoul: Kukhak charyowŏn, 1999.

Kim Sa-ryang. "Zapiski voennogo korrespondenta" [Notes of a War Correspondent]. In *Koreia boretsia* [Korea Is Struggling], 137–150. Moscow: Izdatelstvo inostrannoi literaturu, 1952.

Kim Sŏng-su. *T'ongilŭi munhak pip'yŏng nonli* [A Critical Survey of the Unified Literature]. Seoul: Ch'aek sesang, 2001.

Kim Sŭng-hwan. "Haebang Kongganŭi pukhan munhak: Munhwajŏk minju kiji kŏnsŏl ronŭl chungsim-ŭro" [North Korean Literature after Liberation: A Study of the "Construction of a Democratic Cultural Base" Theory]. *Hanguk hakpo,* no. 63 (Summer 1991): 201–224.

Kim Yun-sik. *Haebang kongganŭi munhak saron* [A Study of the Literature of the Liberation Period]. Seoul: Taehakkyo ch'ulp'anbu, 1989.

———. *Pukhan munhaksaron* [A Study of North Korean Literary History]. Seoul: Saemi, 1995.

———. *Yim Hwa yŏngu* [A Study of Yim Hwa]. Seoul: Munhwa sasangsa, 1989.

Ko Il-hwan. "Sobet'ŭ munhak chakp'umesŏ padŭn yŏnghyang-kwa uri munhak-ŭi sŏnggwa" [The Influence of Soviet Literature and the Successes of Our Literature]. *Munhak yesul,* 1949, no. 10:52–55.

Konovalova, I. "Mikhail Sholohov kak zerkalo russkoi kollectivizatzii" [Mikhail Sholokhov as a Mirror of Russian Collectivization]. *Ogonek,* 1999, no. 25:26–29.

"Koreiskaia literatura" [Korean Literature]. In *Literaturnaia entsiklopediia* [Literary Encyclopedia], 5:460–470. Moscow: Akademiia nauk, 1931.

Kratkaia literaturnaia entsiklopediia [Short Encyclopedia of Literature]. Moscow: Sovetskaia entsiklopediia, 1972.

Ku Sang. *Siwa salmŭi not'ŭ* [Notes on Poetry and Life]. Seoul: Chayu munhaksa, 1988.

K'ŭnak'ŭn uŭi (Ssoryŏn kihaengjip) [The Great Friendship (Travels to the USSR)]. Pyongyang: Chosŏn chakka tongmaeng ch'ulp'ansa, 1954.

Kwŏn Yŏng-min. *Hanguk hyŏndae munhaksa* [History of Contemporary Korean Literature]. Seoul: Midŭmsa, 1993.

Lankov, Andrei. *Crisis in North Korea: The Failure of De-Stalinization, 1956.* Honolulu: University of Hawai`i Press, 2004.

———. *From Stalin to Kim Il Sung: The Formation of North Korea, 1945–1960.* New Brunswick, NJ: Rutgers University Press, 2002.

———. "Kim Il Sung's Campaign against the Soviet Faction in Late 1955 and the Birth of *Chuch'e.*" *Korean Studies* 23 (1999): 43–67.

———. *Severnaia Koreia: Vchera i Segodnia* [North Korea: Yesterday and Today]. Moscow: Vostochnaia literatura, 1995.

Lenin, V. I. "Party Organisation and Party Literature." In *Collected Works,* 10:32–48. Moscow: Foreign Languages Publishing House, 1962.

Li Gien (Yi Ki-yŏng). "O koreiskoi literature" [On Korean Literature] (in Russian translation). *Zvezda,* 1949, no. 12:147–148.

———. *Sud'ba odnoi zhenshchiny* [The Fate of a Woman] (in Russian translation). Pyongyang: Izdatel'stvo literatury na inostrannyh iazykah, 1964.

———. *Zemlia* [Land] (in Russian translation). Moscow: Izdatel'stvo inostrannoi literatury, 1953.

Li Hsiao-t'i. "Making a Name and a Culture for the Masses in Modern China." *East Asia Cultures Critique* 9, no. 1 (2001): 29–68.

Li, V. N. "Koreiskaia assotsiatsija proletarskih pisatelei i prosa 20–30 godov" [The KAPF and the Fiction of the 1920–1930s]. In *Natsional'nye traditsii i genesis sotsialisticheskogo realizma* [National Traditions and the Genesis of Socialist Realism], 581–639. Moscow: Vostochnaja literatura, 1965.

———. "Koreiskaia literatura pervyh let posle osvobozhdeniia (1945–1950)" [Korean Literature in the First Years after Liberation (1945–1950)]. In *Hudozhestvennyi opyt literatur sotsialisticheskih stran* [Artistic Experience in the Literature of Socialist Countries], 339–354. Moscow: Nauka, 1967.

————. *Koreiskaia proletarskaia literatura: Proza 20–30-h godov* [Korean Proletarian Literature: Fiction of the 1920–1930s]. Moscow: Akademiia nauk SSSR, 1967.

————. *Sotsialisticheskii realizm v koreaiskoi literature* [Socialist Realism in Korean Literature]. Tashkent: Fan, 1971.

Lokotkov, K. *Vernost'* [Loyalty]. Novosibirsk: Novosibirskoe knizhnoe izdatel'stvo, 1951.

MacWilliams, Bryon. "Communism at Uncomfortably Close Quarters." *Chronicles of Higher Education,* 26 April 2002, A56.

Maiakovskii, Vladimir. "Pis'mo Tatiane Iakovlevoi" [A Letter to Tatiana Yakovleva]. In *Sobranie sochinenii* [Collected Works], 6:155–157. Moscow: Pravda, 1973.

————. "Pis'mo tovarishchu Kostrovu o sushchnosti liubvi" [A Letter to Comrade Kostrov from Paris about the Essence of Love]. In *Sobranie sochinenii* [Collected Works], 6:150–152. Moscow: Pravda, 1973.

Malaia sovetskaia entsiklopediia [Shorter Soviet Encyclopedia]. Vol. 8. Moscow: Sovetskaia entsiklopediia, 1960.

Margulies, Sylvia. *The Pilgrimage to Russia: The Soviet Union and Treatment of Foreigners, 1924–1937.* Madison, Milwaukee, and London: University of Wisconsin Press, 1968.

Martin, Terry. *The Affirmative Action Empire: Nations and Nationalism in the Soviet Union, 1923–1939.* Ithaca, NY: Cornell University Press, 2001.

Medvedev, Roi. *O Staline i stalinisme* [On Stalin and Stalinism]. Moscow: Progress, 1990.

Min Ch'un-hwan. "Yi T'ae-jun-ŭi chŏngijŏk koch'al" [A Biographical Study of Yi T'ae-jun]. In *Yi T'ae-jun munhak yŏngu* [A Study of Yi T'ae-jun's Literature], 33–54. Seoul: Kip'ŭnsaem, 1993.

Min Pyŏng-gyun. "Leningradesŏ" [In Leningrad]. In *K'ŭnak'ŭn uŭi,* 19–22.

————. "Myŏngnanhan saram" [Merry People]. In *K'ŭnak'ŭn uŭi,* 32–35.

————. "Ŏmŏni" [Mother]. In *K'ŭnak'ŭn uŭi,* 15–18.

————. "Tu suryŏng" [Two Leaders]. In *K'ŭnak'ŭn uŭi,* 12–14.

Mun Sŏk-u. "Rŏsia sasiljuŭi munhak-ŭi suyong-kwa kŭ hakmunjŏk pyŏnyong, torŭsŭtoi chungsim-ŭro" [The Borrowing of Russian Realism and Its Adaptation to Korea, with Special Emphasis on Tolstoy]. In Yi Poyŏng et al., eds., *Hangukmunhak sokŭi segye munhak* [World Literature in Korean Literature], 207–255. Seoul: Kyujanggak, 1998.

————. "Tturŭgenep'ŭ-wa Korikki Munhak-ŭi kyŏngu" [Cases of Turgenev and Gorky]. In Yi Poyŏng et al., eds., *Hangukmunhak sokŭi segye munhak* [World Literature in Korean Literature], 293–335. Seoul: Kyujanggak, 1998.

Munye chŏnsŏne issŏsŏŭi pandongjŏk purŭjyoa sasangŭl pandaehayŏ [Against Reactionary Bourgeois Ideas on the Literary and Artistic Front]. Pyongyang: Chosŏn chakka tongmaeng ch'ulp'ansa, 1956.

Myers, Brian. *Han Sŏr-ya and North Korean Literature: The Failure of Socialist Realism in the DPRK.* Ithaca, NY: East Asia Program, Cornell University, 1994.

————. "Ideology as Smokescreen: North Korea's Juche Thought." *Acta Koreana* 11, no. 3 (December 2008): 161–182.

————. "Kim Jong Il Mania: The Depiction of South Korea in Contemporary North

Korean Propaganda." In Proceedings of the 2006 international conference "North Korean Strategy and Propaganda," Seoul, 19 May 2006.

———. "Mother Russia: Soviet Characters in North Korean Fiction." *Korean Studies* 16 (1992); 82–93.

Na Pyŏng-ch'ŏl. *Munhak-ŭi ihae* [Understanding Literature]. Seoul: Munye ch'ulp'ansa, 1995.

———. *Sosŏl-ŭi ihae* [Understanding the Novel]. Seoul: Munye ch'ulp'ansa, 1998.

Naewoe t'onmgsinsa. "Ch'oegŭn yuhaeng taejung kayo ŏttŏnge inna" [Which Modern Pop Songs Exist (in North Korea)?]. *Taehan maeil,* 23 January 1995, 13.

Nam, S. G. *Formirovanie narodnoi intelligentsii v KNDR* [Formation of the Peoples' Intelligentsia in the DPRK]. Moscow: Nauka, 1970.

Nemzer, Aleksandr. "Razgromlennyi generalnyi" [Destroyed General Secretary]. http://www.ruthenia.ru/nemzer/FAD.html.

O partiinoi i sovetskoi pechati [About Party and Soviet Press]. Moscow: Pravda, 1954.

Ohotnikov, Vadim. *Dorogi vglub'* [Roads to the Depths]. Moscow: Molodaia gvardiia, 1950.

Ŏm Ho-sŏk. "Choguk haebang chŏnjaeng sigi-ŭi uri munhak" [Our Literature in the Period of the War for the Liberation of the Motherland]. In Yi Sŏn-yŏng et al., *Hyŏndae munhak pip'yŏng charyo chip 2 (Ibukp'yŏn),* 185–208.

———. "Munhak chakp'um-ŭi hyŏngsanghwa-e taehayŏ" [On Imagery in Literary Writings]. In *Ch'ŏngnyŏntŭl wihan munhakron* [Literary Theory for the Youth], 70–137. Pyongyang: Minju ch'ŏngnyŏnsa, 1952.

———. "Munhak ch'angjak-e issŏsŏŭi chŏnhyangsŏngŭi munje" [The Problem of Revisionism in Literary Matters]. In *Munhak-ŭi chihyang* [Literary Tendencies], 127–162. Pyongyang: Chosŏn chakka tongmaeng ch'ulp'ansa, 1954.

———. "Munhak paljŏn-ŭi saeroun chingjo" [New Signs of Literary Development]. *Munhak yesul,* 1952, no. 11:92–110.

———. *Munye kibon* [The Basis of Literature and the Arts]. Pyongyang: Kukrip ch'ulp'ansa, 1952.

———. "Nodong kyegŭp-ŭi hyŏngsang-kwa mihaksang-ŭi myŏtkaji munje" [Problems of the Images of the Working Class and Aesthetics]. *Chosŏn munhak,* 1953, no. 11:115–146.

———. "Saenghwal-ŭi chinsil-kwa sasiljuŭi-rŭl wihayŏ" [For the Truth of Life and Realism]. In *Sae hyŏnsilkwa munhak* [New Reality and Literature], 4–46. Pyongyang: Chosŏn chakka tongmaeng ch'ulp'ansa, 1954.

———. "Uri munhak-e issŏsŏ chayŏnjuŭi-wa hyŏngsikjuŭi chanjae-waŭi t'ujaeng" [The Fight with the Remnants of Naturalism and Formalism in Our Literature]. *Nodong sinmun,* 17 January 1952.

———. "Yi T'ae-jun-ŭi munhak-ŭi pandongjŏk chŏngch'e" [The Reactionary in Yi T'ae-jun's Literature]. *Chosŏn munhak,* 1956, no. 3:140–168.

———. "Yi T'ae-jun-ŭi munhak-ŭi pandongjŏk ponjil" [The Reactionary Essence of Yi T'ae-jun's Literature]. In *Munhak-kwa hyŏndae chŏngsin* [Literature and the Spirit of Modernity], 436–477. Pyongyang: Chosŏn chakka tongmaeng ch'ulp'ansa, 1961.

Ostrovskii, Nikolai. *Kak zakalyalas' stal'* [How the Steel Was Tempered]. 1932. Reprint, Moscow: Gosudarstvennoe idatel'stvo detskoi literatury Ministerstva prosveshcheniia, 1948.

Pak Chŏng-ae. "Nae kohyang-ŭi irŭm" [The Name of My Hometown]. In *Yŏngyŏnhan noŭl,* 101–103.

Pak Chong-sik. "Chosŏn munhak-e issŏsŏŭi ssobet'ŭ munhak-ŭi yŏnghyang" [The Influence of Soviet Literature in Korean Literature]. In *Haebang hu 10 nyŏngan-ŭi chosŏn munhak* [Korean Literature during the First Decade after Liberation], 412–461. Pyongyang: Chosŏn chakka tongmaeng ch'ulp'ansa, 1955.

———. "Sovremennaia koreiskaia literatura posle osvobozhdenia: Formirovanie i stanovlenie sotsrealisma v koreiskoi literature po tvorchestvu Li Giena" [Contemporary Korean Literature after Liberation: The Formation and Development of Socialist Realism in Korean Literature—the Case of Yi Ki-yong]. Doctoral thesis, Moscow State University, 1953.

Pak Hŏn-ho. *Yi T'ae-jun-kwa hanguk kŭndae sosŏl-ŭi sŏnggyŏk* [Yi T'ae-jun and the Essence of Modern Korean Literature]. Seoul: Somyŏng ch'ulp'an, 1999.

Pak Hyo-jun. "So" [The Ox]. *Chosŏn munhak,* 1956, no. 3:16–44.

Pak Nam-su. *Chŏkch'i 6 nyŏn-ŭi pukhan mundan* [The North Korean Literary World: Six Years under the Reds' Rule]. Seoul: Pogosa, 1999.

Pak T'ae-sang. *Pukhan munhak-ŭi hyŏnsang* [The Situation in North Korean Literature]. Seoul: Kip'ŭnsaem, 1999.

———. *Pukhan munhak-ŭi tonghyang* [Tendencies in North Korean Literature]. Seoul: Kip'ŭnsaem, 2002.

Pang Chŏng–pae. "Pukhan 'sŏngun chŏngch'I' ŭi chŏngch'ichŏk hamŭi" [The Political Meaning of the North Korean "Military First Policy"]. *T'ongil munje yŏng* 25–26 (2003–2004): 143–162.

Pang Min-ho. "Ilche malgi Yi T'ae-jun tanp'yŏng sosŏlŭi sasosŏl yangsang" [Private Motives in Short Stories of Yi T'ae-jun at the End of the Colonial Period]. *Sanghŏ hakpo* 14, no. 2 (2005): 223–259.

Pastsvet i razvitie koreiskoi kul'tury [The Prosperity and Development of Korean Culture]. Pyongyang: Izdatel'stvo literatury na inostrannyh iazykah, 1959.

Perventsev, Arkadii. *V Koree* [In Korea]. Moscow: Sovetskii pisatel', 1950.

Pervyi Vsesoiuznyi s'ezd sovetskih pisatelei, 1934: Stenograficheskii otchet; Prilozheniia [The First Congress of Soviet Writers, 1934: Stenographic Record; Appendix]. Moscow: Sovetskii pisatel', 1990.

Perzhov, V. O., and I. M. Serebrianskii, eds. *Maiakovskii: Materialy i issliedovaniia* [Maiakovskii: Materials and Research]. Moscow: Gosudarstvennoe izdatel'stvo "Hudozhestvennaia literatura," 1940.

Pihl, Marshall. "Engineers of the Human Soul: North Korean Literature Today." *Korean Studies* 1 (1977): 63–110.

Pit'nanŭn rojŏng [A Brilliant Course]. Pyongyang: Munhakyesul chonghap ch'ulp'ansa, 1998.

Pokpadŭn kangsan [Blessed Rivers and Mountains]. Pyongyang: Kŭmsŏngch'ŏngnyŏn ch'ulp'ansa, 1998.

Pollard, D. E. "The Short Story in the Cultural Revolution." *China Quarterly*, no. 73 (March 1978): 99–121.

Popkin, Samuel L. *The Rational Peasant: The Political Economy of Rural Society in Vietnam.* London: University of California Press, 1979.

Pratt, Keith, and Richard Rutt, with additional material by James Hoare. *Korea: A Historical and Cultural Dictionary.* Richmond, Surrey, UK: University of Durham, Curzon, 1999.

Puk-ŭro kan chakka sŏnjip [Anthology of Writers Who Went to the North]. Vol. 4, *Yi T'ae-jun, Poktŏkpang.* Seoul: Ŭryu munhwa sa, 1988.

Pyŏn Hŭi-gŭn. "Haengbokhan saramdŭl" [Happy People]. *Munhak yesul*, 1953, no. 6:75–85.

Rezolutsiia TsK VKP (b) "O perestroike literaturno-hudozhestvennyh organizatzii" [Resolution of the Central Committee of the All-Russian Communist Party of Bolsheviks (b) "About the Reconstruction of Literary and Artistic Organizations"]. *Pravda*, 24 April 1932, 1.

Ryang, Sonia. *North Koreans in Japan: Language, Ideology, and Identity.* Boulder, CO: Westview, 1997.

Ryu Hŭi-nam. "Han kajŏnge iyagi" [Story about One Family]. *Chosŏn munhak*, 2004, no. 5:26–40.

Ryu Hun. *Study of North Korea.* Seoul: Research Institute of International and External Affairs, 1966.

Scalapino, Robert A., and Chong-sik Lee. *Communism in Korea.* Berkeley and Los Angeles: University of California Press, 1972.

Schmid, Andre. *Korea between Empires, 1895–1919.* New York: Columbia University Press, 2002.

Shin, Gi-Wook. "Agrarianism: A Critique of Colonial Modernity in Korea." *Comparative Studies in Society and History* 41, no. 4 (October 1999): 784–804.

Sholokhov, Mikhail. *Podniataia tselina* [Virgin Land under the Plow]. Moscow: Prosveshchenie, 1973.

———. "Rech' na vruchenii Nobelevskoi premii" [Nobel Speech]. *Literaturnaia gazeta*, 14 December 1965, 1.

Sim Wŏn-sŏp. "1950 nyŏndae pukhan si kaegwan" [A Survey of North Korean Poetry of the 1950s]. In *1950 nyŏndae nampukhan munhak* [Literature of North and South Korea of the 1950s], 100–135. Seoul: P'yŏngminsa, 1991.

Simonov, Konstantin. *Glazami cheloveka moego pokoleniya: Razmyshleniia o I. V. Staline* [Through the Eyes of a Person of My Generation: Contemplations on Stalin]. Moscow: Respublika, 1989.

Sin Hyŏng-gi. "Haebang ihu-ŭi Yi T'ae-jun" [Yi T'ae-jun after Liberation]. In *Kŭndae munhak-kwa Yi T'ae-jun* [Contemporary Literature and Yi T'ae-jun], 63–83. Seoul: Kip'ŭnsaem, 2000.

Sin Hyŏng-gi and O Sŏng-ho. *Pukhan munhaksa* [North Korean Literary History]. Seoul: P'yŏngminsa, 2000.

Sin Ko-song. "Ssobet'ŭ yŏngŭk-esŏ uri-nŭn muŏs-ŭl paeunŭnga?" [What Can We Learn from Soviet Drama?]. *Munhak yesul,* 1949, no. 10:64–69.

————. "Yŏngŭk-e issŏsŏ hyŏngsikjuŭi mit chayŏnjuŭijŏk chanjae-waŭi t'ujaeng" [The Fight against the Remnants of Formalism and Naturalism in North Korean Drama]. In Yi Sŏn-yŏng et al., *Hyŏndae munhak pip'yŏng charyo chip 2 (Ibukp'yŏn),* 164–173.

Sin Ku-hyŏn. *Koreiskaia literatura posle osvobozhdeniia* [Korean Literature after Liberation]. Pyongyang: Izdatel'stvo literatury na inostrannyh iazykah, 1957.

————. "Minch'ŏn Yi Ki-yŏng." In *Hyŏndae chakka ron* [Study of Contemporary Writers], 2:39–169. Pyongyang: Chosŏn chakka tongmaeng ch'ulp'ansa, 1960.

Sin Tong-ho. "Hanguksiesŏ nat'anan paektusan sangjing yŏngu" [A Study of the Symbolism of Paektusan in Korean Poetry]. MA thesis, Chungang University, Chungang taehakkyo yesul taehakwŏn, 1999.

Slonim, Marc. *Soviet Russian Literature: Writers and Problems, 1917–1977.* New York: Oxford University Press, 1977.

Smirnov, M. B., ed. *Sistema ispravitelno-trudovyh lagerei v SSSR* [The System of Penal Correction Camps in the USSR]. Moscow: Zvenia, 1998.

Sŏ Chŏng-in. "Hyŏnsil-ŭl pora!" [Look at the Reality!]. In *Pit'nanŭn rojŏng,* 100–102.

Sŏk In-hae. "Maŭl-ŭi nyŏsŏnsaeng" [The Village Schoolmistress]. *Chosŏn munhak,* 1956, no. 8:80–112.

Sŏk Yu-kyun. "Ryutarŭn p'unggyŏnhwa" [Unusual Landscape]. *Chosŏn munhak,* 2005, no. 5:44–52.

————. "Zvezda I mechta: Is dnevnika byvshego uzdnika yuzhnokoreiskoi tyur'my" [Star and Dream: From the Diary of an Ex-Prisoner in a South Korean Jail]. *Korea segodnya* [Korea Today] (in Russian), 2004, no. 8:37–38; no. 9:36–37; no. 10:42–43.

Sŏng Hye-rang. *Tŭngnamu chip* [A House Covered with Wisteria]. Seoul: Chisik nara, 2000.

Sŏng Man-sil. "Sinjŏng maŭl-ŭi haengbokhan pamiyŏ" [Happy Night in a New Village]. In *Yŏngyŏnhan noŭl,* 128–129.

Song Yŏng. "Chakka minch'ŏn" [The Writer Minch'ŏn]. *Munhak sinmun,* 1960, no. 5:27.

————. "Tu ch'ŏnyŏ" [Two Girls]. *Munhak yesul,* 1953, no. 9:65–79.

Sovetskii entsiklopedicheskii slovar' [Soviet Encyclopedic Dictionary]. 4th ed. Moscow: Sovetskaia entsiklopediia, 1986.

Sovremennaia koreiskaia poeziia [Modern Korean Poetry]. Moscow: Izdatel'stvo inostrannoi literatury, 1950.

Surkov, Aleksei. *Serdtse mira: Stihi o Moskve* [The Heart of the World: Poetical Tributes to Moscow]. Moscow: Moskovskii rabochii, 1946.

Taen, A. N. "Ocherki sovremennoi koreiskoi literatury (demokraticheskie natsional'nye tendentsii i sotsialisticheskii realizm v koreiskoi literature)" [Essays on Contemporary

Korean Literature (Democratic National Tendencies and Socialist Realism in Korean Literature)]. PhD thesis, Herzen Pedagogical Institute, Leningrad, 1954.

Terts, Abram. "Chto takoe sotsialisticheskii realism?" [What Is Socialist Realism?]. In *Fantasticheskii mir Abrama Tertsa* [Fantastic World of Abram Terts], 399–446. New York: Inter-Language Literary Associates, 1967.

Tomomi Wada. "Aeguk munhak-ŭrosŏŭi Yi T'ae-jun munhak" [The Literature of Yi T'ae-jun as Patriotic Literature]. In *Kŭndae munhak-kwa Yi T'ae-jun* [Contemporary Literature and Yi T'ae-jun], 83–119. Seoul: Kip'ŭnsaem, 2000.

Trifonov, Yurii. *Studenty* [Students]. In *Sobranie sochinenii* [Collected Works], 1:12–345. Moscow: Hudozhestvennaia literatura, 1985.

Tsoi, E. M. "Otrazhenie velikih peremen v koreiskoi derevne v romanah Li Giena" [The Reflection of the Great Changes in the Korean Villages in the Novels of Yi Ki-yŏng]. PhD thesis, Moscow State University, 1955.

U Tae-sik. "Haebang hu pukhan mundan-e koch'al" [Study of Post-Liberation North Korean Literary Circles]. Introduction to Pak Nam-su, *Chŏkch'i 6 nyŏn-ŭi pukhan mundan* [The North Korean Literary World: Six Years under the Red's Rule], 9–14. Seoul: Pogosa, 1999.

Usievich, Elena. *Vladimir Maiakovskii.* Moscow: Sovetskii pisatel', 1950.

Van Der Eng-Liedmeier, A. M. *Soviet Literary Characters: An Investigation into the Portrayal of Soviet Men in Russian Prose, 1917–1953.* The Hague: Mouton and Co., 1959.

Vigdorova, Frida. *Moi klass* [My Class]. Novosibirsk: Novosibirskoe knizhnoe izdatel'stvo, 1951.

Wells, Kenneth. *New God, New Nation: Protestants and Self-Reconstruction Nationalism in Korea, 1896–1937.* Sydney: Allen and Unwin, 1990.

———. "The Price of Legitimacy: Women and the Kŭnuhoe Movement, 1927–1931." In Gi-Wook Shin and Michael Robinson, eds., *Colonial Modernity in Korea*, 191–221. Cambridge, MA, and London: Harvard University Press, 1999.

Who's Who in Korean Literature. Published by Korean Culture and Arts Foundation. Seoul: Hollym, 1998.

Wŏlbuk chakka-ŭi taep'yo munhak sŏnjip: Pak T'ae-wŏn, Yi T'ae-jun [A Collection of Representative Literary Works of the Writers Who Went to the North: Pak T'ae-wŏn, Yi T'ae-jun]. Seoul: Munhak-kwa hyŏnsilsa, 1994.

Yang Chae-mo. "Nop'ŭn mokp'yo" [Lofty Goal]. In *Pit'nanŭn rojŏng,* 304–323.

Yi Ch'ang-ju. "Puk-ŭi huip'aram siin Cho Ki-ch'ŏn" [The North Korean "Poet of Whistle"]. *Koryo Times: Weekly Magazine for the Foreign Korean Community,* 10 August 1992, 21.

Yi Chŏl-ju. *Puk-ŭi yesurin* [North Korean Artists]. Seoul: Kyemongsa, 1966.

Yi Ch'ŏng-gu. *Siin Cho Ki-ch'ŏn ron* [Study of the Poet Cho Ki-ch'ŏn]. Pyongyang: Munye ch'ong ch'ulp'ansa, 1953.

Yi Hun. "1930 nyŏndae Yim Hwaŭi munhakron kŭndaesŏng" [A Study of Yim Hwa in the 1930s and Modernity]. In *Minjŏk munhak-kwa kŭndaesŏng* [National Literature and Modernity], 407–427. Seoul: Munhak-kwa chisŏngsa, 1995.

Yi Ki-pong. *Puk-ŭi munhak-kwa yesurin* [North Korean Men of Literature and the Arts]. Seoul: Sasayŏn, 1986.

Yi Ki-yŏng. "Cheji kongjang ch'on" [Paper Factory Village]. In *Hyŏndae chosŏn munhak sŏnjip*, 3:195–213.

————. "Chwi iyagi" [A Story about Mice]. In *Hyŏndae chosŏn munhak sŏnjip*, 3:59–66.

————. *Han nyŏsŏng-ŭi unmyŏng* [The Fate of a Woman]. Pyongyang: Chosŏn sahoejuǔi nodong ch'ŏngnyŏn ch'ulp'ansa, 1965.

————. "Kananhan saram" [Poor People]. In *Hyŏndae chosŏn munhak sŏnjip*, 3:31–58.

————. "KAPF sidae-ŭi hoesanggi" [Recollections of the KAPF]. *Chosŏn munhak*, 1957, no. 8:85–88, 85–91.

————. *Kihaeng munjip* [Collection of Travelogues]. Pyongyang: Chosŏn chakka tongmaeng ch'ulp'ansa, 1960.

————. *Kohyang* [Homeland]. Pyongyang: Chosŏn chakka tongmaeng ch'ulp'ansa, 1955.

————. *Kongsanjuǔi t'aeyang-ŭn pit'nanda* [The Sun of Communism Is Shining]. Pyongyang: Chosso ch'ulp'ansa, 1954.

————. "Minch'on" [Poor Village]. In *Hyŏndae chosŏn munhak sŏnjip* [Anthology of Contemporary Korean Literature], 3:67–100.

————. "Oppa-ŭi pimil p'yŏnji" [Elder Brother's Secret Letter]. In *Hyŏndae chosŏn munhak sŏnjip*, [Anthology of Contemporary Korean Literature], 3:17–30.

————. *Pulgŭn such'ŏp* [Red Pocketbook]. Pyongyang: Minch'ŏng ch'ulp'ansa, 1961.

————. "Silp'aehan ch'ŏnyŏ changp'yŏng" [My First Story as a Failure]. *Chogwang*, 1939, no. 12:32–35.

————. *Ttang* [Land]. Pyongyang: Chosŏn chakka tongmaeng ch'ulp'ansa, 1955.

————. *Ttang* [Land]. Pyongyang: Minch'ŏng ch'ulp'ansa, 1973.

————. *Widaehan saenghwal-ŭl ch'angjohanŭn ssoryŏn* [The USSR Creates a Great Life]. Pyongyang: Chosso munhwahyŏphoe, 1952.

————. "Wŏn-bo." In *Hyŏndae chosŏn munhak sŏnjip* [Anthology of Contemporary Korean Literature], 3:182–194. Pyongyang: Chosŏn chakka tongmaeng ch'ulp'ansa, 1958.

Yi Ki-yŏng and Han Sŏr-ya. *Yisang-kwa noryŏk* [Ideas and Labour]. Pyongyang: Minch'ŏng ch'ulp'ansa, 1958.

Yi Ki-yŏng sŏnjip [Collected works of Yi Ki-yŏng]. Vol.1. Seoul: P'ulpit', 1989.

Yi Kwang-su. *Mujŏng* [Heartlessness]. Seoul: Sŏ mundang, 1997.

Yi Myŏng-hŭi. *Sanghŏ Yi T'ae-jun munhak segye* [The Literary World of Sangho Yi T'ae-jun]. Seoul: Kukhak ch'aryowŏn, 1994.

Yi Myŏng-jae. *Pukhan munhak sajŏn* [A Dictionary of North Korean Literature]. Seoul: Kukhak charyowŏn, 1995.

Yi Pyŏng-ryŏl. "Ch'ŏtchŏnt'u-wa kohyang kilŭi ŭimi" [The Meaning of the (Stories) "The

First Fight" and "The Road to My Native Land"]. In *Yi T'ae-jun munhak chŏnjip* [The Complete Works of Yi T'ae-jun], 3:377–391. Seoul: Kip'ŭnsaem, 2000.

———. "Yi T'ae-jun-ŭi munhaksajŏk uisang" [Yi T'ae-jun's Period in Literary History]. In *Yi T'ae-jun munhak yŏngu* [A Study of Yi T'ae-jun's Literature], 13–26. Seoul: Kip'ŭnsaem, 1993.

Yi Sang-gyŏng. *Yi Ki-yŏng sidae-wa munhak* [Yi Ki-yŏng: His Era and His Literature]. Seoul: P'ulpit', 1994.

Yi Sang-hwa. "P'okp'ung-ŭl kidarinŭn maŭm" [Yearning for the Storm]. http://www2.knu.ac.kr/~psy/kyngsim/space/exhibit/lee_sw/lsw_frm.htm.

Yi Sang-hyŏn. *Namyŏnbaek-esŏ on p'yŏnji* [The Letter That Came from Namyŏnbaek]. *Chosŏn munhak*, 1956, no. 4.:22–35.

Yi Sŏn-yŏng et al., eds. *Hyŏndae munhak pip'yŏng charyo chip 2 (Ibukp'yŏn)* [Collection of Contemporary North Korean Literary Critical Materials]. Seoul: T'aehaksa, 1993.

———, eds. *Hyŏndae munhak pip'yŏng charyŏ chip 3: Pukhan p'yŏn* [Collection of Contemporary North Korean Literary Critical Materials]. Seoul: T'aehaksa, 1993.

Yi T'ae-jun. "38 sŏn ŏnŭ chigu-esŏ" [Somewhere near the 38th Parallel]. In *Yi T'ae-jun munhak chŏnjip,* vol. 3 (2000), 121–129.

———. "Abŏji mosi ot" [Father's Hempen Clothes]. In *Yi T'ae-jun munhak chŏnjip,* vol. 3 (2000), 53–57.

———. "Ch'onttŭgi" [Country Bumpkin]. In *Wŏlbuk chakka-ŭi taep'yo munhak sŏnjip: Pak T'ae-wŏn, Yi T'ae-jun,* 434–445.

———. *Ch'ŏt chŏnt'u* [The First Fight]. In *Yi T'ae-jun munhak chŏnjip,* vol. 3 (1995), 59–103.

———. "Haebang chŏnhu" [Around Liberation]. In *Yi T'ae-jun munhak chŏnjip,* vol. 3 (1995), 13–52.

———. "Haengbok" [Happiness]. In *Puk-ŭro kan chakka sŏnjip,* 4:5–15.

———. "Horangi halmŏni" [Tiger Grandma]. In *Yi T'ae-jun munhak chŏnjip,* vol. 3 (2000), 105–120.

———. "Kisaeng Sandori." In *Puk-ŭro kan chakka sŏnjip,* 4:35–44.

———. "Kkamakui" [Raven]. In *Hanguk myŏngjak tanp'yŏn sosŏl* [Famous Korean Short Stories], 1:247–261. Seoul: Chiphyŏnchŏn, 1992.

———. "Kkoch' namunŭn simŏ nohko" [Planting Flowers]. In *Yi T'ae-jun munhak sŏnjip* [Anthology of Yi T'ae-jun's Works], 76–87. Seoul: Kuiinsa, 1988.

———. "Kogwihan saramdŭl" [Dear People]. In *Yi T'ae-jun munhak chŏnjip,* vol. 3 (1995), 147–159.

———. "Kohyang" [Native Land]. In *Puk-ŭro kan chakka sŏnjip,* 4:61–83.

———. "Kohyang kil" [The Road to My Homeland]. In *Yi T'ae-jun munhak chŏnjip,* vol. 3 (1995), 197–198.

———. "Kŭrimja" [The Shadow]. In *Puk-ŭro kan chakka sŏnjip,* 4:15–35.

———. "Kyŏrhon-ŭi anmasŏng" [The Curse of Marriage]. In *Puk-ŭro kan chakka sŏnjip,* 4:44–61.

————. "Miguk taesagwan" [American Embassy]. In *Yi T'ae-jun munhak chŏnjip,* vol. 3 (1995), 141–146.

————. "Nuga kulbok hanŭnga poja" [Let's See Who Will Surrender]. In *Yi T'ae-jun munhak chŏnjip,* Vol. 3 (1995), 35–140.

————. "Omongnyŏ." In *Wŏlbuk chakka-ŭi taep'yo munhak sŏnjip,* 388–402.

————. "Paekpae ch'ŏnbae-ro" [For One Hundred Times, One Thousand Times]. In *Yi T'ae-jun munhak chŏnjip,* Vol. 3 (1995), 131–134.

————. *Sasangŭi worya* [Moonlit Night of Ideas]. In *Yi T'ae-jun munhak chŏnjip,* vol. 7. Seoul: Kip'ŭn saem, 1988.

————. *Ssoryŏn kihaeng* [A Trip to the Soviet Union]. Pyongyang: Pukchosŏn ch'ulp'ansa, 1947.

————. "T'okki iyagi" [A Story about Rabbits]. In *Yi T'ae-jun munhak sŏnjip* [Anthology of Yi T'ae-jun's Works], 225–237. Seoul: Kuiinsa, 1988.

————. *Yi T'ae-jun munhak chŏnjip* [The Complete Works of Yi T'ae-jun]. Vol. 3 (1995, 2000); vol. 7 (1995). Seoul: Kip'ŭnsaem.

Yim Hwa chŏnjip [Anthology of Yim Hwa's Literature]. Seoul: Pakijŏng, 2000.

Yim Yŏng-t'ae and Ko Yu-han. *Pukhan 50 nyŏnsa* [50 Years of North Korean History]. Seoul: Tŭlnyŏk', 1999.

Yŏngyŏnhan noŭl [Eternal Sunrise]. Pyongyang: Munhakyesul chonghap ch'ulp'ansa, 1998.

Yun Chae-gŭn and Pak Sang-ch'ŏn. *Pukhan-ŭi hyŏndae munhak* [Contemporary North Korean Literature]. Vol. 2. Seoul: Koryŏwŏn, 1990.

Yun Pyŏng-no. *Hanguk-ŭi hyŏndae chakka chakp'umron* [Study of the Works of Modern Korean Writers]. Seoul: Sŏnggyunkwan taehakkyo ch'ulp'anbu, 1993.

Yun Si-ch'ŏl. "Inmin-ŭl pibanghan pandong munhak-ŭi tokso (Kim Nam-ch'ŏn 8.15 haebang hu chakp'um-ŭl chungsim-ŭro)" [The Poison of the Reactionary Literature That Slandered the Korean People (Based on the Post-Liberation Works of Kim Nam-ch'ŏn)]. *Chosŏn munhak,* 1956, no. 5:142–156.

Zaslavskii, D. "Protiv idealizatsii reaktsionnyh vzglyadov Dostoevskogo" [Against the Idealization of Reactionary Worldview of Dostoevskii]. *Kultura I zhizn',* 20 December 1947, 3–4.

Zima, V. F. *Golod v SSSR 1946–1947 godov: Proishozhdenie i posledstviia* [The Famine in the USSR in 1946–1947: Origins and Impact]. Moscow: IRI, 1996.

Zubkova, Elena. *Poslevoennoe sovetskoe obshchestvo: Politika i povsednevnost' 1945–1953* [Postwar Soviet Society: Politics and Everyday Life in 1945–1953]. Moscow: Rosspen, 2000.

Index

About the Author

TATIANA GABROUSSENKO graduated from the Far Eastern State University (Vladivostok, Soviet Union), where she majored in Korean studies and history, and she defended her PhD thesis at the Australian National University. She has been engaged in the field of Korean studies for almost twenty years as a journalist, translator, lecturer, and researcher. She is now a visiting fellow in the Faculty of Asian Studies at the ANU.

Production Notes for Gabroussenko | *Soldiers on the Cultural Front*

Jacket design by Wilson Angel

Text design by University of Hawai'i Press production staff
    with display type in Optima and text type in Garamond 3

Composition by Terri Miyasato

Printing and binding by Edwards Brothers, Inc.

Printed on 60# EB Opaque, 500 ppi